DEVELOPMENT, DEMOCRACY,

AND THE ART OF TRESPASSING

Development, Democracy, and the Art of Trespassing:

Essays in Honor of Albert O. Hirschman

Edited by
Alejandro Foxley,
Michael S. McPherson,
and Guillermo O'Donnell

*Published for the Helen Kellogg Institute
for International Studies by*

UNIVERSITY OF NOTRE DAME PRESS
NOTRE DAME, INDIANA 46556

Library of Congress Cataloging-in-Publication Data

Development, democracy, and the art of
trespassing.

  Bibliography: p.
  1. Economic development. 2. Democracy.
3. Hirschman, Albert O. I. Foxley, Alejandro.
II. McPherson, Michael S. III. O'Donnell,
Guillermo A. IV. Hirschman, Albert O. V. Kellogg
Institute for International Studies.
HD74.D48   1986   338.9   85-41021
ISBN 0-268-00859-0

Manufactured in the United States of America

Contents

Introduction, *Alejandro Foxley, Michael McPherson, and Guillermo O'Donnell*   I

I. Strategies for Economic Development

1. Modes of Industrial Development

Generalized Linkages in Industrial Development:
A Reexamination of Basic Petrochemicals in Brazil,
Peter Evans   7

Changing Models of Economic Efficiency and Their
Implications for Industrialization in the Third World,
Charles F. Sabel   27

The Economics of Fascism and Nazism: Premises and
Performance, *Charles S. Maier*   57

2. Finance and Development

Some Unintended Consequences of Financial
Laissez-Faire, *Carlos F. Díaz-Alejandro*   91

Modes of Financial Development: American Banking
Dynamics and World Financial Crises,
Marcello de Cecco   115

Dependency and the Political Solution of Balance of
Payments Crises: The Italian Case,
Andrea Ginzburg   133

II. Trespassing: Economy, Politics, and Society

1. TENSIONS IN DEMOCRATIC DEVELOPMENT

The Elusive Balance between Stimulation and Constraint
    in Analysis of Development, *John Sheahan*   169

After Authoritarianism: Political Alternatives,
    Alejandro Foxley   191

2. PROBLEMS OF SOCIAL LEARNING AND SOCIAL CONTROL

Strategies for Change in View of Social Learning
    Processes, *Michel Crozier*   219

Against Backsliding, *T. C. Schelling*   233

Suffering from Success, *Paul Streeten*   239

III. *Exit, Voice, and Loyalty*

On the Fruitful Convergences of Hirschman's *Exit, Voice,
    and Loyalty* and *Shifting Involvements:* Reflections
    from the Recent Argentine Experience,
    Guillermo O'Donnell   249

Dismantling Repressive Systems: The Abolition of Slavery
    in Cuba as a Case Study, *Rebecca J. Scott*   269

Exit-Voice Dilemmas in Adolescent Development,
    Carol Gilligan   283

An Antinomy in the Notion of Collective Protest,
    Pierre Bourdieu   301

IV. Essays on Method

The Social Scientist as Constructive Skeptic:
    On Hirschman's Role, *Michael S. McPherson*   305

The Methodological Basis of Hirschman's Development
  Economics: Pattern Model vs. General Laws,
  Charles K. Wilber and Steven Francis   317

Rationality, Interest, and Identity, *Amartya Sen*   343

Some Other Kinds of Otherness: A Critique of "Rational
  Choice" Theories, *Alessandro Pizzorno*   355

Introduction

As Albert Hirschman belatedly confessed,[1] he has been trespassing all his life. With the touch of irony and playfulness which is so often part of his style of saying important things, Hirschman engaged, long before he cared to tell us, in the naughty, somewhat sinful and always intriguing activity of trespassing. His first book, *National Power and the Structure of Foreign Trade*[2] is, as fits an aspiring young economist, about country—and commodity—composition of international trade, and about gains and losses from trade and similar technical topics; but it is also about asymmetries of national power, about states and about foreign policies whose content, he shows, were at least as much dictated by considerations of optimizing international power as by those of economic advantage.

This first book is characteristic of Hirschman's *opus*. The study is textured by the intermixing of economics, of politics, and of actors' ideas concerning what economics and politics are about. This texture is analyzed by means of careful distinctions among several dimensions of economics, politics and ideas. These dimensions are there not because some grand *a priori* scheme demands so, but because they are instruments that the author shapes in his trip toward the discovery of interesting and often surprising conclusions. This first book is also characteristic of Hirschman's *opus* in its remarkable talent for entering unchartered territory, and remaining fresh and alive even after many others have ploughed it. Some of its conclusions formulate themes of national dependency well before the writings on *dependencia* of the 1960s, with none of the dogmatism, one-sidedness and thunderous tone that marred most of the latter. In addition, the problems analyzed, the approach used and the questions asked in this book anticipate the best studies on international political economy from approximately the mid-1970s until today. Yet its importance is not just that of the precursor, to which reviews of the literature respectfully bow in the first footnote before they get into discussing contemporary issues and

1

literature. One has to read *National Power and the Structure of Foreign Trade* because it is remarkably alive: the issues it discusses, and the ways in which it discusses them, have indeed much to tell us today.

Later on, *The Strategy of Economic Development*[3] was apparently "only" about development economics, and deservedly became a classic in this field. But, as the term "strategy" hinted in the title, this book was also about government and society, about perceptions and misperceptions, about apparently good ideas that produced disastrous results, and about more modest ideas that seemed obvious only after somebody formulated them, and often worked much better than the former. Shortly afterwards, *Journeys Toward Progress*[4] was apparently a book about public policy-making and, again, it became a classic in its field. The background for truly understanding it was the vision of economic development displayed in the previous book, which it pushed further by looking at biases, ideas, surprises, opportunities that were missed, problems that for better or for worse were invented, and to opportunities that were purposively created, together with solutions that were unexpectedly found. With its discussion of "reform-mongering," *Journeys* was not only a contribution to studies on policy-making. It was also a crucial contribution to *democratic* policy-making. But for about two decades, the *esprit de géométrie* that Hirschman's Pascalian mind attempts to temper by the *esprit de finesse* led reactionary technocrats, arrogant planners and self-righteous revolutionaries to ignore or dismiss that contribution. Today, when those and other *systèmes* have failed so patently, and democracy is again a vital issue in Latin America, *Journeys* is more relevant and contemporary than ever. It is one of the few intellectual guides available for searching the narrow paths that may allow some fragile democracies to survive in the midst of, and to do something about, the worst socioeconomic crisis Latin America has ever suffered.

We do not need to detail here how much those works, as well as those Hirschman has published since then, have influenced economic, political and social thought. The chapters of this volume bear ample testimony to this influence. There are, however, two aspects we want to stress. The first is that the open-minded and subtle search that Hirschman has been conducting has prevented the emergence of a school, an orthodoxy or a system around his thought—we know how this idea would horrify him. Hirschman's work cannot be totemized because of its disrespect for disciplinary boundaries and a literary style that serves well his attention to *nuance,* his recognition of the ultimate inconclusiveness of social knowledge, and his biases for hope[5] and for what is possible but perhaps not likely.[6] But it is precisely these characteristics that have made his work so influential in so many disciplines and on so many authors that use different, at times contrasting, approaches. Since Hirschman's influence powerfully ramifies in several directions, we felt that the way this volume is organized would be a proper tribute to this great trespasser, mentor and *provocateur*. The sections and subsections of this book embody what, to our mind, are the main (but certainly not the only) lines of Hirschman's work,[7] while the chapters express, in their variety, some of the range of the authors and approaches that he has influenced and inspired.

The second aspect we want to stress is the admirable congruence of Hirschman's life with an *opus* so centrally concerned with development, equity, and democracy. Since his years as an opponent of fascism in Europe, it is easy to trace in his life a line of permanent commitment to crucial values of freedom and decency. In this respect, the numerous Latin American social scientists whom Hirschman has helped and encouraged owe him special gratitude. Furthermore, in the periods of harsh repression that many of our countries underwent (and some are still undergoing), Hirschman generously devoted time and efforts to advising and supporting many of the research institutes that tried to keep some spaces of intellectual freedom. Hirschman also visited those institutes and publicly endorsed their goals, at times when it was personally dangerous to do so. He helped their survival by means not only of his international prestige, but also of the example of his courageous commitment to the same values that had forced him into repeated exile during the rise of fascism.

This amalgam of the man and his work made it particularly easy and pleasant for the three of us, jointly with Fernando Henrique Cardoso,[8] to organize the tribute to Albert Hirschman that is embodied in this volume. The response of very distinguished colleagues working in the United States, Europe and Latin America was immediate and enthusiastic.[9] The Ford Foundation, the Inter-American Foundation and the Helen Kellogg Institute for International Studies of the University of Notre Dame generously agreed to support the initiative. Under the auspices of the latter, we held a conference at the University of Notre Dame, April 15–17, 1984, when the first versions of the chapters of this volume were presented and discussed. After the conference, we were fortunate to count on the valuable contributions, first, of Mrs. Gwen Steege of Williams College and, later on, of Ms. Caroline Domingo of the Helen Kellogg Institute, for the follow-up of the revisions and for the editing of the present volume.

Finally, since we have not blushed in making explicit our friendship and admiration for Albert Hirschman, there is no reason to silence our equivalent feelings for Sarah Hirschman. Her wit, grace, humanity, and sense of humor rhyme admirably well with her husband's and with the *opus* to which the contributors and editors of this volume render tribute.

Alejandro Foxley
Michael McPherson
Guillermo O'Donnell

December, 1985

NOTES

1. Albert O. Hirschman, *Essays in Trespassing: Economics to Politics and Beyond* (Cambridge: Cambridge University Press, 1981).

2. Albert O. Hirschman, *National Power and the Structure of Foreign Trade* (Berkeley and Los Angeles: University of California Press, 1945; written in 1941/2. Reprinted 1969; expanded paperback edition 1980).

3. Albert O. Hirschman, *The Strategy of Economic Development* (New Haven: Yale University Press, 1958, reprinted 1978 by The Norton Library).

4. Albert O. Hirschman, *Journeys Toward Progress: Studies of Economic Policy-Making in Latin America* (New York: Twentieth Century Fund, 1963, reprinted 1973 by The Norton Library).

5. Albert O. Hirschman, *A Bias for Hope: Essays on Development and Latin America* (New Haven: Yale University Press, 1971, reprinted 1985 by Westview Press).

6. See *A Bias for Hope* and *Essays in Trespassing*.

7. As implied from what we say above, this is somewhat of a treason to the characteristic anti-systemic nature of Hirschman's work. But—aside from the fact that for some reason this is what book editors are supposed to do—the apparent thematic rigidity is largely overcome because, in the best Hirschmanian spirit, many of the chapters of this volume commit their own unabashed trespassing.

8. Cardoso's responsibilities as a Senator during the difficult years of the transition to democracy in Brazil prevented him from active participation in the execution of this project, but not from continued solidarity with it.

9. Among those colleagues and contributors to the present volume we must sadly note Carlos Díaz-Alejandro, prematurely deceased at the height of his creative career.

PART I

Strategies for Economic Development

Modes of Industrial Development

Generalized Linkages in Industrial Development: A Reexamination of Basic Petrochemicals in Brazil

Peter Evans

In a recent retrospection, Albert Hirschman suggests that if there were a popularity contest among the various propositions put forward in his early work, "the idea of favoring industries with strong backward and forward linkages would surely receive first prize."[1] As forward and backward linkages became absorbed into the vocabulary of development economics, Hirschman characteristically advanced an even more imaginative formulation of the linkage idea in the form of a "Generalized Linkage Approach."[2] Unlike the original linkage formulations, which not only focused on industry but provided a powerful set of arguments in favor of the "bias" toward industry that tended to characterize policymakers in developing countries,[3] the "generalized" version focused on primary export staples.

In his later generalization, Hirschman crosscuts forward and backward linkages with the "inside-outside" distinction[4]— inside if the forward or backward linkage lends itself to exploitation by the same set of entrepreneurs who instigate the original industry and outside if the linkage is only likely to be taken advantage of by a diffrent group. The generalized approach also adds "fiscal" and "consumption" linkages to production linkages. He closes the discussion of the "Generalized Linkage Approach" with one of his most intriguing and original excursuses, which he labels "micro-Marxism": an "attempt to show how the shape of economic development, including its social and political components, can be traced to the specific economic activities a country takes up."[5] Micro-Marxism takes traditional Marxist concern with the way in which forces of production shape social and political configurations (relations of production), and focuses it at a level of concrete, specific kinds of production.

Surprisingly, there have been relatively few case studies of indus-

7

trial sectors (as opposed to primary products or infrastructure investments) using a linkage approach.[6] More attempts at analyzing advanced
industrial sectors from a linkage perspective should not only provide
new insights into the evolution of the sectors studied but also enrich
our theoretical understanding of linkages. Among the innumerable
candidates for such an attempt, it is hard to imagine one more
appropriate than the Brazilian petrochemical industry.

The basic petrochemical industry in Brazil emerged in São Paulo
in the late sixties on the basis of a complex set of entrepreneurial
initiatives which involved local private capitalists working together
with TNCs and entrepreneurial managers within the state apparatus.
An even more interesting phase of the industry's development began
with the initiation of the Polo Petroquímico do Nordeste in Camacari,
Bahia, one of Brazil's most backward regions, which started in the
early seventies and came on stream in the late seventies. A third,
similar regional complex has since come on stream in Rio Grande
do Sul. Since I have already made several attempts to describe the
general evolution of the industry,[7] the description presented here will
be limited to illustrations of the different kinds of linkages that have
been involved in the development of the industry.

Backward and Forward Linkages in Basic Petrochemicals

What strikes a new observer of basic petrochemical production
most of all are the compelling backward and forward linkages that
bind together the production of feedstocks and the basic products of
the next generation. Within the basic petrochemical industry itself,
at least as far as its most important products are concerned,[8] unbalanced growth is next to impossible. Plants producing polyvinyl chlo-
ride, polyethylene, and polypropylene must have an adjacent source
of olefins. Conversely, a naphtha cracker without such plants close
by to use its output would be unable to operate, almost literally an
industrial "cathedral in the desert." It is precisely because of the
strong compulsion to balanced growth within a petrochemical complex
that the relation between the complex and other industries is so likely
to be "unbalanced." Unless there is already substantial demand for
the products of the third and fourth generation, investments of the
scale necessary to create a petrochemical complex are unlikely. Once
local demand is sufficient to justify a complex, it will almost inevitably
be built with a capacity that is ahead of demand. In short, petro-

chemical complexes are children of backward linkage and depend critically on forward linkages for their future economic viability.

While basic petrochemicals must be understood as fundamentally the products of backward linkages, the principal linkage leading backwards from petrochemical production itself—to oil production—was, at least in the case of Brazil, problematic. Naphtha and energy (traditionally produced by means of oil or natural gas) are the most important raw material inputs in the basic petrochemical industry. Given that oil is in more or less fixed and clearly inadequate local supply,[9] this represents the stimulation of an "infeasible backward linkage."[10] The possible negative implications of this infeasible backward linkage from petrochemicals to oil are minor compared to those of the automobile industry. (Petrochemical consumption accounts for only about 5% of petroleum consumption.) Nonetheless, this particular backward linkage must be counted as a disadvantage of petrochemicals.

The other obvious linkage from basic petrochemicals is to the engineering and capital goods industries. At first, this seemed almost as much of a disadvantage as the link back to oil. When the decision was initially made to go into local olefin production, the balance of payment implications of this linkage were as negative as those of the linkage to oil. Brazilians had no experience whatsoever in producing the equipment for a modern petrochemical plant. Some of the smaller, simpler items (e.g., smaller pumps, boilers and turbines) could be obtained from local suppliers, but the larger more sophisticated equipment had to be purchased abroad. Plant design and construction required experience that only foreign engineering firms could provide. The linkage to capital goods proved, however, much more dynamic than the raw materials' linkage. In the recent additions to the Northeast pole (Camacari) and in the construction of the plants for the Polosul (near Pôrto Alegre), it has not only been possible to source all but the most sophisticated capital goods locally but also to contract local firms to do most of the engineering and design work. What might at first have seemed an infeasible backward linkage had become a developmentally valuable one.

The export potential generated from this kind of backward linkage makes it particularly interesting. Brazil has not yet become an exporter of petrochemical capital goods, but projects like Camacari and the Polosul have been important in the development of a more general comparative advantage in engineering and construction activities in adverse environments. Brazilian construction companies have begun to make major contributions to the balance of payments by

garnering contracts in other third world countries. According to Sercovich, "Brazilian companies are emerging as major contenders in . . .
the export of large-scale engineering projects."[11] Obviously, the petrochemical industry cannot claim to have been the only, or even the
most important, factor in generating this new source of Brazilian
comparative advantage, but the petrochemical poles did play a role
in inducing investment and learning on the part of construction and
engineering companies. One important specific example is the contract
for the construction of the Polosul naphtha cracker. It explicitly requires that the European partner who is supplying the technology will
enable Petroquisa engineers to acquire the expertise necessary to
construct a cracker on their own in the future, and that they will be
allowed to bid on construction contracts for crackers in other countries.[12]

As the example of the steam cracker makes clear, the capacity
of backward linkages from petrochemicals to generate learning in
local infant industries depended on more than the size of the new
market for capital goods. It depended on the existence of an enforceable
administrative preference for "inside" as opposed to "outside" linkages. Letting the contracts without regard for whether they were filled
by local or foreign firms would have allowed some role for local
construction companies, but local equipment producers and engineering companies would never have developed to the same extent. The
link to technological capacity in steam cracker construction was explicitly a negotiated one rather than one entailed by the creation of
the market. Nor is the importance of non-market elements limited
to backward linkages. They are equally salient in the case of forward
linkages.

Forward linkages are generally less compelling and more difficult
to measure than backward linkages, and this is certainly the case in
basic petrochemicals. Nonetheless, analysis of forward linkages is
crucial to any assessment of the industry's developmental impact. By
the time investments in basic petrochemicals were contemplated,
there was already substantial final demand for textiles made of synthetic fibers, parts and consumer goods made of thermoplastic resin,
paints, detergents and the other end products which are based on
petrochemical production. Once investments in basic petrochemicals
were in place, the intermediary industries which transform petrochemical products into inputs for industries currently satisfying this
final demand on the basis of imported inputs should, therefore, have
been subjected to a pincer movement of backward and forward linkages, provided that the initiation of local petrochemical production

actually created some positive forward linkages. Creating a forward linkage depends, however, on whether the locally produced input creates an external economy from the point of view of downstream users. In the case of petrochemicals the existence of the advantage was ambiguous.

The planners, policymakers and entrepreneurs who pushed for the installation of the industry all saw forward linkages as critically important. When the inputs were gases that had to be delivered via pipeline, the forward linkages connecting second and third generation firms had the same compelling character as the links between the first and second generation. In these cases local downstream production, which had not previously been a possibility, became one. Even in these cases, however, local downstream production costs were still likely to be higher than the cost of producing abroad. In cases where transportation of inputs was a possibility, their local availability probably did not create significant external economies in comparison with imported substitutes, if external economies are judged purely on a relative price basis. The nature of the forward linkages envisaged in these cases was rather complex and depended on the kind of downstream producer involved.

Transnational corporations might be induced to begin producing technologically sophisticated fine chemicals that would serve as inputs for the pharmaceutical industry, agricultural chemicals, etc., but it was not primarily lower prices for their inputs that was going to be the incentive. For TNCs with extensive global marketing and supply organizations, international markets were perfectly reasonable sources of supply. Reliance on international markets even had the advantage of facilitating intra-firm transactions. The key to creating forward linkages as far as the downstream TNCs were concerned was setting up a situation which focused attention on the absence of particular products and processes for which local raw materials were now available. Thus it might be appropriate to stimulate the TNCs to think of these activities as ones in which to make defensive investments in anticipation of oligopolistic reaction.

The other set of actors whom local production was designed to stimulate were local entrepreneurs involved in transforming plastics into parts and light consumer goods, making things like PVC plumbing pipes, plastic auto parts, and plastic containers and toys. For these entrepreneurs, the uncertainties of the international market were a potential issue. As small consumers distant from world centers of petrochemical production, local Brazilian manufacturers, especially those outside of São Paulo, could be treated as a spillover market and, therefore, subjected to the vagaries of rapid price rises or lack of supplies created by the volatile petrochemical markets of the seventies. For these producers, it made sense to argue that predictable local supplies were preferable to uncertain international supplies, even if local producers were not internationally competitive in terms of their production costs.

For both kinds of producers the disciplines of basic petrochemical production were important in alleviating problems that might have been created by uncertainties surrounding local production in terms of quality. Process technology of the kind used in basic petrochemicals is very intolerant of substandard construction engineering or maintenance. A substandard plant might quite literally blow up. Such discipline raises the level of backward linkage required to get the industry started in the first place, but, once in place, its very existence is a testimony to its efficiency. Customers are, therefore, less likely to encounter, or have expectations of encountering, problems of substandard products.[13] Even with the diminished quality uncertainty of local inputs provided by the disciplines of basic petrochemical technology, and even with the increased uncertainties surrounding imported inputs as a result of the volatility of international markets during the period, the simple availability of local inputs would probably have been insufficient in itself to induce the desired amount of downstream investment. Market-generated forward linkages had to be administratively enhanced by a variety of incentives in order to become effective. Accessibility to low-cost capital was very important to local firms. "Reservation of the market" through tariff protection was crucial to both locals and TNCs. Generous tax breaks were also important to both. Of course, without the availability of local inputs the incentives would not have made sense, but without administrative enhancement the market signals provided by local availability would not have had the same potency.

Just as in the case of the backward linkage to capital goods production, the linkage effect is not simply a function of prices or the size of the market generated. The linkage effects of market forces are mediated by a complex set of politically constructed administrative mechanisms. These mechanisms are likely to be particularly central in a "politicized market economy"[14] like the Brazilian one, but they are likely to be significant in almost any developing economy. What our analysis suggests then, is that research on backward and forward linkages which tries to reduce them to input-output matrixes is likely to miss the mark.

Inside, Outside, and Spatial Linkages

It should already be clear from the discussion of forward and backward linkages that the question of whether an activity is likely to be induced cannot be considered apart from the question of *who* is targeted as its potential initiator. In Hirschman's terms this is the question of "inside" versus "outside" linkages, that is, whether the new activity induced is carried on by the same actors as the inducing activity or by different actors. Closely related to the inside-outside question is the issue of "spatial linkages." In the generalized formulation, Hirschman suggests that, "With the broader linkage concept a new activity could be defined as one that yields the same product as before but is carried on in a new place."[15] For an industry whose evolution has been as tightly intertwined with questions of stimulating the participation of local capital and rectifying regional imbalances as Brazilian petrochemicals, questions of spatial and inside-outside linkages are central.

In the first stage, the development of basic petrochemical production in São Paulo, basic petrochemicals can be seen as generated by a powerful pincer movement of forward and backward linkages. Since most of the actors were already involved in the industry (either downstream as plastics producers or upstream as refiners), the linkages were primarily inside. When the decision was made to construct the second pole in the Northeast (Camacari), the possibility of getting some of the same actors to undertake production of the same goods in a different locale was the essence of the strategy.[16] Without the existence of local entrepreneurs, skilled labor and experienced organizations in São Paulo, contemplating the construction of a basic petrochemical complex in Camacari would not just have been more difficult, it would probably have been disastrously quixotic. This two-stage strategy in which an important backward linkage is first implemented without any attempt at spatial mobility, and then spatial mobility is attempted while holding the product and producers constant, seems a quite reasonable way of attempting unbalanced growth without allowing the imbalances to become overwhelming.

Trying to add spatial mobility to backwards integration in the creation of the Polo do Nordeste (and later the Polosul) made it more difficult to exploit the backward linkages inherent in the development of the center south markets for plastics and other petrochemically based products. The decision to "do it the hard way" was in part a conscious choice to trade increased regional development "side effects" for greater difficulty in undertaking the initial investment. It would, however, be a mistake to see the regional development effects of these complexes as simply side effects. The projected regional development consequences of both complexes provided a central part of the impetus for their creation. Regional leaders in Bahia took the initiative in generating feasibility studies and political support for the project. Pressure from regional leaders in Rio Grande do Sul was equally central to the initiation of the Polosul. Expected regional development effects can be legitimately argued in both cases to have been "essential to the realization of the project's principal effect and purpose," and, therefore, "mixed side effects" in Hirschman's terminology.[17]

In the third stage, the attempt to use the forward linkages generated by basic petrochemicals to induce the creation of locally owned downstream transforming industries, the question of inside spatial linkages versus outside but spatially compact linkages became more complicated. The first preference of the backers of the regional complexes, especially their local backers, was to limit inside spatial linkages. They wanted to avoid having locally-owned Paulista firms set up branch plants in the Northeast (or Rio Grande do Sul) and instead make space for geographically inside but industrially outside participants, that is, local entrepreneurs currently involved in other activities.[18] Having Paulista firms create subsidiaries in the region of the poles was definitely a second choice, but still one that was strongly preferred over continued expansion of the industry in the geographic confines of São Paulo. The aim, in short, was to try at least to benefit from spatial linkages and to capture the effects of forward linkages within the immediate region of the complexes.

Stimulating spatial linkages proved difficult to do (even with substantial administrative enhancement of forward linkages).[19] The difficulty of attracting local (in the sense of local to the region) entrepreneurs suggests an extension of Hirschman's arguments regarding technological complexity and outside linkages. Hirschman's own discussion focuses on the difficulty of achieving strictly inside forward linkages (that is to say inducing those who are engaged in the upstream activity to move forward, e.g., from sugar cultivation to refining).[20] This example suggests analogous problems when the insiders are defined in regional terms. For instance, when forward linkages lead to activities that are alien in terms of the nature of other entrepreneurial activities common in the region (in the case of the Northeast most entrepreneurial activity is likely to be non-industrial), then "leakage" rather than linkage is likely to result. In this case the possibility is exacerbated by the fact that there is no pincer movement at the regional level (since the principal forward linkages from the transforming industries lead to São Paulo).

The difficulty of attracting Paulista branch plants suggests some interesting ideas regarding the dynamics of spatial inside linkages. Hirschman's original example of a spatial inside linkage is the movement of coffee producers from the Paraíba valley near Rio to the state of São Paulo in response to soil exhaustion. This is a very different case; the possibility of spatial inside linkages depends on the relative weight of the linkages forward from the petrochemical complex to transforming industries as compared to the backward linkages created by the growth of markets for final products in São Paulo (and the center south more generally). The forward linkages from the pole were administratively enhanced (by the various incentive programs) but the administrative enhancements were counterbalanced by the attractiveness of São Paulo as a business environment and the organizational difficulties that would be entailed for any small firm trying to operate in two widely separated geographical locations.

In the end, the difficulties which the pole's planners experienced in attracting "third or fourth generation"[21] firms from the center-south reinforces at a regional level Hirschman's original contention regarding forward linkages in general. They may be powerful as part of a pincer movement which also includes backward linkages, but they are easily overwhelmed by the backward linkages when the two produce opposing incentives.[22]

Extensions: Managerial Linkages and "Inverted Micro-Marxism"

The language of linkages, backwards and forwards, inside and outside, provides a fruitful way of discussing both the origins and effects of the basic petrochemical industry in Brazil. At the same time, this application of linkage thinking has helped elaborate and clarify the nature of forward and backward, inside and outside, and spatial linkages, as well as pointing to some interesting interrelations among the different kinds of linkages. Perhaps most interesting, however, are some extensions of linkage thinking suggested by the case. Two that seem particularly worth exploring might be called "managerial linkages" and "inverted micro-Marxism."

The term managerial linkages provides a way of referring to the tendency for investment in one industry to induce investment in another, not necessarily because the two are connected by buyer-seller relations, but because the second provides an outlet for the skills and organizational capabilities generated in the first. Such linkages might result in a horizontal connection across competing products sharing similiar production technologies or it might join diverse industries sharing the same socio-political climate. Any connection between industries which gives a corporation operating in one reason to see itself as having some kind of comparative advantage in a second creates the possibility of a managerial linkage.

An example of a managerial linkage built around similiar production technologies is the connection between the development of petrochemicals and recent advances in ethanol (alcohol) based technologies for the production of basic feedstocks. Petroquisa has reportly developed an economical, energy-conserving technology for producing ethylene from ethanol.[23] What this represents is investment in a competitive technology (with very different linkage characteristics) by a producer whose ability to make such an investment grew out of its successful investment in a contrasting way of producing the original product.

The managerial linkage in this case is particularly interesting because it may have provided a connection to a potentially fruitful alternative development path. Finding economical ways of using ethanol as the basis of olefin production would have substantial advantages for Brazil. Most important it would dramatically change the negative backward linkages that characterize petrochemical production. Sugar, not oil, is the principal source of ethanol. Ethanol also promises the possibility of more thoroughly internalizing the backward linkages to capital goods while at the same time opening up some potential export markets. Since the scale of ethanol-based olefin plants is less overwhelming than that of naphtha or natural-gas-based plants, this new technology could be very attractive to petroleum-importing LDCs; and, since technologically dominant core country TNCs have little interest in the technology, Brazil could easily end up with a dominant position in ethanol-based techniques of production.

Managerial linkages guided by socio-political as opposed to technological connections are nicely illustrated by the organizational history of the Camacari pole. The corporate vehicle for Petroquisa's involvement in the Northeast pole was a new subsidiary called COPENE. Once the decision to create the third pole had been taken, it was clear that COPENE's further expansion in basic petrochemicals was unlikely. Since COPENE's management, like any other management, has a strong vested interest in expansion (the alternative being to become a "cash cow" for Petroquisa and its downstream partners) they had a strong incentive to discover activities which COPENE, as opposed to some other subsidiary or partner of Petroquisa, would be allowed to undertake.

What was COPENE's comparative advantage *vis-à-vis* their competitors within the Petrobrás family of companies for the use of the cash flow generated by Camacari? Clearly it lay in their new-found "regional identity." The companies involved in Camacari had personnel and technological expertise adapted to the Northeast. In addition, they had the possibility of linking their own aspirations for expansion to the same political forces that made Camacari possible in the first place, as long as they focused on activities in the Northeast. Thus, one of the members of the COPENE management characterized the company as having "a vocation for the Northeast."[24] This "vocation for the Northeast" was subsequently formalized in the creation of NORQUISA, a holding company which became the formal owner of COPENE but which could also invest in other chemical ventures as long as they were in the Northeast. NORQUISA's role is channeling resources from the second generation companies to new chemical investments in the Northeast. One way of reading the name is to say that the "Petro" for "Petroleum" in Petroquisa has been replaced by a "NOR" for "Nordeste." Indeed, one of NORQUISA's new subsidiaries is involved in the production of vinyl acetate on the basis of alcohol and NORQUISA is taking a leading role in the implantation of a "Chloro-chemical" (not petrochemical) complex in the state of Alagoas.[25] If technological learning provided one basis for a managerial linkage leading away from petroleum to other kinds of chemical endeavors, the socio-political logic of organizational competition within the Petrobrás family has provided another.

Whether investment in an industry produces linkages that go backwards, forwards or horizontally from that industry, does not depend simply on the inputs required by the industry or the outputs it generates. The kind of linkages produced may depend even more crucially on how the dominant corporate organizations in the industry are structured. In petrochemicals, the decision to constitute a legally separate company with different owners to form the keystone of the Northeast pole[26] clearly increased the probability that the growth of basic petrochemicals would lead to investments in other branches of the chemical industry, within the geographic boundaries of the Northeast. The decision to create NORQUISA ensured that this would be the case.

Managerial linkages such as those observed in petrochemicals become potentially important as soon as we assume that large corporations in an industry are likely to accumulate at a rate that will exceed investment opportunities in their industry of origin, whether because of market constraints or because of administratively-imposed restrictions. At this point, the "organizational slack"[27] created by the maturation of the corporation's involvement in the first industry becomes a resource to be exploited. In addition, managers are likely to have a strong preference for engaging in new entrepreneurial activities rather than generating dividends that will create only "fiscal linkages"[28] to their industries. They will, therefore, search for other activities that can be plausibly undertaken by the corporate entities they command. In the context of a politicized market economy, linkages like these which run from one activity to another through organizational rather than market channels are likely to be particularly important.

Managerial linkages take the concept of linkages far from the strictly market definitions associated with input-output applications, but the clear success of some of Hirschman's other efforts to join his ideas with an organizational perspective certainly justifies more explicit consideration of the role of organizational factors in the analysis of linkages.[29] Furthermore, such an extension seems very much in the spirit of the 1977 article which goes beyond organizational analysis to broach even broader questions of the socio-political concomitants of industrial choices.

Moving from the level of industrial organization to larger questions of socio-political organization brings us to micro-Marxism. In his generalized linkage formulation, Hirschman raises the possibility of a "particular commodity acting as a multidimensional conspiracy in favor of or against development within a certain historical and socio-political setting" and uses as an example the "special affinity between sugar and slavery in the 16th-century new world."[30] Certainly it is not hard to find affinities between petrochemicals and the forms of socio-political organization that characterize the middle period of Brazil's authoritarian military regime.

The organization of capital associated with petrochemicals is archetypal of those that the Geisel regime tried to construct in the mid-1970s. Given Geisel's intimate association with the development of the industry,[31] it is not at all fanciful to suggest that petrochemicals served at least in part as a model for the regime's more general plans for organizing industrial capital. The essence of the Geisel model is a solidification of the "triple alliance" binding together multinational, state and local capital with a much greater emphasis than in earlier military regimes on the role of the state and particularly on its role as the champion and protector of local capital.[32]

This was essentially the kind of structure that was created in petrochemicals. Control of the raw material (petroleum) and the necessity of tightly "balanced" growth in basic petrochemicals gave the state unusual leverage. Transnational capital did control the production technology, but a good portion of this technology was available from engineering firms, and even when technology was proprietary competition among producers with different national bases (Japanese versus Europeans versus North Americans), it provided more leverage than would have been possible in other industries with the same technological sophistication. The possibility of administratively enhanced forward linkages surrounding the poles provided further opportunity for building relations with local capital.

Geisel's version of the "triple alliance," was compatible with petrochemicals in a way that it would not have been with, for example, automobiles. Since product design is more important than process technology, the hold of the TNCs over the technological essentials is more difficult to break in automobiles. The backward linkages from automobiles connect transnational assemblers with local parts' producers and leave no room for an expanded state role. The fact that the industry produces for a final demand consumer market in which marketing is very important gives the TNCs greater leverage and means so that local capital has no particular interest in controlling the production or pricing policies of the TNCs (as they do in the case of an intermediary industry like petrochemicals for which they are the customers). In short, emphasizing automobiles instead of petrochemicals as a leading sector would have produced a quite different triple alliance.

The existence of correspondences between the characteristics of particular industrial sectors and the overall configuration of relations among different kinds of capital fit the general model laid out in Hirschman's discussion of micro-Marxism for staples. Because the sectors are industrial, however, an additional question is raised which departs fundamentally from the spirit of micro-Marxism. When staples are the focus, and comparative advantage is plausibly related to natural endowments, then it is quite reasonable to start with classic Marxist assumption that the "base" determines the superstructure, that is that the prominence of particular sectors may be at least partially responsible for the prevalance of more general socio-political characteristics. When industrial sectors, especially ones with as little connection to natural endowments, are involved, "inverted Micro-marxism," that is the possibility that the superstructure is determining the base, must also be considered.

In a world of "sectoral targeting" and "constructed comparative advantage," it cannot be taken for granted that the particular sectors are selected for prominence by the invisible hand and that their prominence can serve as a natural starting point for analyzing the social and political components of the surrounding political economy. While there is clearly an economic logic which leads toward the prominence of particular sectors at particular points in a country's economic development, it is also necessary to consider the possibility that particular sectors may be promoted and even developed into leading sectors in part because of the social-political consequences that are perceived as being associated with them. It may well make sense to invert the logic of micro-Marxism. Certainly in the case of Brazilian petrochemicals it makes much more sense to argue that the regime promoted the industry (in part because of its perceived socio-political concomitants) than that the industry was responsible for the emergence of the regime.

The argument should not be overstated. Obviously, the petro-chemical industry was not developed only because of its compatibility with socio-political characteristics considered desirable by the regime. Nor is it the case that only certain kinds of regimes will try to develop petrochemical production. But, holding economic parameters like availability of oil, size of the domestic market, and overall level of industrialization constant, the state's willingness to channel investment into petrochemicals rather than some other industry may well depend in part on the industry's perceived compatibility with general socio-political goals.

The Geisel regime was clearly more willing to invest in petro-chemicals, given that these investments held the promise of an expanded role for state and local private capital, than it would have been if the industry could only have been developed on the basis of wholly-owned TNC subsidiaries. Conversely, the military regime was not deterred by characteristics that might have led a Populist or Social Democratic regime to be more reticent. The fact that the industry would employ almost no unskilled labor after the construction phase and very little skilled labor per dollar of investment might easily have worried a regime in which employment and income distribution were central concerns. The fact that building the industry would entail contracting massive external debt obligations might have worried a regime more concerned with limiting its dependence on international financial capital.

Despite the desire here to draw attention to the possibility of inverting the micro-Marxist analysis, it is also important to underline the reciprocal character of the relation between industries and socio-political regimes. In Hirschman's words, "the connection between the productive activity, be it a staple commodity or an industrial complex, and a social-political regime is not 'unidirectional.' "[33] Just as socio-political concomitants may help explain the state's enthusiasm for promoting a particular industry, the industry's subsequent existence will help reinforce the more general socio-political characteristics that contributed to its birth.

A version of micro-Marxism that includes inverted influences as well as those in the classical direction, is of interest for policy as well as theoretical reasons. If different leading sectors do, in fact, tend to carry different socio-political components in their wake as micro-Marxism suggests, then those interested in fostering social and political change in an era of sectoral targeting and constructed comparative advantage will want to engage in a very careful analysis of the generalized linkage effects of whatever sectoral targeting they might wish to undertake. Put more positively, sectoral targeting may be a way of "smuggling in change via side effects" that should be consciously exploited.[34]

The possibilities should not be exaggerated. The extent to which the state (or for that matter private capitalists) can use sectoral targeting to construct or reinforce larger socio-political structures is rather strictly limited by the logic of prices and profits. Nonetheless, every industrializing regime engages in the promotion of specific industrial sectors, whether by accident or design. Some analysis in a micro-Marxist vein of the probable socio-political concomitants of different sectors is, therefore, both necessary and useful. For example, export promotion must almost inevitably be part of any LDC strategy, but what are the implications of picking different sectors? What are the micro-Marxist implications of soybeans as opposed to beef, or apparel as opposed to consumer electronics? The consequences can, of course, only be projected in a speculative way and international markets will dictate most of the choices, but there is still likely to be a set of rough equivalents. The micro-Marxist differences among them could well prove more important in the long run than the strictly economic differences.

Conclusion

Our discussion of petrochemicals has covered only a portion of the linkages involved and even those deserve a more systematic treatment. Even so, the usefulness of the linkage approach in the analysis of industrial sectors has been fully vindicated. Equally important, the petrochemical example has demonstrated how consideration of an advanced industrial sector can stimulate new ways of thinking about linkages. The fact that an advanced industrial sector rather than a raw material sector was under consideration shaped the treatment of forward and backward linkages, and inside-outside linkages. It was central to the discussion of managerial linkages and was particularly crucial to making a plausible case for inverted micro-Marxism. The aim of drawing the attention of researchers working on advanced industrial sectors to the possibilities of the linkage approach and of those working on linkages to the value of exploring advance industrial sectors seems then to have been served.

At the same time, this attempt to travel the tangled path of forward and backward, inside and outside linkages has generated another, very different kind of conclusion. It has led to a heightened sense of loss on reading Hirschman's statement at the beginning of the generalized linkage article that "the following pages should be read as an outline and preview of the book that might have been *or may yet be.*"[35] When it comes to the examination of specific sequences of linkages and extrapolating from these to general arguments regarding the nature of different types of linkages, there is really not a good substitute for the originator of the concept. The book that "may yet be" could play a crucial role in stimulating new case studies using the approach. It could even be seen as the kind of investment that would in turn induce a variety of related investments in an intellectual industry of great potential profitability. In short, it could be an ideal undertaking for someone who sees development as entailing the "calling forth and enlisting for development purposes resources that are scattered, hidden or badly utilized."

NOTES

1. Albert O. Hirschman, "A Dissenter's Confession: *The Strategy of Economic Development* Revisited" (Washington, D.C.: IBRD, 1982), 20.

2. Albert O. Hirschman, "A Generalized Linkage Approach to Development, with Special Reference to Staples," *Economic Development and Cultural Change* (1977): 67–97. Reprinted in *Essays in Trespassing: Economics to Politics and Beyond* (New York: Cambridge University Press, 1981), Chap. 4.

3. See Albert O. Hirschman, *The Strategy of Economic Development* (New Haven: Yale University Press, 1958), 109: "agriculture certainly stands convicted on the count of its lack of direct stimulus to the setting up of new activities through linkage effects: the superiority of manufacturing in this respect is crushing." It should be noted that Hirschman is more favorably disposed toward agriculture in his later work, characterizing this early statement as an "unhelpful position." See his *Development Projects Observed* (Washington, D.C.: The Brookings Institution, 1977), 184.

4. Hirschman, "Generalized Linkage Approach," 80–87.

5. Hirschman, "Generalized Linkage Approach," 92.

6. Among the earlier works whose "linkage approach" Hirschman cites as exemplars in his 1977 article there are two on primary products (Pearson on oil and Roemer on fishing) and two on infrastructure (Fishlow on railroads and Tendler on hydroelectric power) but none on a manufacturing sector. One of the few attempts to work on manufacturing sectors in the spirit of Hirschman's "micro-Marxism" is James Kurth's "Industrial Change and Political Change: A European Perspective" in Dave Collier, ed., *The New Authoritarianism in Latin America* (Princeton: Princeton University Press, 1979), 319–62.

7. For my own earlier ideas on Brazilian petrochemicals in this period see, *Dependent Development: The Alliance of Multinational, State and Local Capital in Brazil* (Princeton: Princeton University Press, 1979); "Collectivized Capitalism: Integrated Petrochemical Complexes and Capital Accumulation in Brazil" in T. Bruneau and P. Faucher, eds., *Authoritarian Capitalism: Brazil's Contemporary Political and Economic Development* (Boulder, Col.: Westview Press, 1981), 85–126; "Reinventing the Bourgeoisie: State Entrepreneurship and Class Formation in Dependent Capitalist Development," *American Journal of Sociology* 88, S210–47. For some other views see, José Tavares Araujo and Vera Dick, "Governo, Empresas Multinacionais e Empresas Nacionais: O caso da Indústria Petroquímica," *Pesquisa e Planejamento* 4, no. 3 (1974): 629–54; Francisco Sercovich, "State-Owned Enterprises and Dynamic Comparative Advantages in the World Petrochemical Industry: The Case of Commodity Olefins in Brazil," Development Discussion Working Paper No. 96 (Cambridge: Harvard Institute for International Development).

8. The lighter petrochemical fractions, known as olefins (e.g., ethylene, propylene) are very difficult to transport for any distance, requiring very expensive and technologically difficult cryogenic techniques. The highest volume plastics are produced from these fractions. The heavier fractions (aromatics like toluene and xylene) are easier to transport, but since they are co-products along with olefins of the initial cracking process, the compulsion to integrated production of both feedstocks and basic second generation products at the same location is extremely powerful.

9. It is not, of course, strictly true that local supplies of petroleum are "fixed." It is always possible that significant new, economically exploitable reserves will be discovered in Brazil. Were this to happen our vision of the backward linkages from petrochemicals would reverse dramatically. For the

present, however, it is reasonable to view increased investments in petroleum exploration as an essentially quixotic effort to avoid facing the implications of the lack of a key natural resource.

10. The consequences of inducing investment in an industry which cannot, in fact, be developed have not been well explored in the linkage literature. This has, of course, a long tradition in more traditional Latin American thinking on industrial development which is full of invective against "artificial industries," but the implications of this kind of negative linkage effect would seem worth some conceptual elaboration.

11. Francisco Sercovich, "The Exchange and Absorption of Technology in Brazilian Industry," in Bruneau and Faucher, eds., *Authoritarian Capitalism*, 131.

12. The agreement on the cracker requires that the first third-country cracker contracts should be joint ventures with the European partner but subsequent ventures on a wholly Brazilian basis are also possible.

13. The issue of the "latitudes and disciplines" associated with different kinds of economic activities was raised by Hirschman in *Strategy* and is an important theme in *Development Projects Observed* (Chap. 3), but the relation between the degree of "discipline" or "latitude" that characterizes production in an industry and the industry's ability to generate forward or backward linkages remains to be explored. Presumably, high degrees of technologically determined discipline make backward linkages more difficult since the industry is likely to be intolerant of quality variances among its suppliers and therefore to prefer traditional (probably international) sources to incipient local ones. This example suggests, however, that discipline may be an advantage in generating forward linkages.

14. The phrase comes from Michael Barzelay's very interesting study of the interaction of political and market factors in Brazil's alcohol program, *The Politicized Market Economy: Alcohol in the Brazilian Energy Strategy* (Berkeley: University of California Press, forthcoming).

15. Hirschman, "Generalized Linkage Approach," 82.

16. Some change in the specific corporate actors involved was also important to the strategy (see Evans, "Reinventing the Bourgeoisie," S228–29 and "Collectivized Capitalism," 104, 107), but the degree of continuity was still sufficient to make it a case of "inside linkage."

17. See Hirschman. *Development Projects Observed*, 161.

18. The idea of a strictly "inside linkage," that is inducing the same companies involved in basic and intermediary petrochemicals to integrate forward, was rejected from the beginning, both by the companies involved (industry practice includes a general avoidance of "competing with your customers") and by the backers of the project more generally who wanted to make sure a role was preserved for smaller local capitalists.

19. See Evans, "Reinventing the Bourgeoisie," 239.

20. See Hirschman, "Generalized Linkage Approach," 78.

21. The term "generation" refers to the number of steps between the

activity and the production of the basic feedstock. Thus ethylene would be the first generation, polyethylene would be the second generation and molded plastic containers would be the third generation. In the case of other products, like synthetic fibers, additional steps required to produce the petrochemical intermediates make the fibers a fourth generation product.

22. A caveat should be added. Hirschman is careful to insist on the fact that linkage effects "need time to unfold" ("Generalized Linkage Approach," 70). The view offered here is based on looking at the industry immediately after the Camacari project came on stream; forward linkages have hardly had time to unfold. The picture may look quite different after the complex has been in operation for twenty years.

23. See Fernando Baratelli, Jr., "Projeto Eteno de Alcool," *Boletin Técnico Petrobrás*, no. 2 (April–June, 1980): 91–100. See also, Evans, "Collectivized Capitalism," 120–21. Like the earlier discussion of the difficulties involved in realizing the potential for forward linkages in the two regional complexes, this discussion is based on the situation in the industry as of 1979 and needs updating. It should be taken as a somewhat speculative illustration rather than as an empirical description of the current state of the industry.

24. See Evans, "Collectivized Capitalism," 99, 117–18.

25. See Norquisa, *Annual Report 1983*.

26. This may be contrasted to the practice followed by Petrobrás with regard to its refineries which are all operating units within a single legal corporate entity.

27. See James March and Herbert Simon, *Organizations* (New York: John Wiley and Sons, 1959) for the original discussion of organizational slack. See also the subsequent application to firm growth by Edith Penrose.

28. See Hirschman, "Generalized Linkage Approach," 73. Hirschman uses the term to refer to relations between the state and private industry, but the "cash cow" relationship in private industry is closely analogous.

29. The article with Lindblom, "Economic Development, Research and Development and Policymaking: Some Converging Views" (*Behavioral Science*, April 1962) is one example. *Exit, Voice, and Loyalty* (Cambridge: Harvard University Press, 1970) and several aspects of the discussion in *Development Projects Observed* might be considered others.

30. Hirschman, "Generalized Linkage Approach," 96.

31. Geisel was not only president of Petrobrás prior to becoming President of the Republic (and at the time that the development of basic petrochemicals was initiated). He also became the first president of NORQUISA after his term as President of the Republic had ended.

32. See Evans, "Reinventing the Bourgeoisie."

33. Albert O. Hirschman, "Linkages (in Economic Development)" (unpublished ms., 1984), 23.

34. See Hirschman, *Development Projects Observed*, 168–74, for a discussion of smuggling in relation to the design of development projects. A substantial portion of Hirschman's discussion of project design might be

transferred with some modifications to a generalized linkage approach to sectoral targeting.

35. Hirschman, "Generalized Linkage Approach," 71 (emphasis added).

Changing Models of Economic Efficiency and Their Implications for Industrialization in the Third World

Charles F. Sabel

I. Introduction

History seldom settles big questions once and for all. From the last third of the nineteenth century to the present it seemed beyond doubt that mass production—the manufacture of standard goods by means of special-purpose machines and semi-skilled workers—was competitively superior to craft production—the manufacture of specialized goods by means of universal machines and skilled workers. Today, as in the first half of the nineteenth century, mass production no longer seems to be the uniquely efficient form of mechanization. The rapid spread of flexible, often computer-assisted manufacturing techniques in large firms and small, in an astonishing variety of industries and countries, is undermining confidence in the established principles of industrial organization.[1]

This paper argues that by an ironic twist of history these practical and theoretical debates can have important consequences for economic development in the third world. Classical political economy regarded the rise of mass production as a precondition of industrialization (section 2). The view shaped postwar development economics (section 3), and the strategic choices of third-world elites—particularly in Latin America (section 4). The crisis of the 1970s destroyed the preconditions for continued progress down the path of mass production, creating the illusion that no progress in that direction had ever been made (section 5). The crisis also forced firms to experiment with a new, technologically dynamic form of craft organization—flexible specialization—suited to the chronically unstable conditions in which they found themselves (section 6). Surprisingly, I will argue, the way large firms in Latin America have adapted to local markets as well

27

as the spread there of a vast, heterogeneous informal sector have created some of the preconditions for introducing flexible specialization to the region (section 7). Thus the idea—one of the foundations of development economics in the 1950s and 1960s—that change from epoch to epoch and region to region may be indicated in the changed world of the 1980s (section 8).

II. The Classical Model of Development

The classical political economists connected increasing economic efficiency to a logic of specialization (Berg 1980). For Smith, labor productivity was increased by the subdivision of tasks. A top-of-the-widget maker produced more widgets per hour than two whole widget makers. Marx, extending a Leitmotif in Smith's scheme, argued that by reducing tasks to simple motions, the subdivision of labor facilitated design of special-purpose machines that outperformed the human hand. The more work was decomposed, the skill levels reduced, and special-purpose devices substituted for living labor, the more factories resembled a single, automatic apparatus. The end point of this development—symbolized for Marx by the introduction of automatic cotton-spinning equipment in Great Britain in the 1830s—was the modern system of mass production: the use of single-purpose or dedicated machines manned by semi- or unskilled workers to produce vast quantities of standardized goods.

In this vision of development, politics—defined as those conflicts which decide claims to the proceeds of economic activity—influences the progress of specialization insofar as it determines what Smith called the extent of the market. Why would anyone bear the costs of reorganization and run the risks of a more rigid (because product-specific) manufacturing system unless there were customers for the increased output made possible by more efficient methods? Customs barriers, sumptuary laws, taxes, feudal dues—any political intervention in the free exchange of goods which reduced effective demand for a product or reduced the producer's proceeds from its sale—slowed the march of specialization.

But if politics could in this classical view determine the pace and locale of progress, political meddling could not permanently arrest the logic of specialization. That the dynamic of efficiency would triumph in the end was for both Smith and Marx the principal lesson of the fall of feudalism. Despite all their differences, they agreed that history acted through the self-interest of individuals to call forth movements which broadened markets and allowed producers to profit from their efforts. Once there was an efficiency breakthrough anywhere, they agreed further, competition spread it everywhere. Those who could not emulate the new success would be crushed by those who could.

This line of thought was later extended to the analysis of values: convictions about the purpose of life as expressed in everything from prayers to testaments to the organization of the family or village. "Traditional" values (family structures and village communities) were defined in analogy to feudal politics as those that blinded consumers to the infinite possibilities of satisfaction and producers to the limitless profitability of specialization; "modern" values affirmed the necessity and possibility of boundless accumulation. There was dispute as to whether the change of values preceded or followed the change of interests. Did a politically fluky combination of interests call forth new, productive firms whose success redefined the image of the good? Did a theologically fluky change of values encourage accumulation, thereby redefining economic interest?[2] No matter. Whichever came first, there was agreement that once "modern" values appeared, competition assured their generalization no less than that of efficient productive practice.

Capitalism, mass production, and individualism were thus seen as different aspects of the same thing. Capitalism was the form of property which permitted escape from autarky; mass production the form of mechanization which society, thus emancipated, discovered in its search for greater efficiency; and individualism the self-consciousness of the emancipated.

Though it has been criticized innumerable times, this view has had an enduring influence on sophisticated contemporary thought about the watersheds of economic progress. David Landes's *The Unbound Prometheus* (Landes 1972)—until recently the standard textbook account of the first industrial revolution—connects the freedom of British producers and consumers to the country's pioneering successes. The most thoughtful general account of the second industrial revolution, Alfred D. Chandler, Jr.'s *The Visible Hand* (Chandler 1977), connects the geographic extent and political integrity of the U.S. American market to the mass production there in the late nineteenth century of everything from clocks to cigarettes. The writings of the world-system school of Emmanuel Wallerstein connect the third microelectronic industrial revolution to multinational corporations, alone able to exploit global economies of scale to the full (Froebel, Heinrichs, and Kreye 1980).

But what counts more for our purposes is the influence of this story on development economics and the actual course of development in countries that successively followed the pioneers of mechanization. If one measure of an idea's power is its capacity to make alternative ideas unthinkable, then the story of the ineluctable rise of mass production has been powerful indeed. As Hirschman argued in "The Rise and Decline of Development Economics" (Hirschman 1981), the idea of a secular increase in the scale and capital intensity of efficient units of production has decisively shaped modern theories of economic development. Disputes in development economics turned not on whether to accept this general idea but—as we will see next—on what followed practically from it.

III. Development Economics in the Shadow of Mass Production

After World War II classical ideas of the division of labor helped shape and justify the efforts of third-world states to encourage economic development, particularly in the most advanced of the industrializing areas, Latin America. Certainly Smith and Marx would have been nonplussed at the sight of bureaucrats, army officers, and university professors trying to encourage the growth of industrial capitalism rather than giving way before its confident advance. But the twentieth century has been a gigantic lesson in the transformability of theories, political programs, and institutions through their recombination in new contexts. In fact, once the proper combination of interpretations was found, it appeared almost obvious that state promotion of mass-production, mass-consumption society was justified not only by classical teachings but by the experience of nineteenth-century industrialization and the Depression of the 1930s as well.

A direct and important connection between the classical view of the division of labor and postwar ideas about industrialization was Alexander Gerschenkron's work on the economic history of France, Russia, and Germany (Gerschenkron 1972). The later a country began competing with the technological leaders, Gerschenkron argued, the greater would be its need for pools of capital too large to be provided by individuals or rudimentary financial markets. In a hostile world no nation could afford to leave these needs unmet; and the capital would thus have to be provided through large banks in concert with, if not controlled by, the state. He argued further that such public and private efforts would be audibly coordinated by an ideology of development which declared entrepreneurs and officials to be instruments of a progressive nationalism. In Gerschenkron's own ideal world, industrialization would have been managed by the enlightened Josephinian bureaucrats of the old Austro-Hungarian empire (Gerschenkron 1977). Directly and indirectly, this image of a tutelary state helping society industrialize colored the ambitions of the emerging third-world elites. At their most optimistic, indeed, the new leaders could dream of following the German and Japanese examples and leapfrogging industrial powers, investing in best-practice, largest-scale technologies while their competitors amortized older, smaller plants and less efficient organizational techniques (Dore 1973).

A second, more roundabout, yet easily as influential link between classical economics and postwar development strategy was the spread of a suitable reinterpreted form of Keynesianism. Keynes argued that under certain conditions advanced economies, far from being self-equilibrating, topple into a low-equilibrium trap: disruptions in financial markets and changes in the behavior of rentiers could trigger a fall in demand, an increase in unemployment, a further fall in demand, a reduction in investment, and yet another increase in unemployment. If this happened, as it did in the 1930s, markets in the advanced countries would come to resemble the narrow markets of the developing countries, whose expansion was blocked by the classical dilemma of lumpy investments and uncertain demand. Some analogue to the Keynesian techniques of government spending and tax reduction used to relaunch growth in the advanced economies could therefore be used to launch it in industrializing ones (Hirschman 1981). Thus Keynesian legitimation of state intervention in the economy in the first world encouraged its legitimation in the third, while also reinforcing in the latter an association between large-scale production and industrialization which was a marginal theme in the macroeconomic debates of the former.[3]

The pervasiveness of this association and the central strategic conclusions that followed from it were perhaps most clearly revealed in the assumptions shared by contending schools of development economics in the 1950s. All agreed that in light of the stagnation of trade between developed and developing countries in the first postwar decade, industrializing countries could not count on export markets to make good the shortfall of domestic demand. All agreed that investments in efficient equipment would be dauntingly large in relation to existing markets. All agreed that it was necessary to encourage substitution of domestically produced goods for imports by raising tariffs. The divisive questions became: How exactly should the state coordinate the expansion of markets with the necessary increase in investment? Would it be possible to realize this program without radically changing the international economic order?

For advocates of balanced growth, the solution was to create the markets by massive state-financed investments and recover the investments by sales in the new markets (Nurske 1958). If investment funds were allocated among industries in proportion to the potential consumers' preferences, then the capital used to build the new factories would absorb the increased output when it passed as wages through the hands of the workforce. Supply would create its own demand, overcoming the autarkic barriers to specialization. The counterproposal, notably Hirschman's strategy for unbalanced growth (Hirschman 1958), was to attack the problem piecemeal through staggered oversized investment projects, each creating bottlenecks that induced the unmistakable need for further investments.

For advocates of *dependencia,* finally, the question of how investment was timed was subsidiary to the question of how it was controlled (Frank 1967). The *dependistas* argued that the logic of specialization was played out in the world economy as a whole, not in isolated national economies. Increasing specialization of the entire system did not imply increasing specialization of all the parts; on the contrary, the progressive industrialization of some was consistent with and might well depend on the continued provision of raw materials or foodstuffs by others. From this point of view, economic progress depended on emancipation from the political constraints to growth imposed by the developed countries. But in the end these were all disputes within a single family of thought, where kinship was established by descent from the classical view of mass production.

IV. The Disappointing Success of the Mass-Production Model

None of these related development plans worked as their advocates expected, and from the perspective of the near-bankruptcy of Mexico, Brazil, and Argentina in the mid-1980s they might seem like complete failures. But in fact during the 1960s and 1970s the major Latin American countries did progress a surprising distance down the path of import-substitution industrialization. The problem was that progress was more difficult to achieve, more vulnerable to disruption, and less politically benign in its consequences than its architects had imagined it would be.[4]

Some of the difficulties were as obvious in retrospect as the fusion of classical political economy, Keynesian macroeconomics and

Gerschenkronian *etatism* that gave rise to postwar development economics in the first place. The obvious problem with balanced-growth and *dependista* strategies for import substitution was that any country with the resources to change the terms of trade in its own favor and sustain a balanced program of growth could hardly qualify as underdeveloped. If there was to be growth in the developing world, it was going to be unbalanced. The problem with any such strategy, however, was that the first steps often blocked later ones. High tariffs on consumer goods certainly encouraged their domestic production. But domestic production of consumer goods also led to increased imports of everything needed to make them—thus burdening the balance of payments—and encouraged the protected industries to oppose extension of the tariff to their own suppliers: manufacturers of capital and intermediate goods. These later generations of import substitutes were, after all, as likely to be high-cost producers as the first one. But this time it would be the consumer-goods industries, not the consumers, who would pay the bill. The worst result would be stagnation at a slightly higher level of domestic production, not unbalanced growth.

But fitfully and partially the large Latin American countries overcame in practice the obstacles they could not overcome in theory. First, they grew by expanding local production of consumer durables for the home market. Manufacturing output in Brazil, for example, grew at an average annual rate of 8 percent from 1945 to 1962, 3.6 percent from 1964 to 1967, 12.9 percent from 1967 to 1973, and 6.8 percent from 1974 to 1980 (World Bank 1983, iii-iv). These increases exceeded the growth rates in manufacturing output computed at constant prices by the United Nations for the developing and developed market economies as well as the narrower group of Caribbean and Latin American countries in these periods.[5] The scattered information available suggests that by the 1970s this growth was largely due to extension of the domestic markets. It has been estimated, for example, that from 1970 to 1974, growth of domestic demand accounted for 96 percent of the growth of Brazilian manufacturing; between 1974 and 1979 the figure was 86.5 percent (World Bank 1983, vi). Careful studies confirm that this growth was largely attributable to the diffusion of such products as gas and electric stoves, refrigerators, and television sets beyond the conspicuously rich 10 to 20 percent of the population who count as the country's economic elite (Wells 1977).

Second, by the 1970s there was substantial progress towards creating intermediate- and capital-goods industries. The major Latin American countries began to look, in other words, more like complete, self-contained industrial societies than like final assemblers of im-

ported components. Again Brazil was the leader. Its First National
Development Plan in 1971 called for significant direct investments in
production of capital goods and basic industrial inputs. The Second
National Development Plan (1975–1979) continued the investment
program with the aim of establishing national self-sufficiency in the
production of steel and nonferrous metals, pulp and paper, petrochemicals and fertilizers (World Bank 1983, ii. 45). The effects of these
and related programs of import substitution were reflected in the concentration of investment on the core industries and associated infrastructure of mass-production manufacturing. Investments in transport
equipment, chemical products, and metallurgy—some no doubt squan-
dered in, for example, ill-conceived highway projects—accounted for
47.3 percent of total investment in manufacturing in 1969, 62.2 percent
in 1975, and 63.5 percent in 1979 (World Bank 1983, 10).

Third, contrary to the expectations of *dependencia* theorists, at
least some countries were able to loosen the ties that bound them to
subordinate positions in the world division of labor. Mexico and
Brazil borrowed money in the 1970s from the metropoles and lent it
to productive domestic enterprise, public and private. Government
bureaucrats and nationalist entrepreneurs allied to use sovereign power
and divisions among the multinational concerns to reduce foreign
capital's control of domestic developments (Frieden 1981). Studies of
the industrial use of technology in Latin America by Jorge Katz and
his collaborators in the *Programa de investigaciones sobre desarrollo
científico y tecnológico in América Latina* reveal surprising innovative
capacities in large firms that at first glance appear wholly dependent
on foreign expertise (Castano, Katz, and Navajas 1981). None of these
successes, of course, was conclusive. All depended on continued political surefootedness. But they were too robust to discount completely.
Books with ambiguous titles like *Dependent Development* (Evans 1979;
updated, 1982) began to appear in the libraries of area specialists.

There were, however, two conspicuous limits to the successes
of the import-substitution, mass-production model. The first was political. Beginning with the Brazilian coup of 1964—and with the complex exception of Mexico—the largest Latin American countries came
under the control of openly anti-democratic governments. To be sure,
sophisticated attempts by Guillermo O'Donnell and others to connect
the wave of authoritarianism to the model of development remained
unpersuasive. There were too many counterexamples of similar Latin
American countries that did not abandon democracy, and too many
differences in the economic policies of the authoritarian governments
(Canak 1984, 14–16). Nor, as suggested a moment ago, was it even

possible to argue convincingly that success of the mass-production strategy depended on the creation of a politically subsidized middle class through redistribution of income from poor to rich. Wells concluded from his comprehensive study of the diffusion of durables in Brazil that "the main cause of increasing inequality is not particular economic structural requirements nor patterns of resource use, but rather the effectiveness of resistance by the upper-middle and middle classes to a wider distribution of the gains from economic growth" (Wells 1977, 276). But these qualifications are in a sense beside the point. Even if pursuit of the mass-production, import-substitution strategy neither caused nor required a breakdown of democracy or an increase in inequality, it did not automatically promote freedom and equity. For those—and they were many—who associated the progress of the economy with the progress of justice, Latin America's bloody politics made talk of economic success suspicious at best.

The second and ultimately more consequential limit to the postwar development model was the relation between the domestic economy and the world market. At bottom, the import-substitution model implied that developing countries would export only—but at least—so much as they needed to pay for the imports that would ultimately make them self-sufficient. In fact, domestic expansion obviously depended on foreign loans. Even in the 1970s, when the flow of capital from private first-world banks to state development agencies in Latin America become torrential, this lending looked like a good bet to everyone. The borrowers' home markets were, as we saw, expanding; the prices of commodities—their chief exports—were expected to rise (in the second half of the 1970s the Club of Rome was predicting long-term commodity shortages); and their governments guaranteed repayment of loans at floating interest rates usually pegged above those offered to the banks' prime corporate customers (Kuczynski 1982/83, 353–55).

But when the second oil crisis of 1979 pushed the first-world countries into a deep recession, the bets were off. As monetary authorities in the advanced countries raised interest rates to throttle economic activity and slow inflation, they simultaneously increased the debtors' obligation and decreased their ability to repay it by exports to their (now stagnant) traditional customers. If the recession had been as short as commonly anticipated, the debtors' strategy of servicing long-term debt through short-term borrowing might have proved a prudent expedient. As the recession wore on and interest rates rose, it seemed—and seems—like the fatal step on the road to perdition.

No wonder then that by the mid–1980s the import-substitution model of development was losing the power to convince even its former proponents. Not only were its defenders disheartened by political events in Latin America, whatever their precise connection to economic changes. They were further dispirited by the startling growth of countries such as Taiwan, Korea, and Hong Kong. At first glance—but only at first glance (Haggard 1983)—their export successes seemed to depend on the willingness to respond to market incentives and those only. Free market practice, not state interpretation of classical theory, apparently determined their development strategy. Economists such as Ian M.D. Little (1982), who had never trusted the state tutelage of economic growth associated with import substitution, saw all these developments as the revenge of market reason against the academics' and politicians' attempts to second-guess history. The postwar synthesis of classical political economy and modern macroeconomics suddenly appeared so incoherent that it was hard to remember how it could once have been so compelling.

But the foregoing suggests that this ending to the story is a misleading guide to what did and could have happened. There are good reasons for thinking that the mass-production, import-substitution model was succeeding.[7] Its latest reverses were arguably not the inevitable result of government meddling in free markets, but rather of a fundamental, though historically contingent, shift in the conditions of international competition—a shift which threatens mass production in the advanced as well as the developing world. Put another way, the crisis of the import-substitution strategy and the development economics that helped define it may well be just one expression of a broader crisis of the classical ideas of the division of labor on which both the strategy and theory rest. To see how this could be so, and what the implications of these changes might be for third-world strategies of industrialization, it is necessary to backtrack briefly and—drawing on earlier work (Piore and Sabel 1984)—examine first the origins of the crisis of the 1970s, and then its radical effects on firm strategies in many parts of the first world.[8]

V. The Crisis of the 1970s and the Limits of the Mass-Production Model

One way to view the disruptions of the 1970s emphasizes the effects on the advanced capitalist countries of shocks that were at most indirect results of their economic success. Another point of view emphasizes the role of changes in market conditions—especially the saturation of markets for consumer durables—directly connected to the progress of mass production. Ultimately the two explanations are so mutually reinforcing as to be indistinguishable with regard to what concerns us here: the consequences.

The shocks story focuses on the oil-price increases of 1973 and 1979, the surge of labor unrest in Western Europe in the late 1960s and early 1970s, the breakdown of the Bretton Woods regime of fixed exchange rates after 1972, and the fluctuations in world grain prices associated with huge sales of American wheat to the Soviet Union in 1973. In simple versions of this story, the disruptions were caused by political blunders (the failure to calculate the general effects of huge wheat sales, a needlessly provocative delay in raising wages in West Germany during the post–1967 recovery, etc.) or the (mis)calculations of politicians pandering to an overly demanding electorate (President Johnson's inflationary, timorous refusal to raise taxes during the Vietnam War). In either case, the original mistakes were compounded by confused responses to the resulting surges in unemployment and inflation.

More sophisticated variants of this story portray the disruptions as likely accidents reflecting fragilities in the institutions that made possible the postwar boom. The workers' protests are thus alternately explained as a protest against the increasing pace and routinization of factory work, as a revolt of the masses of former farmers, artisans, and shopkeepers deluded by their first encounter with factory work, or as the awakening of a "mature" working class to the extent of its powers and wants in a full-employment economy. Above all, those accounts emphasize the way in which the initial disruptions were amplified by institutions (wage-indexation schemes, master collective bargaining agreements, agricultural price supports) that encouraged the spread of mass production by stabilizing markets and linking increases in productive capacity to increases in purchasing power. In these versions of the story the shocks may or may not have been avoidable, but their effects would almost certainly have been less severe were it not for hidden design flaws in the mass-production model itself—defects which could have been repaired by some combination of technical reform and redistribution of political power.

The market-saturation story, in contrast, focuses on the limits of the international economic framework. It dovetails with an account of the partial success of import-substitution industrialization in the last section. The central idea is that mass-production know-how spread much more rapidly in the 1950s and 1960s than was suggested by the then pervasive talk of unbridgeable technology gaps between the United States and the rest of the first world on the one hand and between the first and third worlds on the other.

By the end of the 1960s, this story goes, competition in technologically sophisticated goods was intensifying among the advanced countries. By the 1970s newly industrializing countries such as Brazil, Mexico, Taiwan, and South Korea had installed so much capacity to manufacture relatively simple standard products that they threatened first-world manufacturers in these lines even when (as was sometimes the case) they had no explicit designs to invade the latters' markets. Since advanced-country markets for consumer durables were close to saturation in any case, both developments discouraged investment and hastened the arrival of a classic crisis of market limitation already on its way. Here too reform could have made a difference. Some form of international Keynesianism that linked increases in third-world purchasing power to global expansion of productive capacity could theoretically have relaunched growth. But the political problems of redistributing wealth from rich to poor nations aside, the advanced countries were too preoccupied with domestic problems to reconsider their collective relation to the third world.

The two explanations of the crisis are complementary. Companies facing higher production costs because of higher oil prices or wages tried to recoup by invading the markets of neighboring countries; the more firms in any one country were squeezed by competitors' export drives, the more vulnerable they became to domestic disturbances. The longer the crisis went on, the more entwined the two strands of causality became, and—as in the analogous case of the Depression of the 1930s—it will therefore probably never be possible to tell them apart.

For our purposes however, this is a negligible problem. The common effects of the economic disturbance were a change in the conditions of competition so fundamental that—at least in the medium term—the restoration of the original situations is out of the question even if the source of the change could be unambiguously identified. The shocks and increasing international competition destroyed the Keynesian confidence in the stability of mass-production economies backed by governments willing to correct whatever disturbances market institutions could not correct themselves. This hardly happened suddenly and all at once. As late as 1978, at the Bonn economic summit, the advanced countries comtemplated a coordinated Keynesian expansion; and Sweden, France, and Austria pursued traditional reflationary policies thereafter, although (Austria partially excepted) with poor results. But by the late 1970s firms were concluding that neither they nor governments could stabilize domestic economies. This conclusion led to experimentation with new forms of production which challenged the mass-production model on which their own success and the ambitions of the third world had been based.

VI. The Shift Toward Flexible Specialization in the First World

Many large firms first reacted to the disruptions of the 1970s by trying to extend the existing model of productive organization (Katz and Sabel 1985). American automobile producers led the way with their world-car strategy. The idea was to design a few basic models suitable for all markets and sharing as many components as possible. The components would be produced in widely dispersed plants sited to take advantage of cheap labor, transportation, or energy costs, and coordinated by a sophisticated communications system from a single home office. The extent of the market would thus be defined by world, not national demand, and the companies could reap previously impossible economies of scale. The strategy was especially appealing because in some cases—particularly in Latin America—foreign production sites were doubly attractive: wage costs were low and the local demand for automobiles was growing faster than the mature markets in the advanced countries.

But demand simply could not be concentrated around the proposed standard models. Fuel prices continued to fluctuate, leaving consumers uncertain as to whether they wanted fuel-efficient cars or not; breakthroughs in the application of semiconductors and new construction materials made it impossible to freeze designs even within the wide range established by fluctuating fuel prices. Manufacturers, furthermore, quickly discovered that long-range decentralization to third-world countries often entailed increased inventory costs (to hedge against possible disruptions of supply) without eliminating the risks of labor militance. By the early 1980s the American automobile firms and the domestic and foreign manufacturers of such goods as clothing and semiconductors who had followed their lead began to retrench. They did not reverse course completely. But hesitantly, then with more decisiveness, they did begin to emulate two convergent, alternative strategies that had evolved partly within, partly outside other large mass-production firms.

The first strategy I will call *kanban* or Japanese mass production. By integrating suppliers more closely into the design and assembly of final products, and training workers to spot and whenever possible eliminate defects, this strategy cuts in-process inventory, reduces the time for model changes, increases quality, and reduces waste. Suppliers, grouped around the assembly plant rather than dispersed, turn out small lots of parts as needed—just in time for production; workers detect problems as they occur, and pass the information to supervisors who solve them in collaboration with suppliers. As the boundaries between final producer and supplier and different grades of workers blur, costs sink and quality rises.

The second strategy shifts competition from price to the definition of the product. Instead of producing a more reliable version of the standard good at a lower cost, firms make specialized products that command a market premium by meeting the needs of particular customers better than the mass-produced article. This second line of defense was not new. Large firms such as Mercedes-Benz or BMW have long used a combination of mass production and traditional craft technologies to distinguish themselves as speciality producers; and industries such as garments and construction, where markets have resisted the standardization required for mass production, are dominated by small craft producers of semi-custom or custom goods. But as the disruptions of the 1970s continued, more and more firms of all sizes began to seek shelter from international competition in market niches.

By the mid-1980s it was clear that the two strategies converged. Firms that cut costs and raised quality in mass production found they had created the preconditions for rapid model changes. Firms that wanted to manufacture a broader and broader range of speciality products at affordable prices found that they were organizing their work force and relations to suppliers along the lines of the *kanban* system. Both found programmable automation technology ideally suited to the twin goals—unthinkable to Adam Smith—of increasing efficiency without sacrificing flexibility.

The fusion of these two strategies led to the practical application and increasingly self-conscious articulation of a new model of production that I will call flexible specialization. This model stands the principles of mass production on their heads, both with regard to the internal organization of the factory and its relation to the broader economy. Mass production is the manufacture of standard products with specialized resources (narrowly-skilled workers and dedicated machines); flexible specialization is the production of specialized products with general resources (broadly skilled labor and universal, typically programmable machines). Mass production thus depends on the increasing separation of conception from execution, flexible specialization on their integration. Mass production is thus a low-trust system—subordinates are expected to do only as they are told; flexible specialization is a high-trust system. Precisely because there is no time to decompose construction of new products into simple tasks, superiors must depend on subordinates to elaborate general directives.

It is possbile to distinguish analytically three major variants of this basic model, though they overlap in practice, and depending on legal and financial conditions, one can easily be transformed into the other. The first, small-firm variant is characteristic of many of the technologically progressive industrial districts producing such goods as machine tools, knit wear, ceramics, shoes, motorcycles, electronic musical instruments, furniture, special machines, and textiles in what has come to be called the Third Italy: the region bounded roughly by Venice, Bologna, Florence, and Ancona. In this system small and medium-sized firms specializing in different manufacturing processes combine to produce final products according to the shifts in demand. The firms form consortia to secure economies of scale in obtaining credit, marketing products, or conducting generally applicable research. If there are economies of scale in one manufacturing operation, a large firm—owned perhaps by a consortia of its customers—is formed to realize them.

Ultimately the success of this first model depends on the institutionalized solidarity of the economically active groups. The municipality or region together with some combination of trade unions, political parties, church and employers' associations must police working conditions and rule out illicit forms. Without such a barrier of institutionalized community sentiment, firms would constantly be tempted to meet the competition by sweating labor, instead of finding innovative uses for machines and skills. If one firm takes this route, others are likely to follow, and the probable result is to undermine the easy exchange of information between workers and managers which is a precondition of the flexible use of machines. Conversely, local government and private associations must cooperate to provide training and other services usual to innovation which are not provided by single firms and consortia.

These forms of solidarity are part cause, part effect of daily practices that tie firms to one another and individuals to the community. Typically, a firm with a winning product this year is willing to subcontract part of the production to a competitor without one in anticipation of the possibility that next year the situation will be reversed. Youngsters grow up learning in everyday life the skills they will need for their working lives. Because a firm is unlikely to take the risks required for survival in these areas unless it can count on its competitors' benevolence, and a youngster who has not already grown into his or her job would be unlikely to risk acquiring the specialized knowledge these districts require, these unobtrusive forms of community also prove indispensable to the production units narrowly defined.

Large firms play a central role in the second and third variants. Thus in the West German version of flexible specialization, large firms are achieving greater flexibility by internal decentralization, while in Japan the large firms are perfecting the *kanban* system of intimate collaboration with an extensive, often local supplier network. In these systems the firm's central administration plays the role of the municipality and consortia in the small-firm variant, providing financial, marketing, and research services to a combination of semi-autonomous internal business units and cooperative external suppliers.

There is a vast amount of impressionistic evidence regarding the spread of these forms of organization and diffusion among managers of an appreciation of their theoretical virtues. The Third Italy is not only an Italian phenomenon. Firms with very different histories but operating according to similar principles clearly contribute to the vitality of regions such as Baden-Würtemberg in West Germany, Salzburg in Austria, and Jutland in Denmark. All are enormously successful judged by the standards of their respective national economies and particularly the standard of domestic mass-production industry. In the United States, West Germany, Italy, and Great Britain, the automobile industry—the very symbol of mass production—has discovered the need for teamwork, highly skilled labor, flexible capital equipment, and disaggregation of mass markets. Case studies documenting the virtues of integration of design and manufacture, closer producer-supplier relations, and high-trust labor relations are standard fare in American business schools—which, for good measure, openly criticize themselves for having taught the opposite lessons only a few years ago. The need for flexibility is becoming axiomatic in the design of machine tools and special machines (including, tellingly, packing machinery, which is now built to accommodate smaller production runs); sales of multipurpose machining centers programmable on the shop floor and ideally suited to the needs of small firms are booming; highly flexible mini-mills that melt scrap in electric arc furnaces are taking over markets from integrated mills organized on mass-production lines; specialty chemical producers are outperforming commodity manufacturers; and the break-up of mass markets is a cliché in modern marketing.

Clearly it would be wrong to conclude from these developments that flexible specialization will completely supplant mass production as the organizing principle of industrial production. First, the macroeconomic background conditions might change. Some forms of international Keynesianism might restabilize markets to the point that standard goods produced on a world scale could be sold at prices low enough to drive niche producers back to the margins of industry. Second, even if flexible specialization does continue to spread, it requires a mass-production sector, just as mass production required a craft sector. Where mass production depended on the craft construction of special machines, flexible specialization would depend on the mass production—pioneered by the Japanese—of flexible machines. A similar argument applies to the volume production of components. In mass production, parts are designed for a particular product or a small family of products. The tendency in flexible specialization is to design standard components that can be recombined in still more various ways. Eventually, the principles of flexible specialization are applied to the production of the standard components, facilitating their customization. But even so at every stage in the development of the system as a whole there is room for volume producers: the manufacturers of commodity computer memories or even personal computers are current examples. Thus it is far from clear that flexible specialization is the wave of the future or that any particular firm or national economy must ride it to keep above water.

Even with these reservations in mind, however, it is also clear that the current reorganization of industry and the strategic reorientation which it sparked will have enormous effects on the international economic order in general, and the industrializing countries in particular. One might be a migration of the remaining mass-production sectors from the first to the third world. A nation's place in the international economic hierarchy would then be defined by how flexibly it used its machines, rather than by its ability to use machines at all. Developing nations—fearful of newcomers with labor costs below their own—would then race each other in adopting the most advanced, computer-based mass-production technology (Coutinho and Belluzzo n.d.)

But a second possibility is that the industrializing nations might themselves adopt to advantage the principles of flexible specialization in at least some sectors of production. In that case, the definition of progress would change with regard to those parts of developing economies already considered modern, as would the definition of modernization with regard to those that were not. In fact, the next and concluding sections argue that in the light of the principles of flexible specialization, the traditional communities, numerous small firms, and seeming inefficiencies of large plants in third-world countries could turn out to facilitate, not obstruct economic progress.

VII. Two Possibilities for Flexible Specialization in the Third World

In much of the developing world, the idea of craft or artisanal production, especially in small firms, has what Americans call a bad press. So long as the efficiency at a plant is presumed to increase with its size and the automaticity of its special-purpose machines, to advocate the use of anything but the largest capacity equipment is to advocate permanent subservience to more efficient producers.

The argument against anything that smacks of artisanal production is familiar from the debate between Marx and Proudhon in the 1840s (Marx 1971; Proudhon 1923). Proudhon was intimately familiar with one of the precursors of modern, computer controlled machinery: the Jacquard loom, which wove complex brocade patterns according to instructions punched on cards. He took it as obvious that machinery could extend a worker's possibilities of self-expression and that competition among small producers did not exclude a more fundamental solidarity. Marx regarded both ideas as ridiculous; and he anticipated later theories of industrial dualism by arguing that small-scale production could survive only as an adjunct to mass production in large factories. As Marx was by far the more prescient observer of actual industrial developments, his authority is always at the service of both critics of cottage industrialization and advocates of mass-production rationalization. From this perspective, small-scale mechanization creates at best a fragile petty bourgeoisie, permanently endangered economically and hence dangerously volatile politically: a group too weak to lead the march to modernity, but powerful enough in alliance with landowners and merchants to block the progress of groups that might otherwise succeed.

The emergence in the late 1960s and 1970s of a movement favoring the use of technologies "appropriate" to developing countries has not, furthermore, changed this picture. The movement based its case on the classical model of industrial growth. Its claim was that the power of the multinationals and the fascination of Western success had brought developing countries to use technologies that were "inappropriately" capital-intensive given their vast reserves of labor. The remedy was, in effect (and sometimes quite explicitly), to use old machines mustered out of service in the advanced countries.[9] But its success, however modest, probably has more to do with the developing countries' disillusionment with the Western growth path than a conviction that there is in fact another road to progress.

That could change. The most appropriate technology could become synonymous with the most modern machines. Successful examples of flexible specialization in the first world and the growth in demand for semi-customized goods which such successes would encourage could well lead third-world countries to experiment with the new model of industrialization in their own economies. Instead of competing against each other in a desperate struggle to conquer first-world markets for mass produced goods or—failing that—running the risks (familiar from the 1930s) of forming autarkic trade blocks with selected first-world partners, at least some developing countries could turn to the production by efficient methods of products truly suited to their own and their neighbors' needs. Whether efforts to do this came to anything would obviously depend on local conditions. In Latin America—to keep attention focused on one of the parts of the developing world where mass production has been most explicitly identified with modernity—two settings in particular seem favorable to the emergence of flexible specialization.

The first is paradoxically enough the large firm itself. The central conclusion of the case studies conducted by the *Programa de investigaciones sobre desarrollo científico y tecnológico en América Latina* is that even the most modern Latin American plants function according to different principles than their first-world models (Katz 1982). Because their design was inspired by factories operating in the large advanced countries, the Latin American plants are typically too big for their own markets. There is, on the one hand, little incentive to cut production costs deliberately because the firms are protected by tariffs from foreign competition; increases in domestic demand, on the other hand, can be met by simply increasing the utilization rate of existing capacity, which automatically reduces unit production costs by reducing the share of fixed expenses charged to each product. Further rationalization on mass-production lines would, in any case, be difficult to achieve because the large firms cannot draw on a network of sophisticated suppliers. They must themselves perform crucial operation in house; and as the classical logic of specialization suggests, responsibility for maintaining the whole manufacturing process reduced their capacity and willingness to rationalize any part of it.

Under these circumstances, Katz and his collaborators found that firms making machines tools, injection-moulding equipment, farm machinery, castings and automobile engines used their slack resources to adapt the original product line to local conditions or develop new products in related lines. Given frequently idle machines, skilled workers used to repairing them, and, as an additional facilitating factor, an abundance of cheap engineering talent, many large Latin American firms are surprisingly well positioned to absorb foreign technology—including programmable equipment—and put it to independent use.

The result is that the Latin American firms following this strategy are systematically different from comparable firms in the advanced countries. Whereas the latter organize operations sequentially on the model of the assembly line or continuous process technology of, say, a petrochemical plant, the former are organized as a collection of semi-autonomous shops under one roof. Each shop specializes in a particular manufacturing operation or the production of a certain family of parts; similar machines or clusters of machines will thus be grouped together, rather than dispersed in sequences defined by the steps required to build a particular product. It is as though the limited extent of the market forced the Latin American manufacturers to reproduce inside the large factory many features of the network of independent craft producers who collaborated in the production of complex goods before the rise of mass production (Sabel and Zeitlin, 1985).

From the point of view of mass-production engineering, this arrangement looks like a makeshift solution to the problems of local backwardness. But from the perspective of flexible specialization, the same arrangement looks like a way to substantially decrease the cost of modifying or introducing new products while minimally increasing the cost of producing any particular good. Indeed first-world firms trying to outflank mass-production competitors are now trying to apply under the name of group technology many of the same organizational principles that emerged spontaneously in oversized third-world plants.

To be sure, internal decentralization is a necessary but not sufficient condition for successful pursuit of flexible specialization. Broader questions of marketing and distribution aside, the firms can only turn their backward organization to full advantage if they introduce programmable automation and establish a network of reliable and flexible suppliers. There is no reason to think that either will happen as a matter of course, but also none to think that either is impossible.

Of the two obstacles, technical modernization seems the easier to solve. The case studies of Latin American firms corroborate the finding of similar studies in Italy (Rolfo 1980), Taiwan (Amsden 1985), Singapore (Fransman 1984), Denmark (Kristensen 1984; Hjalager 1985), and elsewhere that advanced computer technologies can be rapidly mastered by traditionally skilled workers in organizational settings that encourage experimentation with the new equipment. Castano, Katz and Navajas conclude in their study of an Argentine machine-tool firm that the transition to numerically controlled products "was part of an evolutionary process not characterized by great discontinuities" (Castano, Katz, Navajas 1981, 100). Lack of know-how will not block the advance of flexible specialization in this setting, especially if workers and trade unions know right from the start that this form of rationalization depends on, rather than substitutes for, skill.

The problem of subcontractors is more recalcitrant. The large Latin American firms have the flexible internal structure they have partly because they cannot rely on outside suppliers. Worse still, the large firms' internal flexibility sometimes leads them to compete against new small producers—their potential allies— in the tiny market niches which are the natural habitat of young companies (Pack 1980, 22). But to profit fully from their flexibility, the large firms will have to rely on the absent outsiders. To go forward they will have to change the conditions that made them what they are.

But again, the evidence is that this is doable. In Singapore, for example, Japanese and American machine-tool builders created their suppliers almost single-handedly by selling local businessmen equipment at favorable rates, buying their product at above market prices and providing free technical and commercial advice (Fransman 1984, 46–47).

Typically, however, the creation of a supplier network results from the interplay of macroeconomic developments, large-firm strategies, and government policy.[10] Booms and busts, for example, encourage subcontracting: booms because big firms pass on the orders they cannot fill to new satellite suppliers, busts because the big firms convert fixed to variable costs by forcing employees to buy machinery and then paying the newly created shops by the piece. Whether the new producers survive the next turn of the business cycle depends in large measure on how much help they get from their large customers and government agencies at the service of small firms. The more convinced the large firms and the government are of the need to strengthen the supplier network, the more forthcoming they will presumably be, and the more likely it is that the fledglings will survive.

Thus the success of a flexible specialization strategy could be self-reinforcing in the sense that by demonstrating the virtues of federating firms, it would actually make such federations more likely.

The second surprising setting in which flexible specialization might emerge is the immeasurably vast and poorly understood informal sector of the Latin American economies. The informal sector is a residual category. It includes all economic activity that is neither unambiguously modern—the large factory—nor certifiably traditional—the peasant small-holding or artisan's shop. Thus "informal" economic activity ranges from peddling to shopkeeping in urban slums, to homework, to production of automobile parts in backyard shops that look for all the world like factories.

The sector is so heterogeneous that it is possible to illustrate empirically the most various and contradictory theses about its essence (Bromley 1979; Sethuraman 1981). For the Right, the spread of the informal sector reflects either the healthy scorn of the penny-capitalist poor for a paternalist-populist state, or the final degeneration of the urban plebs. For the Left, it represents the resistance of neighborhood or familial solidarity to capitalist dislocation, a further demonstration of capitalism's capacity to turn pre-modern social forms to its own profitable uses, or proof positive that capitalist development leads to mass immiseration.

What these interpretations have with few exceptions overlooked is the possibility that *some* parts of the informal sector could under *some* conditions develop into a Latin American (or Brazilian, or Colombian) variant of the small-firm model of flexible specialization. It would not be the first time such a thing happened: many of the small firms in the Third Italy that today vaunt their numerically controlled machines and foreign customers had their start when large firms decentralized production in the early 1970s to avoid growing union control of the large plants. Only by retooling old machines to make new products and reinvesting all profits in better equipment, and by cooperating with their workers, competitors, and local governments, were the Italian entrepreneurs able to escape dependence on the parent company and enter the "formal" economy. Political, religious, or regional solidarity was clearly a precondition for the necessary cooperation (Bagnasco 1985; Trigilia 1985).

The obvious question is, could something similar happen in Latin America? And the obvious, if unsatisfying answer is, maybe. Studies of the origins of industrial districts organized on the principles of flexible specialization underscore two antagonistic, though not strictly speaking contradictory, conclusions. One is that there are many routes to a permanent-innovation, small-firm economy. The history of the innovative networks of firms in Jutland is different enough from those in Baden-Würtemberg and the Third Italy to make it seem reasonable that a broad range of conditions can produce the high-trust exchanges that put competition in the service of innovation (Kristensen 1985). Perhaps the spectacular success of the small Brazilian shoe factories around Nova Hamburgo, Southern Brazil, is a first sign that such conditions in some places in Latin America already fall with this range. Surely the fact that many of the small-shop owners and those they employ are descendants of South-German shoe makers has something to do with the extensive cooperation among and within firms (Shuster 1985).

But the other conclusion is that broad though it may be, the range of enabling conditions is hardly unlimited: Benton's careful review of research on the informal sector in Spain shows, for example, that the technological vitality of an emergent industrial district can be sapped by anything from unfavorable market conditions to familial traditions that put consumption before investment (Benton 1984). Thus it may be, as some Brazilian observers fear, that the national shoe industry, which now in effect produces to order for large first-world distributors, will be abandoned by the latter for still lower-cost manufacturers, and so deprived of a chance to develop independent design and marketing capacities (Fleury, 1984). Or it could be that even under favorable market conditions the Brazilian shoe industry will fail to adopt microelectronic technologies as rapidly as the first-world countries determined to use flexible manufacturing systems to counter the competitive threat of just such countries as Brazil (Fleury, n.d.). If that happens the low wages and government subsidies for finance which partly explain its current success would become indispensable for its survival. The final result would be mass sweating, not permanent innovation.

But here too public and private choices are likely to make a difference. The knowledge that some such thing as flexible specialization is possible makes it more likely that firms, municipalities, unions, and governments can use their influence to shape the development of those parts of the informal sector that bear some generic resemblance to the flexible-specialization model. Many of the same steps required to build a network of reliable subcontractors, for example, are identical to those required to switch some parts of the informal economy onto the track leading away from sweating and towards technological innovation. And just as in the case of the large firms, success would feed on itself: each success story would enlarge the model's family album, and increase the possibility that some new district would recognize one of its own features in the portraits of the fortunate.

VIII. Many Worlds, Many Economies

The deepest lesson of postwar development economics, Hirschman reminded us in "The Rise and Decline of Development Economics" (Hirschman 1981), was that no system of economic laws applied in all times and places. There may be one physical universe, but there is not one economy. We all want as much of what we want as we can get; yet what we want, how we can get it, and the cumulative effects of our striving are different from region to region and epoch to epoch. But as it constituted itself as a scientific, academic discipline, development economics drew back from an exploration of the full consequences of its own insight. It presented the mass-production, import-substitution model of the 1950s as *the* economics of the developing world, just as American Keynesianism presented itself as *the* economics of the advanced countries. When times and economic conditions changed in the 1970s, development economics and the development strategies derived from the early postwar experience were no less the victims of the doctrine of a universal economics than the most orthodox exponents of the idea.

But the founders of development economics were right from the start. The successes of flexible specialization, partial and fragile though they are, recall the transformative power of their original insight. The world does change and it is different for rich and poor. Yet there is always a way of turning the successes of the strong to the advantage of the weak. There is always a new strategy for growth—and thus reason to share Hirschman's bias for hope.

NOTES

1. As readers who are knowledgeable about Latin America will quickly realize, I am not. In extending ideas developed through study of industry in the first world to this part of the third, I could not rely on what I have always considered indispensable to writing about rapidly changing situations:

personal experience. What I know about Latin America I know through reading and conversations with expert colleagues. Subsequent notes will tell you what I have read, and, perhaps more important, what was beyond the reach of my new curiosity in this area. Here I want to acknowledge the indispensable guidance of Judith Tendler and Beatriz Nofal. But even they could not save me from my beginner's mistakes.

2. The *locus classicus* of this debate and more generally of discussion of the distinction between traditional and modern values is Weber 1958.

3. For an interpretation of the Depression of the 1930s and the rise of Keynesianism which focuses on the increasing lumpiness of investment in the leading industrial countries, see Piore and Sabel 1984.

4. To my knowledge there is no comprehensive account of the relation between the theoretical debates in development economics and the actual economic policies of Latin American countries in this period. Clearly the policymakers did not simply try to enact theories; and on many occasions when they did what one or another theory prescribed, they did so for their own reasons and in ignorance of the coincidence. Nonetheless, policymakers and planners moved in the same world, and to judge by scattered accounts, words and deeds, reflected common assumptions. See for example Lessa 1984 and Mantega 1984.

5. Table I situates Brazil's economic performance more precisely:

TABLE 1

Average Annual Growth Rates of Manufacturing Output at Constant Prices

	Developed Market Economies	Developing Market Economies	Caribbean and Latin American Economies
1950–60	4.5	6.7	6.5
1960–65	6.7	6.8	6.1
1965–69	5.8	7.4	7.2
1970–75	2.5	7.8	7.8
1975–79	5.0	6.8	5.7

	West Germany	United Kingdom	Italy
1950–59	9.2	2.7	9.1
1960–65	6.1	3.6	6.6
1965–69	5.1	2.9	8.3
1970–75	1.7	1.3	3.7
1975–79	3.6	1.1	5.0

	Brazil	Rep. of Korea	Mexico
1950–59	9.7[1]	16.0[2]	–
1960–65	3.9	12.1	8.3
1965–69	9.4	22.6	8.7
1970–75	12.1	19.7	6.4
1975–79	6.8[3]	16.9	7.1

[1] 1950–58
[2] 1953–58
[3] 1974–80

Source: *United Nations Yearbook of National Accounts Statistics* 1960, 1965, 1970, 1977, 1980, 1982.

6. To deny that Brazilian development was founded exclusively on the satiation of a tiny elite is not, of course, to argue that there is no poverty in the country or that a more equitable income distribution would not have led to still faster growth. In any case, Wells's empirical investigations seem to have had little influence on economic debate in Brazil; the prevailing view is that social injustice was the sine qua non of the economic "miracle." See, for example, Furtado 1982, 118.

7. For an argument that Brazil's investment in the infrastructure for a mass-production economy created the preconditions for the country's dramatic successes in export markets in the mid 1980s, see the incisive article in Castro 1985.

8. The argument in the following two sections draws extensively on *The Second Industrial Divide;* readers who want to examine the evidence for the claims made here should consult that book, as well as Katz and Sabel 1985.

9. For a good survey of the literature on these core elements of the debate about appropriate technology, see White 1978. A more peripheral theme in the discussion, which blends into many of the points that follow here, concerns the possibility of increasing efficiency by substituting high technology implements of traditional tools without changing the artisanal character of production. See, for example, the discussion of new spinning techniques in Joshi 1977.

10. An excellent general discussion of the problems of subcontracting under third-world conditions is Amsden 1977.

BIBLIOGRAPHY

Amsden, Alice H. 1985. "The Division of Labour is Limited by the Rate of Growth of the Market." *Cambridge Journal of Economics* (forthcoming).

_____. 1977. "The Division of Labour is Limited by the Type of Market: The Case of the Taiwanese Machine Tool Industry." *World Development* 5, no. 3: 217–33.

Bagnasco, Arnaldo. 1985. "La costruzione soziale del mercato; strategie di impresa e esperimenti di scala in Italia." *Stato e Mercato* (forthcoming).

Benton, Lauren. 1984. "The Informal Sector in the Spanish Economy." Baltimore: Dept. of Anthropology, Johns Hopkins University (mimeo).

Berg, Maxime. 1980. *The Machinery Question and the Making of Political Economy 1815–1848.* Cambridge: Cambridge University Press.

Bromley, Ray, ed. 1979. *The Urban Informal Sector: Critical Perspectives on Employment and Housing Policies.* New York: Pergamon.

Canak, William L. 1984. "The Peripheral State Debate." *Latin America Research Review* no. 1: 3–36.

Castano, Angel, Jorge Katz and Fernando Navajas. 1981. "Etapas históricas y conductas tecnológicas en una planta argentina de máquinas herramienta." Buenos Aires: Programa BID/CEPAL/CIID/PNUB, CEPAL.

Castro, Antonio Barros de. 1985. "Ajustamento transformação: a economia brasileira de 1974 a 1984." In Antonio Barros de Castro and Francisco Eduardo Pires de Souza, *A economia brasileira em marcha forçada*, 11–95. Rio de Janeiro: Paz e Terra.

Chandler, Alfred D. 1977. *The Visible Hand.* Cambridge: Harvard University Press.

Coutinho, Luciano G. and Luis Gonzaga de Mello Belluzzo. n.d. "Reflexoes sobre as tendencias de mundança nos processos de produção." Campinas: UNICAMP (mimeo).

Dore, Ronald P. 1973. *British Factory—Japanese Factory.* Berkeley and Los Angeles: University of California Press.

Evans, Peter. 1979. *Dependent Development.* Princeton: Princeton University Press.

_____. 1982 "Reinventing the Bourgeoisie: State Entrepreneurship and Class Formation in Dependent Capitalist Development." *American Journal of Sociology* 88 (Supplement): S210–47.

Fleury, Fernando Paulo. 1984. "A exportação de calçados do Brasil: uma avaliação dos aspectos gerenciais." *Tecnicouro,* Novo Hamburgo, May/June 1984, 24–32.

_____. n.d. "Exportação, Inovação Tecnológica e Competitividade: Uma Análise dos Manufaturados brasileiros." Relatório Técnico no. 73, COPPEAD/UFRJ.

Frank, André Gunder. 1967. *Capitalism and Underdevelopment in Latin America.* New York: Monthly Review Press.

Fransman, Martin. 1984. "Promoting Technological Capability in the Capital Goods Sector: The Case of Singapore." *Research Policy* 13: 33–54.

Frieden, Jeff. 1983. "Third World Indebted Industrialization." *International Organization,* no. 3: 407–31.

Froebel, Folker, Jürgen Heinrichs, and Otto Kreye. 1980. *The New International Division of Labor.* Cambridge: Cambridge University Press.

Furtado, Celso. 1982. "La dette extérieure brésilienne." *Problèmes d'Amérique Latine* (November): 115–36.

Gerschenkron, Alexander. 1977. *An Economic Spurt that Failed.* (Princeton: Princeton University Press.

———. 1962. *Economic Backwardness in Historical Perspective.* Cambridge: Harvard University Press.

Haggard, Stephan Mark. 1983. "Pathways from the Periphery." Diss. University of California, Berkeley.

Hirschman, Albert O. 1981. "The Rise and Decline of Development Economics." In his *Essays in Trespassing,* 1–24. Cambridge: Cambridge University Press.

———. 1958. *The Strategy of Economic Development.* New Haven: Yale University Press.

HjaLager, Anne-Mette. 1985. "Local Industrial Policy for Small Enterprises: The Case of the Textile Industry in Herning-Ikast." Report prepared for the Bundesforschungsanstalt für Landeskunde und Raumordnung, Bonn, July 1985 (mimeo).

Joshi, Nandini. 1977. "Technological Choice and Socio-Economic Imperatives: A Case Study of Textile Technologies in India." *Research Policy* 6: 202–13.

Katz, Harry, and Charles F. Sabel. 1985. "Industrial Relations and Industrial Adjustment: The World Car Industry." *Industrial Relations* 24 (Fall) (forthcoming).

Katz, Jorge M. 1982. "Technology and Economic Development: An Overview of Research Findings." In Moshe Syrquin and Simon Teitel, eds., *Trade, Stability, Technology, and Equity in Latin America,* 285–315. New York: Academic Press.

Kristensen, Peer Hull. 1984. "Industriel Udvikling i Danmark" (provisional title). Roskilde (mimeo; book manuscript).

Kuczynski, Pedro-Pablo. 1982–83. "Latin American Debt." *Foreign Affairs* (winter): 344–64.

Landes, David S. 1972. *The Unbound Prometheus.* Cambridge: Cambridge University Press.

Lessa, Carlos. 1984. *Quinze Anos de Política Econômica,* 4th ed. São Paulo: Editora Brasiliense.

Little, Ian. 1982. *Economic Development: Theory, Policy and International Relations.* New York: Basic Books.

Mantega, Guido A. 1984. *A Economia Política Brasileira.* São Paulo: Polis/ Voces.

Marx, Karl. 1971. *The Poverty of Philosophy.* New York: International Publishers.

Nurkse, Ragnar. 1984. "The Conflict Between 'Balanced Growth' and International Specialization." In Gerald D. Meier, *Leading Issues in Economic Development,* 4th ed., 373–76. Oxford: Oxford University Press.

Pack, Howard. 1980. "Fostering the Capital-Goods Sector in LDCs: A Survey of Evidence and Requirements." World Bank Staff Working Paper, no. 376. Washington, D.C.: The World Bank.

Piore, Michael J. and Charles F. Sabel. 1984. *The Second Industrial Divide.* New York: Basic Books.

Proudhon, Pierre-Joseph. 1923. *Système des contradictions économiques ou philosophie de la misère.* 2 vol. Paris: Marcel Rivière.

Rolfo, Secondo. 1980. "La diffusione del controllo numerico nella produzione italiana di macchine utensili." *Bolletino CERIS* 5 (September): 125–36.

Sabel, Charles F. and Jonathan Zeitlin. 1985. "Historical Alternatives to Mass Production: Politics, Markets and Technology in Nineteenth-Century Industrialization." *Past and Present,* no. 108 (August): 133–76.

Sethuraman, S.V., ed. 1981. *The Urban Informal Sector in Developing Countries: Employment, Poverty, and Environment.* Geneva: International Labor Office.

Shuster, Lynda. 1985. "Brazil Captures a Big Share of the U.S. Shoe Market." *Wall Street Journal,* August 27, 1985, p. 35.

Trigilia, Carlo. 1985. "Small-Firm Developments, Subcultures, and Neo-Localism in Italy." EUI Working Papers, no. 85/189. Florence: European University Institute.

Weber, Max. 1958. *The Protestant Ethic and the Spirit of Capitalism.* Talcott Parsons, trans. New York: Scribner.

Wells, John. 1977. "The Diffusion of Durables in Brazil and Its Implications for Recent Controversies Concerning Brazilian Development." *Cambridge Journal of Economics* no. 1 (1977): 259–79.

White, Lawrence J. 1978. "The Evidence on Appropriate Factor Proportions for Manufacturing in Less Developed Countries." *Economic Development and Cultural Change,* no. 1: 27–59.

World Bank, Brazil. 1983. *Industrial Policies and Manufactured Exports.* Washington, D.C.: The World Bank.

The Economics of Fascism and Nazism: Premises and Performance

Charles S. Maier

A study of the economics of fascism is appropriate for this occasion on several grounds: first, for its intersection with Albert Hirschman's personal life—as a political opponent of fascism in Germany and Italy; second, for its potential interest to students of development, since fascism is sometimes claimed to be an ideology of development; third, as a test of the general conditions that link economic systems with politics and society. For Hirschman, economic activity is always rooted in a more general context of cultural relations. In contrast to the teaching of neoclassical economics, this cultural context can lead to action that does not always follow from axioms of maximization.

In Hirschman's world people do not always find more of a good to be better than less. Other impulses can be determining. The desire for variety (as explored for example in *Shifting Involvements);* the impulse to conflict as sublimated into interest-group rivalry; the willingness to moderate distributive claims if the future becomes hopeful (Hirschman's "tunnel effect")—all these traits of economic behavior make the psychological models underlying Hirschman's political economy more complex than that of most contemporary theorists.

For this reason, the study of an economic system so determined by supposedly extraneous concerns of power and domination is an appropriate contribution to Hirschman's implicit intellectual agenda. As an economic historian Hirschman has lingered over the Enlightenment, but he knows that capitalism has functioned in less benign political milieus. What, then does fascist economics reveal about the operation of modern capitalism in general, whose underpinnings have so intrigued Hirschman during what Foxley and McPherson call his second career?

In terms of general scholarship this essay can perhaps be justified on the grounds that most students have investigated economic premises and performance either under National Socialism or Italian fascism. Few if any have made any serious effort at systematic comparison or surveyed the economic literature for both systems. This paper represents more of a sketch than an adequate execution of such an ambitious project. But this essay can at least make a start and offer a few theses about the nature and accomplishment of fascist economics. (When I use the term fascist without specific reference to Italy it is intended to refer to Nazi and Italian conditions. Allow me to overlook for the moment the fact that such a bracketing is itself highly contested by many historians.)

The following inquiries can serve to organize comparison. First, was ideology crucial in distinguishing a fascist economic program, and if so what ideology? Second, did the fascist economies represent efforts at modernization? If so, in what sense, and how successful were their efforts? Third, aside from the question of modernization, how did the fascist economies perform, as measured by the quantitative tests that we usually apply to measure performance? How, too, did they perform in mobilizing their countries for war, an activity for which they claimed special competence? Finally, can we define in any meaningful sense a fascist economic system that fundamentally differed from the capitalism practiced by contemporary liberal states?

I. The Question of Ideology

Analysts have rightly discerned a babble of economic preachings in fascism, often contradictory: a celebration of Darwinian struggle, an awareness of common fate; a celebration of heroic entrepreneurs, a condemnation of capitalism; a demand for radical transformation of enterprise, an underwriting of the status quo; a call for genuine socialism, a bitter hostility to social democracy; an evocation of technological progress, a nostalgia for rural roots; a derisive condemnation of state regulation, a summons to an all-embracing corporativism, etc. Faced with these contradictions many have argued that fascism in fact had no ideology worthy of the name and was just an opportunistic series of points that served at different times. The case is easy to make, but not really sufficient. National Socialism and Italian Fascism did present a characteristic range of economic preachings. These varied according to the particular stage that the movement had reached, but not arbitrarily.

It is useful initially to separate the economic program of fascism as a movement in search of power from the concepts proposed once fascism had entrenched itself. Even this distinction proves too clear-cut. At each stage, as the litany of themes cited above suggests, fascist spokesmen presented often conflicting economic programs. Their pronouncements added up to ideology and counter-ideology, as if some contrapuntal doctrine in several movements.

Fascist spokesmen maneuvering for office were capable both of condemning capitalism and of claiming it needed only to be left alone for its own reinvigoration. Both Mussolini and Hitler in the critical months before seizing power praised the capitalist and the entrepreneur. In a celebrated address at Udine on September 19, 1922, and in discussions with industrialists on October 16, Mussolini stressed that fascism meant an end to the state intervention they had complained about since the war. "Basta con lo Stato ferroviere, con lo Stato postino, con lo Stato assicuratore." One had to reemphasize the teachings of Smith, of Say, of Ferrara, the examples of Peel and Cavour. Indeed fascism would create a new doctrine in the liberal spirit.[1] The accent here was an echo of what liberals, such as Einaudi had written for years: Italian industry had to be liberated from the trammels of bureaucracy. Taxes were to be reduced, restrictions lifted: the classical Manchesterite menu of the entrepreneurs. Nor was this accent so different from Hitler's celebrated appeal to Germany's industrial elite who invited him to expound his economic ideas at the Düsseldorf Industrie Klub on January 7, 1932. On that occasion, intended to bridge the distrust that lingered between many industrialists and financiers and the obstreperous National Socialist leader, Hitler praised the entrepreneurial vocation. He insisted that both businessmen and political leadership required a decisionist space; they needed to be liberated from petty restrictions on the exercise of their power. The message was similar, Walther Funk reported later, at Nuremberg: Hitler told businessmen he was an enemy of state socialism and the planned economy. In short, both business leadership and political leadership legitimately claimed liberation from misplaced democratic principles; both needed the power that accrued to proven competence.[2]

Obviously these aspiring dictators, superb at sensing what their listeners wished to be told, shaped the message to the audience. Moreover, many of the potential audience remained skeptical. If the Milanese industrialists active in Confindustria pressed for a coalition government to include Mussolini, Agnelli and the Piedmontese remained more reserved. If Hitler could count on the vanity of Schacht, the ingenuous adhesion of Thyssen or the miscalculation of Hugenberg, other important industrialists vacillated in their support and kept

other options open.[3] But the task here is not to determine how many
of the industrial community welcomed or acquiesced in the new
leadership, but what concepts the Fascist and Nazi parties were bringing. Both leaders understood that their movements at a critical point
must reassure the Establishment if they were to become serious candidates for power. They understood that there were receptive industrial
leaders who nurtured the belief that the fascist leadership might be
tutored in sound industrial principles, that Mussolini or later Hitler
could be separated from the obstreperous radicals who had been their
initial enthusiasts and had been necessary to counter the Marxist
parties and unions that were choking the respective systems.

Nor did Mussolini and Hitler merely play upon Manchesterite
themes in their wooing of business leaders. They plucked deeper and
more intriguing chords. Both men appealed to a technocratic impulse
as they built bridges to industry. Their heroes were not financiers,
but engineers and captains of industry. The dichotomy was a venerable
one and appeared in many of the critiques of capitalism at the turn
of the century, whether Veblen's *Theory of Business Enterprise* or
Sorel's praise of engineers or the crude Populist (German and American) separation of the parasitic financier from the creative inventor
and entrepreneur. Overtones of the distinction exist even in Schum-
peter's 1911 *Theory of Economic Development*. Debased versions would
characterize Gottfried Feder, the roustabout economic tutor of Hitler
in the early Munich years who preached the "breaking of interest
slavery," and even Ezra Pound's paranoid pastoral written in Italian
exile, *Jefferson and/or Mussolini*. Whereas Marxists indicted capitalism as a system of exploitative property relationships, populistic
radicalism focused on the control of credit and money as abusive.
Bankers produced no real value; rather they starved worthy farmers
and small businessmen of credit for their own profits. So too did the
financial organizers of monopolies or large department stores.

To be sure, respectable industrialists who sat on the boards of
banks and mingled with bankers at clubs would not buy this radical
quackery that flourished in the motley undergrowth of fascism and
Nazism. But a more respectable version existed. This stressed the
role of the "productive" industrialist, often the installer of a new
technology, vis-à-vis the mere coupon clipper. Before World War I,
the new Italian Nationalist Association, financed in large measure by
the Ligurian steel magnates of Ansaldo, drew upon fashionable Sorelian
ideas (imported into Italy c. 1908) to urge a national syndicalism.
Alfredo Rocco, who became the drafter of Mussolini's key legislation
of 1925–27, was a key spokesman in the prewar period of the "Marcia

dei Produttori." Industrial leaders together with their workforce in an incipient corporativism would stress discipline, authority, and economic renovation. The state should rest not on the outmoded liberalism and civic ideas of 1789, but on men's functional role in society. Such concepts justified imperialism and a fundamental opposition to social democracy, although they allowed alliances with independent syndicalist leaders, which would be created during the battle for intervention in World War I, and which would form the basis of fascism's labor adherents after the war. The idea of "productivism" gave Mussolini the bridge by which he could cross from his earlier volatile socialism to his new polyvalent fascism of 1919–22. Productivism, moreover, found a special echo among the new industrial leadership and the newly important executive directors of industrial peak associations who were not themselves proprietors. Gino Olivetti, the most able spokesman for Confindustria, and then Antonio Benni, the later president of the association, propagated the gospel of the technocratic industrialist.[4] As Benni declared, "Interference in authority is not possible: the only possible hierarchy in the factory is the technical one required by the productive order. . . . Industry is not personified by the capitalist or the stockholder, but by its directors, its chiefs, and by the organizers of the enterprise."[5]

These technocratic concepts continued to play a role among the more innovative and less intransigent fascists. Massimo Rocca urged a technocratic thrust for the *gruppi di competenza* which he hoped would replace the squads as the grass-roots cadres of the new regime. Fascism would draw upon those with expertise and economic or technological competence no matter what their earlier party preferences. This concept lost out to the militants' insistence on the party's crucial role during the Matteotti crisis in late 1924, but Giuseppe Bottai, the later Minister of Corporations and intellectual gadfly who would play with ideas of planning, continued to sponsor such currents. They remained an important motif of fascist economic thinking during the interwar period, even if they never seriously challenged the hierarchies of industry that were the legacy of earlier capitalist development. At a minimum they suggested that fascism should encourage a technological élan and productive vitality which unified the economy across class lines. They allowed some continuing appeal to young intellectuals at least until the cultural stultification that began to afflict the regime after the mid–1930s.[6]

What equivalent currents existed in Germany? It was harder to maintain an engineering vision in a movement that so stressed the claims of blood and race. Nonetheless, technocratic aspirations continued throughout the regime, later patronized to a degree by such men as Albert Speer. The pre-Nazi concepts of *Konservativer Sozialismus,* held out by Rathenau's assistant, the AEG engineer Wichard von Moellendorff, combined ideals of technical knowledge, and austere dedication to national duty. Similarly Spengler's Prussian Socialism called for a Fichtean collectivism built around a national work ethic and elevating the engineer into a key servant of power. The Verein deutscher Ingenieure remained dedicated to the notion of an apolitical technocracy, which they felt that National Socialism would help realize. Likewise, the movement for *Schönheit der Arbeit* with its effort at a technological aesthetic and sober modernism (growing in part out of the *Neue Sachlichkeit* that marked the late 1920s) meant that technological aspirations remained a constituent of Nazi concepts.[7]

These notions spilled over into ideas of industrial management. The real dividing line in concepts of factory organization came not with the seizure of power in 1933, but with the reversion to an older discipline in the later 1920s. The authoritarian factory order was restored in part in the wake of the great inflation,[8] and during the early 1930s managerial spokesmen began to define authoritarian ideas of factory control that the Nazis had hardly to improve upon. The *Führerprinzip* in the factory might seem an authoritarian analogue of the *Führerprinzip* in government. But it was not merely an assertion of charismatic or non-rational power. Instead it was grafted on top of an encroaching plant authoritarianism that drew upon imported Taylorite and Fordist appeals to scientific management and social engineering. In a similar manner the Nazi use of compulsory arbitration grew naturally out of the Weimar arbitration courts that had already been turned into pro-managerial authorities after 1930.[9]

To summarize, then, we can discern a combination of neoliberal emancipation of the businessman coupled with a technocratic justification of his vocation. "Productivism" and an appeal to managerial engineering constituted the modern message that fascists and Nazis conveyed to the Italian and German economic elites. Moreover, these themes continued after the respective seizures of power and remained recurrent if not dominant motifs. Nonetheless, fascism was a broad enough coalition to nurture aspirations that found technocracy uncongenial. After all, if industrialists could be wooed with a technological gilding of their role in the profit system, their support was crucial only at certain moments. The economic elite had to be cultivated above all during the immediate search for a coalition role in a national cabinet and during the subsequent period of consolidating a regime. Holding power as exclusive rulers seemed initially out of the reach of both fascist leaders. In short, the seizure and consolidation of power (1921–1926 in Italy, 1931–1934 in Germany) required respectability. However, the process of making the movement just a plausible contender of power rested upon a different dynamic. It required mobilizing enough broad-based support to demonstrate the indispensability of the movement as an instrument of popular control. And to mobilize broad support required playing upon the economic grievances of agriculture and of the *ceti medi (Mittelstand)*. Thus both movements encouraged reveries of corporativism. Italian fascist syndicalists advanced plans for organizing the economy into syndicates (later corporations) that could reward dynamic economic leaders, but would also guarantee a social role for all participants in a given professional sector. Nazi propagandists elaborated the small-business and agrarian corporative longings that had long characterized German economic organization.

An important functional distinction persisted, however, between Italian and German corporativist programs. Italian syndicalist theories urged corporative organization as a remedy for economic backwardness, as compensation for the fragmentation of the Italian economy and as a step toward more decisive economic modernization. "The problem of the State thus becomes a formidable problem of *organization* by means of subordinating to the State all its reciprocally co-ordinated social elements."[10] In Germany corporative advocates spoke more in terms of protecting the vulnerable sectors of handicraft, small business, trade, and peasantry from the autonomous tendencies toward oligopoly that were pressing their protagonists to the wall. Italian national syndicalists and corporativists aspired to the very organization that seemed to make the German economy so vigorous and modern. German corporativist spokesmen sought to insulate the *Mittelstand* from the oppressive dominance of big labor and heavy industry. Thus Italian fascist spokesmen for corporativism could easily second the pro-industry thrust of "productivist" rhetoric. (On occasion, however, they did become angry with industrialist efforts to evade control by the corporations: the 1925 debate over what sectors were to be included in the new national "Corporations" demonstrated this divergence of interests.) German corporativists within National Socialism constantly worked to reinforce control of prices, apprenticeship, licensing and the like.

But whether corporativist aspirations represented modernizing or defensive impulses, they had limited results. After long discussion in 1925–26, Mussolini established six corporativist sectors that would interface with the fascist national labor "corporation." He appointed a Minister of Corporations to oversee the structure, but with few budgetary or other assets to vie with the greater bureaucratic resources of the ministries of finance and national economy. This structure still presupposed in effect the representation of syndical or contrasting interests for labor and capital, with disputes to be resolved at the ministerial level, or in the field of labor law by the Magistratura del Lavoro (following the guidelines of the Carta del Lavoro of 1927). In 1930 the National Council of Corporations, envisaged by the 1926 legislation, was instituted, and in 1934 the government called into being the "corporations" for particular economic branches. They were theoretically designed as self-governing organs of economic planning and administration although, since they included labor representatives in the same framework, landlords and industrialists always resisted their claims on real power. At this juncture, elaborating the corporative structures offered some clear political gains. It allowed Mussolini to demonstrate that fascism did incorporate an economic ideal setting it apart from the liberal capitalism that seemed so discredited by the Great Depression. It also provided an agenda for the second decade of the regime, which seemed to have completed its initial historical achievement of stabilization by virtue of the 1929 reconciliation with the Vatican. Intellectuals, such as Ugo Spirito, made the round of fascist-sponsored conferences preaching the virtues of post-capitalist fascism and, in fact, trying to nudge the structure in a "leftist" direction with greater prerogatives of ownership, wage-setting, and collective control. Mussolini looked abroad to find that Franklin Roosevelt was merely seeking to emulate Italy's innovations. In fact the corporations never achieved real regulatory power: *"homo corporativus,* the corporative economy, the corporative state and all the other irridescent formulae, object of such lively discussion and such ample study for a good twenty years, remained a dead letter."[11] Insofar as state intervention increased it did so through the organization of the state holding company, IRI, establishment of the funds for land reclamation *(Bonifica integrale),* creation of national offices for controlling prices and production in cotton, paper and cellulose, regulation of the banking sector, and the build-up for war.

In Germany, corporativist initiatives had even fewer substantive results. Peasants indeed won virtually a return of hereditary entail. But within a year the corporative initiatives fell largely into desuetude (the Nazi development comparable in a sense to the fate of the NRA under the New Deal). Kurt Schmitt, Hugenberg's successor as Minister of Economics in July 1933, retreated on measures that would have enhanced small-business corporatism and halted initiatives, for instance, to regulate the prices of large integrated steel concerns to the smaller finishing industries. This was a setback, not to handicraft, but to secondary industry; however, other initiatives also succumbed, such as plans to curtail department stores and/or to undermine consumer cooperatives. Handicraft chambers and guilds won some relief from discount price competition, though they could not freeze the prices they had to pay their own suppliers nor could they win any continuing authority of their own to impose uniform prices. The same compromise sort of settlement regulated issues of vocational training. The grievances caused by the progress of an advancing large-scale capitalism were attenuated, but *Mittelstand* organizations did not capture the control they had hoped for. Most revealingly, the number of handicraft firms fell by 153,000, approximately 9 percent of the 1.65 million earlier.[12]

Corporativism thus yielded few of the socially protective results its adherents hoped for in Germany and few of the modernizing results (few results, too, in terms of integrating the role of labor with capital) its propagandists tirelessly trumpeted in Italy. For in its different ways it promised what neither regime was prepared to deliver (at least not outside of agriculture). Corporativism envisaged a sort of producers' equality. But neither the large industrial firms nor the fascist states were willing to cede real control over substantive policies. Corporativism as an informal accumulation of power among producer groups remained a continuing tendency of the twentieth century economy. Bureaucratic state intervention in Germany and Italy could delay its advance, or, perhaps to describe its role more precisely, might establish agencies of countervailing corporativist power. But these new state-affiliated centers of countervailing corporativist authority had little to do with formal structures designed to move beyond the lonely individual of 1789 to the integration of man-the-producer.

Nonetheless, as they consolidated power, fascist and Nazi regimes did add a new ideological overlay to their economic program. If corporativism proved less important (at least de facto) than earlier programs had suggested, national self-sufficiency became more so. Both Italian fascism and Nazism built their economic programs upon premises of autarky. And in this respect, the liberalism that they could grant industrialists had to remain limited. We will examine the achievements of autarky below, under the discussion of modernization and preparation for war. For now, however, we can identify crucial points, in fact episodes of crisis, in which the demands of autarky were imposed upon the neo-liberalism that characterized the earlier days of power. For Italy there were two major thrusts toward autarky:

the effort to redress the balance of trade, defend a high exchange-rate for the lire, and move toward self-sufficiency in agriculture marked the first program of the mid–1920s; the move to put the economy on a war footing in 1936 marked the second. In 1925 Mussolini—having moved his regime from its original twilight authoritarianism to decisive dictatorship—likewise switched directions in economic policy. He dropped Alberto De Stefani, the *liberista* Minister of Finance, and added the Venetian industrialist and shipping magnate, Giuseppe Volpi di Misurata. He departed from a non-interventionist course to a far more *dirigiste* control over banking, initiated the Battle for Grain, and drove toward stabilization of the lira at an exchange rate equivalent (the Quota 90) which sharply challenged the preferences of export industry. The program as a whole rallied the southern landlord class (grateful for the protection of grain and the revaluing of the government bonds they held) and created a new web of dependent industries. Above all the chemical and the electricity industry would look toward the protection and contracts of the government.

In 1936 both Mussolini and Hitler would call for autarky. The policy had different effects in the respective countries, however. In Italy state *dirigisme* had been growing in any case since the establishment of IRI and IMI (Istituto per la Ricostruzione Industriale and Istituto Mobiliare Italiano). These public holding companies controlled the major steel conglomerates that had passed into state receivership: Ilva and Terni and Siac (Ansaldo and Cornigliano) under IRI control, Cogne outside IRI. The objective of autarky gave the triumvirate of public steel managers, Arturo Bocciardo, Oscar Sinigaglia and Agostino Rocca, the opportunity to press plans for technical modernization and centralized control over new investment. With the encouragement of Mussolini and the military, sectoral planning progressed in 1937 and 1938. But the imminent approach of war and the perceived need to achieve the highest possible output in the short term allowed jealous private-sector firms to reclaim authorization for their own expansion. Long-term plans for integrated production thus remained only partially fulfilled. Nonetheless, Rocca's alliance with Mussolini would be effectively rewoven in the postwar years when De Gasperi supported Sinigaglia's ambitious plans. Sectoral planning did not require fascism; it would help to have the Marshall Plan. The point is that in a semi-developed Italy, any overriding public economic objective could provide the political impulse to let the spokesmen for modernization make at least some headway against those with investments already sunk in a fragmented and outmoded technology.

The case seems less clear in Germany. The beneficiaries of

autarky were primarily the chemical industries, who benefited from the encouragement given to synthethic fuel development (I. G. Farben had sunk huge costs into hydrogenation development, which without state contracts could not be recouped). The impulse to a declared autarky policy came with the continuing disputes between the Ministry of Agriculture, the Army and such private interests as Farben, on one side, pressing for governmental expenditures and importing the matériel needed for rearmament, and Schacht as Finance Minister, on the other. Schacht remained concerned about balance-of-payments constraints and the inflationary effect of rapid government expenses. For Hitler economic constraints were not insuperable: rearmament was central and political will could prevail over alleged economic difficulties. In the memorandum he prepared at the Obersalzburg in August 1936 he wrote that every consideration must be subordinated to achieving the world's largest army for the struggle against Marxism and Judaism. This meant preparing synthetic rubber supplies and developing the synthetic fuel industry within eighteen months. It further required the development of German iron ore resources: an objective that would justify the development of the low-grade Salzgitter ores in the new public holding company, the "Reichswerke Hermann Goering":[13] "The Volk does not live on behalf of the economy, its economic leadership or economic or finance theories, but rather finance and economy, economic leadership and every theory exist only to serve in the struggle for our people's self-determination."[14] But what results were achieved? Political control was indeed centralized under Goering's nominal leadership as head of the Four-Year Plan. Schacht was pushed toward retirement. But the production quotas set were barely advanced by 1938 and, as we shall see, the economy remained ready to serve only a short war, not a protracted struggle for national existence. In part the difficulty lay in the fact that German economic organization had already reached a high level. Had the regime simply provided the resources for additional hydrogenation development or for expansion of low-grade ore utilization, there might have been better progress. Ruhr steel industrialists such as Ernst Poensgen of the Vereinigte Stahlwerke distrusted the creation of a new steel empire. In contrast to the Italian steel situation, the Four-Year Plan did not allow a nucleus of technocrats to clear the way for decisive modernization. It seems only to have augmented the opportunity for internecine conflict.

Autarky thus represented a policy with clear winners and losers. It moved both regimes beyond liberal economics and established them as activist participants in a mixed capitalism. It established a new, artificially protected role for agriculture. It tended to fray support from the traditional, private metallurgical industries that had usually applauded authoritarian measures. In return it drew on the efforts of a managerial class that saw politics as instrumental to bureaucratic intervention. Nonetheless, it would be wrong to suggest that intervention and autarky severely cost either regime massive industrial support. For if industrial leaders lost the freedom to invest in new plants without approval, in return they had won unprecedented degrees of authoritarian control over labor, which had earlier been a preeminent concern. They also often secured tariff protection or other subsidies. FIAT was one of the more liberal-oriented of Italy's industries, but faced with incursions by Ford in the late 1920s it was happy to win government help in keeping out competition.[15]

Let us pull together the ideological aspects of the fascist and Nazi economic programs. Both preached a neoliberalism in the crucial months before and after attaining power. Both garnished this neoliberalism with motifs of technocratic mission for the entrepreneur and sharply distinguished technological development—the boss as managerial innovator—from financial manipulation. Both included a secondary ideological theme of corporatist protection, although this had a modernizing thrust in Italy and a socially defensive one in Germany. But corporativism had limited impact. The Nazis dropped its *Mittelstand* emphasis and exploited the concept only to seek *Gleichschaltung* of the many private economic associations already in being. The Italians progressively elaborated corporative institutions, but withheld real authority from them, entrusting power to ad hoc instruments of sectoral intervention. If anything, fascism did imply an economy geared for national self-sufficiency and war. Autarky policies thus represented a natural outgrowth of their political premises; they were all the more beckoning when internal contradictions became serious. Faced with a tug of war among conflicting priorities and bureaucratic interests, Mussolini (in 1925 and 1936), and Hitler (in 1935–36) seized upon autarky to impose a more comprehensive authority over disputing factions. Because the Italian economy was less advanced in many sectors, autarky could provide cover for more substantive efforts at modernization. In the German situation it merely licensed a new set of bureaucratic conflicts.

To be sure, this account has not yet listed what, along with nationalist economic objectives, remained the crucial premise of both movements: the destruction of an independent labor movement. This achievement, too, was far from complete given both outright resistance and the recreation of autonomous impulses *within* the new official union structures. But it was complete enough to win the adherence of most industrial groups (of course, not of all individual industrialists!) even as the regimes moved toward unwelcome degrees of interventionism. To a large degree, despite the technocratic veneer, the suppression of labor remained what these movements were about.

In a larger sense, however, fascist economics was not really economics at all. Fascist and Nazi economics had to respond, as Hitler wrote, to political will. The original appeal of fascism consisted in part in its promise to adherents that they need not be powerless against what often seemed inevitable economic trends. German voters chose National Socialism, not for its economic program, but from despair at what the autonomy of the market and of industry seemed to have wrought: whether the emergence of a powerful (Marxist) working class, or the continuing power of organized industry, in either case, the predominance of selfish interest groups. Hitler promised, in Tim Mason's phrase, the primacy of politics over the "system."[16] The contrast was less stark in Italy, for there the society seemed insufficiently organized, "invertebrate" in the term Ortega chose for Spain. But here, too, clear political direction was required to impose the organization upon a capitalist economy that many felt was lacking. Fascism's underlying economic message was that economic society was malleable and to be shaped by political will. In this sense, fascism was an extreme form of the recourse to political vs. market solutions that Hirschman has seen as one pole of the spectrum of social action in *Shifting Involvements.*

II. The Issue of Modernization and Development

The fate of the government steel sector that was discussed above introduces the more general question: in what sense was fascism modernizing? The issue is occasionally posed for Germany, more often with respect to Italy. Hitler, after all, inherited an economy recognized as one of the two or three most technologically advanced, even if the farming population (as in the United States) remained far higher than in Britain or Belgium. The task facing the National Socialists was to resume industrial progress, not to transform the structures of production. So the question of whether fascism was modernizing must really be addressed to Italian fascism. The strongest positive response is that of A. James Gregor, who has declared Italian fascism to be a precursor of the nationalist modernizing ideologies that seemed prevalent in much of the third world during the 1950s and 1960s. On the other hand, Nazism is often labelled as an archaic search to arrest the consequences of modernization, as a utopian railing against progress.[17] The debate is often carried on in confused terms. It rarely distinguishes political and economic modernization, usually fails to distinguish between different indices of transformation, and almost inevitably fails to ask what the plausible trajectory of development would have been had the respective societies remained non-authoritarian. As one of the few Marxist analyses to stress the productive side of fascism argues: "Under Fascist rule, Italy underwent rapid capitalist development with the electrification of the whole country, the blossoming of automobile and silk industries, the creation of an up-to-date banking system, the prospering of agriculture. . . . Italy's rapid progress after World War II . . . would have been unimaginable without the social processes begun during the Fascist period."[18] But certainly for analyses of development as for other events, post hoc, propter hoc represents flawed reasoning.

The argument for *political* modernization can perhaps be made more easily than for economic modernization. It can also be made for the case of Germany; perhaps Ralf Dahrendorf has done so most plausibly.[19] He has argued that despite whatever visions of *Gemeinschaft* Nazism conjured up, its major political contribution was to shatter the older elites through persecution and war so that on the debris of fragmented hierarchies the pluralist society of the Federal Republic could be built more easily. In this sense, of course, every political leadership that pulverizes its enemies lays the groundwork for modernization, and one tends to stretch the dialectical cunning of history to its breaking point. Nonetheless, there is a case to be made that the intrusion of new, uncouth leadership, the denigration of older, honorific entitlements (as in academics), or the decimation wrought in the wake of the July 20 assassination attempt, helped prepare for a more modern society, even while Nazi ideology appealed to values allegedly deriving from less splintered communities.

Italian fascism exerted far less of a pulverizing role; it left intact the monarchy and made a treaty with the Church. Dealing with elites in being, whether the industrial leadership of Lombardy or the political class of the Mezzogiorno, it suborned rather than smashed. On the other hand, Mussolini and the Italian fascists appealed less frequently to what might be called *Vergangenheitsmusik*. Certainly they did not like the political systems of liberal democracy and Marxist-derived ideology. But they did not glorify handwork and guilds; instead they suggested that corporativism as a functional arrangement of political economy was the wave of the future. My own assessment is that

Italian fascism was "neutral" with respect to political modernization or reversion. The decisive episodes of Italian political modernization came during the years between 1912 and 1922: the removal of male suffrage restrictions at the beginning of this decade made political party overhaul necessary; the controversy over entering World War I and the impressive mobilization of manpower and resources that Italy carried out between 1915 and 1918 (far more successful than during the Second World War); and finally the quasi-civil war of 1919–22, all contributed as much or more to political modernization than the subsequent fascist *ventennio*.

Nor did Mussolini's rhetoric and the other velleities of technocracy make fascism a modernizing ideology as such. It remained a prescription for ruling a society riven by internal cleavages. Perhaps one can rescue a weak connection between fascism and modernization in the sense that A.F.K. Organski sought to do fifteen years ago, when he argued that facism was "a last-ditch stand by the elites, both modern and traditional, to prevent the expansion of the [domestic] system over which they exercise hegemony. The attempt always fails and in some ways the fascist system merely postpones some of the effects it seeks to prevent."[20] This view, however, implies that fascism represents the expression of a crisis of modernization, not a cause of it, a view similar to that of Barrington Moore, Jr.[21] The fascist recourse, Moore suggests, arose in a society whose elites had attempted economic modernization—tantamount to the introduction of market society—while limiting democratization. Ultimately, in this view, fascism emerged from the Right's recognition of the fact that a channeled and plebiscitary mass mobilization was required, if a more authentic democratic representation was to be forestalled. Fascism, however, was not itself the agent of political modernization.

The issue of economic modernization per se is addressed less cleanly in the literature. By and large scholars have compounded confusion. Some have cited overall rates of economic growth, as if the vicissitudes of the interwar economy did not have any bearing on these statistics. Others cite indices of industrialization, without asking what the appropriate trend lines might be. To establish a connection between fascism and economic modernization or "development," however, we need to seek for better indices. First if we use rates of economic growth, we must compare them with the growth rates chalked up before and after. At the same time we must posit a longer-term trend development so we can discount the effect of the wars and the depression. This is hardly a simple question. Economic historians, for example, have suggested two basic trend lines for

German economic development: one would be the secular growth and employment tendencies of, say, 1900 to 1960; the other would treat the interwar period as one of "delayed catching up" that is normal after most major wars. Unless we resolve which model should serve as the trend, it is hard to evaluate the Nazi contribution.[22] Finally, we must avoid oversimplified notions of what the development process entails. Just to look at the exodus of labor from the countryside can also be misleading. Both Nazism and Italian fascism believed that the countryside should not be depopulated further. Their vision of modernization included maintenance of a significant agrarian sector. The proper indices to apply, then, might include rates of agricultural productivity, but hardly a mere percentage of workers on farms.

Granted these cautions, let us examine a few rudimentary indices. Starting with real per capita growth of GNP, we can (following Toniolo)[23] place Italy and Germany in an international comparison.

	1897–1913	1922–1938
Italy	2.7	1.9
Germany	2.6	3.8
UK	1.9	2.2
Sweden	3.5	4.1
W. Europe	2.1	2.5

For Italy, therefore, the economy progressed, but one can hardly credit a growth performance superior to that of the Giolittian period (and of course inferior to that of the decades 1950–70, which averaged 5–6 percent per annum). Nor can one claim that fascist Italy did distinguish itself in comparison with European standards during the fascist *ventennio*.

Does the record suggest better results in terms of structural change? If we examine agricultural output, which was a target sector of the regime, the results are not encouraging. Mussolini spotlighted the battle for grain as he switched to a more interventionist and autarkic policy in the mid–1920s. Arrigo Serpieri, one of the most interesting technocrats of the era, was placed in charge of the extensive land-reclamation schemes (the *bonifica integrale*). Malarial swamps were drained, and major investment made in agrarian production. After the free-trade interim of 1918–25, tariffs were raised again on cereals. But agricultural productivity slowed despite the effort: per-worker growth of agricultural output went from 2.2 percent in the

1897–1913 period to 1.6 percent in the years 1921–38, then rose in the postwar era (1949–67) to 6.2 percent.[24]

In fact the reclamation program underway after 1928—essentially the commitment of state investment funds for agrarian modernization by landlords—produced ambiguous results by other measures as well. As recent work shows, yield per hectare did increase in response to investment, but regional yields did not rise, nor did the labor supported on the countryside in the reclamation areas reverse its tendency to fall. The fact that the land area given over to grain cultivation went up about 9 percent testifies, however, neither to a growth in productivity nor to a rational allocation of resources, even assuming that self-sufficiency and arresting the migration from the land could be construed as rational developmental objectives.[25] Moreover, the contribution of agriculture to the overall growth of the economy was not always thought through. To encourage expansion of grain output, tariffs were designed to keep prices high. But high internal food prices made little sense in terms of encouraging industrial investment. Only because food consumption, especially of food richer in protein, actually dropped after 1927 could the new costs be absorbed. Finally, it turned out that government-guaranteed loan funds made their way disproportionally to the *latifondisti;* when the architect of the program, Serpieri, sought to impose requirements for the landlord recipients of loans to commit their own funds for improvements he lost his job. Without the *bonifica* program, agricultural investment would have fallen as sharply in the depression as in the rest of the economy. Finally, of course, the concentration on grain probably impeded greater diversification, although more attention to non-cereal vegetables and fruits made sense only for a free-trade regime that looked toward higher exports and imports.[26] In the last analysis, one is tempted to make a comparison of Italian agricultural policy with that of the Soviet Union. In different ways both tended to conceptualize political problems—the demand for autarky and ruralization in Italy, subjugation of an independent peasantry in Russia—as economic constraints. Both chose inefficient approaches to extracting more return from the countryside because market allocation was politically unacceptable. Both convinced themselves and many foreign observers that the results were a success in economic terms and not just a victory for the ruling groups.[27]

Did industrial development make notable qualitative strides in Italy? Again the results suggest progress, but no particular improvement over earlier or later periods, nor any better record than other countries. Manufacturing output rose about 4 percent per year between

1921 and 1937, but about 4.6 percent in Germany, 4.1 in France, 5.3 in the United Kingdom, 6.6 in Sweden, and 3.9 in the United States where the depression took its greatest toll (-20.6%, 1929–32). Output per worker climbed modestly; on the other hand the engineering industry *(meccanica:* which includes machine tools, autos, etc.) and the chemical industry grew about as strongly in Italy (7.6 and 7.1 percent per annum) as in any of the other industrial countries. Moreover, these branches created employment. If 1929 employment is indexed at 100.00, then by 1939 the steel industry climbed to 166, "meccanica" to 170, while the aggregate of manufacturing sectors stood only at 107. The autarky program that Mussolini announced in March 1936, during the Ethiopian crisis, probably contributed to the most clear-cut sectoral results, as discussion of the steel industry above has already suggested.[28]

But dramatic percentual rises of output were still higher before the first war and after the second. Primary steel production averaged 367,000 tons (=100) per year between 1901 and 1910; 961,000 tons (=262), 1911–20; 1.517m tons (=414), 1921–30; 1.961m tons (=534), 1931–40; 1.653m tons (=450), 1941–50 (which of course includes wartime disruption); and 3.940m tons (=1074) per year during the first half of the 1950s. Finally as an index of development, one might cite the growth of electrical power during the same time intervals: 750m KWH (=100), 1901–10; 3,190m KWH (=425), 1911–20; 7,640m KWH (=1187) in the 1920s; 14,158m KWH (=1888) in the thirties; 19,165m KWH (=2555) across the war years; and 33,277m KWH (=4437) in the first half of the 1950s.[29] The rhythm of Italian industrial development thus does not seem particularly tied to the fascist regime. Italian growth has traditionally been a progression of spurts and slowdowns, surges of technical transformation that yield to constraints of a more refractory social structure, then to be followed in turn by a resumption of rapid growth often in the wake of decisive liberalizing or *dirigiste* intervention. The Giolittian decade brought sustained development; the hothouse industrialization during the First World War led to postwar crisis but then rapid export-led growth during the early *liberista* phase of the regime (1922–25). Slowdown in the latter 1920s, induced in part by the high revaluation of the lira, introduced the doldrums of the depression, which did hit Italy harder than often depicted.[30] Finally, after a decade of often painful orientation toward the domestic market, state investments stimulated renewed growth on the basis of autarky in the latter 1930s, a period that in many ways laid the infrastructural basis for the spurt of the 1950s once wartime dislocations were overcome. Fascist interventions appear as part of a longer pattern of periodic initiatives. When they put power in the hands of intelligent entrepreneurs and engineers they meant progress; when they responded to entrenched or politicized constituencies they led to slowdown. In this sense fascist leadership resembled the clientelistic approach of its liberal predecessors and its Christian Democratic successors.

III. Other Aspects of Performance: Employment, Wages and Recovery from the Depression.

Italian fascism, the above discussion suggests, performed with intermittent vigor. The fascist experience produced no results in terms of modernization that other governments would not have achieved. Although Nazi Germany gives the impression of greater vigor, it is arguable that it, too, brought no great qualitative changes in the economy. Productivity gains were meager in comparison with those scored in the United States, Sweden, and even France and Italy— moreover, this lag occurred at a point in the business cycle when it is usually easiest to register such gains. They also lagged in comparison with the pre–1914 or post–1950 achievement.[31] The Nazi regime harnessed the underemployed labor of the German economy but hardly pushed through any structural transformations.

Still, recovery from the world depression needs evaluation on its own terms. In a world that found it difficult to utilize productive resources, how did the German record stack up? Since recovery was apparently six months underway when Hitler was named Chancellor— indeed his nomination was not unavoidable, even granted the need for recovery from the depression[32]—one might consider the Nazis more as beneficiaries of an economic revival that had its own autonomous impulse. But let us grant the National Socialists the credit for the trends that occurred during their administration. How do we measure their performance?

Along with the United States, Germany was the country that suffered most catastrophically from the depression. However, it emerged far more quickly. Nor was it rearmament that triggered this success, although rearmament probably helped sustain and advance the boom after 1936–38. Admittedly, there were other "Keynesian" measures undertaken under the "Immediate" Program (conceived under the Papen government and committing RM 600m) and the

Reinhardt program of 1933–34, including the construction projects of the Autobahn. Between 1933 and 1936 the government appears to have committed about RM 3b for work-creation projects and allowing for other spending perhaps a total of 5.2b.[33] Nonetheless, recovery seems to have outpaced whatever contribution this deficit spending might account for, even allowing for a generous multiplier effect.[34]

To be sure recovery had begun in Germany and might have continued vigorously. The Papen cabinet had already abandoned the deflationary policies of Brüning and had initiated disguised financing of industrial recovery through the issue of Mefo notes (bills of exchange for the metallurgical industries that the government would discount and accept in lieu of taxes). But private initiative was probably the major motor of recovery, and the wage policy of the new regime may well have contributed more to this result than government spending. Whether correctly or not, German industrialists had felt they labored under a crippling profit squeeze by the end of the late 1920s. The rapid real wage increases of the post-inflationary period (1924–29) and the imposition of new social-insurance charges convinced them that they faced higher labor costs than their competitors. Above all they blamed the Weimar state for this condition. Its constitutional provisions for compulsory arbitration and workers' representation; the leading role that the Social Democratic party had played in its establishment; its weakness in front of Allied reparation demands—all seemed to condemn the entire political structure. So long as the "system" remained intact, social democracy and organized labor would always be able to press for wage settlements that precluded adequate profits and investment. Even Chancellor Brüning's rule by Article 48 and the exclusion of the Social Democrats from governing circles could not appease their distrust of the republic. The National Socialist accession promised a more durable redressal. If "confidence" really does play a role in business decision-making, then a Hitler-Papen-Hugenberg cabinet seemed to generate confidence.[35]

Real wage behavior bore out their expectations. Essentially the Nazi government froze wages at their 1932 level. While wages had not dropped so drastically as prices in the years since 1929, real wages were still lower than they had been during that best year of the 1920s. Until the approach of war with its "overemployment" and bidding for labor, they remained extraordinarily stable.[36] Likewise, the wage-and-salary share of national income also dropped from its high point of 1932 from about 66 percent to about 55 percent by 1938, while the share of profits rose concomitantly.[37] Essentially the new regime allowed much of the recovery of national income to flow toward investment and profits. Workers could earn more as the work week increased and certainly the work force as a whole gained through re-employment, but labor could not expand its compensation per hour. Needless to say, the destruction of the traditional trade unions, the change in arbitration procedures from results that were predictably pro-labor to pro-management, the failure of even the Nazi autonomous shopfloor delegates (the NSBO) to hold their own against the centralized and bureaucratic Labor Front, the legislation of 1934 which made the manager the "leader" of a community of work, all helped generate confidence. Management would find that it might recover profit margins, but not investment autonomy. Increasingly firms had to use their earnings to purchase government bonds and seek approval for investment projects according to the competing priorities of government agencies, as in the Four-Year Plan.[38]

Nonetheless, the restrictions proved vexatious only later and they probably mattered less than the availability of contracts and unchallenged control within the enterprise. Whatever the reasons, the Nazi regime achieved a rate of growth from 1933 to 1939 that averaged 8.2 percent. However, if the 1939 national income exceeded that of 1936 by a third, this increment went increasingly into military applications. Perhaps even more impressive than the increase in output (by 1937–38 Britain had also risen 20 percent over 1932) was the pace of re-employment, which seems to have been the most rapid in the West. By 1938, as Germany approached a scarcity of labor, the United States still had 20 percent unemployed, the UK, 10 percent.[39]

The Italian fascists imposed restrictions similar in kind on the role of labor. They undermined the old unions and then in 1928–29 effectively cut the autonomy of new fascist confederations. As did Hitler in 1933, Mussolini had decreed 10 percent wage and price reductions in the late 1920s. Wages showed the same compression, but the results in terms of gross national product were not so impressive. First of all, the cost of high revaluation of the lira in 1926 was a period of stagnation that ended the export-led growth of the period 1922–25. Until the mid 1930s, however, no domestic demand surged forth to replace foreign purchasers. But the government did not rely on market slack alone to keep prices down; once upward pressure appeared after the revaluation of the lire, the regime decreed a 10 percent wage cut in May 1927 and in October a further reduction to bring the cumulative reduction to 20 percent. Further reductions of about 7 to 12 percent each followed in 1930 and 1934. In each case the government announced it was trying to keep purchasing power constant as prices descended, although the wage reductions probably led the fall in prices. Only after 1935, as Italy moved toward rearmament, did wage pressure resume.[40]

Both Italian fascism and National Socialism thus performed a similar economic function. In each country these governments came to power after a period of rapid rise of real wages had been brought to a conclusion by a deflationary crisis. In Italy the sharp recession of 1921–22 ended the giddy wage increases of the postwar inflationary ebullience. The lay-offs in 1921–22 contributed in fact to the weakness of the working class in the face of the fascist offensive; unemployment undercut socialist and trade union influence in economic terms even as fascist violence shattered their political cadres. The task of the new rulers was to prevent any renewal of the earlier wage pressure that had accompanied the *biennio rosso* of 1919–21. The German situation showed similarities. In Germany the end of the 1923 inflation had led to a sharp stabilization crisis and massive unemployment in early 1924. Real wages were stabilized at a level far lower than that of 1913. Nonetheless, with the relative prosperity of the next five years, based in part on the influx of American capital, wages jumped quickly. While Germany's real unit labor costs in the mid–1920s lagged behind those of Britain, by 1929 rapid wage increases had removed that slack. German entrepreneurs looked for a force to cap the rise of money wages, which they felt were not to be contained within the permissive constitutional framework of the Weimar Republic. The depression broke the economic trend, but at a great cost to profits as well. The Nazi regime, however, provided wage stability for the renewed post–1932 expansion. Of course, it would be crude to say that management chose fascism to contain real wage movements. Many industrialists resisted fascism. But the logic of the two movements and of the support they drew did give them similar roles. Still, it did not require fascism to contain the revival of wage pressure; in Britain wages remained low after the deflation of 1921 despite major labor efforts to contest wage cuts and plant closings. But in contrast to Britain, Weimar Germany and post–1918 Italy did not seem to have the institutions that capital could rely on without an authoritarian recourse. Stabilization crises might arrest the rapid advance of pay, but they alone could not perpetuate the rollback of the wage share they briefly achieved. To this degree fascism and Nazism allowed for the possibilities of accumulation once again. They seemed to make capitalism a workable proposition in the eyes of those who wanted it to work. This achievement, more than any technical overhaul of their respective economies, more than any qualitative innovations or structural transformations, constituted their claim to economic success. In a world where sectoral conflict between the claims of labor and capital appeared inevitable, the fascist regimes suggested that labor's advance need not inevitably undermine the possibilities for profit and investment. This accomplishment rested more on coercion than inventiveness however.

IV. Other Aspects of Performance: Mobilization and War

Pressure of time and space precludes devoting adequate attention to the economic mobilization for war. By and large both Italy and Germany devoted impressive efforts to prepare for the Second World War. While Great Britain was rapidly accelerating her military expenditure by the end of the 1930s, Germany by 1939 was investing about 17 percent of her GNP into rearmament. Even Italy devoted an impressive 10–12 percent of GNP to military preparations. The view that has tended to dominate from the work of Burton Klein to that of Alan Milward, which denigrates German commitment and argues that Hitler prepared at best for quick Blitzkrieg victories, has now been persuasively challenged by R. J. Overy and others. Commitment of national resources to war continued smoothly from the late 1930s until allied bombing and invasion finally and only belatedly dislocated the German economy. If civilian expenditure later seemed to have been only slightly infringed, part of the reason lay in the great exploitation of foreign labor and resources.[41]

Obviously these efforts were not sufficient. First of all Axis production just could not keep up with Soviet, British, and above all American output. The production of airplanes is revealing. In 1940, Germany turned out 10,247 planes, the United States 12,804, Russia 10,565, and Britain 15,049 (up from 7,940 the previous year). Despite continuing effort, the balance had to shift. In 1944, the year of maximum production, Germany turned out 39,807 planes, Britain 26,461, Russia 40,300, and the United States, 96,318. Being outdistanced by nations with larger populations was to be expected (although Hitler had obviously dismissed such obvious calculations), and does not reflect per se on the mobilization of resources for war. On the other hand, the Western powers worked more efficiently with what they mobilized. In 1941 German workers produced aircraft at 81 percent the volume of American workers (pounds of aircraft per day); by 1942 they dropped to 69 percent, recovered to 80 percent the following year and in 1944 fell back to 45 percent.[42]

Nonetheless, it was increasingly clear that quantitative mobilization did not assure efficient utilization of the capacities that were at hand. If there is any consistent report about the German, and even more, the Italian war effort, it is one of administrative confusion, and bureaucratic interference and ineptitude. General Thomas on the German side and General Favagrossa on the Italian provide testimony of how different agencies quarreled with each other in a war of all against all. For Italy old weapons were trundled out for parades; new ones were produced at best in prototype; army units remained skeletal and underequipped. Delusions about strength and modernity were cultivated by Mussolini and permeated the defense establishment.[43] The fact that the fascist states had begun their rearmament years before the war probably also diminished the incentive of the military to work with industry. They relied on their own expertise and links with traditional suppliers. Only when Todt and later Speer arrogated control of the German war economy in 1942–43 could a successful turnabout be improvised. In the Western countries the need to catch up rapidly led to much more of an interchange with civilian experts quickly. In this sense, as in so many others, the capacity for improvisation and not the skills of long-term planning proved more useful for modern war.[44]

This is not to argue that improvisation and planning were necessarily at odds. But it seems clear that despite the massive apparatus on paper for planning in Germany, in fact planning was fragmentary at best. Too many agencies collided inside government circles; too many jealous hierarchs saw their power and prerogatives at stake; too much deference was given to civilian managers who resisted conversion; too much revery was allowed the dictators. In contrast, Great Britain, the political economy most resistant to governmental intervention of any during the 1930s, proved far more successful at wartime planning. In part Britain could not afford the seeming indulgences that a victorious Germany in 1940–41 could permit herself. Moreover the constraints in terms of labor supply and necessary imports were so glaring that all economic processes were maximized in terms of labor and/or shipping. Britain could see what sort of maximization problem she faced because a couple of constraints were so obvious. If she planned targets around tonnages of shipping or available manpower, then her administrators harnessed resources far more efficiently than her adversaries on the continent. Moreover, the system of committees and joint boards that Britain developed proved flexible and resilient; Todt and Speer developed the functionally equivalent "ring" system only belatedly.[45] "Planning" proved to be an ambiguous term. It might signify a rational mobilization of resources and harnessing of effort. But for Germany, and even more for Italy, too often it amounted only to a proliferation of decrees and exhortations that foundered outside the walls of government ministries.

V. Conclusions

What were the successes of the fascist economies? Wherein lay their failures? They produced indifferent records of development if development is taken to mean a structural modernization that leaves tracks in greater productivity or an evolving industrial base, and not merely the resumption of growth. Indeed, the Italian economy probably underwent more qualitative change under fascism that did the German. To be fair, it must be pointed out that the Italian fascists took charge in a country still dualist in its structure, still susceptible of the major transformations associated with industrialization. Nonetheless, the Italian fascists did not really succeed in pushing through transformation outside the regions already on their way to development. Moreover, the governments before and after the fascist intermezzo chalked up more impressive records. The Italian fascists in effect presided over further advances, at a moderate pace, in the already modern regions of the country. Likewise their performance in terms of quantitative growth was typical of other eras. The regime was distinguished by two growth spurts: 1922–25 and 1935–39; between the two, the fascists suffered from the same stagnation that afflicted all the capitalist economies. The Nazis had a decade less of power. Their major achievement was the rapid reduction of unemployment and toward the end of the decade a hothouse investment in projects that looked toward war. Sometimes these could mean modernization of infrastructure, especially in the hydroelectric and steel plants that were constructed in Austria after the Anschluss.

In the case of both regimes, control of labor was the clearest achievement. And yet even here other less repressive regimes were to score just as well. Postwar Germany and Italy enjoyed labor compliance (measured by wage stability) that was just as great, and liberal Britain had already contained labor demands in the 1920s by deflation and unemployment. Obviously no value judgement is intended here; but whether labor restraint is useful or not, fascism was not alone in providing it.

The clear lesson is that fascism did not really introduce either economic achievements or an economic system different in kind from that of liberal capitalism. In terms of their approach to the economy, fascist officials behaved like those in the other Western countries during the depression and the war. Fascism legitimated the ad hoc intervention that massive unemployment or wartime demands did elsewhere. Obviously fascist administrators had an ideological justification for intervention upon which they could draw. But we err, I believe, in looking for a fascist economic vision as such. Fascism remained the expression of a political ideology and a political drive. Its economic expedients were byproducts and their results were consistent with the mixed results that their respective societies traditionally achieved in the economic sphere. Perhaps their mixed performance remains as a warning not to justify future authoritarian regimes in terms of alleged economic results. Only if the overriding aim must be the regimentation of labor should this variant of repression be credentialed as an economic remedy.

Fascism had middling results in pulling out of the depression. But both regimes showed revealing difficulties in mobilizing for war. Germany's performance was impressive more in purely military terms than economic ones. Why should regimes that so prided themselves on the capacity to make war have done relatively poorly in the economic preparations and conduct of it (certainly less efficiently than their despised democratic enemies)?

The answer, I think, is that fascism proved unsuccessful at operations that demanded setting priorities. It was better at tasks that involved mobilization of popular efforts from a situation of underutilization of human resources to one of fuller utilization. But once near that threshold, neither its ideology nor its procedures indicated how to make the necessary choices. The ideology of fascism was a non-zero-sum celebration of the national or racial unit. It called for subordinating all traditional cleavages to the maximization of national power and energy, presumably at the cost either of fictive internal enemies (the Jews) or outside adversaries. It was not an ideology that provided guidance for situations in which, to use the jargon, Pareto optimality had already been achieved. Second, its institutional structure also militated against clear tradeoffs. It consisted increasingly, especially in Germany, of official satraps who competed for the thaumaturgic command of the Führer. Hitler was hardly prepared to adjudicate most of these disputes; he had tended to avoid them by planning a new conquest or new chancellery. But when the expansionist recourse failed, choice was difficult.

If war sets a people any challenge it is that of choice. With resources strained to the utmost, war requires setting priorities. In military terms this involves the art of strategy. Hitler and Mussolini found this task of choosing unfamiliar, for they had come to power by smashing traditional restraints. But those were the restraints set by liberals and social democrats, the restraints of civilization. The constraints set by total war did not yield so easily. Thus fascism, which could exhort a people to climb out of a depression (and could provide the classic remedy of lower real wages to facilitate the process!), did less well in meeting the task it always claimed as its own. Fascist economics was not an autonomous doctrine or systematic approach. It was an adjunct of fascist politics. Happily the politics proved incapable of mastering the situations which it insisted upon loosing on the world.

NOTES

1. Ernesto Rossi, *I padroni del vapore* (Bari: Laterza, 1966), 46.

2. Alan Bullock, *Hitler: A Study in Tyranny* (New York: Harper and Row, 1952), 155.

3. Reinhard Neebe, *Grossindustrie, Staat und NSDAP* (Göttingen: Vanderhoeck & Ruprecht, 1981); Mario Abrate, *La lotta sindacale nell'industrializzazione d'Italia 1906–1926* (Turin, 1967) for the most pro-industry account. These works replace the earlier, sometimes rather crude Marxist accounts of fascism as a capitalist conspiracy.

4. For Rocco, see Paolo Ungari, *Alfredo Rocco e l'ideologia giuridica del fascismo* (Brescia: Morcelliana, 1963); for Olivetti see Frank Adler articles in *Telos*.

5. Statement to the Grand Council, March 1926, in Segr. Part. del Duce, 242/R, Gran Consiglio, National Archives Film T586/1122/074296–309.

6. See on these trends, David D. Roberts, *The Syndicalist Tradition and Italian Fascism* (Chapel Hill: University of North Carolina Press, 1979), 257 ff. on syndicalist productivism, with emphasis on the role of Panunzio; also Alberto Aquarone, "Aspriazioni tecnocratiche del primo fascismo," *Nord e Sud* 11, no. 52 (April 1964), 109–28; Sabino Cassese, "Un programmatore degli anni trenta: Guiseppe Bottai," *Politica del Diritto*, n. 3 (1970), 404–47.

7. Cf. Gerd Hortleder, *Das Gesellschaftbild des Ingenieurs* (Frankfurt/M: Suhrkamp Verlag); also Anson Rabinbach, "The Aesthetics of Production in the Third Reich: Schönheit der Arbeit," *Journal of Contemporary History* 11 (1976); and Jeffrey Herf, *Reactionary Modernism* (Cambridge University Press: forthcoming); *Wichard von Moellendorff, Konservativer Sozialismus* (Berlin, 1932).

8. Cf. Otto Neuloh, *Die Betriebsverfassung, 1955.*

9. Cf. Johannes Ewerling, *Vom Einigungsamt zum Treuhänder der*

Arbeit (Düsseldorf, 1935); also, T. W. Mason, *Sozialpolitik im Dritten Reich. Arbeiterklasse und Volksgemeinschaft* (Opladen: Westdeutscher Verlag, 1977), 117–23; also Mason, "Zur Entstehung des Gesetzes zur Ordnung der nationalen Arbeit vom 20. Januar 1934: Ein Versuch über das Verhältnis 'archäischer' und 'moderner' Momente in der neuesten deutschen Geschichte," in Hans Mommsen, et al., *Industrielles System und politische Entwicklung in der Weimarer Republik* (Düsseldorf: Droste Verlag, 1974), 322–51.

10. Giuseppe Bottai, "Ancora dello Stato Corporativo," in *Critica Fascista,* (June 15, 1928), 221–22; now included in Anna Panicali, ed., *Bottai: Il Fascismo come rivoluzione del capitale* (Bologna: Cappelli, 1978), 140.

11. Sabino Cassese, "Corporazione e intervento pubblico nell'economia," in Alberto Aquarone e Maurizio Vernassa, *Il regime fascista* (Bologna: Il Mulino, 1974), 327–56, citation from p. 351. Cf. in the same volume, Silvio Lanaro, "Appunti sul fascismo 'di sinistra.' La dottrina corporativa di Ugo Spirito." 357–88. For the political context, cf. Renzo De Felice, *Mussolini il Duce: Gli anni del consenso 1929–1936* (Turin: Einaudi, 1974). The corporative structure was completed in 1939 with the transformation of the parliament into a Chamber of Corporations. For the limited achievement of corporativist approaches in labor disputes see Gian Carlo Jocteau, *La magistratura e i conflitti di lavoro durante il fascismo 1926/34* (Milan: Feltrinelli, 1978).

12. Arthur Schweitzer, *Big Business in the Third Reich* (Bloomington: Indiana University Press, 1964), 110–238.

13. On these developments see Franco Bonelli, A. Carparelli, and M. Pozzoboni, "La riforma siderurgica Iri tra autarchia e mercato (1935–1942)," in F. Bonelli, ed., *Accaio per l'industrializzazione* (Turin: Einaudi, 1982), 215–333. Cf. also Paride Rugafiori, *Uomini macchine capitale. L'Ansaldo durante il facismo 1922/1945* (Milan: Feltrinelli, 1981).

14. Dieter Petzina, *Autarkiepolitik im Dritten Reich. Der nationalsozialistische Vierjahresplan* (Stuttgart: Deutsche Verlags–Anstalt, 1968), 50–51.

15. Valerio Castronovo, *Giovanni Agnelli* (Turin: UTET, 1971).

16. T. W. Mason, "The Primacy of Politics—Politics and Economics in National Socialist Germany," in Stuart Woolf, ed., *The Nature of Fascism* (New York: Vintage, 1969): 165–95.

17. See A. James Gregor, *The Ideology of Fascism* (New York: Free Press, (1969); Henry A. Turner, Jr., "Fascism and Modernization," *World Politics* 24 (1972), 547–64.

18. Mihaly Vajda, "The Rise of Fascism in Italy and Germany," *Telos,* 12 (1972), 3–26, quote p. 12.

19. Ralf Dahrendorf, *Society and Democracy in Germany* (Garden City, New York: Doubleday, 1967), 416–18.

20. A. F. K. Organski, "Fascism and Modernization," in S. J. Woolf, ed., *The Nature of Fascism* (New York: Vintage, 1969), 41.

21. *Social Origins of Dictatorship and Democracy* (Boston: Beacon Press, 1964), Chap. 8.

22. For the secular trend evaluation see Knut Borchardt: "Trend, Zyklus,

Strukturbrüche, Zufälle: Was bestimmt die deutsche Wirtschaftsgeschichte des 20. Jahrhunderts?" in Borchardt, *Wachstum, Krisen, Handlungspielräume der Wirtschaftspolitik* (Göttingen: Vandenhoeck & Ruprecht, 1982), 100–124. For a catching-up model *(verzögerte Rekonstruktion),* see Werner Abelshauser and Dietmar Petzina, "Krise und Rekonstruktion: Zur Interpretation der gesamtwirtschaftlichen Entwicklung im 20. Jahrhundert," in Abelshauser and Petzina, eds., *Deutsche Wirtschaftsgeschichte im Industriezeitalter* (Königstein/Ts.: Athenäum, 1981), 47–93. No single source of statistics was used for the various data cited in this paper; hence there may exist discrepancies among certain indices. Nonetheless each individual comparison (e. g., growth rates, manufacturing indices, etc.) has been drawn from a single source and should provide a valid measure of cross-national performance.

23. Gianni Toniolo, *L'Economia dell'Italia Fascista* (Bari: Laterza, 1980), 6.

24. Toniolo, *L'Economia,* 9. Drawn from G. Fuà, *Formazione, distributione e impiego del reddito dal 1861: sintesi statistica* (Rome: ISCO, 1972).

25. J. S. Cohen, "Un esame statistico delle opere di bonifica intraprese durante il regime fascista," in Gianni Toniolo, ed., *Lo sviluppo economico italiano 1861–1940* (Bari: Laterza, 1973), 351–71. Hectare statistics in Giuseppe Tattara, "Cerealicoltura e politica agraria durante il fascismo"; also in Toniolo, p. 379.

26. J. S. Cohen, "Rapporti agricoltura-industria e sviluppo agricolo," in Piero Ciocca and Gianni Toniolo, eds., *L'economia italiana nel periodo fascista* (Bologna: Il Mulino, 1976), 379–407. Cohen seeks to break down investment results further, but admits difficulties. If net investment in agriculture is a higher proportion of national investment in the 1930s than before or after, does this suggest success of the agrarian program or just the attrition of industrial capital formation?

27. For Soviet options see Alexander Erlich, *The Soviet Industrialization Debate, 1924–1928* (Cambridge: Harvard University Press, 1967); Stephen F. Cohen, *Bukharin and the Bolshevik Revolution* (New York: Vintage, 1971), Chaps. 5–6 among other sources.

28. Tattara e G. Toniolo, "L'industria manifattureria: cicli politiche e mutamenti di struttura (1921–37)," in Ciocca and Toniolo, eds., *L'economia italiana nel periodo fascista,* 103–69, esp. 103–9, 140–43, 160 (Tavola A.1). For the progress made in some key industries such as the Cornigliano steel works, the FIAT's Mirafiori plant, and the general technological enthusiasm of the 1930s, see Giulio Sapelli, *Organizzazione lavoro e innovazione industriale nell'Italia tra le due guerre* (Turin: Rosenberg and Sellier, 1978), 261–70.

29. Statistics from Rosario Romeo, *Breve storia della grande industria in Italia* (Bologna: Cappelli, 1963), tables 12, 17.

30. Cf. Gianni Toniolo, *L'economia dell'Italia fascista* (Bari: Laterza, 1980), 139–146. With an index of 1929 of 100, per capita GNP in 1933 was 95.9 in the U.K., 93.0 in Germany, 95.1 in Europe generally, and 95.2 in Italy. But this setback in Italy was concentrated above all in manufacturing, not

agriculture. The manufacturing indices of 1932 were 89.2 in the U.K., 60.8 in Germany, and either 85.6 for Italy (ISTAT estimate) or 74.9 (OECD criteria) (Tables 4.2 and 4.3). W. Arthur Lewis, *Economic Survey 1919–1939* (London: Allen & Unwin, 1949), 61, suggests a sharper drop for industrial production. With an index of 1929=100, 1932 figures were 84 for the U.K., 67 for Italy, 53 for both Germany and the U.S.

31. See R. S. Overy, *The Nazi Economic Experience, 1933–1938* (London: Macmillan, 1980), tables.

32. On this issue see Werner Conze and H. Raupach, eds., *Die Staats- und Wirtschaftskrise des deutschen Reiches 1929/33* (Stuttgart: Klett Verlag, 1967).

33. Dietmar Petzina, *Die deutsche Wirtschaft in der Zwischenkriegszeit* (Wiesbaden: Franz Steiner Verlag, 1977), 112–13.

34. Knut Borchardt suggests that the 1932 shortfall in national income as compared with a potential full-employment situation was RM 30b. Even a large deficit program would have comprised only RM 2b. See Borchardt, "Zwangslagen und Handlungsspielräume in der grossen Weltwirtschaftskrise der frühen dreissiger Jahre," in Borchardt, *Wachstum, Krisen, Handlungsspielräume*, esp. 174 and 270–71 (n. 29), 276–79 (nn. 59, 63). Petzina's statistics, above n. 32, suggest that during the years 1933–34, the government was spending about RM 2b per year. For a general account of Nazi measures see C. W. Guillebaud, *The Economic Recovery of Germany, 1933–1938* (London, 1939). In general, recent work suggests that currency devaluation played a more effective role in the recovery process than Keynesian policies that were intermittent (as in the U.S.), feeble (as in Britain, which showed a strong resurgence in the 1930s, or late in coming on stream (as in Sweden). Germany, however, did not devalue the Reichsmark; she resorted to bilateral agreements and internal demand.

35. Borchardt's essay, cited n. 33 above, has generated considerable controversy by implying that real wages really were excessive during Weimar, and industrialists could see no remedy within the system. For a review of the argument and now large literature, see C. S. Maier, "Knut Borchardt's 'Sick Economy' of the Weimar Republic," forthcoming in *Geschichte und Gesellschaft* (Spring 1985).

36. See Gerhard Bry, *Wages in Germany, 1871–1945* (Princeton: Princeton University Press and NBER, 1960), 233–65. Average real wage rates in all industry went from 100 in 1932 to 99.4 (1933), 96.8 (1934), 95.2 (1935), 94.5 (1936), 93.9 (1937), 93.6 (1938), 94.0 (1939). Weekly earnings rose from 100 (1932) to 113.7 (1936) and 126.0 (1939). Bry, 262, Table 67.

37. Wage share cited by Borchardt, "Handlungsspielräume," 281 (n. 72); cf. Rainer Skiba and H. Adam, *Das westdeutsche Lohnniveau zwischen den beiden Weltkriegen und nach der Währungsreform* (Cologne: Bund Verlag, 1974), 107, figure 8, for the quotients of dependent labor in gross national income (corrected for changes in occupational structure).

38. See on these policies, René Erbe, *Die nationalsozialistische Wirt-*

schaftspolitik 1933–1939 im Lichte der modernen Theorie (Zurich, 1958).

39. Petzina, *Die deutsche Wirtschaft,* 108.

40. The most recent and reliable resumé of wage movements—pulling together earlier series by Salvemini, Buozzi, Mortara and others is that of Vera Zamagni, "La dinamica dei salari nel settore industriale," in Ciocca and Toniolo, eds., *L'economia italiana nel periodo fascista,* 329–78. From her Tables 1 and 2, the following data can be extracted:

Indexed Real Wages
(based on 1938 lire)

	DAILY WAGES	HOURLY WAGES
1913	100	100
1918	91	81
1919	118	147
1920	130	162
1921	135	179
1922	128	160
1924	132	155
1925	126	148
1927	112	162
1929	110	157
1932	110	170
1934	119	179

41. See R. J. Overy, "Hitler's War and the German Economy: A Reinterpretation," in *The Economic History Review,* 2nd ser., XXXV, no. 2 (May 1982), 272–91. For the older views see Burton Klein, *Germany's Economic Preparations for War* (Cambridge: Harvard University Press, 1959); Alan S. Milward, *The German Economy at War* (1965); cf. also the essays in F. Forstmeier and H. E. Volkmann, eds., *Wirtschaft und Rüstung am Vorabend des Zweiten Weltkrieges* (Düsseldorf: Droste, 1975); and Berenice Carroll, *Design for Total War* (The Hague: 1968). For industrial mobilization, W. Birkenfeld, *Der synthetische Treibstoff, 1933–1943* (Göttingen, 1963), and Manfred Riedel, *Eisen und Kohle für das Dritte Reich* (Göttingen, 1973).

For an idea of the commitment of resources, Overy cites the proportion of military expenditure to national income in current prices: 1938–39: RM 17.2/RM98b. 1939–40: 38/109b. 1940–41: 55.9/120b. 1941–42: 72.3/125b. 1942–43: 86.2/134b. 1943–44: 99.4/130b. (p. 283). I remain skeptical about the late wartime figures, however.

42. R. J. Overy, *The Air War 1939–1945* (London: Europa, 1978), 150, table 12, for planes; 168, for output per worker.

43. Carlo Favagrossa, *Perché perdemmo la guerra* (Milan: Rizzoli, 1946); General Georg Thomas, *Geschichte der deutschen Wehr- und Rüstungswirtschaft (1918–1943/45)* (Boppard/Rh.: Schriften des Bundesarchivs, no. 14, 1966).

44. Cf. Overy, *The Air War,* 162ff. Also, Albert Speer, *Inside the Third Reich* (New York, 1970), and for a revisionist view of Speer, primarily to credit his predecessor, Fritz Todt, see G. Jansens, *Das Ministerium Speer. Deutschlands Rüstung im Krieg* (Berlin: Ullstein, 1968).

45. See W. K. Hancock and M. M. Gowing, *The British War Economy* (London: HMSO, 1949); and D. N. Chester, ed., *Lessons of the British War Economy* (Cambridge: Cambridge University Press and NIESR, 1951).

Finance and Development

Some Unintended Consequences of Financial Laissez-Faire[1]

Carlos F. Díaz-Alejandro

I. Introduction

The notion of unintended consequences of human action can be found in several of Hirschman's writings. This theme, in Hirschman's hands, is turned into a general foundation for possibilism, as well as a source of mind-expanding paradoxes.[2] This essay is in the latter spirit, as it seeks to understand why financial reforms carried out in the Southern Cone of Latin America during the 1970s and intended to free domestic capital markets from government regulations, yielded, by 1983, domestic financial sectors very much under government control. The clearest example of this paradox is Chile, which, guided by able economists committed to laissez-faire, showed the world yet another road to a de facto socialized banking system. Argentina and Uruguay show similar trends, which can be detected less neatly in other developing countries.

This paper will do two things. It will first examine the stylized facts of Latin American domestic financial history and of recent Southern Cone financial liberalization experiments. Secondly, it will indulge in reform-mongering, suggesting alternative ways of organizing domestic capital markets under Latin American conditions.

II. Notes on the Financial History of Latin America and Southern Cone Experiments

While the financial history of Latin America remains to be written, it appears that by the 1920s most countries had succeeded in establishing commercial banks of the (then) traditional sort. Several countries carried out banking reforms during those years following the advice of Professor E. W. Kemmerer, of Princeton University, and of visitors from the Bank of England. The banking system of South American countries already included institutions owned by national and provincial governments; Argentina, for example, had an important government-owned mortgage bank and several other public banks. The late 1920s were characterized in most Latin American countries by fixed exchange rates, convertibility and price stability. Domestic interest rates were closely linked to those in New York and London. Although there was no "financial repression," critics pointed to a lack of medium- and long-term credit, particularly to finance industry and non-export agriculture. Within agriculture, those without real estate collateral also complained about non-availability of credit. Domestic stock and bond markets were small; only Argentina seems to have had a promising formal domestic financial market, dominated by mortgage paper.

The 1930s brought exchange controls and the expansion of government financial institutions, which at the height of the crisis proved their usefulness in decreasing the incidence of panics and runs; the massive bank bankruptcies which occurred in the United States during the early 1930s were not witnessed in the large Latin American countries, thanks apparently to the presence of state banks plus an activist policy of rescuing most private banks in trouble. By the 1940s many countries had development banks granting medium- and long-term credits to non-traditional agriculture, industry and construction. Those credits, at least during the 1930s and early 1940s, seemed to have been granted at interest rates still ahead of domestic inflation, or at least not too far behind it, and in most cases contributed to an upsurge in capital formation. Public development banks remained, often through the 1950s, relatively small and efficient, as in the case of the Brazilian Banco Nacional de Desenvolvimento Econômico (BNDE). The drying up of external sources of finance during the 1930s and 1940s encouraged these efforts to mobilize local savings.

By the 1950s however, it was clear that in South American countries experiencing inflation, the development banks created to solve one form of perceived market failure (lack of long-term credit for socially profitable non-traditional activities) had led to another; i.e., a segmented domestic financial market, in which some obtained (rationed) credits at very negative real interest rates while non-favored borrowers had to obtain funds in expensive and unstable informal credit markets. Public controls over the banking system typically led to negative real interest rates for depositors. "Financial repression" became an obstacle to domestic savings and their efficient allocation, and financial intermediation languished.

In inflation-prone countries, financial reforms were introduced during the 1960s in the form of indexing of some loans and deposits; those involving the housing market were a particularly popular field for these new policies. Post-1964 Brazil is the clearest example of a sustained effort to revive the domestic financial system and domestic savings using a number of indexing devices, while at the same time maintaining close government supervision of financial institutions and of interest rates charged in formal markets. The results of the Brazilian reforms have been mixed: domestic financial savings have been encouraged relative to the pre-1964 situation, in spite of continuing inflation, and the new policies have supported impressive rates of capital formation. But attempts to encourage a significant stock market have failed, and the financial market remains heavily dominated by public securities. Private agents have shown reluctance to offer indexed securities. Credit to some sectors, such as agriculture, has been heavily subsidized for long periods of time. Brazil has also retained controls over the links between domestic and international financial markets, while following a passive crawling peg exchange rate policy, with sporadic jumps and other innovations.

In Central American countries, with a tradition of price stability and conservative macroeconomic management (before the 1970s), bank concentration and an association of a few private banks with dominant economic groups, historically raised concerns about monopoly power. Writing in 1979, Vicente Galbis noted:

> The experience of El Salvador suggests that interest rate freedom cannot be expected to be a panacea and automatically produce interest rate equilibrium in countries that have a relatively concentrated and unsophisticated financial system, which is the typical case in small, less developed countries. Positive policy actions to avoid market distortions might be required (Galbis 1979, 349).

This type of concern led to the nationalization of the banking system in Costa Rica in the late 1940s and in El Salvador in 1979. Government regulation, including selective credit allocations, over such oligopolistic structures may make matters worse, consolidating access by a few favored businesses to subsidized credit; post-Second-World-War Greece is said to be an example of inefficient and inequitable regulation of a concentrated banking sector.

Southern Cone countries, coming out of sundry populist experiences around the mid-1970s, undertook financial reforms going beyond those of Brazil in a laissez-faire direction. Post-1973 Chile provides the clearest example of this type of financial liberation.[3] That experiment started with a fully nationalized banking sector; a first task was to return most banks to the private sector. This was done by auctioning them off, with generous credit arrangements, or by returning them to previous owners; apparently little effort was spent on investigating the banking credentials of new entrants. At an early stage, interest rates were freed and *financieras* were allowed to operate with practically no restrictions or supervisions; early bankruptcies in December 1976 and January 1977 of the more adventurous and unregulated *financieras* led to the establishment of minimum capital requirements for entry. Authorities repeatedly warned the public that deposits were not guaranteed, beyond very small deposits with banks, and that financial intermediaries, like any other private firm, could go bankrupt; it was explicitly stated that there would not be a "bailing out" of banks and other financial intermediaries. Since 1974 multipurpose banking was allowed on the ground that the Chilean market is too small to sustain specialized financial institutions of efficient size. Reserve requirements were steadily reduced, reaching less than ten per cent of deposits by 1980.

During 1977 it became apparent that an important bank (the Banco Osorno) was in serious trouble. The authorities, fearing that its bankruptcy would tarnish external and internal confidence in Chilean financial institutions, intervened, and rescued all depositors and the institution. Apparently, the fear that external loans would decrease if the Osorno had been allowed to go bankrupt was the crucial argument for intervention. Naturally, fresh warnings were issued that, from then on, financial intermediaries would not be rescued. At that stage practically no inspection or supervision of bank portfolios existed; only in 1981 were significant regulatory powers given to the Superintendency of Banks. One may conjecture that after this event most depositors felt, de facto, fully insured and foreign lenders felt that their loans to the private Chilean sector were, in fact, guaranteed by the state. After 1977, banks, rather than *financieras,* became predominant in the financial system.

During 1979 the Chilean economic authorities started a process expected to culminate in a pseudo-exchange-rate union (Corden 1972) with the United States. The nominal exchange rate between the peso and the U.S. dollar was fixed in July 1979, and restrictions over convertibility and capital movements were relaxed; by 1981 those restrictions had been considerably weakened, and Chile witnessed a massive capital inflow. Presumably the hope was to make lending to Chile subject to no more currency risk than lending to Puerto Rico or Panama; the nominal exchange rate was supposed to last "for many years." Some of the economic authorities dreamed of doing away with the national currency altogether, but feared that the military might not wish to go that far. The theoretical underpinning of these policies included a special version of the monetary approach to the balance of payments, plus the hypothesis that financial markets, domestic and international, were no different from the market for apples and meat. Voluntary financial transactions between private lenders and borrowers were their own business, and presumably Pareto-optimal. Indeed, the nationality of those private agents was regarded as almost irrelevant. The then Director of the Western Hemisphere Division of the International Monetary Fund put it this way at a meeting held in Santiago de Chile during January 1980:

> In the case of the private sector, I would argue that the difference between domestic and foreign debt is not significant—barring governmental interference with the transfer of service payments or other clearly inappropriate public policies—if it exists at all. The exchange risks associated with foreign borrowing are presumably taken into account as are the other risks associated with borrowing, whether it be from domestic or foreign sources. More generally, private firms can be expected to be careful in assessing the net return to be derived from borrowed funds as compared with the net cost since their survival as enterprises is at stake. (Robichek 1981, 171).

The same author went on to argue that overborrowing by the private sector, even with official guarantees, was very unlikely, provided official guarantees were given on a selective basis; only public borrowing on international financial markets was regarded as posing more serious debt service risks (Robichek 1981, 172).

Convergence of domestic inflation and interest rates toward international ones proved to be a slow process, during which the fixed "permanent" nominal exchange rate yielded great incentives for private capital inflows into Chile: during 1981 the current account deficit reached an astonishing 14 percent of Chilean Gross National Product, with international reserves holding their own, while domestic savings appeared to collapse. The process of financial liberation had also led to a widely noted (by opposition economists) concentration of potential economic power in the hands of a few conglomerates or economic groups, which combined financial and non-financial corporations. Before 1981, the official view seems to have been that those economic groups must reflect some economies of scale, and could be regarded as one special type of apple or butcher shop, disciplined by free entry and other competitive pressures. Their allocation of credit resources, often heavily loaded in favor of companies associated with the group, was presumed to be more efficient than that which government bureaucrats could achieve.

As late as March 1981, international business publications were writing that "Chile's free-enterprise banking environment" was proving to be a powerful magnet for foreign banks, and that more entrants into the thriving sector were lining up *(Business Latin America,* March 11, 1981, 79). By June 1981 the same publications were noting with concern the cessation of payments on local credits by CRAV, a Chilean sugar company, as well as other blemishes on the economic miracle, but argued that "the problem areas pose no immediate threat to growth" *(Business Latin America,* June 3, 1981, 173). Following the CRAV news, the Central Bank supported financial institutions to stem incipient "runs." By November 1981 the position of two important private Chilean banks and several *financieras* became critical: they were "intervened" by the Central Bank. Further interventions of financial intermediaries occurred during the first half of 1982; rather than harsh bankruptcy proceedings, these actions apparently involved a generous expansion of credit to the private sector. Between the end of December of 1981 and the end of June 1982, domestic credit in Chilean pesos expanded by 41 percent; of the net increase in domestic credit, 92 percent went to the private sector (International Monetary Fund, 1983, 118–119, lines 32 and 32d).

The massive use of Central Bank credit to "bail out" private agents raises doubts about the validity of pre-1982 analyses of the fiscal position and debt of the Chilean public sector. The recorded public sector budget deficit was nonexistent or miniscule for several years through 1981, and moderate during 1982.[4] The declining importance of ostensible public debt in the national balance sheet was celebrated by some observers; indeed it was argued that public sector assets, such as remaining public corporations, exceeded its liabilities. Ex post it turned out that the public sector, including the Central Bank, had been accumulating an explosive amount of contingent liabilities to both foreign and domestic agents who held deposits in, or made loans to, the rickety domestic financial sector. This hidden public debt could be turned into cash, domestic or foreign, thanks to the fixed exchange rate, as the financial system threatened to collapse and the government was forced to intervene as lender of last resort. Eminent students of fiscal and financial systems, who were involved in the Chilean reforms, apparently overlooked this potential debt bomb.[5]

By late 1981 and early 1982 Chile was also feeling the full force of the international economic crisis and discovering that it was not a "small country" in international financial markets, in the sense of being able to borrow, in either public or private account, all it wished at a given interest rate, even including a generous spread. Pressures mounted on the already overvalued nominal exchange rate, fixed with respect to the U.S. dollar since July 1979. In June 1982 the unthinkable devaluation was carried out in haste, initiating a period of experimentation, which has included clean and dirty floating, a crawling peg, multiple rates, and a tightening of exchange controls.

The official exchange rate rose rapidly from 39 pesos per U.S. dollar to a range of from 74 to 80 pesos by January 1983; the free rate went substantially above official quotation. Those who had dollar debts were placed under stress; financial difficulties contributed to and were aggravated by a drop in real Gross National Product of about 14 percent during 1982. The Central Bank undertook rescue operations of banks and other financial intermediaries during the second half of 1982, to avoid a breakdown of the financial system. In January 1983 a controversial, massive intervention in five banks, the liquidation of another three, and the direct supervision of another two left the government in control of a good share of the Chilean corporate sector, as well as of its domestic and foreign debts. It has been estimated that non-performing assets of banks rose from 11 percent of their capital and reserves at the end of 1980, to 22 percent at the end of 1981, to 47 percent at the end of 1982, and to 113 percent in May 1983 (Arellano 1983a, 192).

Many of those linked to the intervened banks and associated companies, including ex-ministers of the Pinochet regime, charged that the January 1983 measures by the Central Bank and its now active superintendency of banks were unnecessary, arbitrary and politically motivated: they hinted, too, that rival economic groups stood to profit from the measures. General Pinochet himself took the lead in charging the troubled economic groups with a number of sins, including betrayal of the General's good faith. During 1983 and 1984 some well-known financiers and ex-ministers were jailed and charged with fraud. Specifically, it was charged that Banco de Chile and three other private Santiago banks set up in Panama a new bank, which was used to circumvent limits on how much a bank could loan to members of its own group, when those measures were belatedly (during 1981) imposed to control "the conglomerates' rampant self-lending tactics" (The Wall Street Journal, March 6, 1984, p. 38).

Whatever the merits of these charges, it was clear that the

domestic financial crisis in Chile had thrown into question not only the future of many existing banks and corporations but also the rules of the game as they had been understood during the years of the "Chilean miracle." The opaqueness of the intervention procedures, and of the announced processes to settle the tangled web of inter-company and bank debts, even raised questions about the regime's respect for property rights or at least its willingness to provide effective mechanisms for the efficient exercise of those rights. On the other hand, only the depositors with the three liquidated banks underwent any direct losses (up to 30 percent of their deposits); all other depositors were assured that they could get their money back.

The 1982–83 breakdown of rules, and the reliance on discretion by Chilean officials extended to the handling of private external debts. In contrast with other heavy borrowers, such as Brazil, a large share of the pre-1982 capital inflow into Chile went directly to private banks and corporations, borrowing abroad without government guarantees. Indeed, both private borrowers and lenders were warned by govern-ment officials that they were on their own, and that such debt could in no way be regarded as a Chilean *national* debt. In spite of these ex-ante announcements, during early 1983 external debts of private banks were taken over by the government, which announced its intention to continue servicing them. Those private debts have been included in the debt rescheduling being negotiated between the Chilean state and the foreign bank advisory committee for Chile. Apparently the Chilean government caved in under pressure from the bank advi-sory committee, which argued that it would be extremely difficult for the international financial community to focus its attention on the pressing needs of Chile while an increasing number of companies and their associated Chilean banks were experiencing or approaching a suspension of their payments and subsequent bankruptcy. To make their viewpoint absolutely clear, foreign banks apparently tightened up their granting of very short-term commercial credits to Chile during the first quarter of 1983, a technique reportedly used with some success ten years earlier vis-à-vis the same country. The International Monetary Fund, also active in the debt rescheduling exercise, has not publicly objected to this threat to the Robichek doctrine.

In sum, the ad hoc actions undertaken during 1982–83 in Chile to handle the domestic and external financial crisis carry with them an enormous potential for arbitrary wealth redistribution. The lessons private agents are likely to draw from these events are unlikely to be compatible with a reconstruction of a domestic financial sector relying on credible threats of bankrupcty to discipline borrowing and lending.

In spite of the ex–post government guarantees to peso deposits, private individuals decreased their demand for peso-denominated assets as domestic inflation picked up and expectations grew that the clearing up of the domestic debt tangle would involve additional inflation, exchange-rate depreciation and arbitrary controls. Faith in orderly judicial proceedings to clear up debts and claims on assets appeared to be quite low; stories abounded of debtors fleeing the country, and of petty and grand financial chicanery going unpunished.

Argentine and Uruguayan domestic financial experiences offer a number of similarities and some contrasts to the narrated Chilean events (Frenkel 1984). In those countries domestic financial intermediation also flourished and then collapsed. Major comparative points are the following:

1. Whether or not deposits are explicitly insured, the public expects governments to intervene to save most depositors from losses when financial intermediaries run into trouble. Warnings that intervention will not be forthcoming appear simply not to be believable. Roque B. Fernandez (1983) has blamed explicit insurance for financial deposits by Central Bank authorities in explaining the Argentine financial crash of 1980–82. But, as we have seen, explicit insurance was much less used in Chile, where nevertheless many firms and households apparently felt that their deposits were implicitly guaranteed by the Central Bank (Arellano, 1983 b).

2. The central banks, either because of a misguided belief that banks are like butcher shops, or because of lack of trained personnel, neglected prudential regulations over financial intermediaries. Not surprisingly, the assets held by Argentine and Chilean banks and *financieras* around 1980–81 appeared to have been substantially riskier relative to those held by similar institutions in the United States or in Western Europe, and relative to plausible counterfactuals of sensibly regulated financial intermediaries in those countries. It has been argued that in Uruguay the presence of U.S.-owned banks, regulated indirectly by the Federal Reserve, reduced the magnitude of risk-taking by banks.

3. The new financial institutions in the Southern Cone attracted fresh entrepreneurs and stimulated the creation of new conglomerates and economic groups. While new entrepreneurial blood has an attractive aura, experience indicates that such venturesome animal spirits are better channeled toward non-financial endeavors, where the disciplining threat of bankruptcy could be more credible.

4. In economies characterized by intractable market and informational imperfections, conglomerates and economic groups, even as they may correct government-induced financial repression imperfec-

tions, could exacerbate others, particularly via the creation of oligopolistic power. The close association of financial intermediaries with non-financial corporations, frowned upon by U.S. regulations, can indeed lead to distortions in the allocation of credit, as shown by the Argentine and Chilean experiences. Linkages in both countries between banks and firms, which were hardly arms' length, were responsible for the high use of debt by private firms. In Chile by late 1982 private firms were more indebted than state enterprises; within the private sector, extreme indebtedness was found among those that controlled banks (and that had acquired from CORFO those firms nationalized under the Allende presidency). Between 1975 and 1982, Chile went from a financially shallow economy, where inflation had wiped out the real value of debt, to an excessively financially deep economy where creditors owned a very large share of real wealth, a clear case of "too much debt and too little equity." Interpenetration of economic and financial power appears to have reached extraordinary levels. The two largest business groups in Chile by late 1982 controlled the principal insurance companies, mutual funds, brokerage houses, the largest private company pension funds and the two largest private commercial banks; about half of all private external debt was channelled through the domestic banking system, so control of banks allowed ready access both to domestic and foreign credit. By late 1982 many banks had lent one quarter or more of their resources to affiliates.

5. The freeing of interest rates and the relaxation of controls over financial intermediation will not necessarily encourage intermediation beyond short-term maturities. The flourishing of private financial intermediaries in the Southern Cone, even at the height of the boom, was limited to deposits and loans of less than six months duration. Longer-term intermediation via banks or bonds, not to mention via active stock markets, remained very weak. Insofar as the new policies destroy pre-existing government-supported long-term intermediation arrangements, as in the case of the Chilean housing system, SINAP, financial liberation will reduce available long-term financial intruments. Stock markets may witness short booms, but will mobilize very few funds; charges of manipulation and fraud, plus lack of protection for minority stockholders, will reduce public interest in buying stocks in unregulated or badly regulated stock markets. It has been charged in the Chilean case that false stock transactions were an important component in the growth of financial intermediaries during 1977 through 1981. It is argued that market prices of shares owned by large business groups were manipulated upwards, via phony transactions, to increase the value of collateral used to secure loans

and to induce fresh inflows into captive mutual funds.

6. The end of financial repression undoubtedly encouraged many types of financial savings; Arellano (1983a and 1983b) documents the boom in Chilean financial savings and intermediation, especially during 1977 through 1982. Paradoxically, however, total domestic savings did *not* increase in the South American experiments in financial liberation, in spite of handsome returns to savings. Chilean gross national savings *fell* from an average of 16.3 percent of Gross National Product during the decade of the 1960s to 12.4 percent during 1975 through 1981 (Arellano 1983b, 12). Arellano cogently argues that the expansion in Chilean financial savings came mainly from the foreign capital inflow, the recording on both sides of the ledger of accumulated interest and of capital gains, and a reorientation of saving flows from the public to the private sector.[6] In 1980–81 reforms of the social security system gave a further boost to funds flowing into private financial institutions, by changing the pay-as-you-go government-managed system into a capitalization scheme, in which pension funds were to be managed by private financial institutions.

7. Aggregate investment performance showed no clear sign of either improving or of becoming more efficient in the South American countries undergoing financial liberation. In Chile gross fixed investment during the 1960s averaged 20.2 percent of Gross Domestic Product; during 1974 through 1982 it reached only 15.5 percent of GDP (Arellano 1983a, 226). Argentine and Uruguayan performance was better on the investment front, partly because public sector capital formation did not shrink as in the Chilean case.

8. Foreign lenders take government announcements that it will not rescue local private debtors, especially banks, with non-guaranteed external (or domestic) liabilities even less seriously than depositors take the threat of a loss of their money. The alleged Japanese attitude of not differentiating between the public and private external debt of a developing country appears to have been upheld ex-post as a sounder guide to action than the Robichek doctrine. Foreign banks lending to both the public and private sectors of a country have considerable leverage to convince governments to take over ex-post bad private debts, especially those of financial intermediaries. There appear to be no international referees to keep them from exercising such leverage. The substantive differences between the nationalization of Mexican private banks during 1982 and the intervention in Chilean private banks during 1983 may be less than one would think by reading the editorials of the international financial press. International banks, knowing they are regulated at home, where they also have close

political connections with their governments, expect the same in borrowing countries.

While debts of private Chilean banks to foreign banks were fully assumed by the government, other operations by Southern Cone banks carried out abroad do not seem to have received the protective mantle of home-government support. For example, the Argentine authorities declined to accept responsibility for claims on the New York branch of the failing Banco Intercambio Regional, which was taken over by the New York State Banking Department (Johnson and Abrams, 1983, 23). Given this experience, it is unlikely that Southern Cone banks will emerge as important competitors in international banking in the near future.

9. The combination of a pre-announced or fixed nominal exchange rate, relatively free capital movements, and domestic and external financial systems characterized by the moral hazard and other imperfections set the stage not only for significant microeconomic misallocation of credit, but also for macroeconomic instability, including the explosive growth of external debt, most of which was incurred by private Chilean banks, followed by abrupt cessation of capital inflows. The macroeconomic instability would occur even assuming tranquil circumstances, but it is of course exacerbated by external shocks hitting economies made particularly brittle and vulnerable by that combination of policies and institutions. Contrary to some old and new notions, the experiences of Argentina, Chile and Uruguay show that what happens to the *nominal* exchange rate does affect the *real* exchange rate, at least in the short and medium runs, and that changes in the exchange rate can be an important and efficient mechanism of adjusting the balance of payments. Faulty exchange-rate policy appears much more important in explaining financial turbulence and the severity of the Chilean 1982–83 depression than the reduction in import barriers. The credibility of the latter was reduced by peso overvaluation, inducing an import binge and reducing local savings.

10. Short-term real interest rates, plausibly defined, on the whole remained very high in Argentina, Chile and Uruguay, even during periods of massive capital inflow. A number of hypotheses have been offered to explain this phenomenon: macroeconomic policy; expectations of devaluation and inflation, which in the short run did not materialize; a change in the real productivity of capital; and even excessive spreads orginating in Central Bank reserve requirements. As in the case of explanations for the high, but less spectacular, real interest rates recorded in the United States during the early 1980s, none of the hypotheses are fully satisfactory (Litterman and Weiss

1984). From the viewpoint of this paper, the most intriguing hypotheses for explaining extravagant Southern Cone real interest rates (which in Chile reached 32 percent per annum on the average during 1976 through 1982 according to Arellano)[7] focus on the nature of financial deregulation and imperfections in those markets. It was noted earlier that the high Chilean interest rates were reflected mainly in double-entry bookkeeping. It can be argued that firms and households borrowing at extravagant rates either expected them to last for very brief periods, or, if they did not, borrowers expected the government to bail them out, knowing as they did that many other borrowers were in a similar situation. Such expectations, of course, favored "distress borrowing": either interest rates fell, or government would "bail out" everyone. Whatever the validity of these arguments may be, it is clear from the Southern Cone experience that the type of deregulation experienced by those countries gives no assurance of stable real interest rates hovering around reasonable estimates of the socially optimal shadow real interest rate. Some observers have argued that the main function of high real interest rates was to transfer the ownership of real enterprise wealth from debtors to creditors, a mechanism doomed to stop when no more shareholders' wealth was left.

11. As elsewhere in Latin America, the decline in real Gross Domestic Product in Argentina (11 percent between 1980 and 1982), in Chile (15 percent between 1981 and 1983), and in Uruguay (14 percent between 1980 and 1983) may be said to be the result of unfavorable external circumstances during the early 1980s, combined with less than optimal domestic policies. As noted earlier, policy-induced stickiness in nominal exchange rates delayed adjustment to changes in external terms of trade and changes in capital flows. The brittle Southern Cone domestic financial sectors must also bear blame for first exaggerating the boom, then aggravating the recession and finally delaying recovery. The consequences of the Chilean financial crash have been the most spectacular and have led to a massive rearranging of the national balance sheet. Such a rearranging, however, has been a slow and opaque process, leaving many economic entities not knowing who owns what, or who owes what to whom, hardly ideal circumstances for encouraging a revival of private investment.

12. As with international debt, the sorting out and allocation of losses and blame for "mistakes" (only clear ex post) by borrowers and lenders in the domestic financial markets present monumental conceptual and legal problems, especially when "mistakes" are widespread. Since 1982 Argentina appears to have taken the time-honored route of washing out old financial mistakes via inflation (which is

not allowed to be reflected in interest rates); this approach favors
borrowers over lenders. As noted earlier, in the Chilean case the path
out of the morass remains unclear; inflation accelerated, but "only"
to around 25–30 percent during 1983. There are few precedents and
less accepted doctrine regarding financial processes as bizarre as those
experienced by Chile during 1975 through 1983. Bankruptcies, financial
distress and confusions delay recovery beyond what would be necessary
to achieve real adjustment to the new international terms of trade,
capital market realities and expectations about growth in the international economy.

III. Options For Latin American Domestic Financial Systems

Southern Cone domestic financial systems of the late 1970s and
early 1980s ended up with a *pessimum* "middle way": de facto public
guarantees to depositors, lenders and borrowers, and no effective
supervision and control (until it was too late) of the practices of
financial intermediaries. Reform could logically head in two opposite
directions: more laissez-faire with binding commitments against future
bailouts, or toward more public controls, possibly culminating in
nationalization of the banking system, as in Costa Rica, El Salvador,
India and France. Other Latin American countries outside the Southern Cone, such as Brazil and Colombia, have domestic financial
systems that, while showing signs of stress during the last few years,
have not undergone Southern-Cone-type crises; their experiences (including their post-1981 troubles) could be useful in sketching desirable
characteristics of domestic financial arrangements.

As noted earlier, the credibility of a government commitment
to a truly laissez-faire domestic financial system is very low. Firstly,
as illustrated in the recent Chilean experience, foreign financial agents
will not accept a separation of private and public debts when a crisis
arrives; financial laissez-faire in one peripheral country does not seem
viable. Secondly, "public opinion," including generals and their aunts,
simply does not believe that the state would (or could) allow most
depositors to be wiped out by the failure of banks and financial
intermediaries. It may be that private financial agents, domestic and
foreign, lenders, borrowers and intermediaries, whether or not related
to generals, know that the domestic political and judicial systems are
not compatible with laissez-faire commitments which a misguided
minister of finance or central bank president may occasionally utter
in a moment of dogmatic exaltation. When a crisis hits, borrowers

and lenders will reason, bankruptcy courts will break down; when most everyone (who counts) is bankrupt, nobody is! Thus, even if one believed, à la Hayek, that the externalities and public good characteristics of the domestic monetary and financial system are negligible, one may conclude that the political and social infrastructure found in many developing (and developed?) countries conspires against the viability of such a pure laissez-faire financial system. The zealot may conclude that the nation does not measure up to the purity of the model.

So should one move back to good old 1950s style financial repression; extensive controls and perhaps full nationalization of the domestic financial system? It can be argued that a *believable* alternative system could be designed, avoiding many of the inefficiencies of financial repression while avoiding those of the Southern Cone experience, and blending both public and private financial agents. What follows sketches some features of that eclectic system.

Negative real rates of interest became common in Latin America during the 1940s and 1950s as inflation gained momentum and many monetary authorities maintained ceilings on nominal interest rates offered and charged by the banking and financial system. At that time most South American countries (but not Mexico, Venezuela, Central America and the Caribbean) also maintained extensive exchange controls. Limited international capital mobility buttressed the taxing of cash balances and financial repression; the then prevalent Keynesian orthodoxy also encouraged these developments. While persistently negative real rates of interest in the formal financial market occurred only when the government imposed rate ceilings and exchange controls, it is not obvious that public regulation and participation in the domestic financial market necessarily had to lead to negative rates of interest. The Mexican financial system of the 1950s and 1960s, praised by development scholars, contained both public institutions and substantial government regulations. As already noted, the post-1964 Brazilian indexing and other financial reforms could hardly be described as involving a laissez-faire approach. The celebrated South Korean financial reforms of the 1960s were carried out with a high degree of public ownership and control of the formal financial sector (Gurley, Patrick and Shaw 1965, 45).

Assuming that a country intends to maintain monetary sovereignty but that significant, yet not explosive, inflationary expectations persist, there is a strong case for making sure that firms and households have available a domestic liquid financial asset yielding a real interest rate which is not far below, nor much above, zero. The inflationary tax borne by currency balances may result from the inability of the fiscal system to find non-inflationary sources of revenues, or it may be simply a by-product of an inflationary spiral, whose inertial momentum could only be halted by a severe real contraction. Presumably the transactions convenience provided by domestic currency will be enough to generate some demand for it, even under moderate inflation, an assumption supported by South American experiences. But without a liquid and safe store of value denominated in domestic currency which at least maintains its purchasing power, a national monetary and financial system will have little long-run credibility, short of draconian controls. It could also be argued that without such an asset the system would not meet the most elementary tests of social equity.

It should be emphasized that introducing a "zero-real-rate asset" next to a zero-nominal-rate asset involves a delicate trade-off, which may increase welfare only if the inflation tax on money remains "reasonable." The zero-real-rate asset will reduce the demand for money, but may also reduce the demand for assets denominated in foreign currencies. An inflation which accelerated sharply above historical norms, introducing massive currency substitution, could destroy the credibility of all domestic financial assets.

There are many possible ways to supply a zero-real-rate asset. The banking system, for example, could provide indexed savings accounts; depending on practical considerations, they could be used partly as checking accounts. At least that segment of the banking system would have explicit and full deposit insurance, perhaps only for accounts below a certain (generous) limit; insurance for larger accounts could be partial. Naturally, the use by banks of funds coming from those accounts would be tightly regulated by a flinty-eyed superintendency of banks. Indeed, practical considerations could lead to the requirement of 100-percent reserves on that type of deposits, to be placed in very safe assets.

Enormous potential power is given by this scheme to the regulatory agencies: it could end up with the central bank controlling each loan. Experiences in Latin America and elsewhere with a public monopoly of credit have not been so encouraging as to make one indifferent to this possibility. Safeguards against the monopoly scenario would include allowance for the legal supply of alternative financial assets, by either private agents or decentralized public ones, plus an active congressional supervision of the regulatory agencies and the public banks. The latter point suggests that democracy, whatever its more fundamental virtues, is an important technical input for a healthy domestic financial system. Austrian and French experiences could also provide lessons in how to combine public ownership with decentralization and non-politization of credit allocation by public banks.

Suppliers of riskier financial assets would not have available public deposit insurance but would be subject to less regulation. Nevertheless, these would still include minimum capital requirements, strict "transparency" informational rules (regarding both assets and connections with other firms), and clear "risk-may-be-hazardous-for your-health" warnings to the general public. After recent experiences it is probably better to proceed cautiously in this segment of the domestic financial market, but not so cautiously as to make it an empty set. Interest rates offered and charged by these intermediaries would be expected to show significant real rates. At least on an experimental basis those rates would not be set by the monetary authorities, but spreads between rates paid to depositors and those charged to borrowers would be subject to antitrust vigilance (as entry into this sector would not be completely free). Those spreads would depend, inter alia, on possible official reserve requirements; these could be presumed to be quite low for this segment of the market. Both foreign and private institutions would be expected to participate, but entry regulations and antitrust vigilance would be on guard against interlocking directorates among financial and non-financial firms and would lean against the creation of dominating economic groups and conglomerates. Prohibitions against the mingling of financial and non-financial firms, as in the Unites State's Glass-Steagall Act, appear particularly desirable where markets are relatively small.

Latin American experience, and indeed that of Continental Europe in the last century, makes one skeptical that private markets alone will generate a flow of financial intermediation high enough to support a rate of long-term fixed capital formation which fully exploits available high social rates of return to long-term investments. Private uncertainties and skepticism of all sorts, which will not disappear by freeing interest rates, reduce the scope for private long-term finance and for stock markets; the latter have continued to languish even when encouraged by various subsidies, as in Brazil. It will be recalled that this was the original motivation for the creation of public development banks in Latin America during the 1930s and 1940s. The need remains to close gaps left in long-term capital markets by acute uncertainties found in Latin American societies, and public development banks remain a plausible solution, in spite of the abuses and errors in their management registered over the last fifty years. Not all experiences have been negative; as noted earlier, public mortgage banks obtaining funds by issuing indexed obligations yielding modest real rates of interest and correspondingly pricing their mortgages, have registered important accomplishments in a number of countries. The crucial lessons remain the avoidance of real interest rates too far from plausible estimates of the shadow opportunity cost of capital, plus political mechanisms to check potential abuses of those public agencies.

Decentralized, efficiently run public financial intermediaries operating together with private intermediaries could play several important functions, besides merely plugging gaps in the long-term segment of the market. As recent Latin American experiences have shown, confirming the evidence of the early 1930s, during financial crises the public appears to turn to public banks for greater security. (The "flight to quality" in the Latin American context also benefits large, well-known foreign banks.) Public banks could help focus market interest rates around the social opportunity cost of capital, decreasing instability in real interest rates. Those institutions could channel external funds, helping to keep tabs on the foreign debt and improve borrowing terms. Their operating costs would give evidence and provide a yardstick on reasonable spreads between interest rates paid to depositors and those charged to borrowers. By providing long-term credit to new, non-traditional activities, development banks would eliminate one of the excuses frequently given for extravagant protection against imports. Indeed, the valid cases for infant-industry protection or promotion are likely to be most efficiently handled under Latin American conditions using public credit instruments, suitably priced, rather than by barriers against imports. Needless to say, public banks will not yield these results without a great deal of effort and pressure by those in charge of their management and supervision. Considerable experimentation is also likely to be needed, particularly regarding the establishment of a structure of interest rates compatible with both a vigorous rate of fixed capital formation, a matching flow of voluntary domestic savings and the avoidance of destabilizing portfolio shifts by depositors.

The real exchange rate, no less than the real interest rate, remains a crucial price for Latin American economies. The Southern Cone emphasis on exchange-rate management as an instrument to achieve nominal targets, letting market forces settle the real exchange rate, emerges from recent experience as less successful than the Brazilian-Colombian crawling peg practice, which targets the real exchange rate as an explicit objective of policy. As with the real interest rate, the correct real exchange rate is not easy to define and calculate exactly, but grossly over- or under-valued real exchange rates, like giraffes, are not so difficult to recognize on sight. "The correct real exchange rate" would be that compatible with expected current account deficits, output levels and long-term capital inflows, given commercial and other policies. These are *real* considerations; what about the role of the exchange rate (and of expected changes in its *nominal* level) as a crucial link between domestic and international financial markets, and its impact on the capital account of the balance of payments?

Domestic policies targeting real interest rates and real exchange rates will not be compatible with free or untaxed capital movements and unrestricted convertibility, except by fluke (or short of extravagant average levels of reserves). This is not a pleasant conclusion for those familiar with past experiences with exchange controls over international flows in Latin America or elsewhere. Limitations on unconditional capital-account convertibility, however, may have greater or smaller inefficiencies, inequities and effectiveness depending on the context in which they are undertaken. (No exchange control system, of course, will be free of leaks and absurdities.) A real exchange rate hovering around its long-run equilibrium level will do much to reduce pressure on convertibility limitations; it would be absolutely essential to avoid the temptation of manipulating convertibility restrictions to buttress overvalued exchange rates, as in the past. The heterodox tool of exchange controls must be managed with orthodox concern for the real exchange rate. Note, incidentally, that even without convertibility restrictions, overvalued exchange rates can be propped by manipulating the capital account of the balance of payments, i.e., high interest rates went along in the Southern Cone with overvaluation. Particularly during times of stress, a realistic exchange rate for most current account transactions could be supplemented with a legal and freely fluctuating rate for all other transactions. Large and persistent gaps between those two rates would signal the need to move the basic rate, or adjust fiscal and monetary policies.

The prudential regulatory machinery could be used to discourage volatile international financial flows relying primarily on taxes or tax-like requirements, i.e., via special reserve requirements for certain types of unwanted international financial transactions, as is the practice in several Western European countries. Taxes would also be expected to capture arbitrage profits from borrowing abroad and lending domestically, under "normal" circumstances. Persistent subsidies to encourage foreign borrowing would be a sign that either the real exchange rate or domestic real interest rates have drifted from their equilibrium levels.

Unrestrained convertibility in the capital account is in fact a luxury, desirable in itself, enjoyed only by a handful of countries which have either a very developed or very underdeveloped domestic financial system. It is neither the usual practice in OECD countries (Bertrand 1981), nor was it the expectation of at least some of the architects of the Bretton Woods system (Crotty 1983). So long as domestic currency balances may be burdened by an inflation tax higher than those levied on foreign currencies, some limitations on convertibility are widely perceived as a necessary part of transitional policy package (see for example McKinnon and Mathieson 1981).

The case for some limitations on free capital account movements rests partly on macroeconomic considerations and partly on the need to correct microeconomic imperfections in domestic and international financial markets. Events during 1982 must have put an end to the notion that there are small countries in international financial markets, in the sense that those countries could borrow all they want at a given interest rate. Currency and sovereign risks will inevitably tilt the supply schedule of foreign funds to any country in an upward-sloping direction, and may even give it a kinkier look, so that there will be a gap between private and social costs of borrowing.[8] Moral-hazard considerations on both sides of the market, or expectations of bailouts, reinforce the case for home-country supervision of inter-national financial flows; if home countries do not undertake that supervision others will do it for them.

These considerations also cast doubt on the desirability of allow-ing the domestic financial system to offer deposits denominated in foreign currencies, either to domestic residents or to foreigners. Such deposits sharply curtail the freedom of maneuver of monetary authori-ties, for the sake of maintaining the credibility and reputation of the banks offering them. (The point is partly applicable to any country whose banks have an international scope, even if deposits are denomi-nated in home currency.) The Mexican and Uruguayan experiences suggest that deposits denominated in foreign currencies and insured by the home central bank enhance vulnerability to crises, introducing the likehood of sharp discontinuities in the rules of the game. At any rate, in general that type of deposit would not be compatible with limitations on capital account convertibility, limitations which would also rule out the feasibility of a totally clean float for the exchange rate, including both spot and future quotations.

IV. A Final Caveat

Recent Chilean experience shows that a balanced budget by itself will prevent neither a serious financial crisis nor acute macroeconomic turbulence. Yet previous Chilean experiences, and those of other Latin

American countries, also show that fiscal extravagance is a sure way to bring about not only economic dislocation, but also the weakening and even collapse of fragile democratic institutions. This paper has discussed neither fiscal policy nor strategies on how to eliminate inflation. Implicitly, it has assumed that Latin American inflations may be sustained by many sources, not just budgetary laxity, that in most countries for the foreseeable future "living with inflation" will be a more credible policy goal than eliminating it, and that this must be taken into account when designing desirable domestic financial policies, as well as other measures.

Nevertheless, there are inflations (and budget deficits) which no domestic financial system with a minimum of coherence could live with. Examples include inflations which accelerate for more than, say, three years in a row, reaching levels substantially above historical norms, or inflationary rates which fluctuate unpredictably from year to year. Under either circumstance relative prices will become very volatile, and real and financial calculations very difficult. The stage would be set for wild swings in depositors' preferences as between private and public financial institutions, and as between domestic and foreign financial assets. It would be nearly impossible to design reasonable financial systems, in a mixed-economy context, which could be compatible with sustained public expenditures and budget deficits of the magnitude of those registered in Chile during 1971–72, in Argentina during 1974–75, or in Mexico during 1981–82.

NOTES

1. A version of this paper was first presented at a conference held in Bogotá on November 22 and 23, 1982, sponsored by the Universidad de Los Andes and the Banco de la República. Visits to CIVES, in Montevideo, and CIEPLAN, in Santiago de Chile, during March 1983, were also very helpful for extending that early version. The joyous Notre Dame conference in honor of Albert O. Hirschman, held April 16 and 17, 1984, provided yet another stimulating source of comments. I am grateful to all these institutions and to numerous individuals who shared with me their views of the events narrated and of the issues discussed in the text. Among those who are unlikely to find embarrassing my acknowledgement of their help, I mention José Pablo Arellano, Edmar L. Bacha, Alex Cairncross, Guillermo Calvo, Jonathan Eaton, Ricardo Ffrench-Davis, Alejandro Foxley, Arminio Fraga Netto, Jeff Frieden, Eduardo García d'Acuña, José Antonio Ocampo, Hugh Patrick, Gustav Ranis, Patricio Meller, Miguel Urrutia and Laurence M. Weiss. My gratitude is no

less for the often extraordinarily generous cooperation of those not explicitly named.

2. See especially Hirschman 1971, 31–37.

3. For a careful narrative see Arellano, 1983a and 1983b.

4. For evidence on the apparent Chilean fiscal performance, see McKinnon 1982.

5. Present at the creation and early development of the new Chilean financial system were experts brought together by the Organization of American States Program for the Development of Capital Markets. Together with the Chilean Central Bank, this program sponsored seminars on capital markets in Santiago during 1974, 1976 and 1977.

6. See also Harberger 1982 for a discussion of the poor performance of Chilean savings.

7. Arellano 1983b, 31; this is the rate charged for short-term loans.

8. For an early, but apparently unheeded exposition, see Harberger 1981.

REFERENCES

Arellano, José P. 1983a. "El financiamento del desarrollo." In CIEPLAN, *Reconstrucción Económica Para La Democracia,* 189–237. Santiago de Chile: Editorial Aconcagua.

———. 1983b. "De la liberalización a la Intervención: El Mercado de capitales en Chile: 1974–83." *Estudios CIEPLAN,* no. 11 (Estudio No. 74, Diciembre): 5–49.

Bertrand, Raymond. 1981. "The Liberalization of Capital Movements: An Insight." *The Three Banks Review,* no. 132 (December).

Business Latin America, March 11 and June 3, 1981.

Corden, W. Max. 1972. "Monetary Integration." *Princeton Essays in International Finance.* No. 93. Princeton, N.J.: International Finance Section, Princeton University.

Crotty, James R. 1983. "On Keynes and Capital Flight." *Journal of Economic Literature* 21 (March): 59–65.

Fernandez, Roque B. 1983. "La Crisis Financiera Argentina: 1980–1982." *Desarrollo Económico* 23 (April-June): 79–98.

Frenkel, Roberto. 1984. "Notas para una investigación sobre el sistema financiero en Argentina." Buenos Aires: CEDES (processor).

Galbis, Vicente. 1979. "Inflation and Interest-rate Policies in Latin America, 1967–76." *International Monetary Fund Staff Papers* 26 (June): 334–66.

Gurley, John G., Hugh T. Patrick, and E. S. Shaw. 1965. *The Financial Structure of Korea.* The Bank of Korea (reprint).

Harberger, Arnold C. 1981. "Comentarios." In Banco Central de Chile, *Alternativas de Políticas Financieras en Economías Pequeñas y Abiertas al Exterior; Estudios Monetarios VII,* 181–88. Santiago de Chile: Banco Central de Chile.

————. 1982. "The Chilean Economy in the 1970s: Crisis, Stabilization, Liberalization, Reform." In Karl Brunner and Allen H. Meltzer, eds., *Economic Policy in a World of Change,* Vol. 17, 115–52. Amsterdam: North-Holland Publishing Company.

Hirschman, Albert, 1971. *A Bias for Hope: Essays on Development and Latin America.* New Haven: Yale University Press.

International Monetary Fund. 1983. *International Financial Statistics* (March). Washington, D.C.

Johnson, G. C., and Richard L. Abrams. 1983. *Aspects of the International Banking Safety Net.* International Monetary Fund Occasional Paper. no. 17, March.

Litterman, Robert B., and Laurence Weiss. 1984. "Money, Real Interest Rates, and Output: A Reinterpretation of Postwar U.S. Data." Federal Reserve Bank of Minneapolis (processor).

McKinnon, Ronald I. 1982. "The Order of Economic Liberalization: Lessons from Chile and Argentina." In Karl Brunner and Allan H. Meltzer, eds., *Economic Policy in a World of Change,* 179–84. Amsterdam: North-Holland Publishing Company.

McKinnon, Ronald I., and Donald J. Mathieson. 1981. "How to Manage a Repressed Economy." *Princeton Essays in International Finance,* no. 145 (December). Princeton, N.J.: International Finance Section, Princeton University.

Robichek, E. Walter. 1981. "Some reflections about External Public Debt Management." In Banco Central de Chile, *Alternativas de Políticas Financieras en Economías Pequeñas y Abiertas al Exterior; Estudios Monetarios VII* (December), 171–83. Santiago de Chile: Banco Central de Chile.

The Wall Street Journal. 1984.

Modes of Financial Development: American Banking Dynamics and World Financial Crises

Marcello de Cecco

I

In this paper I shall try to suggest that, from a largely homogeneous, theoretical and practical banking tradition, the different interaction of political and economic forces led the British and American banking systems to develop according to different modes. The American banking system, after a start which followed British lines, radically changed course in the Jacksonian era, and it has increased its differences from the British system, and from other major banking systems, as time has passed. The non-existence, in the United States, of a strong coalition of lenders, and the structural bias of the country towards using more savings than it generated, blended with a banking theory and a legal tradition totally similar to the British ones, have modelled the U.S. banking system in a way which, if it has favored the fast growth of the American economy, has also given it a tendency to deep financial instability.

The structural imbalance of the American financial system has been a most important generator of crises of the international financial system in the last 150 years. In this paper I shall give a rapid sketch of how American financial instability has recurred throughout the period and spread to the rest of the world financial system. In a short piece like the present one, many questions are left unanswered and many links are missing. But the field is now being extensively ploughed by many able scholars, and more detailed and persuasive works, which will help fill the gaps, will certainly appear in the near future.

My main aim is to show how the same cultural tradition can generate wildly different results, if applied to different socio-political and economic circumstances. Or, as Pasteur taught, the receiving environment is even more important than the virus that infects it.

II

Even more than is the case with nuclear power and, of course, long before it, in the United States banking has been subject to extensive regulation. As elsewhere, regulation has been imposed on American banking by political forces. And, more often than not, regulation has been skillfully manipulated by some sectors of the financial community so that it may work to their own advantage, and to the detriment of their competitors. In order to do this, industrialists, farmers and other large blocks of the American political body have been used to serve the purposes of this or that section of the financial community. This, however, has been true of regulation in most countries. The interesting thing to discover is what interplay of political and economic forces led the American financial system to develop in a mode different from that in which the financial systems of other industrial countries developed. It is equally interesting to trace the impact of the peculiar mode of American financial development on the world financial and economic system.

Americans, and foreigners, still tend to think of the United States as a new country, with young institutions. But as far as banking is concerned, the United States has had an experience synchronous with that of every other developed country. Modern banking developed on these shores exactly when it was developing in England; it therefore even preceded banking development in the rest of Europe. The same can be said of banking and monetary theory, as the United States and Britain were a homogeneous intellectual community.

As to central banking, it is fair to say that in the United States it developed, in its most modern and accomplished form, before it did everywhere else. The First and the Second Banks of the United States resembled modern central banks more than the early nineteenth-century Bank of England did.[1]

The Second Bank of the United States was partly owned by the federal state, managed only secondarily for profit, and it acted as the fiscal agent of the federal government. After only a decade of existence, it had become one of the largest banks in the world. And it is generally recognized that the 1820s, the period in which the Bank of the United States was extending its operations, was, perhaps, before the 1940s and 1950s, the quietest period in American banking history. The Bank of the United States successfully managed to control the state banks by checking their overissue of bank notes. It thus stabilized economic activity.

The United States government, however, having scored a first in world financial history until the 1820s, proceeded, in the next decade, to destroy its own achievement by denying the Bank of the United States a renewal of its federal charter.

As of 1836, as a result, one of the linchpins of Hamiltonian state-building and one of the most innovative ones, was destroyed. The United States had to wait until 1913 to have a central bank, and this time it was an institution different from all other central banks: the Federal Reserve Systems.

III

The coalition that brought about the demise of the Bank of the United States is worthy of careful study, as it was composed of the elements whose influence would set, and keep, the United States on its path of financial instability for much of the following period.

The *masse de maneuvre* of the coalition were the farmers. Unlike its European counterpart, American agriculture was, since the early decades of the nineteenth century, a highly innovative and highly indebted sector of the economy. When we read the financial history of the main European countries, in particular British financial history, we are always treated to an account of savings flowing from agriculture to other sectors, especially industry. A part of the rent which is extracted from agriculture is transferred, via financial intermediaries, to the industrial entrepreneurs and to the government. In the United States, on the contrary, agriculture *absorbs* credit, to buy land and to make it yield its fruits. Throughout the nineteenth century, agriculture remains an innovative sector of the American economy and a highly capital-intensive one. It is also the sector that absorbs the largest share of manpower and it is the largest exporter. American farmers, like all farmers, would like to be paid in sound, stable money for their crops. But they would also like easy, freely flowing credit available on tap and at stable rates. It is this peculiar contradiction that makes the U.S. farmers the ready raw material for manipulation, by politicians and by adventurous financiers.[2]

The Bank of the United States, because of the financial underdevelopment of the agricultural states, soon gained a foothold there. It helped to move the crops, in particular cotton, and put itself between the Southern farmers, the Eastern merchants and bankers, and the English financial institutions which financed the exports of cotton to its users in Lancashire. In its conservative management of the American paper currency, the Bank of the United States was, at one and the same time, exercising a restraining influence on the farmers, on its Eastern banking competitors and on the Bank of England, whose coffers it tended to deprive of gold. But these were potential enemies, and before they were mobilized, Congress renewed its charter. The Congressional decision, however, was vetoed by President Andrew Jackson, who had been elected on a platform which included a return to a sound metal-based currency, and a drastic decrease of the regulatory influence of government, and who took advice from enterprising financiers like Kendall and Van Buren. One year after the scrapping of the federal bank, the world experienced the first full-scale financial crisis of predominantly American domestic origins. In order to deliver on his electoral promises, President Jackson not only had vetoed the renewal of the federal charter for the Bank of the United States. He also had ruled that all sales of federal land be paid for in gold, that the surplus of the federal budget be redistributed to the states, and that the fiscal revenue of the federal government be deposited with a large number of banks—the so-called "pet banks," many of which were owned by government supporters. From the point of view of monetary management, a series of financial measures nearer to pure folly would be difficult to imagine. The scattering of financial ammunitions, which had been so wisely centralized before, resulted in an immediate run on the banks and a suspension of specie payments on their part when the Bank of England cut the American banks' discount facilities in London.

The clique of financiers which had skillfully manipulated the actions of General Jackson thus managed to destroy their main competitor and to move the financial center of the country to Wall Street from Philadelphia. But it did so at the cost of engendering a world crisis, whose worst effects were experienced in the cotton-producing South of the United States and in the cotton-using North of England. They also re-established freedom of banking operations but at the cost of precipitating the country into a financial anarchy which, if it was useful to promoters, speculators and robber barons, and thus to the fast growth of the U.S. economy, definitely wove the pattern of 150 years of world financial instability.

It is worth asking why the Bank of the United States had so few friends. Part of the answer must surely be found in its peculiar charter. It was owned in part by the government and in part by private investors, some of them foreigners. It could not, as a result, be described as a public agency, to be defended as part of the Constitution. But its main weakness was that it could not represent, like the Bank of England, a great coalition of landed aristocracy who provided a part of the capital, of gentry and middle-class savers who provided another part, and of merchant bankers of the city of London who manged the bank, staffed the court of directors, and elected from it the governor.[3] With a coalition like that behind it, the Bank of England could stand the repeated attacks that Northern industrialists, country bankers and farmers waged against it in the same years when Nicholas Biddle and his Bank of the United States succumbed to Andrew Jackson and his checkered but unbeatable army of banking adventurers, who could mobilize the ill feelings of the indebted farmers. Deprived of its federal charter, the Bank of the United States could have re-emerged in a purely private incarnation, and run the U.S. banking system by the force of its sheer size. This was the course adopted, after all, by the Bank of England in the next thirty to forty years in order to keep its primacy. But Biddle could not rely on a coalition of savers. He thus tried to beat his adversaries at their own game. He attempted to corner the cotton market and to bring about a general suspension of cash payments. He failed in both enterprises, thus showing, as would be often shown in the future, that central bankers are not very successful when they try their hand at being real financial adventurers.

John Law's adventures in France can be read in much the same vein. But, apart from this personal failure, the structural reason for the failure of the Bank of the United States is that it was created without a natural constituency, just when the country was at a watershed of its history and was embarking upon the dazzling development of the huge American continent. How could an institution imitating that great coalition of savers and lenders, the Bank of England, succeed in a country where, for many future decades, borrowers prevailed?

In fact, perhaps the most useful interpretative key to the financial instability which the United States has shown through a great part of its history is the dynamism of the American development process. Financial stability depends on the existence of a consolidated coalition of creditors. How could such a coalition form and thrive in a country where land was not scarce, especially because of a moving frontier, and where development continuously changed the game, the place where it was played, the people it suddenly made rich?

After the dismantling of the first experiment at financial centralism, in the 1830s, the oscillations of political coalitions formed to deal with banks and banking resulted in a complete fragmentation of the American banking system. The fragmentation was increased by the establishment of the independent treasury which centralized government revenue and had no officially devised way of recycling it back to the banking system. This was because it had been designed to fulfill the voters' dream of ridding the bankers of federal money, over which they might spin a web of unfair control.

The independent treasury managed to make the federal gold reserve virtually unusable, and a net hindrance on the working of the national and international monetary system, as funds were locked away and could not be recycled to the economy. The system thus needed a much higher quantity of gold to keep moving than it would have needed without the independent treasury.

The fragmentation of the American financial system which followed the 1830s, and the lack of a lender of last resort, joined with the rise of the powerful American export, agriculture, to create another structural problem: the so-called seasonal fluctuations in the demand for cash. This lasted until the First World War and even beyond it.

Every summer, crops were moved from the farming states to the East or to foreign countries. Cash would move the other way to pay the farmers, thus depriving New York of its funds and sending the interest rate to very high levels. As there was no central bank, the financial strategy was communicated to the rest of the world. The Bank of England, which, in order to behave as a normal, profit-making institution, subsisted on the smallest possible gold reserve, would put up its bank rate, and hope that money would come from Europe, so that it might be sent to New York to relieve the dearth of funds that was experienced there.[4]

Whenever bad luck ordained that another negative factor intervene, in the United States, or elsewhere, at the time of the "autumn drain," a major financial crisis would break out.

This annual pattern of financial stringency, which shook the world financial system with weather-like periodicity, could not be altered as long as the American financial system remained without a center which might function as lender of last resort.

We can safely say that the lender of last resort function is one of the most unambiguously defined *public* functions, as it is certain that it cannot be efficiently performed by a profit-maximizing institution. In times of crisis the lender of last resort has to provide funds, at punitive rates, to borrowers in need, against collateral of acceptable quality so that the banking system may not contract too adversely or even collapse. The essential features of the function are, first, that the institution which performs it must be generally known to have unlimited funds at its disposal. And *second,* that the operation must be performed quickly, with only scant probability of inspecting the quality of the property accepted as collateral. After the crisis period is passed, therefore, this paper may take a long time in being liquidated.[5]

Hence the impossibility for a profit-maximizing bank to perform this function without endangering its profitability. Hence the very marked difficulty the Bank of England encountered in performing it every year. What happened in practice was that, aware of the peculiar structure of the U.S. banking system, and of the inevitable recurrence of the so-called autumn drains, the Bank of England would protect its gold reserve by devices which amounted to partial inconvertibility, or to a fluctuating gold-sterling rate. In the twenty-five years before 1914, the Bank of England could also rely on the reserves the Indian Empire earned in world markets and was compelled to hold as deposits in London.

In the 1860s the American banking system was reformed, with the passage of the National Banking Act. It was a further step in the process of differentiation of the American financial system from those of the main European countries. Like many monetary reforms, it was the product of war finance and outmoded monetary theory.[6] It tried to bring all banks under national, i.e., federal, charter, by imposing a punitive tax on state bank notes. All national bank notes were to be secured by federal obligations. No central bank was provided however, to give elasticity to the money supply, no rules were given to regulate the creation of deposits, the more modern banking device, and individual states were still allowed to charter banks. As a result, the *dual* banking system, which exists even today, was founded.

Thus in the decades before the end of the century, while the U.S. economy advanced by leaps and bounds to become the largest and richest in the world, the American banking system grew as fast as the economy, but according to a model different from that according to which the major European financial systems were developing.

The National Banking Act forbade branching, with the result that small banks mushroomed everywhere, while some New York and Chicago banks reached gigantic size. The small banks, following what the Act prescribed, deposited funds with the large ones, and these funds, which were considered as reserves by the small banks, were either invested by the large banks in stock exchange speculation or lent on short term to the stock exchange speculators. Thus what the small banks considered as their reserves were funds which were lent for the most risky and unstable use. When a cloud appeared over the financial horizon, this system would contract credit as fast as it had expanded it. Small banks would call in their loans to large banks, and large banks would recall their loans from the stock exchange brokers. As a multiplier was in operation, there was not enough money to satisfy every bank that claimed its funds back. Interest rates soared, the stock market plunged, and in the absence of a lender of last resort, money was supposed to come from abroad to re-establish equilibrium.

The tendency to crisis of this inverted financial pyramid increased as the financial sophistication of the country increased. We have to remember that financial sophistication is not necessarily by itself conducive to the balanced growth of the economy. Quite to the contrary, it is an attempt, on the part of financial operators, to maximize the volume of transactions with respect to basic financial resources. And this, while it induces fast growth, also causes deep cyclical oscillations. In the last quarter of the nineteenth century and in the years before the Great War, fast technological advances united the United States to a far greater degree; the improvement in communications and transportation was tremendous. But this, for the financial system, only meant that small banks could proliferate even more than before, and that the whole system could be connected by a web of inter-bank deposits which, the system still being headless, increased the rate of credit expansion but also that of credit contraction.

The coexistence of very small banks and very large banks contributed to instability by giving depositors little trust in small banks, to which they were lured by high deposit rates. Competition drove up the cost of inter-bank deposits and encouraged large banks to lend funds to lucrative but risky stock exchange adventures. Large banks were not in favor of a branch banking reform that might squeeze the small banks out because, by their existence, the fixed costs implied by branch banking were avoided. Large banks would solicit inter-bank deposits when they needed them and get rid of them when they did not.

In this period, banking was being extended to larger and larger sections of the population, thus involving people who could be easily exploited but who also more easily got frightened and wanted their money back, if the shadow of a panic appeared.

And panics were frequent. Between the establishment of the national banking system and the First World War there was a panic every ten years, with an increase in frequency towards the end of the period. They ushered in widespread bank failures and industrial depression, and spread quickly to the rest of the world, as transatlantic communications became much better and new possibilities for international speculation opened up.

IV

If we compare financial development in the United States in the two decades preceding the Great War with financial development in Europe, we find that a common feature to all national experiences was the rise of large banks. But, while in Europe banks became large by establishing huge national branch networks, in the United States banks became large by increasing the size of their wholesale operations, on the asset side, and by getting more and more inter-bank deposits from small banks, on the liability side.

There was, therefore, in the United States, a growth of financial instability associated with the rise of large banks, as they engaged in fierce oligopoly battles for customers and for funds and did not have any central bank to restrain them or to get them out of the trouble in which they frequently placed themselves.

In addition, those were the decades when trust companies grew in the United States to challenge the operations of large banks, unfettered by even the scant controls the national banking system exercised on federally chartered banks. Financial innovation, in the form of the enormous development of stock exchange transactions, favored the peculiar type of financial development the United States experienced in this period.

Rapid financial innovation, together with diffusion of growth and with improvement in communications, coupled with the interest of the large financial institutions in maintaining the institutional status quo would, however, not be enough to explain a course of financial development which was peculiar to the United States. As I said earlier, in all major European countries branch banking had spread to the remotest corners, and central banks had been established to rule over an oligopolistic banking structure. The degree of autonomy of the banking system from the political world varied according to the countries. But the banking structure prevailing everywhere was the same.

One has, therefore, to look again at the peculiar political coalition prevailing in the United States, and to the even more peculiar regulation it imposed and maintained on banking, if one wants to explain the different course financial development took there in the four decades preceding the First World War. As I said, branch banking was, in fact, almost universally prohibited, at state and federal levels. And the prohibition suited very well the local interests politicians were inclined to bow to, as it would allow enterprising individuals to try their hands at banking. Deposit insurance was the answer to the riskiness of this course of financial development, and it was duly adopted in several states, after the panic of 1907.

The main feature of the dual banking system, created by the National Banking Act and still in function today, was and is that it allows banks to arbitrage between federal and state regulations in the search for an optimal result which will not necessarily agree with public welfare or macroeconomic stability. I do not want to imply that the European mode of financial development had no problems. In its British incarnation, for instance, which is the one morphologically nearest to the American, it witnessed, in the twenty-five years before the First War, the great and increasing difficulties of the Bank of England to organize a working relationship with the giant clearing banks which had resulted from the merger movement. These banks were a new force in the traditional City landscape. They were outside the *sancta sanctorum* of British finance and threatened to organize themselves in a way that would do away with the services of the Bank of England. As lender of last resort this function was performed by the Bank of England with increasing difficulty because the Bank had to maximize profits and to keep a large gold reserve, which reduced profitability. The bank also threatened to invade the field of operations of the merchant banks, from which the directors of the Bank of England and its governors were chosen. The crisis of July 1914 showed how advanced was the degradation of the British financial system's control network. On the news of Sarajevo, and before war had broken out, the clearing banks organized a run on the City, by withdrawing money from the Stock Exchange and even by trying to get gold from the Bank of England.

But, again, the coalition, which stood behind the inner sanctum of the City, intervened powerfully and swiftly with all the weight of the British government to rap the uncouth clearing banks' fingers and to rescue the Bank of England and the merchant banks. From the minutes of the "crisis conferences" Lloyd George held to stem the financial panic, the picture emerges clearly of the financially powerful but politically unprotected clearing bankers being pushed back into their place.[8]

They had been treated not very differently a quarter of a century before, at the time of the Baring Crisis. It is worth noting, moreover, that on the same occasion, July 1914, there was wild financial panic on Wall Street. The stock market collapsed, the foreign exchange market was closed. Bond prices sank. The finance of foreign trade virtually ceased. And the United States was not involved in the war.

V

In 1914, the Federal Reserve Act had been in force for one year, but in spite of its formal passage, the new control structure it had created would not start to operate until November 16, 1914. Consequently, it had not been able to avert the panic in July 1914 which, as in previous cases, preceded the crisis in London and contributed decisively to its outbreak and added to its gravity. It was in fact on learning that the markets had closed in New York that the British clearing bankers took fright, as London was New York's largest creditor and the interruption of transactions there meant that London merchant banks and other financial institutions would not be able to recover the short-term funds they had lent to New York in the immediate future.

The Federal Reserve System was once more the product of a compromise between the main political and economic forces in the United States.[9]

After the panic of 1907, a large coalition had formed in favor of financial reform. Prominent in the coalition, however, were the proponents of the *real bills doctrine,* a banking theory fallacious but capable of attracting the fervor of industrialists, small bankers and farmers.

The real bills doctrine's main contention is that banking will be conducted without problems if bank loans are supported by *real bills,* that is to say, if money is lent on the collateral of paper proving a real mercantile transaction, which will be "self-liquidating." Henry Thornton, as early as 1807, had proved the fallacious nature of the doctrine, showing how the same sum of money could be used to finance a very large number of real bills, thus causing an uncontrollable expansion of credit. What was really at issue was, of course, the central bank's power to exercise *quantitative* control of credit. Real bills proponents maintained that quantitative control was impossible and that *quality* control over the real transactions which credit financed was all that mattered.[10]

As everyone is against bad debts and everyone thinks his own debt is good and socially necessary while the next guy's debt is bad, the real bills doctrine has traditionally been a great social catalyst. A battle was fought over it in Britain in the first half of the nineteenth century, but the real bills supporters were effectively incapacitated as a political force by Peel's Act and never recovered again, essentially because of the political weakness of industrialists, country bankers and small farmers. In the United States, however, the charm of the real bills doctrine still worked. The 1907 crisis had awakened the public to the extremes of financial speculation and people were therefore inclined to believe a doctrine that maintained that there was nothing wrong with any quantity of credit the banks generated, provided it financed honest and productive transactions and not the financial speculations of stock exchange promoters.

The Federal Reserve Act was, as a result, based on the principles of free banking, of qualitative credit controls, of the choice by bankers between state banking and federal banking. In the spirit of pluralism, it also mandated that no less than twelve Federal Reserve Banks be set up. And to cap it all, the Federal Reserve Act incorporated the United States' adherence to a rigid version of the gold standard, such as had never functioned anywhere in the world.

With such internally contradictory foundations, the new system began to operate, after the big parenthesis of war and war finance, in a way that helped induce and certainly did not prevent the financial crises of 1920, 1929, 1930, 1932 and 1933.

VI

If we compare the performance of the Federal Reserve System with that of its predecessor, we must draw a prima facie conclusion that the interwar performance was even worse than the prewar one. This may be unfair, because the structural problems of the international economic system, and in particular of the American economy, were far greater in the interwar period.

Some of these problems are so well known and so well studied that it would be useless to go over them again. For my purposes here, however, it is useful to focus on one aspect of the interwar scene which has received less attention. In the 1920s and early 1930s, the American banking system went through one of its most dynamic phases. The instability of Europe in this period, added to the huge demand for credit on the part of European and Latin American countries, found large American banks ready to take up the challenge. We must appreciate that in the 1920s the demand for bank loans on the part of American corporations declined very substantially, as they found it more profitable to finance themselves out of retained profits and to finance their sales by trade credit and cash discounts.[11]

At the same time, a whole new world had opened up for American banks in personal financial management. Because of the extremely large gains all sectors of the American economy had made by supplying first all European warring nations and then the Allies, a new dimension of prosperity had been reached, and millions of American citizens were now in a position where they had money saved and money to be invested.

The banks, especially the large banks, had acquired expertise in dealing with this new demand when they had been given the task of retailing Liberty Bonds and then government war debts. After the war they found it very profitable to maintain and increase this activity by selling the same clientele foreign bonds and by entering en masse the field of trust and security operations. Large American banks, in the same years, also began to attract short-term deposits from, and to make short-term loans to, foreign individuals and governments. In this period, as a result, we see the American banking system and, in particular, its most dynamic components, become at the same time international bankers and investment bankers. The Federal Reserve Act, much more than the National Banking Act, had been a product of large banks' pressure on their traditional allies. Having satisfied the other partners of the coalition with the offal of the real bills doctrine and the twelve Reserve Banks, the Act went a long way towards giving the large money market banks more than proportional representation in the twelve Federal Reserve Banks' open market committees and on the Board of Governors.

It is thus natural that, in the 1920s and early 1930s, the monetary policy of the United States was motivated by the needs of the banking community, as perceived by large money center bankers.

The level of interest rates thus became heavily influenced by the need to maintain the values of their security portfolios which was common to all banks and to keep a hold on the notoriously volatile and interest-elastic foreign short-term deposits, a need especially felt by large money center banks. Thus in the 1920s, the American large banks happily lent to foreign governments and other public and private foreign customers, in an attempt to replace declining home business demand and to expand their trust and securities operations with American families. And, starting in 1928, they switched to domestic stocks and bonds placements, stoking the fires of the Wall Street boom and at the same time inducing, by the sudden withdrawal of loans, the default of their foreign customers.

European financial turmoil and major banking crisis followed in 1931. The sudden drop of foreign demand for American goods which the drying up of American foreign loans induced reverberated upon American industry and was an important cause of the Depression. But it is fair to say that, in an attempt to prevent the withdrawal of foreign balances which was one of the results of the cessation of American loans abroad, the Federal Reserve put up interest rates and thus busted the Wall Street boom. In the following years interest rates were kept high, in spite of the huge fall in economic activity, because to have lowered them would have meant decreasing the banks' prof-

itability and accelerating the flight from the dollar, which was taking
place after the devaluation of sterling. Foreign owners of sterling
balances, scalded by the experience, expected the same fate for their
dollar balances.

VII

The New Deal banking legislation is commonly credited with
the "reining in" of banks. But it does not seem to have been capable
of giving the American economy a stable financial system. Stability
in this field was achieved in the 1940s and 1950s, but this came largely
because the banks were innundated with war bonds and transformed,
for a long time, into *rentiers*. This, however, was not true of all banks,
but mainly of provincial banks, while the large money market banks
plunged more deeply into foreign operations, to gain a competitive
edge on the rest of the financial system.

With the return of the Western financial system to convertibility
in the late 1950s, and with the start of the Great American Inflation
a few years later, the large banks found themselves exposed to external
as well as internal threats.[12] Convertibility had revived the possibility
of arbitrage, i.e., of shifting funds between financial centers following
interest differentials and of international speculation based on exchange rate changes. The large banks thus found themselves exposed
to sudden withdrawals of foreign-owned balances if American interest
rates went, for purely domestic reasons, out of alignment with foreign
ones.

The Great American Inflation meant that the financial resources
of the United States grew at very high speed.[13] The large banks found
themselves at a disadvantage vis-à-vis non-bank financial intermediaries as they were saddled with reserve requirements. Against small
local banks they had difficulty in competing, as they were deprived
of branches to attract deposits and generally to look after the financial
needs of provincial communities enriched by the migration of industry
and populated by families who had been made financially sophisticated
by the growing inflation.

To fight this battle for a share of the fast-growing financial cake,
large banks have resorted to the invention of means to increase their
domestic competitiveness, like Certificates of Deposit, and to the
exporting of more and more of their operations to the offshore money
markets, where reserve requirements do not apply. At the same time
they have tried to specialize in loans to genuine foreign borrowers.

In addition, they have been clamoring for the repeal of the New Deal banking legislation, and they have largely won the deregulation battle with the passage of the Depository Institution Deregulation and Monetary Control Act of 1980, which treats all depository institutions on the same footing for what concerns reserve and other requirements.

As in 1928, the freeing of the domestic market in 1980 has induced American banks to expand their operation at home relative to their foreign loans. This, in addition to the Federal Reserve restrictive policy, has meant a drastic reduction of their foreign lending. The sudden dearth of funds thus induced has in turn placed the large banks' biggest foreign customers in near bankruptcy position. To relieve the situation, the Federal Reserve was compelled, in August 1982, to climb down from its restrictive stance, reducing interest rates. This brought about a stock market boom, and a revival of the domestic economy. But the attraction of a very high real interest rate remained, as prices slowed down and as the main foreign countries tried to revive their economies by dropping interest rates in step with the United States. The resulting strength of the dollar has induced a huge balance of trade deficit.

The parallel with the end of the 1920s is inevitable. We are again at the end of an extremely dynamic phase for the American financial system, which has again changed the name of the game, the place where it is played, and the people who are made rich by playing it. The large money center banks have reacted to a domestic and international challenge with a behavior which, if it has helped them to keep their market shares, has increased the instability of the U.S. financial system.

The Great American Inflation, superimposed on the New Deal banking legislation, has resulted in a complicated scramble for a very much expanded financial cake, with running battles between thrift institutions, large and small banks and non-bank financial intermediaries. The increase in anarchy was much facilitated by the great breakthrough in communications achieved by the electronics revolution. And, as I said earlier, innovation is not necessarily by itself conducive to more order. To retain their hold on the financial system, the American monetary authorities have been compelled to stretch dangerously the interest rates instrument. Historically, interest rate policy is viable only if, by small changes, large results are obtained. If the oscillations become wide, history teaches us that direct control weapons have to be used.

We are now clearly at a watershed. But whether direct control will be resorted to before or after a disastrous financial crisis, we shall learn before the end of this year. Western financial history, however, teaches us that controls are usually introduced only to stem a crisis which is actually taking place.

NOTES

1. On the First and Second Banks of the United States, the *locus classicus* is Bray Hammond, *Banks and Politics in America* (Princeton: Princeton University Press, 1957).

2. What I have just written could be read as going against the well-reasoned argument Bray Hammond develops in his classic book to prove that it was not the farmers but other social forces which fussed for free banking and cheap money in colonial America and in the early decades of the Republic. My argument, however, is that the size and peculiar character of American farming made it easy prey to political manipulation because it had, by its nature, to take a contradictory position vis-à-vis bank credit and currency. As a result of their needing long-term loans and at the same time payment for their crops in sound money, American farmers' allegiances could be made to swing between "cheap money," "no banks" and "sound currency." That they were the most powerful force in the political arena is undeniable, and the mutual inconsistency of their needs was used by other forces to obtain political actions with regard to banking and currency, which, if they did not benefit farmers, still were achieved with their essential support.

I would therefore heavily qualify some of Hammond's stronger statements on the issue. The farmers' support could be won in campaigns against banks and in favor of a gold currency, essentially because farmers were convinced that credit, as administered by American banks, was not of the revolving type they needed—and not because they were against credit per se. American banks would solicit loans to farmers in times of high prices, and foreclose on them in times of low prices. Still, the need for loans *was* there. Credit was essential to American agriculture but could not be given on terms farmers could find equitable. At the same time, the vagaries of crop prices were often attributed to unsound currency, hence the farmers' attention to sound currency campaigns.

These contradictions are not experienced exclusively by American society. In his *The Passions and the Interests* (Princeton: Princeton University Press, c. 1977), Albert O. Hirschman has written some very illuminating passages on the problem of the "mobilization" of land control in eighteenth-century France. And the very high capital intensity and reliance on credit of American farming was noticed from the very early decades of the nineteenth century. While in Britain agriculture had already fallen to employing a very low share of total labor by 1841, in America it kept swelling in absolute terms as an employer, and maintained its share of total employment, between 1820 and 1870. American farmers had to rely on credit exactly because so many people still *became* farmers, and had to *buy* land and then the capital to work it. In his splendid book on American agriculture, *Change in Agriculture* (Cambridge: Harvard University Press, 1968), Clarence Danhof tells us very clearly with many references to contemporary sources, how generalized farmers' indebtedness was as early as 1830. He conveys very well the feeling of need, and at the same time of hatred, the farmer had for the banker from the very start of the nineteenth century, and the contradiction between easy money and hard currency, two things the farmers wanted simultaneously. That is why I have used the expression *"masse de maneuvre"* in the text.

The basis of understanding the environment in which U.S. banking developed is to contrast European agriculture—characterized by its pressure of people on the land, by its high rents, and hence by its inevitable financial surpluses—with American agriculture, perhaps the most dynamic sector throughout American economic history—characterized by its low rents, by the high rate of owner-workers, and by the resulting net absorption of financial resources. This is so in spite of Bray Hammond's exhortation not to project back on the earlier age the designation of "cheap money advocates" which farmers received in the last part of the nineteenth and the early decades of the twentieth centuries. This position is simply not logical. Other authoritative sources, like Danhof and his references, prove the early indebtedness, and thus the contradictory feelings, of farmers concerning banking and currency problems.

3. On the Bank of England's shareholders, see John Harold Clapham, *The Bank of England* (Cambridge: Cambridge University Press, 1945), I.

4. On the seasonal fluctuations and their consequences, the reader can be referred to my *The International Gold Standard* (Totowa, N.J.: St. Martin Press, 1984), where he will find further references.

5. If we make use of one of Albert O. Hirschman's most useful contributions to economic thought, the lender of last resort function can be considered as a contradiction of the rules of "exit" and "arms' length relations" predicated by the market system. To be exercised wisely, the lender of last resort function, in fact, requires that, first of all, "exit" (or bankruptcy) be suspended, and funds be advanced against collateral of an illiquid nature, i.e., against the normal rules of banking conduct. The intervention of the central bank, in effect, is meant to save the money market as an essential institution, against its short-run illiquidity. By negating the "exit" rules in the case of a crisis, the central bank ensures that institutions remain in existence in normal times, when their operation may prove useful for the economic system's general efficiency. It was, in fact, Albert Hirschman, who in his *Strategy of Economic Development* (New Haven: Yale University Press, 1958, p. 64, footnote), called the central banker a sort of honorary member of the market forces.

6. On the Act, see Eugene N. White's excellent *The Regulation and*

Reform of the American Banking System (Princeton: Princeton University Press, 1981).

7. See White, *Regulation and Reform.*

8. See de Cecco, *International Gold Standard.*

9. For all the references to the literature on the origins of the Federal Reserve System, see White, *Regulation and Reform.*

10. It is interesting to note that among American writers on banking and currency problems, a strong predominance exists, since the earliest times and until quite late in the twentieth century, of supporters of the real bills doctrine. This has been noticed and exhaustively commented upon by the two main students of American banking theory, Miller and Mints. They have both remarked on the scarcity of quantity theory supporters among American economists. This can be contrasted with the British literature, but is not very different from German experience in the same period, as analyzed for instance, by Howard S. Ellis in his *German Monetary Theory* (Cambridge: Harvard University Press, 1934). There does not seem to have been, however, an American version of the *Staatliche Theorie des Geldes.* Writers on early American banking seem often to devote a lot of attention to the credit problems of farmers. And it is interesting to see how they manage to reconcile the farmers' credit needs and the real bills doctrine, with its insistence on "self-liquidation." Eligibility of agriculture finance paper for rediscount would overcome most real bill supporters' requirements, such was its political importance, and be specifically mentioned in the most important pieces of U.S. banking legislation. See, for the relevant literature, Lloyd W. Mints, *A History of Banking Theory in Great Britain and the United States* (Chicago: University of Chicago Press, 1945) and Harry Edward Miller, *Banking Theories in the United States before 1860* (Cambridge: Harvard University Press, 1927), to be contrasted with F. W. Fetter, *The Development of British Monetary Orthodoxy* (Cambridge: Harvard University Press, 1965).

11. I have dealt at greater length with this subject in "The International Debt Problem in the Inter-War Period" in Miles Kahler, ed., *The International Debt Problem* (forthcoming) where I have also given the relevant bibliography.

12. See my "International Financial Markets and U.S. Domestic Policy Since 1946," *International Affairs* 52 (July 1976), 381–99. Also, C. A. E. Goodhart, "Structural Changes in the Banking System and the Determination of the Stock of Money," presented to the Conference on Western European Priorities, Brussels, December 1982; in mimeo.

13. See Henry Kaufman, *Complexities of U.S. Stabilization Policies in an International Context* (Salomon Brothers International, October 1983).

Dependency and the Political Solution of Balance of Payments Crises: The Italian Case

Andrea Ginzburg[1]

Introduction

Examination of the relationship between macroeconomic performance and political coalitions of a heterogeneous group of twelve Western countries (including Italy) in the period 1960–69 led D. A. Hibbs to the conclusion that "governments pursue macroeconomic policies broadly in accordance with the objective economic interests and subjective preferences of their class-defined core political constituencies" (Hibbs 1977). This is supposedly proved by relatively low rates of unemployment (and relatively high rates of inflation) in countries governed by coalitions with left-wing tendencies as opposed to those governed by moderate or conservative parties. Hibbs's conclusions may probably serve to reaffirm, in general, the importance of political choices and actions in determining the course of economic events where (as, for example, in the United States) this principle has, in certain quarters, been brought into question. The obvious validity of the principle, however, does not rest on the universal validity of such conclusions. It would be difficult, for example, to seek confirmation of the general conclusions Hibbs reached in the experience of postwar Italy. As stated by De Vivo and Pivetti in an article to which I shall refer later, "throughout the postwar period high levels of employment never represented an objective of Italian economic policy" (Pivetti 1979, 120).[2] And yet, after 1947, Italy had a succession of coalition governments of varying political persuasions. The center-party governments with a Christian Democrat majority that ruled between 1947 and July 1960 gave way in 1963, after a number of transition governments, to center-left coalitions (which included among the major parties, alongside the Christian Democrats, the Socialist party). Center-left political coalitions have governed practically uninterruptedly in Italy from 1963 to the present day. The only interruption of note in these two decades of center-left government was a moderate-center coalition between the summer of 1972 and the summer of 1973. (I shall come back later to the long-term effects of the economic policy decisions taken during this brief period of time.)

The continued absence of an economic policy aimed at the achievement of high levels of employment seems to me to deserve an attempt at explanation, at the same time bearing in mind that during this period neither the economy, nor society, nor Italian politics stood still. Two factors, in particular, need to be recalled: 1) the strong wave of social struggles both in the early sixties and, above all, after 1968—at the beginning of the seventies this resulted in important gains in pay and conditions and in radical changes in customs, beliefs and way of life; 2) the consequent weakening, in relative terms, of the electoral popularity of the Christian Democrat party after 1976, which has led to significant shifts of political bias towards the left within the same center-left coalitions.

Is it possible that in the Italian case, and in the postwar period, there is a relationship between phases of industrialization and "elective affinities" of political models, as is claimed for Latin America?[3]

Interaction between phases of development of productive forces and political models is excluded, for opposite reasons, both by those who interpret Italian economic affairs in the postwar period from a cyclical standpoint, and by those who, on the other hand, take an exclusively long-term view. The former tend to have the economy (or, rather, a particular interpretation of it) "taking command": they stress the seriousness of the recurrent crises in the balance of payments and tend to regard domestic deflation and expansion of exports as a mandatory path that any political coalition would have to follow. (In the long term, this point of view gives rise to the hope that a deflationary policy can set in motion a virtuous circle of exports-investments-productivity-exports.) Those who concentrate their attention on the long-term and structural aspects, however, also tend to exclude interactive elements between economics and politics: they focus on the intervals between one crisis and the next to show that the reduction in the balance of payments deficit has not brought about an increase in internal demand. In this case, it is politics, aimed at preserving the internal balance of power between the classes but regardless of the changing political coalitions, which is entirely responsible for the economic policy adopted.

For all the importance of the insights deriving from the long-term point of view, it is difficult to avoid the impression that, if it is coupled with an anthropomorphic view of power (one that almost postulates the existence of a plan devised by a single person to keep the levels of unemployment high), one winds up casting reality in a static mold, and is regularly destined to notice changes in progress only after the event.

The limitation of one or the other formulation may perhaps be overcome, at least in part, if, like François Simiand, we view development as the *overall* result of phases of expansion and stabilization.[4] If we adopt this point of view, we come up with a paradoxical result: the phases of expansion (1959–62, 1972–73 and 1979–80) correspond with moderate political coalitions. The balance of payments crisis that occurs at the culmination of the phase of expansion is met with a policy of monetary and, more rarely, fiscal restriction (sometimes these measures are adopted by governments considered weak and provisional, *governi balneari,* "summer-holiday" governments, as they are known in Italian political jargon). In the subsequent phase of recession (and growth of employment), we find the country being governed by coalitions with a stronger bias to the left. A pattern emerges that is sufficiently systematic to suggest the presence of underlying forces which, in the case of Italy, tend to mold the relationship between phases of development and policies adopted in a given form.

The paper that follows is divided into three parts. The first contains a brief analysis of the major critical moments in the Italian balance of payments in the period 1960–80. Its main aim is to show that these crises coincide with acceleration phases in the "dependent" accumulation of the Italian economy. In the discussion of certain short-term and long-term aspects of this dependence, the fact that Italy belongs among the countries defined by Hirschman as "late-late industrializers" will become important.[5] One feature of this group of countries, namely the incomplete development of significant "backward linkages" in the sector of investment goods, determines a high import content of investment demand which tends to be especially evident during the acceleration phases of accumulation. The second part deals with the relationship between expansion of exports and increase in the import content of demand (a similar phenomenon seems to have occurred in Brazil between 1968 and 1974). It is argued that in the case of Italy the other face of export-led growth has been its markedly import-intensive character. This has endowed Italian development with certain features that can be found, *mutatis mutandis,* in what Hirschman has called "import enclave economies" (cf. A. O. Hirschman 1958, 111). However much they differ in certain important aspects (especially by the presence of possible inducement mechanisms for the development of the internal market) from the better known and more studied export enclave economies, the presence in both of strong links with the international market engenders a point of contact between them. In fact, in the third part it will be argued that, as in the export enclave economies (cf, for example, P. Klarén 1973, and D. Collier 1976), but obviously in less drastic form, Italian political life is permeated by cycles of exclusion and (relative) incorporation which can be traced back to different phases in the process of international integration. The first-named of these cycles corresponds to "waves of accumulation" and, simultaneously, to critical moments in the balance of payments; the second to phases of compression of internal demand and of import-intensive growth of exports. If this assertion is accepted, one can then put forward the hypothesis that absorption of oppositions (*trasformismo*) is a political model that has an "elective affinity" with the phases of stabilization in the dependent development of the Italian economy.

I. Towards the First Center-Left Government: The Crisis of 1963

1. When the EEC came into being with the ratification of the Treaty of Rome in 1959, the Italian economy presented certain features that set it apart quite clearly from the other European countries. Despite the substantial emigration abroad and the growth of industrial employment supported by public investment in infrastructures in the first half of the 1950s, the official rate of unemployment was higher than in the other European countries (6.5% in 1958). Italian income was 50–60% of the European average. The exchange rate, already undervalued in 1949, was even more undervalued ten years later, given the movement of relative prices. The decision to go for an early liberalization of the economy, which took effect from the beginning of the 1950s (but which excluded the transport sector), involved the abandonment of an industrial policy of completion of the inter-industrial matrix, in particular in the basic capital goods sector (cf. De Cecco 1971). Between 1959 and 1960, following the rapid expansion in EEC exports (+37% at constant prices), there was a boom in investments. The rate of accumulation (22.6%) was the highest of the postwar period. In part, though to a decreasing extent, it was a question of state investment in facilities in support of the private car industry (roads and motorways) and generally of the mechanical sectors (Taranto steelworks) and building trade (cement). To a much greater extent it was a question of private investment in modernizing and extending

plant in view of the liberalization of the home and foreign markets. The increase in the productive capacity of sectors producing consumer durables, notably in the urban centers which attracted a steady flow of immigrants from the South, went hand in hand with processes of restructuring in the so-called "traditional" sectors, namely the light consumer goods industries (textiles, clothing, footwear). Through a process of backward linkage, starting from these two groups of sectors producing consumer goods, there emerged small and medium-sized firms producing components and capital goods "close" to the stage of final consumption. This period saw the shaping of certain features of the Italian economy's specialization on home and foreign markets which, in their essentials, were destined to become more marked and to evolve along the same lines (e.g., expansion in the domestic appliances industries), but without radical change, in the years to come (cf. De Cecco 1971).

We can interpret this period of expansion as the result of the overlapping of a phase of backward-linkage industrialization (which was to be aimed at the growth of exports) onto a waning phase of infrastructure development.

As Hirschman noted (1958, 95), the characteristic assumed by the phases of import substitution in "late-late industrializers" is that of adding last touches to a host of imported products and of concentrating on consumer rather than producer goods. The development of further significant backward linkages was never actually to be realized. This can be seen in the considerable increase in the import of machines and equipment (in particular from Germany) that henceforth was to accompany each "wave of accumulation." The effort to industrialize and export manufactured goods was accompanied from the end of the 1950s by a reduced interest in agricultural reform; this was underlined by those clauses in the Common Agricultural Policy that granted France (and the "rich" agriculture of Northern Italy) favorable price conditions in exchange for her acceptance of the common market in industrial products. (From 1963 onwards the agricultural deficit was to grow in proportion to the surplus on industrial products.) The increase in industrial employment, which was concentrated in the cities of the industrial triangle of Northern Italy, was accompanied in the early 1960s by a strenthening of the bargaining power of the working classes, above all in medium-sized and large industries. The result was that salaries increased more rapidly than productivity for the first time (in 1963 the unit cost of work in industry increased by 9.8%). Increasing prices and high demand (food imports increased by 55% in value and 37% in quantity), together with substantial flights of capital, brought about, in 1963, a deficit in the balance of payments of 1,250 million dollars. (On the other hand, the worsening of the current balance was equal to the total official export of capital for 1962 and 1963.) Meanwhile, on the political front, an abortive attempt at authoritarianism at the beginning of 1960 sparked off long negotiations aimed at including the socialists in government. In September 1963, a "weak" transitional government effected a sharp credit squeeze by restricting the banks' loan facilities abroad. In December 1963 the first center-left government was installed. The usual time-lag that occurs before the effects of any monetary policy can begin to be felt obscured the fact that the picture had been largely predetermined by previous decisions: first in the pattern of international integration and accumulation, later in the drastic monetary restrictions. (They were also overdue, but elections took place in 1963.) In the following two years the number of people employed in industry dropped by 300,000 (only in 1980 was the total employment level to return to that of 1963).

2. It has been stated (cf., for example, M. D'Antonio 1973, 14) that, from 1958 onwards, when Italy broke away from the influence of the United States cycles, the cyclical behavior of the Italian economy "has predominantly internal causes and may be regarded as being governed essentially by the economic effects of the workers' struggles," it being argued that there is a chain of cause and effect: increase in wages = fall in investments = reduction of the increase in wages.

To postulate a cause and effect relationship of this nature is, other considerations apart, to obscure the fact that the process of accumulation (and, indirectly, the commercial balance) in Italy has been linked since the beginning of the 1960s (but no doubt it has a much longer history than that) to the same process in Europe, and in Germany in particular (cf. Table 4).

It has been acknowledged that such a dependence has existed in more recent years, albeit as an exclusively short-term relationship (the locomotive theory). However, it should be stressed that the relationship between the waves of accumulation occurring in Germany and those regularly occurring thereafter in Italy is threefold. On one hand, there is the short-term mechanism, mentioned above, whereby investments adjust to the reduction in unutilized capacity caused by an increase in Italian exports to Germany (and the rest of Europe). On the other hand, there are the stimuli given to the Italian economy by the variations in the *composition,* not only the level, of German investments. These variations enable the Italian economic system to find a foothold in market sectors, and segments within sectors, with a relatively low value-added/sales ratio, which in Germany are gradually being abandoned, not least because of the repeated revaluations of the mark; the sectors in question are those that generally produce specialized consumer and capital goods, normally in small batches. Finally, the high level of importation of capital goods coinciding with each "wave of investment" in Italy causes a reduction in the multiplier (and thus of the investment/income ratio) but also a substantial transfer of "alien technology," with repercussions on employment, rate of work and the organization of labor.

It is no coincidence, therefore, that with Germany's increased specialization in the capital goods sector after the recession of 1967, small and medium-sized firms in the northeastern regions of Italy found entry into the international market at intermediate technological levels.

The fact, on the other hand, that the Italian and German economies are out of phase, and that their areas of industrial specialization are complementary, helps to explain, therefore reducing the importance of relative prices, the sudden drops (corresponding to German recession) and the "spectacular" successes (corresponding to shrinking demand on the home market) of Italian exports.

II. The Balance of Payments Crises in the 1970s

1. The 1970s in Italy saw three main crises in the balance of payments: in 1973–74, in 1976 (on a smaller scale) and in 1979–80. At first glance one may be tempted to explain the first and third crises by the increases in the price of oil that occurred in those years. One must remember, in this connection, Italy's close dependence on energy imports: in 1973 oil supplied 73% of energy utilized. But such an explanation would be incomplete. Indeed, the onset of the first crisis predates the rise in the price of oil. Furthermore, the first and third crises coincide with waves of accumulation again out of phase with respect to the German cycle accompanied by a growth in the total import coefficient, and in particular in the proportion of imports of capital goods in the total investment demand. From the political point of view, the oscillation is wider than in the 1960s, but it faithfully respects the relationship between political coalitions and lines of economic policy mentioned above (cf. Table 1).

Let us briefly run over the events of this period. After 1969 the distribution of income shifted in favor of industrial workers. A series of factors led to a rightwards swing in the political situation of Italy (to be redressed in 1974). The center coalition, formed in the summer of 1972, found itself with a balance of current account still in credit, partly because of a slackening of demand. In that year the big producers of consumer durables, suffering as they were from years of under-investment, came under pressure not only from foreign competitors but also from the claims of the workers (in 1972 imports of motor vehicles increased by 29%, exports by 10%). One of the first actions of the center government was to demand a revision of the clauses of the monetary "snake." This aroused fears of devaluation and led to substantial flights of capital. The move towards devaluation took effect at the beginning of 1973: the lira was left to float. Between February and July of 1973 the lira lost about 20% against the principal European currencies (9.2 and 17.5% as a weighted average reckoned in 1973 and 1974, respectively). Given the composition of Italian imports (and the rise in the cost of raw materials in the period in question) this led inevitably to soaring inflation, which, following subsequent devalu-ations and increases in oil prices, still afflicts the Italian economy. Devaluation was accompanied by a policy of strong stimulation of demand: gross investments increased by 15% (22.6% in machinery and equipment, the highest rate since 1950), while the commercial balance in relation to the GNP reached the highest negative level since 1952. In July 1973 a center-left coalition (said to be of the "more advanced equilibria") took over. Credit squeezes (including a deposit on imports in 1974, to be renewed in 1976) and restrictive fiscal measures, at first moderate but later, in 1974, more drastic, reduced consumption and, even more, investment: the speed with which the process of adjustment took place is indicated by the fact that in the second half of 1974 the commercial balance, excluding oil, improved by 1600 billion lire and went into credit.

Similar events, but without an increase in investments and with a higher incidence of capital speculation, took place between the autumn of 1975 and the beginning of 1976. When, after the elections of the summer of 1976, the first government to be formed with the crucial parliamentary abstention of the Communist party was sworn in, restrictive monetary measures had already been adopted and were followed in the autumn by increases in indirect taxation and moves to reduce the cost of labor. International loans granted by the IMF and the EEC were conditional upon the implementation of a strict monetary policy and of tight budget control. The joint program of the parties supporting the government was ambitious: it set out to combine precise short-term aims (high growth rate, anti-inflationary moves, increased employment) with long-term objectives (industrial reorganization, investment in the South, substitution of imports) in a climate of austerity and sacrifice (cf. *Mondo economico,* July 1977). With the exception of some measures aimed at rationalizing the administration of the public budget, the results were modest as regards curbing inflation, non-existent as regards the other plans and negative as regards unemployment, which rose in the South and among young people. The improvement in the balance of current accounts was outstanding, however; it moved from a deficit of 2,365 billion lire in 1976 to a surplus of 2,175 and 5,400 billion in 1977 and 1978 respectively. This improvement was due not only to the squeeze on home demand, but also to a policy of revaluation against the dollar and of devaluation against the deutschmark. In the medium term, however, this policy tends to increase Italy's economic dependence on Germany and, thanks to the way in which the Monetary Compensation Amounts system works, to aggravate, in particular, the Italian food deficit. Moreover, during this period Banca d'Italia allowed Italian banks to increase their debt abroad in order to finance, by means of commercial loans, the foreign trade in capital goods.

The currency reserves built up in this period were to be used in the expansion cycle of 1979–80 by the subsequent coalition government, which did not rely on the support of the Communist party and was led by the Christian Democrats. The elections held in the summer of 1979 marked a defeat for the Communist party (and a weakening of the Christian Democrat party). This time international finance allowed the Italian government to face the second oil price increase by expanding the economy "against the wind": with the result that, together with a sharp increase in investments, which had been stagnant for several years, the government set a new record for the commercial balance deficit, in relation to the GNP. From 1981 onwards, with coalitions led by figures from outside the Christian Democrat party, the Italian economy was brought into line with the recessive pattern of the major European economies.

2. The periods of major devaluation of the exchange rate (1973, 1976 and, in part, 1979) coincide both with substantial flights of capital and with the renewal of the three-year work contracts of important categories in industry. It is reasonable to argue, therefore, that the devaluation ploy enabled the profit margins squeezed by the workers' struggles to be recovered by means of inflation. Given the existing means of indexing wage rates (renegotiated in 1975), the higher the inflation, the greater the reduction in the proportion of wages protected by the escalator clause. Repeated, sharp devaluations, together with curbs on internal demand, thus enabled the relative prices of exports

to be reduced, despite inflation. After 1974, as in the 1960s, it once again fell to exports, together with tourism, to maintain the level of economic activity (cf. De Vivo and Pivetti 1980, 11 and 14).

The Italian experience of this period suggests two considerations. On the one hand, it emphasizes the importance of the decisions taken during the phase of expansion (especially in 1972–73) which would almost appear to have predetermined, or at least strongly influenced, the succeeding phase. On the other hand, it suggests a re-examination of the traditional, close association between orthodox or conservative policies and policies aimed at maintaining stability of prices—this not only because devaluation may be directed towards recovering profit margins. In a lucid article of 1945, G. Harberler came close to advocating inflation, and thus devaluation, as an instrument whereby the direct control of prices, wages, foreign trade, etc. in Europe might be rendered vain and the free market be re-established. From the second half of 1946 onwards, this suggestion was destined to be put into practice by the Italian monetary authorities (cf. V. Lutz 1950, 306): thus, with the exclusion of the Communist party at the peak of the inflationary phase, a more traditional relationship was established between political coalitions and economic phases, i.e., exactly the opposite of the one described here for the 1960s and the 1970s. Besides the economic tools employed (the sequence of export of capital= devaluation=inflation=stabilization), this distant experience (on which see also A. O. Hirschman 1948, and G. Amato, 1972, 22–25) had in common with the 1970s the general aim of restoring the free market and, in particular, reshaping public intervention within such limits that it could not interfere with the decisions of private industry.

The 1970s had opened with a bitter controversy waged by private groups of the North against the investment strategy being carried out in the South by state-controlled industries (in the sectors of special steels and motorcars). They ended with a drastic reduction in the importance and scope of public industry, dogged as it was by inefficiency, debts and the burden of the lame-duck sectors (steel, shipyards, artificial fibers). The turnaround in favor of private groups came in 1973 when, during a period of inflation, an increase in public spending was accompanied by a relative drop in fiscal revenue. This served as justification for a reduction in the amount of public money available for industrial investment in the South (and as a whole), though probably the fact that such investments would have proved less fruitful in terms of votes for the ruling coalition should not be overlooked. Subsequently (in 1975 and 1976), the funds needed for industrial renewal were reduced in real terms. Despite their programs, the coalition governments in office between 1976 and 1978, who achieved such spectacular successes in boosting the monetary reserves, were unable to reverse this tendency.

III. Specialization and "Vulnerability"

Viewed in the longer term, the Italian economy seems to be trying to imitate *with other means* (including inflation)—and obviously on a smaller scale and in a very different social situation—a central aim of the German economy, namely, the accrual of huge current account surpluses accompanied both by the extensive use of commercial credits to promote the export of capital goods—especially towards lower income countries—and by an increasing international financial integration.[6]

This imitative pattern arises from the complementarity, established with the founding of the EEC and since developed, between the productive specialization of Italy and Europe, and particularly Germany.

That same complementarity also explains both the rhythm of growth and the increasing vulnerability of the Italian economy. The vulnerability of the Italian economic system can be classified under two headings: "external" and "internal." External vulnerability has two sides to it: the first, as is obvious, concerns the degree of specialization and refers to the effects of a drop in foreign demand in a system in which a high and increasing proportion of production is exported; the second concerns the form of specialization. It is usual, in this case, to recall the fact that Italian exports are very rigid in relation to income and very elastic in relation to price.[7]

De Vivo and Pivetti (1980, 5) put forward another argument which, in the terms in which they have formulated it, does not seem to me to be convincing, yet which can be developed in another direction. The authors emphasize that the *negative* aspects of specialization are generally neglected because the marginal theory of distribution denies the existence of a problem of effective demand, so that the attention focusses on the "advantages of efficiency" accruing from specialization itself. But "if specialization leads to lower levels of overall activity, the customary argument concerning the 'advantages of efficiency' loses its force." According to the authors, the particular vulnerability of Italian specialization derives from the fact that it concentrates on "broadly non-basic goods," that is to say, luxury consumer goods and the means of production directly involved in producing them. As they see it, the relatively fickle demand for these goods is due to the fact that "there are clearly greater possibilities of insulating the growth of the economy from an insufficient rise in its import capacity if dependence on imports chiefly concerns 'luxury goods' and their specific means of production." This explanation does not seem to me to be convincing: it is difficult to imagine the industrialized countries with which Italy trades resorting to selective measures aimed at "insulating the growth of the economy." Moreover, it is anything but obvious that "light" consumer goods and the machines "employed in the direct production of these goods" should be considered "non-basic" goods, that is to say that they should not be thought to constitute "wage goods" of foreign workers. Rather, growth in the demand for these goods will be influenced by the factors that speed up or slow down the movement of the Germany economy towards the "high technology" sectors. Reduction in demand will depend, amongst other things, on: the difficulty of competing with the United States in the advanced field (cf. De Cecco, 1976a), the demand by the OPEC countries for intermediate technology goods, and the international decentralization of production, particularly in those sectors that produce light consumer goods. As Simonnot pointed out, this process of decentralization was favored by EEC approval, in 1971, of the Generalized System of Preference (cf. Simonnot 1971a and 1971b). If international decentralization and the opening up of the European market to developing countries producing light consumer goods help to explain, on the one hand, the drop in Italy's exports of these goods to European markets in 1973 and 1974, they also stimulated the expansion of small firms in Italy and internal decentralization of production (cf. S. Brusco 1982).

In the case of Italy, a certain significance would appear to attach to an internal mechanism of vulnerability, which is also connected with the specialization in the production of capital goods close to final consumption. The process of accumulation in Italy appears schematically to adopt two modes (cf. *Tendenze reali* 1983 and Table 7). The first, which can be defined as accumulation concerning the enlargement of productive capacity or "light restructuring" (and which mainly concerns small and medium-sized industries) is largely met by internal production. This seems to have happened, for example, in the wave of accumulation in 1973.[8] An abrupt expansion of this component of investment demand has the effect of deflecting a proportion of production previously exported onto the home market and thereby tends to have an adverse influence on the commercial balance.[9]

Expansion of internal production, on the other hand, similarly *reduces* the *proportion,* relative to home demand, of imported capital goods. The process is reversed, however, when home demand flags.

In the case of a process of accumulation directed at a "deeper" renewal of productive techniques, on the other hand (such as that of 1979–81, which involved more the large factories), the absence of "backward linkages" manifests itself directly in an increase of imports. Here, the worsening of the commercial balance shows itself in an *increase* in the import quota. It follows that the worsening (or improvement) of the commercial balance will depend on the degree of coincidence and *interdependence* of the two processes of expansion (or restriction) of the components of investment demand.

In that this mechanism indicates the existence of a trade-off between exports and investments, it helps to explain why it is so difficult in the Italian economy to find a "virtuous" circle connecting exports and investments, so that increases in productivity are often obtained in other ways (cf. De Cecco 1971, F. Vianello 1975). On the other hand, an expansion of exports achieved systematically by means 1974–78—will tend eventually to emphasize the incompleteness of the productive matrix. The result will be an increase in the incidence of "deep" restructuring, and hence a permanent increase in the import content of demand.

IV. Foreign Exchange Illusions

1. The policy followed by postwar Italian governments has been described as "a restrained domestic growth strategy" (De Vivo and Pivetti 190). Indeed, between 1960 and 1973 (and in the period 1976–78) the average growth rate of exports had been allowed ... to exceed the average growth rate of domestic demand by the largest percentage diffential of the major capitalist industrial countries" (De Vivo and Pivetti 1980, 3). The same authors note that, contrary to general opinion, the chief problem affecting Italian economic policy has not been one of making "increases in employment compatible with the external constraint," but how to "cope with the economy's tendency towards large external surpluses, without impairing ... the expansion of exports. *The solution of this problem has been the rapid increase in the import content of demand* and the ample freedom allowed to capital movements" (p. 5, my italics). It is interesting to note that a similar phenomenon of growth in the import content of demand together with a sustained increase in exports appears to have

occurred in Brazil between 1968 and 1974. J. Serra writes: "the Brazilian experience... points to an interesting paradox that could, *mutatis mutandis,* be extended to the other Latin American countries with more diversified economies. This experience seems to suggest that the pattern of domestic growth tends to be readjusted in response to the poselasticities for imports increase rapidly as those opportunities (due to the pronounced growth of exports) increase, until the problem of external disequilibrium again returns" (cf. J. Serra, in D. Collier, ed., 1979, 156)

In the case of Italy, while De Vivo's and Pivetti's comments regarding the freedom granted to movements of capital can be fully endorsed, the absence of an analysis of the forces underlying the increase both in the import content of demand and in exports may open the way to an anthropomorphic explanation of this paradox: it may suggest, that is to say, the existence of a deliberate plan to keep levels of unemployment high. But before accepting such an explanation, one will need to assure oneself that there are no other socio-economic automatisms leading in the direction of an increase in import content. First and foremost, it should be noted that the assets and liabilities on the foreign balance are not always independent of each other. Two instances of this—which are important in the case of Italy—have already been mentioned: the relationship between the import of foodstuffs and the export of Italian manufactured goods, favored by CAP agreements, and that between exports (particularly capital goods) and commercial credits.

Yet there is an even more direct relationship, namely, that which links exports to the imports directly and indirectly necessary to produce them. This obvious relationship is far from having become a matter of common sense. As Gramsci observed, the power of "dominant conceptions" lies precisely in the fact that they have succeeded in asserting themselves as "common sense." In this case, the relationship has been overlooked for two reasons: the first is the indiscriminate inheritance of analytical models devised for "advanced" economic systems, in which this aspect was not important, at least in the past; the second is that the majority of theoretical and applied studies in international commerce subscribe to the hypothesis of the marginal theory—as H. Johnson himself acknowledged—of "a world in which all goods are final goods, goods destined for final consumption, and are produced entirely by means of originary production factors" (H. Johnson 1971, 307).

The theory of the product cycle, which was also put forward in the latter half of the 1960s in order to introduce some elements of realism into the analysis, does not differ in essence from this hypothesis.[10] The "product cycle theory," considered as a theory of stages of development, shares with other theories of "stages" (for example, that of Rostow) the limitation that they take into account sectors defined exclusively on the basis of the final stage of production (e.g., textiles, motorcars, steel). (Here we ignore the fact that the "mix" of products in any given statistical sector may differ widely from country to country.) A definition of this type would be justified if all countries had a complete (or equally incomplete) interindustrial matrix, as well as being the same size. As Hirschman emphasized, "the apparently similar patterns of the earlier and late-industrializers . . . conceals an essential qualitative difference," namely, the capacity of the former to produce "their own capital goods" and the need (and possibility) of the latter to import them. For this reason "one must be on guard against studies purporting to show that the history of industrialization is substantially the same in all countries, working its way from light consumer goods industries to heavy capital goods industries and eventually to consumer durables" (Hirschman 1968; 1971 ed., 93). The definition of phases of industrialization based on sectors identified in this manner excludes a priori consideration of the different effects that the manufacture of a given product in different countries may have (both in the individual countries and in the asymmetric system of interdependence of the countries), depending on the degree of completeness of the interindustrial matrices. To formulate the same idea in another way, the object of the theory is the final product and not the process defined by the vertically integrated sector which, in the country in question, achieves it, both directly and indirectly. In *Strategy,* Hirschman (1958; 1961 ed., 168) pointed to the existence, particularly in "small countries that start out with the 'final touches'," of a "foreign exchange illusion." In these economies, as distinct from the economies with a complete productive matrix, the single "user of imported products" is led to formulate plans which completely ignore the existence of "supply limitations": "the *real* supply limitation" of these economies, that is, the "the ability *of the country* to earn additional foreign exchange through exports," will never be perceived in advance by the single user, but only after the balance of payments crisis through devaluations and exchange controls.

A similar contrast between the perspective of the single "import user" and the perspective of the system as a whole is reflected in the difference between the nominal value of exports and actual value added to the economy (obtained by subtracting from the export value the value of imports necessary to produce them). The importance of this difference for the "import enclave" economies that export primary products is well-known and has given rise to estimates of the "retained value" deriving from exports. Yet there are two circumstances by virtue of which considerable, and increasing, importance has to be attached to this difference to a greater or lesser extent in the industrialized economies as well (cf. Tables 12–14). The first concerns the significance attaching to the decentralization of production from the early 1970s onwards (cf., for example, G. Adam 1973). The second concerns not so much a generic process of international integration, as the particular way in which it comes about.

A considerable part of the expansion of exports in the "export-led" dependent economies is due to the filling-in of gaps left free by a gradual process of "negative import substitution" in the economies of the "center." As has been pointed out previously, among the factors influencing this process of movement (and abandonment) of sectors, not only the speed and stability of growth in demand but also the value-added content per unit produced will play an important part. In the transfer of production (and hence of export) quotas to the dependent economies, the import content, which is already relatively high in relation to that of the "new" sectors in the central economies, does not remain unchanged: it is reasonable to suppose that it increases owing to the incompleteness of the interindustrial matrix of these economies—and this would emerge even more clearly if it were possible to make adequate provision, in the calculation of import content, for the capital goods that have to be imported. (We do not intend to embark here on a discussion of the limitations of the hypotheses upon which the input-output tables have been constructed.)

As in the case of the "effective protection rate," one can therefore speak of an "effective specialization" (and of "effective" sectorial balances) as opposed to the "apparent" specialization and balances normally taken into account in exchange-rate policies, industrial policies, etc. (cf. A. Cauchin 1982, 68). An indication of the significance of these phenomena for the Italian economy is contained in Table 14 (cf. also A. Ginzburg 1981). This table compares, over a period of some years, the value-added content per export unit in the same sectors in Italy and Germany. It shows that, in a comparison between countries and sectors, the value-added content is lower, in the case of the Italian economy, in those sectors in which there has been a greater relative expansion of exports (textiles, foodstuffs, footwear and leather goods). The sectors are arranged in three groups according to the traditional classification adopted by the exponents of the "product cycle" theory and refer to "advanced," "intermediate" and "mature" products (as is known, this classification reflects the list of the expenses of R & D incurred during the 1960s *in the United States)*. If one compares the sectors within the same country, it can be seen that, as far as the value-added content is concerned, a "dependent" economy need not necessarily expand the final production of the "advanced" sectors, should it fall at the same time to modify the vertically-integrated sector corresponding to it.

Another implication of what has been said is that the "social prestige" attaching to export sectors which seem to make important contributions to the expansion of the country (for examples, cf. Hirschman 1968; 1971 ed., 97, note) may, from this standpoint, hardly be justified, or at least severely diminished (cf. in the case of Italy, for example, the motor vehicle industry).

V. Incorporation and Exclusion

It has been stated in the preceding pages that economic development in postwar Italy may be described as the result of (short) phases of accumulation alternating with (longer) phases of export growth and stabilization of domestic demand (not necessarily of prices, as has been seen). In homage to Simiand, we shall call these subsequent phases Phase A (Accumulation) and Phase B (Current Account Positive Balance). (Cf. for an overall picture Table 15.) To associate these successive phases with a fixed political pattern inevitably implies running the risk of schematism. I would point out that I am fully aware of this risk (indeed it is much more than a risk). I could attempt to blur (or conceal) this schematism by pointing out deviations, variants, complications, counterforces at work hindering the development of the rigid sequence suggested here. But my aim is here above all to show how necessary it is to go beyond other schematisms (to two of which I shall refer later on) which offer an even more static view of Italian society than the one suggested here. Thus I shall make no attempt to disguise the rigidity of the scheme.

On the basis of what I have said about the bottlenecks in the structure of production in the period under consideration, a proposition of J. D. Sachs can be applied to Italy: according to this, in the 1970s, "current account movements" tend to be dominated by "shifts in domestic investment rates."[11]

In Phase A the most dynamic element is afforded by investments. Bearing in mind what I said in the first part of this paper: 1) the accumulation phases correspond to moments of acceleration in the complementary integration of Italy in the European division of labor. In particular, the timing and composition of investments are linked with the medium-term tendencies of accumulation in the German economy; 2) the non-synchronization of the cycle requires that the reduction in unutilized capacity, necessary in order for investments to be made, be engendered also by stimulation of private and/or public consumption; 3) the expansion of internal demand and employment in this phase is accompanied by the activation of "horizontal coalitions" among employed workers, i.e., coalitions established on a class basis, which succeed in obtaining real wage increases; 4) the import content of investment demand, for reasons already mentioned, is very high; 5) both the non-synchronization of the cycle and, at a given level of world demand, the circumstances behind the expansion of internal demand (high employment rates and high real wages) tend to have a negative effect on exports (cf. M. Pivetti 1979, 55).

The resulting crisis in the balance of payments may be exacerbated or become dramatic by reason of the flight of capital encouraged, or at any rate not opposed, by the monetary authorities. Against this background the adoption of strictly orthodox economic measures is accompanied by attempts to establish a broader basis of consensus in order to soften the political impact of such measures (in these periods of transition and negotiation, authoritarian solutions, real or imagined, may be threatened). Thus Phase B begins.

The incorporation of political forces of a more left-wing persuasion, anxious for legitimization, given the previous phase of exclusion, does not detract from the fact that the Christian Democrat party (the party with the relative majority) nevertheless maintains a central role in both phases. The felicitous image of the Italian political system as a system of *inamovibilità sussultoria* conveys the idea of a system characterized by more than thirty years of Christian Democrat presence in the governing coalitions and of continuous instability of these coalitions (cf. G. Galli 1975, 33).

In Phase B, the most dynamic element of global demand is represented—even in the absence of devaluation—by exports. 1) The fall in investments and employment, caused by deflationary measures, gives rise by itself to a swift improvement in the balance of payments; the fact that, at least at first, it is the small and medium-sized less-unionized firms that largely contribute to this improvement allows the large firms, harder hit by the workers' struggles, to undertake a slower, direct restructuring (however, they are quick to take advantage of the restructuring of contractors and subcontractors). 2) The export of "import intensive" products finds an outlet which is easier the more the markets of the "center" countries have operated a "negative import substitution" in order to specialize in other sectors or segments of the market with higher value added. 3) The high import content of export increases the amount of exports necessary to finance a given level (or increase) of internal demand: this results in a current account surplus lower than the surplus that would occur with parity of import content. To the extent that this increase narrows or completely eliminates all room for public intervention aimed at lowering unemployment or overcoming structural bottlenecks and inefficiency, it also softens or altogether cuts out the conflicts that may arise thereby. By contributing indirectly to the immobility of policies in the face of extremely mobile coalitions, it thus gives support to political stability.[12] Like emigration and, in certain cases, inflation (cf. A. O. Hirschman 1977; 1981 ed., 201), the absorption of the room for expansion of internal demand thus acts as a safety valve which eases political pressure (even if, by itself, it tends to increase the social pressure). 4) The drop in employment, especially in those areas of the South excluded from the growth in exports, legitimates intervention in support of public money.[13]

The Left-inclined political forces incorporated in the coalition are faced with an alternative that, whatever the outcome, will lose them their consensus: either they must accept the role of managing "austerity" and "restoring national finance to a state of health," or they must try to divert resources to the periphery. With the first of these alternatives tension and unrest will arise among various social strata; with the second the Christian Democrats' firm control over the pipelines through which these resources are distributed (key ministries, local bodies, banks) enables that party to foster—in the absence of stable employment outlets—"vertical coalitions," i.e., based on the "defence of individual or family interests through relationships across class lines" (cf. M. Attalides 1977, 137).

Oscillation of expansion and stabilization may indeed ultimately help to strengthen "clientelistic" networks. As J. Chubb wrote in a study on politics in Southern Italy, "the control of *access* to resources" may be more important than "the quantity of resources distributed." "Once all centers of both local and extralocal power are centralized in the hands of one party, *an expanding stock of resources is no longer necessary.*" Indeed, "when during an economic crisis, the already restricted resource base of the society shrinks even further, the role of the dominant party may actually be enhanced" (cf. J. Chubb 1982, 247 and 213-4, italics mine).

On the one hand, disappointment and social unrest and on the other, in the less stably inclined segments of society, the shift of the importance of ties based on class to that of ties based on other principles of aggregation and social stratification eventually open the way to a new phase in the political sequence.

The "complexity of the aggregations and disgregation of the subaltern classes in Italian society" requires an analysis of the way in which, in the different phases and areas of development, different principles of social stratification are interwoven (cf. G. Levi 1979, 728 and J. Davis 1977). This suggests the unconvincing nature both of analyses based on excessively mechanical class stratifications and of interpretations based on the hypothesis that *trasformismo* be the residue of a system, *typical of pre-industrial societies,* of absorption of oppositions through "patrimonial political practices" and vast use of "patronage and benefits" (cf., for example, J. F. Kurth 1979a, 324). For the rest, as early as 1882, *trasformismo* had been born as an instrument whereby to remove the radical threat emanating from the more industrialized areas of the country (cf. G. Carocci 1956, 300).

If patronage is simply one of a number of "modes of representation—such as bureaucratic control and class struggle—of forms and idioms of social stratification," it must be interpreted as "a *sui generis* political form which coexists with other political forms and is influenced by them." Since patronage is "a near-universal form of manipulation which cannot be explained by referring to its particular manifestations," "those who attribute the origins or causes of patronage to the imperfect industrialization of Mediterranean communities, to their imperfect integration into national economies (J. Schneider and L. Graziano) are wrong" (J. Davis 1977, 150).

Given the autonomy and great flexibility of the patronage system, it can happen that the specific form in which development in Italy manifests itself leads to the constitution of hybrid forms, such as, for example, "bureaucratic patronage," and hence to a strengthening, rather than to a weakening of this social form of construction of material differences.

TABLE 1

Average Growth Rates (1970 Constant Prices)
in the Italian Economy and Political Coalitions

	1959–63	1964–71	1972–73	1974–75	1976–78	1979–80
GNP	+6.65	+4.81	+5.11	+0.25	+3.48	+4.41
Consumption	+6.33	+5.13	+5.41	+1.11	+2.82	+4.23
Fixed Investment	+10.21	+2.52	+4.31	−4.7	+0.63	+7.60
Exports (goods and serv.)	+14.56	+12.77	+7.64	+6.78	+9.97	+2.36
Imports (goods and serv.)	+20.49	+8.30	+10.93	−3.73	+7.80	+10.24
Political coalition oriented towards	Center	Left	Center	Left	Left	Center

Source: Elaborations on ISTAT.

TABLE 2

Italy — Balance of Payments (Mill. Dollars) 1960–72

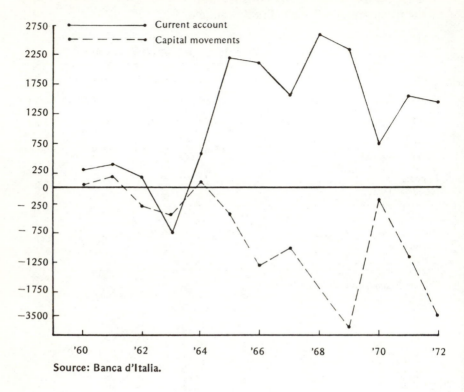

Source: Banca d'Italia.

TABLE 3

Total Employment, Yearly Changes ('000) — 1960–72

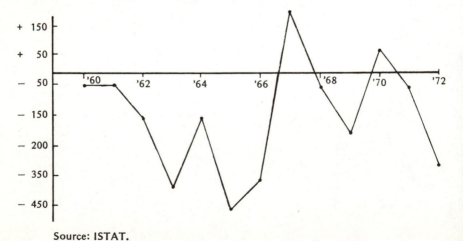

Source: ISTAT.

TABLE 4

Gross Fixed Investment in Germany and Italy (% changes, 1970 constant prices)

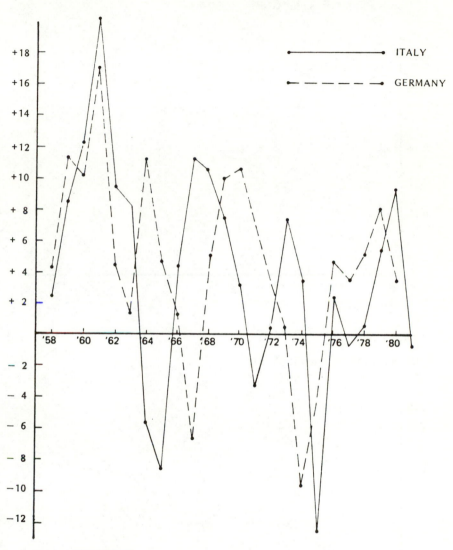

Source: EUROSTAT.

TABLE 5

Import Coefficient (Imports of Goods and Services divided by Imports of
   Goods and Services plus GNP) - 1960–81

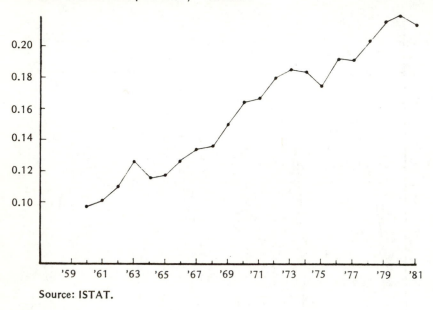

Source: ISTAT.

TABLE 6

Unemployment Rate (1960–81)

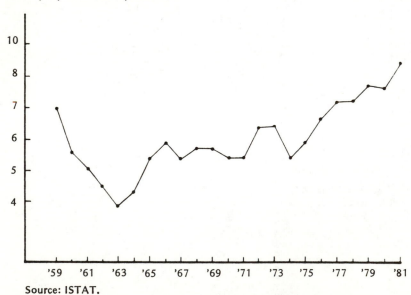

Source: ISTAT.

TABLE 7

Investment Goods (volume terms; 1970 = 100)

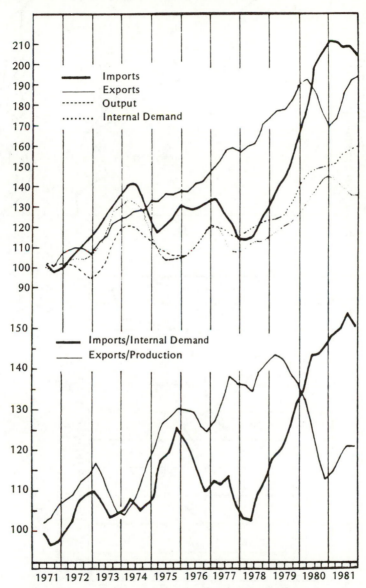

Top: Import, Export, Output and Internal Demand.
Bottom: Imports/Investment and Export/Production Ratios.
Source: Tendenze reali.

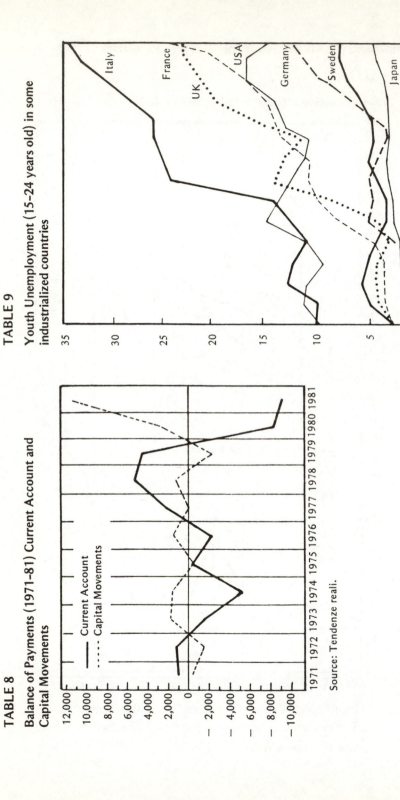

TABLE 8

Balance of Payments (1971–81) Current Account and Capital Movements

12,000
10,000
8,000
6,000
4,000
2,000
0
− 2,000
− 4,000
− 6,000
− 8,000
− 10,000

——— Current Account
·········· Capital Movements

1971 1972 1973 1974 1975 1976 1977 1978 1979 1980 1981

Source: Tendenze reali.

TABLE 9

Youth Unemployment (15–24 years old) in some industrialized countries

35
30
25
20
15
10
5
0

Italy
France
UK
USA
Germany
Sweden
Japan

Source: OCSE.

TABLE 10

Imports of Machinery and Equipment as a Percentage of Investment in Machinery and Equipment (Current Prices), 1971–1980

1971	26.3	1976	42.9
1972	28.0	1977	45.0
1973	28.8	1978	47.0
1974	34.5	1979	48.6
1975	35.3	1980	50.3

Source: ISTAT.

TABLE 11

Italian Trade to and from Germany (as a Percentage of Trade in Each SITC Category, and Total), Selected Years

	1959		1963		1973		1980	
SITC	Export	Import	Export	Import	Export	Import	Export	Import
0	31.2	2.8	35.3	2.5	37.5	11.9	31.0	16.9
1	21.9	2.7	25.3	11.5	28.6	12.5	26.3	27.8
2	23.4	5.9	21.2	5.8	26.4	9.4	20.0	8.4
3	2.4	6.3	4.8	4.3	9.1	2.4	1.5	1.5
4	7.8	5.5	9.5	2.5	16.9	7.6	16.3	10.9
5	8.1	30.5	9.1	30.1	12.6	35.3	11.9	28.5
6	13.4	20.8	16.7	23.1	24.2	23.8	20.6	20.1
7	12.7	40.0	22.2	37.2	15.0	39.2	13.0	33.8
8	14.9	35.9	20.9	32.7	32.0	27.2	26.5	19.1
9	0	11.6	29.1	7.2	18.8	49.2	9.3	9.7
Total	16.2	13.9	17.9	16.9	21.7	20.3	18.1	16.7

Source: OCSE.

TABLE 12

Intermediate Import Content of Final Demand Components

	EXPORTS	INTERNAL DEMAND
Italy 1959	0.180	0.101
France 1959	0.132	0.078
Italy 1965	0.194	0.109
France 1965	0.143	0.091
Germany 1965	0.161	0.122
Italy 1970	0.214	0.133
France 1970	0.167	0.106
Germany 1970	0.176	0.131
Italy 1974	0.305	0.199

Source: Elaborations on EUROSTAT, Tableau Entrées-Sorties, 1978, and, for 1974 data, ISTAT.

TABLE 13

Final, Intermediate, and Total Import Content of Internal Demand

	CONSUMPTION			INVESTMENT		
	Final	Interm.	Total	Final	Interm.	Total
Italy 1965	0.0269	0.0917	0.1186	0.067	0.100	0.168
Italy 1970	0.0338	0.1079	0.1417	0.099	0.123	0.223
Germany 1970	0.0537	0.1144	0.1681	0.064	0.111	0.175
Italy 1974	0.0450	0.1588	0.2038	0.111	0.166	0.278

Source: I. Lavanda (1980).

TABLE 14

Export Net of Import Content Per Unit of Export

	1965		1970		1974
	Italy	Germany	Italy	Germany	Italy
I Group					
Chemistry	0.807	0.818	0.777	0.787	0.683
Office m.	0.827	0.886	0.834	0.862	0.782
Electr. m.	0.773	0.862	0.752	0.836	0.703
Aircraft	0.801	0.841	0.753	0.741	0.702
Photo etc.	0.771	0.789	0.651	0.748	0.544
II Group					
Petrol. der.	0.667	0.677	0.638	0.652	0.321
Rubber	0.778	0.831	0.780	0.812	0.662
Non el. m.	0.847	0.864	0.794	0.865	0.753
Vehicles	0.799	0.850	0.754	0.837	0.690
III Group					
Leather, etc.	0.765	0.769	0.751	0.799	0.696
Wood	0.776	0.816	0.780	0.848	0.723
Paper	0.826	0.835	0.812	0.850	0.761
Text. cloth.	0.783	0.759	0.793	0.756	0.737
Non met. min.	0.902	0.919	0.887	0.887	0.809
Iron, steel	0.698	0.662	0.607	0.739	0.527
Metal prod.	0.821	0.861	0.763	0.815	0.711
Food-Meat	0.815	0.875	0.701	0.839	0.699
Milk	0.931	0.895	0.914	0.854	0.872
Oth. f.	0.779	0.675	0.752	0.667	0.642
Drinks	0.910	0.894	0.891	0.896	0.844
Tobacco	0.963	0.867	0.963	0.892	0.945

Source: See Table 12.

TABLE 15

Gross Fixed Investment and Current Account Balance, as a percentage of GDP,
and periods of political coalitions oriented towards Center (C) and Left (L)

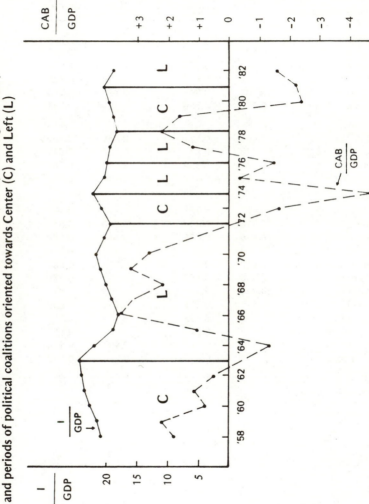

Source: Elaborations on ISTAT.

NOTES

1. I wish to thank Guillermo O'Donnell and Fernando Vianello for helpful comments to a previous version of this paper.

2. There is a slightly different English version in G. DeVivo and M. Pivetti 1980.

3. Cf., for example, the lively debate regarding the theories of O'Donnell in the second half of the seventies in D. Collier, ed., 1979, and in the same volume, in a wider historical perspective, J. R. Kurth's analysis of European events in the nineteenth and twentieth centuries.

4. Cf., for example, F. Simiand 1934. For a similar idea, differently motivated, cf. A. O. Hirschman 1982. It may be of interest to recall that Hirschman, who emigrated to France in 1933, numbered Simiand himself among his teachers in Paris.

5. Cf. A. O. Hirschman 1968, 95, and, for a discussion, J. Kurth 1979b, 322 et. seq.

6. On the importance of commercial credits in Italian foreign trade, cf. A. Simonazzi 1983.

7. Cf., for example, F. Pierelli 1983. But for evidence to the contrary, see P. Modino and F. Onida 1983.

8. For a confirmation of S. Linder's hypothesis of the impact of the home market on the Italian pattern of export specialization of capital goods cf. E. S. Andersen et. al., 1981.

9. For a discussion of the limits of the "domestic demand pressure" hypothesis in the Italian case, see A. Simonazzi 1978, 155.

10. The basic ideas underlying the theory had been anticipated, but in a determined historical and temporal context, by A. O. Hirschman 1960.

11. Although Sachs's general scheme of interpretation is itself unconvincing, the statistical evidence he supplies confirms that this proposition is particularly relevant to the case of Italy: cf. J. D. Sachs 1981, 229 and 236.

12. One may argue along similar lines with reference to the role played by export of capital in the absorption of current surplus, wherever this export is considered as a flux in some way necessary and/or unstoppable: cf. on this point, the remarks of M. Pivetti 1979, 24.

13. On the use of planning jargon by the "old world of the South" after 1963, see S. Tarrow 1969, 299.

REFERENCES

Adam, G. 1973. "Multinational Corporations and Worldwide Sourcing." In H. Radice, ed., *International Firms and Modern Imperialism*. London, 1975.

Amato, G., ed. 1972. *Il governo dell'industria in Italia*. Bologna.

Andersen, E. S. et al. 1981. *International Specialization and the Home Market*. Industrial Development Research Series no. 19, Aalborg.

Attalides, M. 1977. "Forms of Peasant Incorporation in Cyprus during the Last Century." In E. Gellner and J. Waterbury, eds., *Patrons and Clients in Mediterranean Societies*. London.

Brusco, S. 1982. "The Emilian Model: Productive Decentralisation and Social Integration." *Cambridge Journal of Economics*, no. 6.

Carocci, G. 1956. *Agostino Depretis e la politica interna italiana dal 1876 al 1887* Torino.

Cauchin, A. 1982. "Pour une théorie de la spécialisation effective." In H. Bourguinat, ed., *Internationalisation et autonomie de décision*. Paris.

Chubb, J. 1982. *Patronage, Power, and Poverty in Southern Italy*. Cambridge: Cambridge University Press.

Collier, D. 1976. *Squatters and Oligarchs: Authoritarian Rule and Policy Change in Peru*. Baltimore.

Collier, D., ed. 1979. *The New Authoritarianism in Latin America*. Princeton: Princeton University Press.

D'Antonio, M. 1973. *Sviluppo e crisi del capitalismo italiano*. Bari.

Davis, J. 1977. *People of the Mediterranean: An Essay in Comparative Social Anthropology*. London: Routledge and K. Paul.

DeCecco, M. 1971. "Lo sviluppo dell'economia italiana e la sua collocazione internazionale." *Rivista internazionale di scienze economiche e commerciali*, 983–88.

––––––. 1976a. "Aspetti e tendenze della divisione internazionale del lavoro." In AA.VV., *Crisi economica e condizionamenti internazionale dell'Italia*. Roma.

––––––. 1976b. "Banca d'Italia e 'conquista politica' del sistema del credito." In AA.VV., *Il governo democratico dell'economia*. Bari.

DeVivo, G., and M. Pivetti. 1979. "L'Italia e il vincolo della bilancia dei pagamenti." In M. Pivetti, *Bilancia dei pagamenti e occupazione in Italia*. Torino.

––––––. 1980. "International Integration and the Balance of Payment Constraint: the Case of Italy." *Cambridge Journal of Economics*, no. 4: 1–22.

Galli, G. 1975. *Dal bipartitismo imperfetto alla possibile alternativa*. Bologna.

Ginzburg, A. 1981. "Struttura produttiva e commercio internazionale." *Studi e ricerche dell'Istituto Economico*, n. 8, Facoltà di Economia e Commercio, Università di Modena.

Haberler, G. 1945. "The Choice of Exchange Rates after the War." *American Economic Review*.

Hibbs, D.A. 1977. "Political Parties and Macroeconomic Policy." *American Political Science Review*.

Hirschman, A.O. 1948. "Inflation and Deflation in Italy." *American Economic Review*, 599–605.

––––––. 1958. *The Strategy of Economic Development*. New Haven: Yale University Press.

————. 1960. "Invitation to Theorizing about the Dollar Glut." *Review of Economics and Statistics* Feb.: 100–102.

————. 1968. "The Political Economy of Import-Substituting Industrialization in Latin America." Now in *A Bias for Hope*, New Haven: Yale University Press, 1971.

————. 1977. "A Generalized Linkage Approach to Development, with Special Reference to Staples." Now in *Essays in Trespassing,* Cambridge and New York: Cambridge University Press, 1981.

————. 1982. "A Dissenter's Confession." In G. Meier and D. Seers, eds., *Pioneers in Development.* New York: Oxford University Press, 1984.

Johnson, H. 1971. "The Theory of Tariff Structure with Special Reference to World Trade and Development." In *Aspect of the Theory of Tariffs.* Cambridge: Harvard University Press.

Klarén, P.F. 1973. *Modernization, Dislocation and Aprismo.* Austin and London.

Kurth, J.R. 1979a. "Industrial Change and Political Change: a European Perspective." In D. Collier, ed., *The New Authoritarianism in Latin America.* Princeton: Princeton University Press, 1979.

————. 1979b. "The Political Consequences of the Product Cycle: Industrial History and Political Outcomes." *International Organization* (Winter).

Lavanda, I. 1980. "Una nota sulla dipendenza esterna dell'economia italiana." *Rivista internazionale di scienze sociali,* n. 1.

Levi, G. 1979. "Regioni e cultura delle classi popolari." *Quaderni Storici,* n. 41.

Lutz, V. 1950. "Italy: Economic Recovery and Development." In H. Ellis, *The Economics of Freedom,* introduction by D. O. Eisenhover. New York.

Modiano, P., and F. Onida. 1983. "Un'analisi disaggregata delle funzioni di domanda di esportazioni dell'Italia e dei principali paesi industriali." *Giornale degli Economisti.*

Pierelli, F. 1983. "I mutamenti nella struttura degli scambi mondiali e la 'posizione italiana.' " *Contributi alla ricerca economica,* temi di discussione n. 16, Banca d'Italia, n. 16 (March).

Pivetti, M. 1979. *Bilancia dei pagamenti e occupazione in Italia.* Torino.

Sachs, J.D. 1981. "The Current Account and Macroeconomic Adjustment in the 1970s." *Brookings Papers on Economic Activity.*

Serra, J. 1979. "Three Mistaken Theses Regarding the Connection between Industrialization and Authoritarian Regimes." In D. Collier, ed., *The New Authoritarianism in Latin America.* Princeton: Princeton University Press.

Simiand, F. 1934. *Inflation et stabilisation alternées: le développement économique des Etats Unis.* Paris.

Simonazzi, A. 1978. "Domestic Demand Pressure and Export Performance: the Case of Selected Italian Industries." *Economic Notes.*

————. 1983. *Governi, banchieri e mercanti.* Milano.

Simonnot, P. 1971a. "Pourquoi les Six sont-ils si pressés d'appliquer les préférences généralisées au Tiers-Monde?" *le Monde* (6 avril).

————. 1971b. "Les préférences tariffaire en faveur du Tiers-Monde: relations nouvelles entre pays riches et pays pauvres." *Tiers Monde* (octobre-décembre).

Sylos, Labini. 1971. "Investimenti, produttività e politica finanziaria." *Note economiche* 3.

Tarrow, S. 1969. *Partito comunista e contadini nel Mezzogiorno.* Torino.

Tendenze Reali. 1983. Banca Commerciale Italiana, Ufficio Studi, luglio.

UCIMU. 1977. *Il parco macchine utensili nell'industria italiana.* Milano.

Vianello, F. 1975. "I meccanismi di recupero del profitto: l'esperienza italiana 1963–73." Now in *Il profitto e il potere.* Torino, 1979.

Wolf, E. R. 1966. "Kinship, Friendship and Patron-Client Relations in Complex Societies." In M. Banton, ed., *The Social Anthropology of Complex Societies.* New York: F. A. Praeger.

PART II

Trespassing: Economy Politics, and Society

Tensions in Democratic Development

The Elusive Balance between Stimulation and Constraint in Analysis of Development[1]

John Sheahan

In *The Seventeenth Century Background* Basil Willey explores in imaginative ways the question of what it means to "explain" reality.[2] In that period in Western Europe, long-accepted explanations in terms of the medieval religious-scholastic synthesis were giving way, slowly, to a new set of explanations based on deduction of behavioral regularities. The old explanations were dominated by questions of human and divine purpose, essence, and moral values; the new ones simply stopped explaining purpose and essence in favor of identifying regularities. For many people they were not explanations at all, just mechanical descriptions which left out the essential questions. Then more and more people began to accept the idea that the mechanical explanation of the circulation of the blood or the movement of the planets or the way prices change in response to changes in the stock of gold was *really* what an explanation is and should be. Concerns for values, or for ultimate purpose, came to be seen as personal matters best kept out of attempts to explain reality.

The foundations of modern economics grew directly out of the new conceptions of search for systematic cause and effect, excluding questions of ultimate purpose or relationships to moral values. The economic system does not guide people to do the right thing because they want to do the right thing; charity, concern for others or for one's own soul, imaginative personal expression, and all such distractions become likely sources of confusion if they are allowed to intrude. Economists rarely have as much fun as when they are pointing out how generous intentions can have consequences exactly opposite to those desired. At times, the game of overturning popular misconceptions of economic issues leads close to a conclusion that a society which pays too much attention to popular preferences is almost bound to get into trouble; a modest dose of authoritarianism, guided by respect for economic constraints, may give better practical results.

Willey suggests that this more mechanical-systematic approach won out not because it explained everything which people wanted to understand but rather because it gave answers on the particular side of reality least well answered by existing explanations. It "explained" in ways which worked to give greater control over physical and social events, not, perhaps, to get people into heaven any more effectively than the value-charged medieval synthesis. But the empirical evidence on that question has never been clear in any case. The new approach just left aside the unknowable, to be considered by those so inclined in the idle years after retirement, or not at all by those with the stamina to keep on accumulating utility right up to the final moment.

In economics the new kind of explanation certainly did work, in the main, to raise the wealth of nations. It worked by directing attention to the concepts of efficiency, incentives, and thrift. Because it worked in this sense, and because good intentions and romantic spirits trying to break out of the system almost always came to grief, it became extremely difficult for anyone to accomplish the miracle of combining respect for basic economic principles with analysis questioning their effects on other human concerns. The rare value of Albert Hirschman's work to all of us is that he manages to achieve such a combination. He keeps reopening the questions in ways which escape the boundaries within economics which act to block off inquiry into wider values.[3] His explanations rise beyond the mechanical principles to questions of purpose. He does it in part by taking up for serious examination the very kinds of popular conceptions which so much of economics serves to deride—by searching for the hidden truth, or partial truth, rather than the weakness which could be used to discredit. Instead of the negative and potentially authoritarian strand within economics he brings out a more open sense of constructive possibilities.

This kind of reorientation can be marvelously stimulating and it can also cause trouble. The following discussion is in part a confession of doubt and resistance mixed with fascination—of reasons for concern that the effort can favor costly misdirection at the same time that it opens up splendid new avenues of thought. The discussion is directed to three sets of issues concerned with problems of developing countries, and in particular of Latin American countries: (1) analysis of linkages, (2) response to inflation and the survival of democratic regimes, and (3) "antagonistic growth."[4]

I. Linkages and Limits

Development economics was from its inception concerned with activation of potential, with changing the response mechanism of the economic system, as opposed to preoccupation with efficiency in the sense of resource allocation through markets and prices. It ran head on against the traditional theme of "economizing": against emphasis on the need to restrain demand to fit productive capacity, to limit government intervention and protection, to restrain the rate of growth of government spending and the money supply to avoid inflation, and to hold real wages and consumption down to free resources for investment. In the lively period of early postwar development analysis these conservative considerations were attacked from many different angles, not so much with the idea that they are inexorably wrong as that they leave too much out. A key theme was that a broader vision would take into account the possibility of action to stimulate potential which otherwise well-functioning private markets allow to go to waste.

The models of W. Arthur Lewis and Ragnar Nurkse centered on excess labor and the possibilities for growth inherent in creating productive employment; Raúl Prebisch and CEPAL emphasized closely similar questions combined with failures of changing relative prices to correct structural problems of supply; Hirschman identified problems of entrepreneurship and the need for destabilizing pressures to force both entrepreneurs and the state to act in new directions.[5] All such supply-side questions lead naturally to social and political variables: class structures and social mobility, land ownership and access to capital, impediments to the acquisition of education and skills, the role of the international system, and the forces acting to determine choices by the state. They lead attention toward fundamental concerns of social goals and social control, away from issues of economic efficiency and consistency.

The orientation of the Lewis and Nurkse models, which postulated excess labor and productive potential which could be made effective by increased investment, matched all too well the Prebisch conceptions of using protection as a means to stimulate industrial investment for the home market. By "too well" I mean that they did not pay much attention to limits and the need for selectivity. The intellectual system did not specify why any particular kind of investment or level of protection should be chosen; it did not provide any brakes on a process which had to be carried out within some very real constraints. The constraints showed up promptly and keep on showing up every time promotional policies are pursued without selective guidance, chiefly as foreign exchange crises and inflation.

Hirschman agreed with the others on the reality of underutilized potential but went further to formulate a theoretical principle which might be used to guide selection. The theoretical principle was a step upward from the conception of marginal adjustments in existing activities to the circular process through which individual decisions affect the economic system as a whole and thereby change the pressures acting on the following set of individual choices. Where traditional economics takes as given the capacity of entrepreneurs to respond to profitable opportunities, and of the government to implement public sector policies to facilitate economic performance, Hirschman postulated that the capacity to respond has another dimension for both of them. In addition to questions of profitability, pressure or compulsion to initiate action may reveal potential that would otherwise have been blocked. The fact that actions are not being undertaken—that the pipeline or the shoe factory is not being built—may in some cases mean simply that the expected returns are too low but it may in many others mean instead that the pressure to take action is not strong enough. Whatever the existing base of objectively available resources and skills, an underdeveloped country is likely to be able to do more than it is actually doing, to move its production possibility frontier outward, if business and the government are put under pressure to take the discontinuous steps needed to start movement in new directions.

In Hirschman's model, the process of development could be stimulated by creating disequilibria which would compel new actions, thereby creating new needs and further response. Glaring shortages of infrastructure compelling state action would show up as a result of industrial investment requiring more transport and power; shortages of inputs for one line of activity would stimulate investment in order to provide the input; and shortages in final product markets would compel new production to meet them. The consequent creation of needs for new inputs would then extend the chain of imbalance and response. No country need ever come to "the end of import substitution," or any other closure. The linkages between each individual action and the rest of the economic system provide an ongoing series of stimuli.

Analysis of linkages inverted the Nurkse type of argument in favor of "balanced growth." Each approach emphasizes the system of connections among markets but they differ on what to do. For Nurkse, the solution seemed to be to do everything at once, to expand all lines of production simultaneously at rates matching the pattern of increase in demand. That comes close to a counsel of impossibility: it implies either unacceptable diseconomies of scale or a sense of despair because the upper limit of possible investment in any period is too low to permit expansion in every direction simultaneously. Hirschman's alternative does not demand doing everything at once but would instead foster disequilibrium by selective promotion. And it gives what could be seen as a principle of selection: the greater the linkages implied in any new activity, the more favorable it is as a channel through which to stimulate development. Instead of a counsel of unhelpful generality, or of despair, it suggests a selective line of action. But the idea brought in a new kind of trouble of its own. It does not provide guidance to make sure of its consistency with a well-functioning economic system.

Intensity or variety of linkages do not measure desirability of promotional action. Linkages can be harmful as well as helpful. Harmful linkages can be of many different kinds, including those which lead straight to new import requirements without any accompanying increase in capacity to pay for them, those which provoke high-cost domestic production wasting scarce resources, and those which involve technical or managerial skills which can only be answered through recourse to foreign investment short-circuiting possibilities of domestic learning and control. Hirschman's own presentation does not disregard costs. It distinguishes among linkages according to the degree to which they lead to production levels above minimum efficient scales. It does not call for unlimited protection but, very circumspectly, for "perhaps, some infant industry protection."[6] But which cases warrant protection and whether there should be any upper limit, why some and not others, whether differential implications for employment or for foreign exchange requirements should be considered, what to do when linkages imply technology which is at the time beyond any likely possibility for domestic firms, or how additional costs should be distributed within the society, remain open questions. As Hirschman ruefully notes, even the fact that such questions are relevant disappears in some of the applications of the general principle.[7]

The concept of linkages might be seen as a major step forward in Willey's sense of an explanation which clarifies essence, which makes people more aware of connections in a complex world. It draws attention to possibilities for constructive stimulus which could be hidden by conventional investment criteria. That is not the same thing as a set of operational rules about what to do next. Each of the included links needs to be considered in terms of the constraints bearing on the particular economy at the time, and should also be considered in terms of the goals of the society. The problem of choice changes character. The outer limits can be seen as more flexible but the input implications of the whole linked package raise new problems of dealing with constraints. These problems could block economic growth, or shape it in directions adverse for autonomy or reduction of poverty, if the fact of linkages were taken as a certificate of desirability.

II. Inflation and the Survival of Democratic Regimes

The side of development analysis which emphasizes stimulation of underutilized potential, the need for structural change more than concern for constraints, naturally favors tolerance for some degree of inflation. This fits well with a preference for government responsive to popular pressures, willing to listen to competing claims for help even if the claims add up to excess demand. A moderate degree of inflation can be seen as a stimulus for investment and change at the same time as it lessens the pressure for direct confrontation of interest groups. But is that approach favorable for the survival of open political systems? Focusing the question on Latin America in the postwar period, do democracies have a better chance to survive if their governments accept moderately high inflation or if instead they exert continuous effort to keep it down? Where authoritarian regimes are in place, would the chances of restoring open political systems be better if these regimes were encouraged to maintain strict anti-inflationary policies or if instead they were to relax such economic restraints?

Democracies are not common among developing countries anywhere but Latin America has had a good many, of which Chile and Uruguay were for many years among the leading examples. Further, the drive to get back to democracy after periods of authoritarian rule is clearly strong in most countries of the region, successfully so at the moment in many cases. But "at the moment" must be said with an uneasy sense that for many of them it is touch and go. That sense is especially disquieting because of the *nature* of authoritarian rule in the dramatic examples of Brazil since 1964, Chile and Uruguay since 1973, and Argentina from 1976 until 1983. Authoritarian states can vary a great deal in character; these have been among the most vicious in the modern world, in the sense of their degrees of systematic violence against their own people. At the same time, they have been

unusual in terms of their economic policies: all of them were from
the start emphatically oriented toward support for free markets and
determined opposition to inflation.[8]

The background and special character of these "bureaucratic
authoritarian" regimes raise complex questions of causation in many
domains, analyzed particularly well by Guillermo O'Donnell.[9] Inflation is only one of many strands in the picture, of less immediate
significance than fears about communism and the survival of private
ownership, breakdowns of personal security in conditions of terrorism,
breakdowns of the capacity of the economic system to function, and
pressures from the United States through national military forces to
overturn distrusted civilian governments. Considered separately, inflation may be seen as a distinctly secondary concern. Still, for many
people, with some foundation, it is an expression of a society's loss
of control, both a result and a contribution to social breakdown.

Carlos Díaz-Alejandro emphasizes that all four of the overturns
of democratic regimes in Brazil and the Southern Cone followed loss
of control over accelerating inflation.[10] He does not argue that this
was the dominant factor involved but suggests that one try the mental
experiment of subtracting inflation from everything else going on: if
Goulart, the Peróns, and Allende had managed to keep it down would
the violence of the opposition which swept out democracy in these
countries have been as great, or public acceptance of the overturns
as broadly based? The question might be applied in reverse to countries
which did not suffer these violent overturns: would Colombia have
been able to keep its always-threatened democracy if inflation had
gone twice as high as it did in the 1960s or 1970s?

The association between exceptional levels of inflation and subsequent bureaucratic authoritarian regimes is not just a matter of
immediate pre-coup bursts of hyperinflation. In the late 1950s and
the 1960s four Latin American countries stood out as exceptionally
inflation-prone. They were Argentina, Brazil, Chile, and Uruguay.
Their inflation rates varied a great deal among periods but taking the
decade of the 1960s as a whole they had the four highest averages in
the region.[11] Apart from Bolivia and Paraguay in the early 1950s, the
rest of Latin America—those countries which have not become bureaucratic authoritarian regimes, or at least not yet—had dispersed
inflation rates similar to those in other developing regions.

From one point of view this relationship between exceptionally
high inflation and exceptionally severe political repression might be
regarded as support for a conclusion that inability to respect restraints
and to control inflation is a major contributor to the breakdown of

democracies. But from another point of view it might be seen instead as raising a different question: what is it about these particular countries which gave rise to such severe difficulties in dealing with inflation in the first place? If they are subject to special strains which made them inflation-prone then they were in danger of political violence in any case, and if that is so then perhaps the optimal course for them was to allow inflation as a means of dealing with these strains. Instead of a cause of breakdown, acceptance of inflation might have been a way to stave off repressive political response.

This second way of looking at the inflation-repression relationship owes a great deal to Hirschman's explorations of the issues. He agrees with many others in emphasizing the political dangers of hyperinflation but then adds to that a compelling argument in favor of viewing inflation as something of a safety valve.[12] Governments which are trying to build up more stable institutions in difficult conditions cannot risk too many head-on conflicts with the country's major interest groups. A business sector always worried about possible destruction from major changes in economic policies, and practically always pressed for liquidity if the government tries seriously to restrain inflation, becomes a threat to the survival of the system if its taxes are increased or it is refused support in the form of protection or subsidies. Massive disaffection over wages by the labor force, or over agricultural policies by landowners, can lead either to outright violence or the intensified pressure for a political overturn if the government rejects all claims inconsistent with price stability. To accept claims which are excessive in nominal terms but are then scaled back by inflation can defuse social conflict. Against the conservative criticism that inflation is the temptation of the devil—the insidious way out by resorting to a hidden tax—Hirschman opposes the principle that institutions, like people, can stand only finite doses of direct conflict. The costs of being forthrightly negative can be too high for a democratic system to bear.

Both the conservative warning that failure to restrain inflation can become a serious threat to democracy and the counter-thought that excessive zeal in attacking it can have exactly the same negative effect clearly embody important truths. Is it possible to say which one is the better guide, under what circumstances? In some cases, perhaps yes. Two examples which fit more the Hirschman view are the contrasting strategies of Brazil from 1967 and of Chile under its authoritarian regime. Two which in some respects go the other way are the examples of democratic Chile in the Frei administration and Colombia.

In Brazil in 1967 the conflict was between the conservative IMF-supported view of the need for continued deflation, after three years of aggressive restraint had brought the inflation rate down from ninety to about thirty percent, and the contrary option for expansion accepting the existing thirty percent inflation. The decision taken was to accept the inflation and promote expansion, within monetary constraints set at a rate likely to prevent any rise in inflation, and with the exchange rate moving to keep exports growing along with rising imports.[13] From 1967 to 1974 this combination gave Brazil one of the best economic performances in Latin American history. It became possible because the ongoing rate of inflation was correctly seen to be more a matter of persisting behavioral patterns in which each group tried to defend its real income than of any excess demand or excessive pressure from wages. To accept the existing rate of inflation, rather than to keep on beating it down by further contraction, facilitated growth and eventually a turn toward a less repressive political system.

The anti-inflation strategy of the Chilean military government provides a direct contrast to the Brazilian choice in 1967. After a period of severe contraction had brought inflation down from an annual rate of around a thousand percent at the start to about forty percent by 1978, some economic expansion was allowed but under continued strong pressure to eliminate inflation. In addition to very high real interest rates and budgetary balance, the regime chose to fix the exchange rate while almost eliminating protection, in order to restrain prices by import competition. That approach cut inflation further but it fostered rapidly rising imports, stopped the growth of non-traditional exports, and led to a foreign exchange crisis followed by another steep plunge in production and employment.[14] The obsession with stopping inflation at all costs proved to be so expensive it made the inflation itself a comparatively minor problem. The option for continued economic repression went hand in hand with continued political repression: Chile got a much weaker economic performance than Brazil did and has so far shown no signs of movement to a more open political system.

Considering a case of democratic government under great pressure—the Frei administration in Chile from 1964 to 1970—the view of inflation as a danger to democracy seems more nearly valid. It would be difficult to find an example of a higher quality economic program at the start.[15] Frei inherited a rate of inflation of forty-nine percent and was determined to reduce it. But the reduction was attempted with a fully worked out program based on increasing production and employment, promotion of non-traditional exports through a variable exchange rate, increased taxation of middle and higher income groups, use of some price controls, and a target rate of increase in real wages calculated to fit actual production possibilities. In its first three years these policies helped cut the rate of inflation almost in half while production, exports, tax revenue, employment and real wages all increased. It would not have been possible to accomplish all that if the inflation had been answered simply by deflation of demand, or if the expansion had been pushed beyond rates consistent with productive capacity. Frei avoided both of these mistakes for three years. But then he lost the struggle in the fourth year by allowing, or encouraging, a much faster rate of wage increase than that specified in his own program. The increases pushed up production costs and widened the government's deficit. Inflation started right back up again, and growth slowed down as investment programs were cut to lessen the inflationary pressures coming from the wage increases.

Any explanation of why the Frei government undermined its own program by ignoring its wage targets would need to go far afield into all the factors bearing on Chilean society in this fateful period, but one of the key considerations is straightforwardly political: the Christian Democratic party was engaged in a struggle against the radical Left for the support of the country's workers. Frei concluded that wage restraints could not be maintained without paying too high a political price. Heaven knows whether the opposite choice of staying with the wage restraints would have worked. The consequences of failing to stick with the restraints were that the program broke down and the stage was set for the country's traumatic experiences in the 1970s.

What are the main circumstances in this case which made accommodation to inflationary pressures work so badly? One factor may have been the evidence of governmental inability to maintain its own clearly defined and successful program. While most groups in the society accepted it, the government broke it selectively to appeal to a special interest. Another important consideration is that the accommodation could not do anything positive for the growth of real income: it had to mean heightened conflict over income shares. Brazil in 1967 could move more freely because it was coming out of a recession induced by strong prior deflation. Arguments for continuing deflation were simply wrong to insist on any need to keep down demand in real terms. But Chile under Frei was achieving a successful expansion pushing close to the limits of productive capacity. That left little room for a positive supply response to yet faster growth of demand. Under such conditions the concessions intended to lessen social conflict served to destroy a balanced program of expansion and helped set in motion a chain of extreme reactions decidedly adverse for democracy in Chile.

Colombia has not had dramatic episodes of system breakdown in recent years. It returned to a democracy in 1960, after a decade of violence and a semi-populist kind of authoritarianism. In the 1960s it had the fifth highest rate of inflation in Latin America, after Brazil and the Southern Cone. But it turned more toward monetary restraint than the other four, and also turned away from increasing protection for industrialization while still at much lower levels than those in Argentina and Brazil. It also adopted a moving peg exchange rate to promote new exports at the same time as Brazil, without needing an authoritarian system to make this critical change.[16] The new set of policies proved highly favorable for growth of employment from 1967 through the 1970s but probably contributed to a decline in industrial real wages in the course of the 1970s. It was much more favorable for increases in the real wages of rural labor, construction workers, and even household servants, all of whom began to catch up on higher levels of industrial wages.[17] All this could be regarded on balance as either a successful or an unduly conservative strategy but in the present context the question is how Colombia, with a democratic system much less firmly established than those of Chile and Uruguay as of the beginning of the 1960s, could get away with the kinds of restraint the others seemed unable to apply.

Among the countless possible factors bearing on this difference, two different themes might be suggested. One is a matter of policy balance: the fact that Colombia never went anywhere near as far as Argentina, Brazil, and Chile in disconnecting its industrial structure from world markets through protection in the early postwar period, and never adopted anything like Argentina's direct attack on agricultural export incomes, helped keep its economic system more responsive to normal incentives and also kept down the level of social conflict. The second consideration is at once a weakness and a factor easing tensions: the country has never been able to extend its educational system as completely and bring all social groups into political participation to the degree of the Southern Cone countries, and its labor force has never been able to achieve the degrees of organization of theirs. Its backwardness in social terms has meant that it has not yet needed to meet acid tests of the kind which broke down Frei.

These factors certainly do not exhaust the matter but they help account for survival in a mine-strewn field. They suggest a two-sided position on the preceding questions about inflation and democracy: (1)

if the structure of production can be kept from becoming severely unbalanced in the first place, and if the inevitable conflicts among economic groups can be moderated by compromise rather than pointed toward combat as they were in the Southern Cone, then it is *easier* to restrain inflation without traumatic consequences; (2) given such conditions in the first place then it is *safer* for democracy to bend toward restraint on inflation than to lean toward accepting it. The counterpart of (2) is of course that when the basic context has become much more difficult, as it became in Brazil and the Southern Cone, then the argument for acceptance of even fairly high ongoing rates of inflation becomes more appropriate, and probably more favorable for the survival of democracy. It could be a costly mistake to carry over this partial truth to application in conditions, such as those in Colombia, where the otherwise defensible leaning toward acceptance of inflation could undermine a real possibility of sustained growth free of authoritarianism.

III. "Discipline as the Central Objective of Economy Policy"[18]

The darkest years of political repression and state-authorized violence against the people of Chile and Uruguay from 1973 and of Argentina from 1976 to 1982 were periods in which these governments emphasized the efficiency-oriented character of their economic policies. Adolfo Canitrot has explained the Argentine economic model of 1976—removing industrial protection and discrimination against agriculture, eliminating regulation and subsidies, and restraining monetary growth—in terms of a double objective: (1) to get rid of many existing causes of inefficiency in the sense normally intended by economists, and (2) to reverse history, to sweep away group interests which had torn Argentina apart from the late 1940s on, to nurture "a farsighted and remote authoritarianism, possessed of a moral authority and discipline higher than that of a surrounding society made sick by years of mismanagement."[19] The economic strategy and the application of political repression were not viewed by the government as accidental associations.

The vision in Chile has been much the same, combining great zeal in the application of traditional principles of economic efficiency with a ruthless effort to weed out proponents of radical reform, to eliminate any Left-oriented teaching from the universities, to suppress prior labor organizations and create a restrictive new legal system governing labor relations, and to go far beyond mere deregulation toward an all out "privatization" of everything possible in the economy.[20] The mixture has included the same two types of measures: one set which could be seen as normal under democratic conditions in many countries, and a second which constitutes something more like a vengeful drive to restructure the society in order to destroy the economic power and the political channels of expression of both organized labor and domestic industrialists.

Alejandro Foxley characterizes the kind of thinking behind this program as belonging to *"los ideologismos económicos totalisantes."* [21] Arnold Harberger argues that there is nothing anti-democratic about the economic measures themselves, as distinct from the political regime which imposed them. It is a case of "guilt by association" to identify efficiency-oriented economic stabilization with authoritarianism. Harberger's opinion is that, "no single component of policy in the Southern Cone countries is without its precedents in a democratic setting."[22] That objection could be seen as helpful and valid if limited to questions of individual economic policies such as export promotion or the elimination of price controls. But what is a strictly economic policy in these specific contexts? Does an overall set of policies which generates such persistently high levels of unemployment that they could never be held in place without political repression constitute a strictly economic question?[23] Do attempts to change the legal system and institutional framework of the society, in order to reduce the power of special interest groups to interfere in formulating economic policy, belong inside or outside such a domain?

Perhaps the most difficult of all the problems of reconciliation between efficiency criteria and democratic institutions is precisely this issue of conflicting interest groups. They can paralyze a society, as they have done in Argentina. In all countries, democratic or not, "special interest organizations and collusions reduce efficiency and aggregate income in the societies in which they operate and make political life more divisive."[24] Mancur Olson's stress on the high costs of pressures exerted by special interest groups was not intended as a call for authoritarian solutions: his emphasis is on the need for import competition and free movement of capital to undercut the blocking power of interest groups. But it should be noted that the problem is exactly the one that the Argentine generals considered themselves to be called upon to answer.

The Southern Cone countries have been extreme examples of the frustrations of trying to deal with conflicting interest groups. It is not only a matter of traditional class conflict: factions within the labor movements of Argentina and Chile can be at their most ruthless in dealing with each other, capitalists dependent on protection have been perfectly willing to undermine the capacity to function of market systems, and all sides have proven ready to resort to direct violence. Without meaning to suggest any defense whatsoever of the vengeful character of the authoritarian responses, the prior conditions of these countries *had* reached degrees of interacting hostility difficult for any society to bear.

What course of action can possibly succeed when societies become caught in such tight corners between bitter group conflict and the forces making for violent repression? In the other Latin American countries which have not yet reached such degrees of conflict, what kinds of choices might help to reduce the dangers?

These concerns have been central for the economists associated with CIEPLAN, which has published a wealth of positive suggestions.[25] Their ability to deal in original ways with complex economic issues cutting across wide social concerns has much in common with Albert Hirschman's discussions related to these questions. Among the touchstones they share are a consistent concern for the social implications of economic policies, and an emphasis on a return toward industrial growth, within a vision of relatively elastic possibilities for response on the side of production. In his recent writing on these issues Hirschman has added discussion of a role for periods of "antagonistic growth," in which particular groups advance their objectives at real cost to opposing interests, normally followed by years in which the injured groups recover the initiative and redress the imbalance.[26] The discussion supports toleration of group conflict, in direct contrast to the Argentine vision of disciplining "a society made sick by years of mismanagment." His argument is as always on the more humane side. But as developed so far it leaves open some troublesome questions.

On one level, recognition of the possibilities of growth in "antagonistic" cycles could help lead away from dangerous appeals for repression in the name of necessary discipline and for radical social restructuring to eliminate the strength of competing groups. By calling attention to the ways in which democracies manage to survive and advance, going through pro-labor or pro-expansion swings for a time and then back to caution or pro-business periods when the balance of public preferences changes, the concept clarifies the healthy function of imbalance and reaction. But it seems to presume that the winning side will not change the rules and stop the election process, or destroy the economic base of the opposition, or rule particular people and ideas out of the competition. It presumes a healthy democracy in the first place, with respect for limits. In such a context group conflicts are often likely to be constructive. But the idea of desirability needs more boundaries. A goal of avoiding breakdown and repression requires that the degree, or character, of group conflict be held within safe limits. Imbalances need to be restrained. That is true for unbalanced growth in an economic sense and equally true for economic conflict which aggravates social tensions. Latin America might have avoided the brutalities of the repressive regimes if the societies had been able to moderate group conflict in the first place.

Historically, the upper income groups usually dominant before the 1930s did not hesitate to step on the poor, and by doing so they helped build up profound antagonism to the kinds of market systems identified with extreme inequalities. The first labor-oriented government of the postwar period, that of Perón in Argentina, proved to be just as extreme in the opposite direction in its attack on incomes of landowner-exporters, stimulating a process of ever more violent conflict. In one period, the second half of the 1960s, it seemed briefly possible that Argentina might break out of the impasse: a conservative government finally did manage to put together a coherent growth strategy, including export promotion, some protection, wage and price control, and enough monetary expansion to favor investment but not so much as to provoke inflation. That approach almost pulled the economy out of its prolonged morass.[27] But the conservative side could not resist using controls over wages to force them down in real terms, setting off the fierce labor upheaval which led shortly afterwards to the return of Perón, and shortly after that to the nightmare reaction to the breakdown under the Peróns.[28] The Argentine experience has been supremely antagonistic, but not in the sense of healthy swings between civilized kinds of imbalance. We need clearer distinctions between (a) desirable group conflict of the kind Hirschman means, and (b) the kind of social warfare which could, unhappily, be fostered by economic policies seen as understandable parts of a necessarily conflicting process.

Growth within a non-repressive framework in Latin American conditions probably requires conscious effort to bend economic policies in directions which reduce group conflict. That may at times mean sacrificing efficiency. To insist on dominance of efficiency criteria and of macroeconomic restraint over any compromises lessening social conflict is at least as dangerous as forgetting about them. Much as Hirschman's concept seems problematic for Latin American conditions, Harberger's defense of the economic policies of the repressive regimes raises serious doubt. He is right that the individual economic policies adopted by the repressive regimes have been used within stable democratic societies in the North. But that does not mean that they have the same consequences. There are several reasons why they might be more dangerous for democracy in the South than in the North: (1) differences in the objective characteristics of the economies; (2) differences between the carefully limited reliance on market forces in the northern democracies and the belligerent extremes imposed in the Southern Cone, and (3) differences in the strength of democratic institutions.

The major difference between Latin America and northern democracies with respect to the consequences of market forces is that in much of Latin America they foster extreme inequality and leave high shares of the population almost entirely out of the gains of growth, while in the North they have for the most part been consistent with at least stable degrees of inequality and with increasing real incomes for practically everyone. If an economic system provides gains to the majority of the population it has a high chance of being protected by all sides in freely elective political systems. If it concentrates the gains on a minority then either the majority has to be kept in ignorance of what is going on or, if it becomes aware, the system has to be crushed as a political force.

The second special factor in Latin American experience which has linked insistence on efficiency principles to destruction of democratic protections has been the intensity or *degree* of the changes in this direction. The Chilean military government could have promoted greater industrialization and industrial employment at the same time as it was sweeping away the tangle of distortions adverse for economic growth. It could have moderated the loss of output and employment in 1974–75 and again in 1981–83 with some elements of fiscal stimulus. It could with less inegalitarian changes in taxation and public services have avoided the glaring contrast between falling consumption for the poor and increasing consumption by the higher income groups.[29] Actions to moderate such extremes might have cost something in terms of lost efficiency but it is hard to be enthusiastic about any conception of efficiency which has the effect over a full decade of reducing industrial production, employment, and the real income of the poor.[30]

The third special factor distinguishing Latin America from the North in terms of the social consequences of economic policies is the relative weakness of the former's democratic institutions. Economists in the North have strongly entrenched habits of criticizing the ways in which politicians give in to special interests. We do not often stop to ask if such criticisms imply a fundamental distrust of democracy itself; we can under normal conditions take for granted that our own structure of protection for personal freedoms is firmly established. That assumption is not valid in Latin America. Long-continued concentration of wealth and privilege on one side, fearful of limitations likely to be imposed by majority preferences, and bitter resentment on the other side because the cards are stacked against them, greatly reduce the base of public support for democratic institutions. When that part of the informed population which can influence events hears constantly from the outside world, and perhaps especially from its own younger technicians, that popular preferences need to be kept in check for any successful economic management, the remaining core of patience for the negotiation and compromise needed for democracy is seriously undermined.[31]

IV. Two Suggestions for Making the Odds Less Fearsome

Questions of balance between economic stimulation and constraint closely parallel conflicts between tolerance for inflation and for competing groups as opposed to insistence on efficiency and social order. These would not be such eternal questions if there were any compelling, universally applicable, answer to them. Since there isn't, it might at least be of some help to make two suggestions directed to the particular context of contemporary Latin America.

The first concerns a distinction running through the preceding discussion between appropriate policies for societies which have become seriously handicapped by distortions of the system of production and by internal group conflict, as in Brazil and the Southern Cone, and societies which have not as yet gone to such extremes. Balances between the side of emphasis on stimulation and toleration of inflation, and the side of greater concern for economic constraints, probably should differ between the two groups. For the first, existing tensions are almost bound to be explosive if too much stress is placed on eliminating inflation and on institutional restructuring guided mainly by efficiency criteria. For the other countries, safety might lie more on the side of traditional restraints, paying closer attention to efficiency criteria and macroeconomic balance, so that they may avoid becoming too much like the first group.

The second suggestion is applicable to both sets of countries. It is to avoid placing all the burden of necessary downward adjustments on any one group—whether agriculture or urban labor or industrialists

—and to avoid using institutional changes to force drastic reductions in the real income of any one group for the sake of raising others. Such guidelines would go counter to at least some of the possible implications of Hirschman's "antagonistic growth." It would preclude both Peronist wage and agricultural policies and a Pinochet-type repression of workers in favor of property owners, both of which either demand a totalitarian system in the first place or greatly increase the odds in favor of violent reaction. It could conflict with efficiency criteria when prices or wages have been arbitrarily set too low or moved too high in the first place.

Much of the strain in Latin American experience has been related to efforts to get out of prior distortions of prices, wages, and the structure of production. Governments concerned with efficiency and ability to export must do something to offset these conditions. But there are many ways to go about it. Most of the technical criticisms of the economic policies followed in early postwar Latin America were justified and were being heard. Many countries shifted over from extremes of protection toward more export promotion, from arbitrary wage setting in the industrial sector toward wage policies more nearly related to output growth, and from negative to more positive policies toward agriculture. Reforms within democratic systems necessarily involve compromises to moderate negative impacts on particular groups. The Colombian style has been to reduce protection gradually, in the context of progressively higher prices for foreign exchange, and in most years also in the context of adequate liquidity and rising aggregate demand. But the authoritarian regimes in Brazil from 1964 and the Southern Cone in the 1970s all started with drastic reductions of real wages and a wide range of institutional changes favorable for property owners. They persecuted the leaders of labor and peasant groups and went a long way toward elimination of the groups themselves. That kind of strategy is unlikely ever to be compatible with democracy.

V. Conclusions

The concepts of linkages and of antagonistic growth, and of inflation as a possible safety valve reducing social tensions, all share a wonderful quality of releasing fixed ideas about necessary constraints. They counteract a built-in tendency in economic analysis to establish firm boundaries for the sake of reaching firm conclusions, short-circuiting the infinite complexities of reality. They exemplify what

Basil Willey considered to be the kind of explanation unduly neglected in the modern world and therefore the most valuable—rising above mechanical connections to illuminate essence and purpose. And they share the problems of all such open-ended thought: they invite a host of diculties if taken as sucient guides.

At the same time as they free ideas which conventional economic principles would foreclose, they become possible rationalizations for costly mistakes which those principles might have prevented. What we need is not a choice between the innovative and the constraining visions but ways to use both of them, sometimes more that of free-moving stimulation and sometimes more that of restraint. Which side more under what conditions? That is a never-ending question to examine in the context of particular countries and periods. The main suggestions here are as follows: (1) Never apply linkages as a guide to action without asking both what the costs are and what goals are intended; linkages are vital facts to explore but they can embody negative as well as positive values. (2) Acceptance of inflation as a social safety valve may often be desirable in countries as tied up by distorted structures of production and internal conflict as Brazil and the Southern Cone have been, both because the costs of confrontation are greater and because under such conditions inflation may have little to do with objective limits on productive capacity, but it is likely to be unhealthy medicine in countries under less intense strain in the first place; it can intensify conflict just as easily as moderate it. (3) The concept of antagonistic growth could help counteract a dangerous sense that authoritarian surgery is needed to clean out quarrelsome interest groups, or might instead be used to defend economic policies which aggravate social conflict by making the advance of one side dependent on pulling down everyone else. I hope that Hirschman will develop the concept further; no one else is as likely to turn it in ways which are both constructive and unexpected.

The fundamental question intended here might be seen as a three-way tangle of alliances rather than as a two-way conflict between stimulation and restraint. The third side of the picture is the Southern Cone style of resolving conflicts in favor of orthodox economic policy by recourse to direct repression. If conventional demands to respect economic constraints shade into alliance with this third way the social costs will be incalculable. To escape that third way requires instead a coalition between the first two, seeking a kind of moving imbalance which rises above conventional restraints but keeps them constantly in sight.

NOTES

1. Thanks are due to all the participants in the Hirschman conference who registered objections to the original version of this essay; to Albert Hirschman for his unmatchably civilized reply to my doubts about some of his ideas; to Lee Alston, Henry Bruton, Paul Clark, and Michael McPherson at Williams College; and most especially to Rebecca Scott for her incisive criticism of a point which I consider to be crucial.

2. Basil Willey, *The Seventeenth Century Background* (London: Chatto and Windus, 1934).

3. This is a constant feature of Hirschman's writing but it comes out with exceptional clarity and force in his recent statement, "Against Parsimony: Three Easy Ways of Complicating Some Categories of Economic Discourse," *American Economic Review* (May 1984), 89–96.

4. This concept is introduced and explained in Albert O. Hirschman, "A Dissenter's Confession: *The Strategy of Economic Development* Revisited," World Bank, forthcoming.

5. Albert O. Hirschman, *The Strategy of Economic Development* (New Haven: Yale, 1958) and "Dissenter's Confession"; W. Arthur Lewis, "Economic Development with Unlimited Supplies of Labour," *Manchester School* 22, (1954) 139–91, and *The Theory of Economic Growth* (Homewood, Illinois: Richard D. Irwin, 1955); Ragnar Nurkse, *Problems of Capital Formation in Underdevelped Countries* (New York: Oxford University Press, 1955); Raúl Prebisch, *The Economic Development of Latin America and its Principal Problems* (New York: United Nations, 1950), and *Towards a Dynamic Development Policy for Latin America* (New York: United Nations, 1963).

6. Hirschman, *Strategy,* 101.

7. Hirschman, "Dissenter's Confession."

8. John Sheahan, "Market-oriented Economic Policies and Political Repression in Latin America," *Economic Development and Cultural Change,* 28 (1980), 267–91.

9. Guillermo O'Donnell, *Modernization and Bureaucratic-Authoritarianism, Studies in South American Politics* (Berkeley: University of California, Institute of International Studies, 1973). The same questions are analyzed from many different angles by O'Donnell and others in David Collier, ed., *The New Authoritarianism in Latin America* (Princeton: Princeton University Press, 1979).

10. Carlos Díaz-Alejandro, "Open Economy, Closed Polity?" in D. Tussie, ed., *Latin America in the World Economy* (London: Gower, 1983).

11. For the decade of the 1960s Brazil and Uruguay had the region's highest average rates of increase in the cost of living, at forty-four percent, Chile was next at twenty-eight percent, and Argentina was fourth with a rate brought down to fifteen percent by a period of intense restraint from 1966 to 1969 IMF, *International Financial Statistics, 1983 Yearbook.*

12. Albert O. Hirschman, "The Turn to Authoritarianism in Latin America and the Search for its Economic Determinants," and "The Social and Political Matrix of Inflation: Elaborations on Latin American Experience," in Hirschman, *Essays in Trespassing, Economics to Politics and Beyond* (Cambridge and New York: Cambridge University Press, 1981).

13. Albert Fishlow, "Reflections on Post-1964 Economic Policy in Brazil," in Alfred Stepan, ed., *Authoritarian Brazil* (New Haven: Yale, 1973).

14. Alejandro Foxley, *Latin American Experiments in Neo-conservative Economics* (Berkeley: University of California, 1983).

15. Ricardo Ffrench-Davis, *Políticas económicas en Chile, 1952–1970.* Santiago: Centro de Estudios de Planificación Nacional, Ediciones Nueva Universidad.

16. Miguel Urrutia, "Winners and Losers in Colombia's Recent Growth Experience," World Bank research report, July 1981.

17. Sheahan, "Market-oriented Economic Policies"; R. Albert Berry, ed., *Essays on Industrialization in Colombia* (Tempe: Arizona State, 1983); Berry and Francisco Thoumi, chapters 10 and 11 in Berry, Ronald Hellman, and Mauricio Solaún, eds., *Politics of Compromise* (New Brunswick: Transaction Books, 1980); Franciso Thoumi, "International Trade Strategies, Employment, and Income Distribution in Colombia," in Anne O. Krueger et al., *Trade and Employment in Developing Countries* (Chicago: Chicago University Press, 1981), 135–79.

18. The quotation is from the title of Adolfo Canitrot (1980), "Discipline as the Central Objective of Economic Policy: an Essay on the Economic Programme of the Argentine Government Since 1976," *World Development* 8 (1980), 913–28.

19. Canitrot, "Discipline," 916.

20. Alejandro Foxley, *Latin American Experiments,* and "Stabilization Policies and Their Effects on Employment and Income Distribution: A Latin American Perspective," in William R. Cline, and Sidney Weintraub, eds., *Economic Stabilization in Developing Countries* (Washington: The Brookings Institution, 1981), 191–225.

21. Alejandro Foxley, "Cinco Lecciones de la crisis actual," *Colección estudios CIEPLAN,* no. 8, (julio 1982), 161–71.

22. Arnold Harberger, "Comment" on Foxley, in Cline and Weintraub, 229.

23. Oscar Munoz, "Hacia una nueva industrialización: elementos de una estrategia de desarrollo para la democracia," *Apuntes CIEPLAN,* no. 33 (marzo 1982).

24. Mancur Olson, *The Rise and Fall of Nations* (New Haven: Yale, 1983).

25. These issues are treated in practically every issue of *Colección estudios CIEPLAN,* and have been brought together in Foxley et al, *Reconstrucción Económica Para la Democracia* (Santiago: CIEPLAN, 1983).

26. Hirschman, "Dissenter's Confession."

27. Richard Mallon and Juan Sourouille, *Economic Policy Making in*

a Conflict Society: the Argentine Case (Cambridge: Harvard University Press, 1955).

28. Canitrot; Sheahan, "Early Industrialization and Violent Reaction: Argentina and Brazil," Institute of Development Studies, University of Sussex, Discussion Paper no. 126, 1982; Juan Carlos Torres, "El movimiento laboral en Argentina: 1955–76—de la exclusión a la participación en el poder," in Jean Carrière, ed., *Industrialization and the State in Latin America* (Amsterdam: Center for Latin American Research and Documentation, 1979).

29. René Cortázar, "Distribución del ingreso, empleo, y remuneraciones en Chile, 1970–78," *Colección estudios CIEPLAN,* no. 3 (junio 1980), 5–24.

30. Foxley, *Latin American Experiments,* Oscar Muñoz, "Crecimento y desequilibrios en una economía abierta: el caso chileno, 1976–81, *Colección estudios CIEPLAN,* no. 8 (julio 1982), 19–41.

31. Hirschman, *Essays in Trespassing,* 113–14.

After Authoritarianism: Political Alternatives[1]

Alejandro Foxley

I. Introduction

In a recent work in which he attempts to bring together the central themes of his vast work, Albert Hirschman introduces the concept of "Antagonistic Development." In so doing, the originator of the theory of unbalanced growth closely examines the conflicting and potentially destructive nature of the process of development. In particular, Hirschman examines clashes between various sectors which lead to a worsening of overall economic conditions; a situation he describes as "a negative sum game" (Hirschman 1963).

Applying this concept to the political sphere, Hirschman analyzes a pluralistic democracy in which two political parties alternately apply programs which are mutually antagonistic. In political affairs, he asserts, as in economic development, negative sum games can raise the level of antagonism and increase the tendency to look for "radical solutions, such as putting an end to the destructive struggle between political parties" (Hirschman 1984).

In earlier work, Hirschman explored factors which would explain the transition from antagonistic development to authoritarian politics in Latin America (Hirschman 1981a), and outlined three variables which help explain the collapse of democracies in this part of the world. The first condition relates to the tendency of policymakers not to defer to economic constraints when designing economic policies. This omission results in huge economic imbalances. This was particularly true during certain episodes of import substitution industrialization (ISI). The second condition arises in intellectual processes in Latin America which have frequently been characterized by a high propensity towards "escalation" in diagnosis and in solutions when faced with difficult problems of economic growth. This escalation in "fundamental remedies" brings on a confrontation between alternative solutions that tend to be strongly ideological, mutually exclusive and characterized by continued recourse to "global solutions" calling for the total replacement of the existing economic system.[2]

A third characteristic of antagonistic development and its eventual catastrophic outcome, results from the contradictory and partially superposed relation between what Hirschman calls the entrepreneurial function (which by emphasizing accumulation increases inequality) and the always latent inclination of an unequal society to favor reforms that would alter this tendency in favor of a more equal society (Hirschman 1981a). The premature "breaking in" of the reformist cycle limits the possibilities of accumulation in the economy, affecting negatively its development and growth.

When taken together, these tensions and contradictions in the process of development help explain, at least in part, "the political catastrophes that shook a number of third world countries since the 1970s" (Hirschman 1981b) and caused great confusion among those economists and politicians who believed firmly in economic development as a stabilizing factor in both social systems and democratic politics.

The economists' lack of attention to development processes that are increasingly antagonistic and polarized has been somewhat compensated by valuable contributions by political scientists (Dahl 1982). But the connections between political, economic and ideological aspects of the collapse of democracy have not been well explored, with the exception of work by O'Donnell (1983) and by Hirschman himself.

This paper will study some of these themes, in particular the processes of escalation and radicalization of political and economic solutions that have characterized preauthoritarian politics in various Latin American countries. As Hirschman points out, these processes are directly related to the high propensity of these countries to embark on political experiments. What has been the interrelation between ideological escalation and the high propensity to undertake political experiments? The first section of the paper will explore this theme from a very personal perspective: that of an observer and participant in these processes during the 1970s in Chile. I will attempt to describe, starting from an almost subjective perception, the processes of ideological escalation in Chile. Thus, what follows necessarily represents a partial view of the problem. It also involves a profound critique of the connection between politics and forms of intellectual reflection in Latin America that has sometimes contributed inadvertently to the weakening of democracy and its eventual substitution by brutally repressive political regimes in the area.

Three successive experiments which took place in Chile form a context within which this intellectual development and its relation to political projects can be studied: the Christian Democratic government of Frei, the Popular Unity (Unidad Popular—UP) experiment under Allende, and the military government that came to power in the 1973 coup. The paper will attempt to relate the lessons that can be learned from these past experiments to the present-day dilemmas and options regarding alternative forms for post-authoritarian politics. In the final sections of the paper, several possible alternatives for the democratization process in Chile will be examined in the context of a comparative analysis drawing mainly from European experience.

II. The Radicalization of Ideas and Its Relation to Antagonistic Development and Political Catastrophes

The recent history of Chile provides perhaps the best of all possible case studies through which to discuss the interrelation between ideological escalation and political polarization. During the last twenty years Chile has been subjected to successive social and political experiments that eventually led to a total crisis and collapse of the democratic institutions in the country (Garretón 1983).

The historical background for our story begins in the 1920s when Chilean society entered into an accelerated process of change in rebellion against the century-old domination of the power structures by a land-based oligarchy (Vial 1981). At this point in time, the "middle sectors" gradually emerged into political life and slowly began to displace the oligarchic sectors until, in 1937, a new political alliance was formed between the middle class and urban labor. Known as the Popular Front, the group consisted of the Radical party and Socialist and Communist parties. The Popular Front was an alliance which implied a class compromise directed towards joint participation in a national-democratic project. The central elements consisted of an economic program of industrialization and of political reform aimed at the gradual democratization of Chilean society (Cavarozzi 1975; Pinto 1973; Stevenson 1942).

The collapse of the Popular Front in 1947 and the subsequent failure of a populist attempt in 1952 produced a marked turning point in the ideology and programs of the Left, particularly the Socialist party. Later reinforced by the Cuban revolution, the ideology of the Left in Chile thus evolved from nationalistic and reformist, to orthodox revolutionary. This trend was evident as early as 1956 when the

Popular Action Front (Frente de Acción Popular—FRAP) was formed.
FRAP denounced the alliance of classes and re-oriented itself towards
"proletarian internationalism" (Moulian 1983).

The political Center also underwent significant changes. The old
Radical party, characterized by pragmatic and coalitionist tendencies,
was displaced by a Christian Democratic party (CDP) which was
ideologically rigid and alternativist. The CDP did not seek coalitions
but rather sought to make alliances unnecessary by trying to develop
its own broad popular support (Valenzuela 1978).

From this point on, the Left and the Center traveled parallel
paths, each attempting by way of a bitter political struggle to articulate
a hegemonic coalition to replace the previously dominant oligarchy.
With this background, we can attempt to analyze the subsequent
process of radicalization of ideology and programs experienced by
both political groups during the 1960s and early 1970s.

During those years, a powerful political class had consolidated.
This political class was able to penetrate and manipulate social organizations in order to take control not only of the state but of civil
society as well (Garretón 1983). Intellectuals exercised a powerful
influence over these processes, particularly in defining the agenda of
problems and solutions that the political elite would eventually propose to the country (Moulian 1983).

The process, similar to that described by Hirschman in "Journeys," was characterized by a disturbingly short path between the
conception of new ideas and their subsequent acceptance as fundamental parts of governmental programs, or in Hirschman's words,
by "exaggerated and hasty claims made to supply a basic explanation
and cure." In this way, a "pseudo-creative form of solving problems"
was invented (Hirschman 1983).

The political class, in particular that fraction that had acceded
to power, rapidly adopted these "solutions" and implemented them
with rigor and zeal. Thus, a succession of political "experiments"
applied by the state were unleashed upon society. The proposed solutions suffered from "an inflation in fundamental remedies" and
hence the proposed tasks were more and more global and antagonistic.
This culminated in the belief shared at the time by a large number
of intellectuals and politicians that the fundamental problems of Chilean development were to be found mainly in the prevailing structure
of private property, rather than in more conventional factors.

If discussions that prevailed in the second half of the 1960s are
followed, it will be seen that Chilean intellectuals at the time heatedly
debated alternative schemes for ownership of the means of production

which they saw as the determinant variable of the possibilities of future development for the country. While engaging in these discussions, intellectuals were decisively influencing the public agenda proposed to the country in the 1970s both by the political Left and by the political Center as the three "narrations" that follow will suggest.

The First Narration

The writings of T. Moulian, a well respected intellectual in the Chilean Left who participated actively during the Popular Unity government, aid in understanding this process. Moulian states that "up until the military coup of 1973, nationalization was considered to be one of the central axes of Popular Unity politics. The spontaneous response to the problems of Chilean development, from the left and even the center, was to increase the ability of the state to control the economy and transfer property towards the state." He goes on: "The area of social property had, during the period of the Popular Unity, an almost mythical significance: It represented for many (or most) the heart and soul of the revolutionary process. Programs emphasized development in this area as if it was thought that the only requirement for the existence of socialism was state ownership of the means of production, without any consideration of the possible negative ideological effects of the massive expropriation policies over the non-monopolistic bourgeois sectors" (Moulian 1983).

Moulian now asserts that this simplistic view flourished because "we nourished ourselves on a religious vision of politics which caused us to think of Marxism as the source of all knowledge . . . hypnotized by what we believed to be laws of revolutionary development: the rigid distinction between reform and revolution, the lack of confidence in gradual reform, the necessity to destroy the bourgeois state, the impossibility of capitalist development in a country of the periphery, and the need for political subordination of the middle sectors" (Moulian 1983). This *"rage de vouloir conclure"*[3] was supported by "an imitative and dependent manner of thinking that created habits of dogmatism by the neglect of empirical investigation, and by a tendency to repeat slogans or theories without concern for the specificity of historical events in Chile . . . Chile was thought to be equivalent to Russia—the capitalist development of Chile was discussed using the words of Lenin, more than in terms of its own specific history" (Moulian 1983).

Through the powerful intellectual influence of the most orthodox Marxism, public discussion in Chile was increasingly oriented towards the theme of property and expropriations. And, as Moulian maintains, this emphasis was characteristic not only of the Marxist Left, but of those political groups and intellectuals closely associated with the CDP as well.

The Second Narration

Even though Chilean Christian Democracy is usually identified with developmental reformism along the lines of the Alliance for Progress (which in fact predominated under the Frei Government), in truth, this political group had been searching since the mid–1960s for more radical approaches to ideology as well as to programs. As in the case of the Marxist Left, both diagnoses and propositions had a marked emphasis on property relationships. In part, this reflected the need to counter the theoretical paradigm of the Marxist Left. But it was also related to an ideological effort to give concrete meaning to the Christian "communitarian" philosophy that had characterized the Chilean Christian Democratic party since its inception, an effort crystalized in the idea of communitarian socialism. The second narration is a description of how these ideas were developed in the late 1960s.

The theory had two bases. The first involved accepting the diagnosis of the Left, namely, that the strong concentration of property in private hands severely limited the possibility of a more equal development. The second emphasized the need for a decentralized system of social property, making possible a more egalitarian economic development, along with the existence of political democracy.

During those years, intellectuals close to the Christian Democratic party, and later those who conducted the economic policy of the Popular Unity government, wrote extensively about socialism, democracy and decentralization. These discussions were reflected in a book that was somewhat pretentiously entitled *Chile, búsqueda de un nuevo socialismo* (Foxley 1971). As a result of the intellectual effort of many groups and research centers, the alternatives of decentralized socialism took shape. Self-managed socialism was incorporated into the Christian Democrats' platform during the presidential campaign of Radomiro Tomic in 1970. Later it became a point of reference in multiple negotiations at both the official party level and in parliament between the Popular Unity and Christian Democrats. The objective of these negotiations was to reach a compromise on the extent of and institutional framework for the expropriation policies that were at the core of the UP program.

Compromise was never reached. Self-management was discarded

as a reformist scheme by the UP parties and the statist, more centralized model prevailed. In retrospect, the elaboration of self-
management by the CDP was incomplete at best, and left serious
theoretical questions unresolved. For instance, when self-management
was proposed as "the" desirable system in terms of property relationships and as the specific form that workers' participation would take,
nothing was said about how the existing capitalist system in Chile
would evolve towards self-managed socialism.

In fact, the formulation of the self-management proposal was
strongly influenced by the Yugoslavian experience. But no proper
account was taken of the historical evidence indicating that in the
Yugoslav case, self-management came about only after a long transition period during which the means of production were integrally
expropriated by the state and maintained for years under centralized
state management. If the Yugoslavian experience was at all valid, it
showed that the centralized Soviet model seemed to be a prerequisite
for the establishment of self-management. Therefore, once power and
property were concentrated in government hands, only an enlightened
state would voluntarily transfer the factories to the workers.

On the other hand, historical experience also demonstrated that
at least in the case of Yugoslavia, self-management was imposed and
preserved through the existence of just one political party, the Communist party. A question thus arose. In the case of Chile, which was
a pluralistic democracy where multiple and antagonistic political and
ideological currents were constantly contesting for power, could self-
management actually be made to function? How could a Yugoslav-type
self-managed economic system be made compatible with pluralistic
democracy, which was also a key political objective? The solution we
proposed was simple enough. First, one had to accept the fact that
political pluralism meant also plurality in the forms of property ownership. This in turn implied the acceptance of a mixed economy
model instead of a purely self-managed one. Thus, we in fact avoided
the initial problem (how to transform capitalist property relations
into self-management) by postulating that the mixed economy would
only gradually evolve towards self-managed forms of property ownership, within the framework of a mixed economy.[4]

Inherent within this postulation was an inevitable series of consequences. First, as we know from comparative experience, the mere
announcement of a deep, albeit gradual, transformation in property
relationships tends to be perceived as a major threat by capitalist
sectors. The unavoidable result in Chile of the late 1960s was that
property owners radicalized their political positions and withdrew

resources from investment. Second, given this private sector reaction, obviously only the state could undertake investment since the self-managed sector was by then weak and rather marginal. In addition, financing the new public investment necessitated an increased tax burden on the private sector which, in turn forced a further retreat of private enterprise. This crowding out confirmed the capitalist sector's worst fears: that is, the inevitability of a systematic expansion of the state, once the self-management formula in a mixed-economy context was accepted.

The Socialist experiment of the Popular Unity began in this climate, where fundamental questions of property and the relations-of-production were disputed. And the disputes intensified. The increasingly volatile popular mobilizations served to reinforce the fears of the business sector, while the Popular Unity further radicalized its positions in order to maintain the support of the mobilized masses. By the middle of 1973, public property represented 70 percent of total assets in the industrial sector and 45 percent of all industrial production (Bitar 1979).

The Third Narration

In 1972 a group of thirty economists, influenced by ideas from the University of Chicago and supported by the anti-UP political Right, began to meet. These economists were motivated by a profound discontent with the course of political affairs and the socialist direction of the economic transformation. The third narration describes their impact in Chile after 1973.

By the end of 1972 these economists discussed ideas and authored documents for circulation among the most radicalized groups of the right, which had by that time begun to think in terms of a "military solution" to the problem of the Popular Unity experiment. They elaborated a diagnosis that was at first totally technocratic, as it concentrated on proposing how to re-establish the fundamental economic equilibrium which had been profoundly altered by the Socialist experiment. To do so, they argued, it was necessary to return to orthodox policies, including "sound" fiscal and monetary policies freeing up prices in order to ensure their allocative role, and opening the economy to free trade with the rest of the world. Theirs was a "neutral and technocratic" solution, applicable under any political system. This intellectual group filled a vacuum at that time and provided the ideas which would subsequently constitute the "program" of the military government at the time of the coup.

As is well known, upon taking power, the military junta suspended all political parties and organizations which had played major roles during the UP regime. Instead of the previous state of affairs that implied that *todo es político,* (everything is political), it was now stated that *todo es económico* (economics is everything). Not only did the military feel they had the self-imposed task of "cleaning up" politics and repressing social organizations but also of returning "rationality" to the market and re-establishing the basic economic equilibria. In so doing, they followed the suggestions previously elaborated by the "Chicago" economists. The latter would increasingly fill the key government positions.

The economic model began as a mere program of economic stabilization. As it was applied in a political vacuum with absolute state control over all social and political life, it soon began a subtle process of transformation. The economic goals became increasingly ambitious, especially with regard to the transformation of the country's economic structure. It was soon argued that the macroeconomic ills (inflation, balance of payment deficits, etc.) were ultimately due to an excessively large government sector. The "privatization" of more and more economic activities was proposed as a requirement for a revitalized economy. On the other hand, increasingly drastic and ambitious goals were set for a process of tariff reductions, so that full integration to "free" world trade would be achieved over a period of four years.

This process of structural change in the economy and of ideological escalation, which has been described elsewhere (Foxley 1983a), finds a receptive echo in both the Right and in the business community which supported the authoritarian regime. It was also well received in the military itself. The latter would again and again demonstrate a marked propensity for "overkill," not only in the political arena but also in the area of economic policies. Filled with "revolutionary zeal," the military was in fact attempting to eliminate all vestiges of socialism and Marxism in Chile through a curious blend of political repression and free-market ideas. The latter were embraced with truly religious fervor. The "new" economic truths were incessantly preached to the public through the media that was—with very few exceptions—controlled by a repressive state. Friedman was giving lectures on national television, as were many of the local Chicago boys. Harberger's press conferences were given the space usually reserved for visiting heads of state. Each of his words was used by the official press as an endorsement of Pinochet's economic policies. By these means, plus the fact that politics were not allowed to be discussed, Chicago economics became the official ideology of the regime.

To be sure, the process of indoctrination was not an easy one.

The difficulties were certainly compounded by the Chicago boys themselves because at one time they were talking about "closed-economy monetarism," then about "global monetarism," and the policy prescriptions resulting from both versions of the theory were at least partially opposed.[5] At one moment they were arguing for supply-side economics, the next for the "public choice" doctrines.

While this was happening, both the military and the business communities were making serious efforts to digest all these new doctrines that were thrown at them as scientific, immovable truths. This ideological paroxysm of the technocratic Right seemed to provide an answer for every question. When the economic model collapsed in 1981–82, advocates contended that the observed massive bankruptcies of firms were but a manifestation of the healthy effects of the free market as it improves the utilization of available resources. Thirty percent unemployment was thought to be caused by the still lingering effects of a labor market with less than perfectly flexible wages. The enormous balance of payments deficit, that would be equivalent to 21 percent of GDP in 1981, only reflected the spontaneous adaptation of the economy to the needed absorption of huge amounts of foreign capital. The availability of these foreign loans was thought to be, in fact, a confirmation of the model's success. The exorbitant domestic interest, between 30 and 40 percent in real terms, was nothing but a signal that a process of automatic adjustment in financial markets was in full operation. And most importantly, the slow reaction of the economy to the new free market stimuli only reflected the inherited irrationality of existing economic agents. The discipline of the free market, reinforced by the military, was the only force capable of inducing the rationality that was needed in order for the country and its economy to come out of the crisis and function as "the model" predicts.

But politics—suppressed for a while as a condition for the success of the neo-conservative transformation—came back with a vengeance. The suppression of politics eliminated social feedback. As a consequence, the economic crisis was worsening—without the government fully realizing it—to the point that the legitimacy of the military government was at stake. The government reacted by reaffirming the same economic policies, and increasing political repression to new, higher levels.[6]

III. The Alternatives for Post-Authoritarian Politics

Our narrations in the previous section are meant to illuminate from a subjective perspective, the nature of politics in the period that preceded the political disaster in Chile: the exacerbated antagonism and the extremely competitive polarization and radicalization of ideas that, when added together, produced the tragic and well-known outcome. In this section, we would like to explore the issue of the "quality" of politics in its various alternative forms.

To start with, we accept the fundamental lesson of our three narrations: an improved quality of politics requires a certain tuning up with society's real problems, which are not identical with problems as perceived by ideologized intellectuals. As several authors have pointed out (Touraine 1983; Garretón 1983), the Chilean political class utilized out-bidding and social mobilization as the principal instruments for increasing its quota of power and gaining control of the state. Politically-amplified, unrealistic demands were made upon the state while the manipulation of social organizations by political parties accentuated conflicts and polarized and politicized each and every level of society.

On the other hand, when there exists a political class which monopolizes all forms of intermediation between society and the state and shares with intellectuals the tendency for embracing utopian solutions, the need arises to allow for a wider representation of interests and participation in public decisions and to give a voice to the principal social actors. What are the possibilities for developing new forms of interaction between political parties, social organizations and the state so that the pattern of interaction helps in consolidating democracy and not the opposite?

These questions are quite broad and have received a good deal of attention from contemporary political science. Our objective here is not to repeat this discussion but rather to explore the options in the particular case of post-authoritarian Chile.

The Four Options

In order to analyze the alternative political options, a framework proposed by Schmitter (1982) will be modified and used here. The reason we chose this particular scheme is that it focuses not only on the state and the political parties—the focus of traditional politics in Chile—but it enlarges it to include as well the relationship between the corporate interests in society and the state and political parties.

It is our basic contention that the renewal of politics and a concurrent strengthening of democratic processes in Chile have to deal with the issue of interest intermediation and with the alternative channels by means of which labor and business organizations may represent their demands and participate in some key public decisions. On the other hand, concerted action may improve efficiency in decision-making and reinforce political stability, as European experience seems to show (Schmitter 1984).

Table 1 describes four alternatives. They are defined as a function of two main variables: the mode of interest representation—pluralist or corporatist;[7] and the process of policy formulation—statist (policies decided by government and imposed from above) or concerted policies (with participation of organized interest groups). Each of these alternatives can be related to concrete historical experience, particularly in post-war Europe. That is why our discussion, in what follows, will make continous reference to comparative historical analysis.

TABLE 1

Political Alternatives

		FORMATION OF PUBLIC POLICY	
		Statist	Concerted
Representation	Pluralist	1	4
of Interests	Corporatist	3	2

Alternative #1: Pluralism and Competitive Politics

The authoritarian experience generates in society a strong demand, not only to reconstruct politics and parties, but also for spaces which make possible the autonomous development of individuals and social movements. Political parties return to public life full of competitive vigor. In its naive version, free competition among parties is seen as having the same virtues that orthodox economists grant to the free market: it will eventually lead society towards an optimizing equilibrium. Parties compete with each other for the favor of the electorate, until hopefully a stable equilibrium is reached. Interest representation is pluralistic in the sense that any group can voice its demands in competition with others, but there are no established institutional mechanisms to process these demands or orchestrate decisions between corporate or social organizations and the state.

Post-Franco Spain appears to have followed this model. Even though the democratic regime there arose out of an initial and transitory pact—the pacts de la Moncloa—the political system rapidly evolved toward a system of highly competitive parties in which social organizations were increasingly fragmented (Linz 1981).

The homogeneity and "unity" imposed on social organizations by Franco gave way to multiple divisions during the first phase of democratic reconstruction in Spain. For example, at one point the workers' movement gave rise to twelve different national organizations. None of these confederations, however, was strong enough to constitute a valid spokesman for labor. On the other hand, political parties did not maintain institutional ties with social organizations. These factors combined led to a form of politics in which state action appears dissociated from the principal social and economic factors. The regime is pluralistic in the sense that it allows for the representation of multiple interests; and it is statist in the formulation of public policy. This corresponds to entry 1 in Table 1: decisions are taken by the government alone and are implemented from above, without the participation of groups affected by the policies.

It would be easy to speculate that this is a course that Chile could follow. In fact, the modest opening up of the political system in Chile after the national protests of 1983 permitted the partial and transitory reconstruction of the powerful Chilean "political class," which has always been extremely competitive. On the other hand, more than ten years of harsh repression of social organizations has inevitably led to a weak and divided labor movement, ineffectual business organizations and a virtually nonexistent peasant movement.

In keeping with our analysis under this scenario, we can project that this political class could again corner the spaces made available by the gradual opening, and penetrate social organizations with the intention of increasing its political power, until it is again in a position to take control of the state. In addition, if pre- and post-authoritarian electoral conduct is consistent, it is probable that the political scene would be characterized by three clearly differentiated blocks, with the Leninist revolutionary Left again advocating maximalist solutions, including massive expropriations. The traumatic memory of the recent past, refreshed by these radical positions, would probably initiate a new cycle of political polarization between the authoritarian Right and the more radical Left.

In this scenario the process of democratization would not bring about a stable political system. Rather, politics would be characterized by permanent instability and "the political game" could result in any of a number of outcomes. The wide range of possible outcomes would breed the same kind of uncertainty that rendered impossible the long-term survival of the previous democratic regime, and caused the military to intervene.

Alternative #2: Consociational Democracy

The precarious equilibrium of forces that characterizes post-authoritarian situations, with the always-present risk of reversion to authoritarianism, may act as a dissuasive factor against the development of the harshest forms of confrontation in post-authoritarian politics. The total crisis of society at the point when the regime is replaced forces people to face certain basic questions, such as the likelihood of democracy's survival after authoritarianism. On the other hand, the systematic abuse of basic rights under the military makes democracy appear more precious to thousands of citizens who see their rights threatened. For these reasons, a strong demand is likely to emerge for cooperation among parties and social groups, with the objective of reducing the probability of returning to authoritarian government.

Due to the fact that democracy only institutionalizes uncertainty (to use Przeworski's expression), tendencies develop in society that attempt to reduce uncertainty by regulating the results of the democratic process through pacts and alliances. A new theme emerges in these weak democracies: consociational pacts. They are perceived as a means of eliminating the rough edges from confrontation over ideology and over the mutually exclusive programs that are a feature in sharply segmented and polarized societies. The experiences of Holland and especially Austria in the postwar period seem pertinent in this context, as is the case of Colombia after "the violence" (Castles 1978; Stephens 1979; Wilde 1982).

In the Austrian consociational scheme, political-ideological conflicts are regulated by way of political pacts which involve the principal parties. Subordinate to these pacts, an understanding is structured between corporate organizations. Institutions representing business and labor negotiate with the government and even participate in the implementation of economic policy. Areas of negotiation and participation include incomes policy, modernization and expansion of industry, export strategies, etc.

The attractive feature of this scheme is that it appears to improve economic performance as well as to contribute to the "governability" of society (Schmitter 1984). The troublesome features are also obvious. By definition, these pacts exclude groups and sectors of society that are not formally organized. These may be large and, in many developing countries, they may even form the majority of the population.

The difficulties for a scheme such as this in Chile, or more generally in Latin America, are varied. The existences of weak and fragmented corporate organizations which represent only a small fraction of the labor force or of the producers is but one of the limitations of the scheme. On the other hand, if the consociational pact is conceived only as a means to avoid "internal war," it tends to reinforce the status quo, thus making it more difficult to advance towards the solution of the more fundamental problems of post-authoritarian society: the reincorporation of the marginalized sectors of the population and the acceleration of economic growth (Dos Santos and Grossi 1983).

In other words, the consociational pact fortifies the transition by reducing uncertainty. But it also excludes political sectors that are forced to operate outside the system (i.e., the revolutionary Left). These sectors capitalize on the demands of the discontent, gradually increasing their power and constituting a powerful opposition not controlled by the pact. In the end the military, which has the balance of power, sees this development as a threat and promotes actions to "protect" the democratic regime from the perceived threat. Almost inevitably, this leads to a "hardening" of the new democratic regime.

Does this *"democradura"*[8] (with an increasing emphasis on the "dura") represent a better option than the one previously analyzed (pluralistic and competitive, less certain of the possible outcomes but more democratic in the institutions controlling the political process)?

Without doubt, there is a complicated trade-off between these two options. The trade-off becomes even more complicated when one considers the economic limitations imposed by the heritage of the monetarist experiment and the low tolerance for error or poor performance implied by these limits. From this point of view, concerted action to achieve the most urgent economic goals—reconstruction of productive capacity, improved international competitiveness, increased employment, etc.—seems like a most useful instrument.

Alternative #3: Statist Corporatist with Limited Pluralism

A third alternative for post-authoritarian politics is a regime with marked class characteristics that would, therefore, seek the collaboration of just one sector (labor or industry, depending on the bent of the government) for the purpose of better achieving the policy objectives set by the state. This regime is characterized by partial representation of corporate interests and corresponds to a statist regime in terms of the formulation of policy. See entry 3 in Table 1.

Scenario 1: The Left-Wing Version

There are two alternative scenarios in which these characteristics would be present. Scenario 1 would be the following. If the initial process of democratization is arrived at as a consequence of a simultaneous crisis in both the economic model and in the political regime, then it is probable that the objective economic conditions will point in the direction of rather drastic and radical solutions. This may, in turn, generate serious political repercussions.

Let us illustrate the argument by drawing on recent Chilean experience. The economic crisis in Chile, after ten years of monetarism, has led to a forced government intervention into most banks, financial companies and many industries, in order to avoid their bankruptcy. The significance of the government-intervened sector's output relative to Chile's GDP is almost equivalent to the size of that of the nationalized sector according to Allende's plan in 1971, as shown by figures in Table 2.[9]

TABLE 2

Area of Social Property in 1971 (approx.)
and Government Intervened Firms in 1982

	APPROXIMATE – 1971	INTERVENED – 1982
	% of Sector Value Added	% of Sector Value Added
Industry	19.6	9.6
Construction	–	0.8
Transportation	18.8	9.2
Commerce	14.3	14.9
Financial	13.8	34.3
Services	–	–
Total	9.3	8.6

What stands out in Table 2 is that after ten years of the most radical privatizing free-market experiment, the erroneous conception of economic policy forced the conservative government of Pinochet to intervene a percentage of production activities similar to that which had been planned by the socialist government of the Unidad Popular.

This gigantic failure has a devastating effect on public opinion. The neo-conservative ideology becomes discredited. The economic failure predisposes the general public towards a total change in public policy. On the one hand the material and even legal conditions for major socialization of the means of production and financial activities are now present, since so many bankrupt firms are de facto in government hands. Because of the failure of the private enterprise model, nationalization might appear again as a legitimate option.

What type of regime would be ready to take up this option and use it to its full advantage, nationalizing all of the intervened sector? It would probably be a leftist statist regime of the kind that the military sought to eradicate in 1973. Polarized economic and political conditions do exist in 1985's Chile to the extent that a radical swing to the left after democratization is a not unlikely possibility, given the enormous failure of Pinochet's policies.

The nature of the regime, in terms of Table 1, would be statist as far as policy formulation is concerned, with participation in policy implementation limited to government-supporting labor organizations.[10] The scheme would polarize the political spectrum further, perhaps pushing the business sector more to the right. A relapse into authoritarian solutions would not be impossible under these circumstances.

A Second Alternative Scenario: The Center-Right Coalition

An alternative—the opposite of that just described, yet sharing the statist character of public policymaking and partial corporative representation—would consist of a right-of-center government that would correspond to the typical liberalizing coalition observed in several processes of transition to democracy (Kaufman 1980; Prezworski 1984).

With regard to interest representation, the regime would tend to seek mechanisms for the participation of the business sector, while excluding workers' organizations, and would retain the centralized ability to define and implement public policy from above. This governmental form contains elements of restricted pluralism and would be situated between entries 3 and 4 in Table 1. Typical examples include Chile's rightist governments, such as Alessandri's, and the center-right governments of the 5th Republic in France.

The French case is especially illuminating. France, like Chile, has a long tradition of centralized state administration and of workers' confederations which are divided along ideological lines and which cannot represent workers as a whole. Industrial organizations in both countries are weak, even though they do possess a marked capacity to mobilize when threatened by adverse political coalitions. Both political systems are characterized by a multiplicity of parties with strong ideological differences, and a Marxist Left which represents at least one-third of the electorate.

Beginning with the government of DeGaulle, the center-right coalition secured control of a stable electoral majority for more than twenty years. The state maintained strong control, while at the same time attempting to assure coherent policies and improved implementation of programs by way of informal participation from representatives of business organizations and from executives from the largest public firms (Flanagan, Soskice, and Ullman 1983; Lehmbruch 1982). Formal organizations such as a "Social and Economic Council," modernization committees, and hundreds of smaller committees and councils functioned with the representation of both the private sector and public firms and institutions. In DeGaulle's France, however, there was no scheme for delegating authority to corporate organizations as in the better known cases of concerted action observed in the Scandinavian countries, and in Holland, Austria, and Switzerland.

Perhaps the most illuminating mechanisms in the French case were the "Contrats de Programme"—production agreements between the state and leading private firms. These were often secret agreements between the government and big firms. For example, a leading enterprise agreed to pursue technology improvements and better methods of production as proposed by the government. The firm also agreed to help apply the government's incomes policy—if a firm conceded salary increases greater than the government's goals, then price controls would be imposed on the enterprise. As a quid pro quo, the firm had access to preferential and guaranteed state subsidized credit; the government and public firms would purchase needed inputs from that firm and not from others. Selected enterprises could freely manipulate prices to increase profits, as long as they were compatible with the government's plans for modernization and expansion (Flanagan, Soskice and Ullman 1983). This arrangement signified the institutionalization of a close corporate alliance between a strong state and a private sector that adhered to the state's plans in exchange for a privileged status which implied the protection of its economic interest.

Labor organizations were excluded from the agreements. The rightist government attempted to discipline unions by adopting recessionary policies and indirectly controlling salaries through leading firms in each sector. In addition, government deliberately pursued a strategy of ignoring unions' demands until accumulated problems exploded in a wave of strikes. After a prudent waiting period, the government increased nominal salaries only to follow with monetary expansion and devaluation of the franc. The result was that wage increases were eaten up by higher price rises (Flanagan, Soskice and Ullman 1983).

This type of government and corporate organizational relationship corresponds roughly to that in Chile during the Alessandri administration in the last half of the 1950s.

Alternative #4: Concerted Policies in a Pluralist Framework

The fourth alternative, which corresponds to Box 4 in Table 1, allows for the coexistence of a pluralist system of interest representation with informal but systematic participation of corporate organizations—both labor and business—in selected areas of governmental decisions.

Perhaps the best illustration of how this alternative works is given by Italy in the 1970s and 1980s. In the last decades, Italy has evolved from a competitive and pluralistic system (which corresponds to entry 1 in Table 1) towards an alternative which is best represented by entry 4 in the same table. Beginning with the emergence of center-left coalitions, a gradual process of non-institutionalized informal consultations with labor organizations, and in other cases with business organizations, was initiated. These organizations were usually consulted regarding key legislative initiatives and government actions.

The coalition between a multi-class Christian Democratic party, with an electorate covering a wide spectrum of Italy's social structure, and a Socialist party in competition on the left with the Communist party, provided the political conditions for the development of concerted action, particularly between the key labor organizations and the government.

The participation of labor organizations evolved gradually. Beginning with the transfer of majority control of the board of Social Security Institutions to labor representatives, it continued with labor incorporation into numerous local and national committees that sketch out specific sectorial and regional policies, including participation in management of public firms (Regini 1982; Flanagan, Soskice and Ullman 1983).

The inclusion of labor organizations in the state's decision-making was facilitated by the economic crisis that Italy faced in the 1970s. This forced the labor unions to focus not only on labor-related issues, but more and more on global economic problems: industrial revitalization, strategies to reduce unemployment in general and especially among the young, retraining of permanently displaced workers,

international competitiveness of Italian industry, and the need to
increase investment, especially in the south. All of these themes
appeared in negotiations between the labor confederations and the
government during the late 1970s.

A practical result of consultations with labor seems to have been
that they accepted policies which implied a reduction in living standards, in exchange for a future perspective promising an improved
economy through higher investment and increased international competitiveness of Italian industry. These arrangements have become
increasingly important in Italy during the 1980s and they helped
explain that country's notorious ability to recover from major political
and economic crises.

It must be stressed that, in the context of our discussion here,
the Italian system's versatility and its ability to adjust to changing
conditions are particularly attractive features that are not abundant
in most of Latin America. Rather, rigid ideological confrontations
and antagonistic politics seem to have characterized the recent past,
at least in the Southern Cone of Latin America. Even though the
Italian case has been described by some as one of "dismal politics,"
it is not at all dismal when compared to the way politics has been
conducted in Latin America.

Perhaps an approximation to the Italian model could be found
in the experience of the Popular Front in Chile. The Front represented
a broad center-left coalition which included the Radical, Socialist and
Communist parties; it governed from 1938 until 1947. Politically, this
was a pluralist scheme with participation by business and worker
organizations on certain public decisions. Strictly speaking, the former
had a more significant participation, particularly on the boards of all
major public corporations. Representation of labor organizations was
minimal. Their demands were mainly voiced through leftist parties
in Parliament, where they pushed for changes in social legislation and
achieved an increase in social service for workers. The emergence of
a welfare state and the gradual democratization of Chilean society,
while a mode of capitalist development was retained, were the substantive contents of the class compromise represented by the Popular
Front.

IV. Tendencies and Perspectives

Although the previous section explored some alternative forms
of political life after authoritarianism in Chile, almost no reference
was made to the probability of occurrence of any one of these alter-

natives. This will depend on the likely behavior of the respective political forces, social actors, and, if we accept the argument presented in the first section of this paper, the role played by the intellectual-politicians in the definition of the tasks and agenda that post-authoritarian society imposes on itself. What is clear at this point about the Chilean case is that the future behavior of the pertinent forces and actors cannot be accurately predicted. For this reason it is only possible to suggest some of the pieces of the complicated mosaic that is beginning to form.

Twelve years after the military coup, the political class shows some signs of taking up politics where it left off: with bitter internal conflict where each group seeks to maximize its own short-term gains, without sufficient considerations for the long-term stability of the democratic system. Within this scheme there is a premium placed on the ability of a group to differentiate itself from all others. According to this fiercely competitive logic, the more similarities there are between the programs proposed by two groups, the more they try artificially to differentiate from each other, a goal often achieved by radicalizing one's own party positions. Outbidding becomes the name of the game. This already occurred in Chile during the 1960s. When the CDP took up the banners of agrarian reform and the nationalization of copper, the Popular Unity reacted by radicalizing its positions on these issues and introducing new themes, such as the need to expropriate a significant fraction of industry. We will call this principle of political behavior "the risk of excessive coincidence." The result, when it is in operation, is that long-term political agreements are difficult to achieve.

Of course, ex-ante programmatic coincidences tend to become highly significant in the post-authoritarian phase. Thus, the economic crisis in Chile—characterized by unemployment rates of 30 percent of the labor force, by per-capita output levels in 1983 equivalent to those already achieved in 1966, by the destruction of one out of seven industries and by an external debt per capita that duplicates the average for Latin America—generates a wide consensus over what was wrong with the monetarist model and what now needs to be done (Foxley 1983 b).

Political and social conditions contribute to this convergence of proposed programs. After suffering political repression from the authoritarian state, political parties in the opposition place a new value on the need to strengthen civil society so that respect for human rights is ensured, and autonomous spaces for social movements are possible. There is also agreement on the need to decentralize decision-making in order to avoid the recurrence of authoritarian forms of centralized government and hence to procure the development of truly participatory democracy (Pinto 1983).

These coincidences, already evident within the so-called "Alianza democrática," a center-left coalition established in 1983, do not ensure non-competitive behavior. In fact, one can already observe a tendency towards political differentiation even within this coalition.

Another possible tendency of Chilean politics has already been described in alternative 3 of Table 1. The collapse of the financial system and the involuntary intervention of a large number of productive enterprises by the authoritarian state in Chile as a result of the failure of monetarist economics, creates structural conditions which make maximalist expropriation schemes a possibility. This is reinforced by the influence of events on the international scene. Just as the Cuban revolution had a strong, radicalizing effect on the Chilean Socialist party during the 1960s, the Communist party now absorbs and adopts as its own another imported scheme—that of the Nicaraguan Revolution. Thus, objective conditions, which favor statism in the economic sphere, and the Sandinista ideology provide a political framework which legitimizes the thesis, new to the Communist party, of popular insurrection and violence. An extreme left coalition (the Popular Democratic Movement) is the instrument created by the Communist party as an answer to the challenge posed by the reformist Alianza democrática. The Popular Democratic Movement seeks to outflank the opposition on the left.

This Communist party strategy induces the expected response from the Right which is aligned with the military regime—a more cautious advancement towards liberalization is proposed, as well as a more rigorous definition of what constitutes "acceptable" political behavior, before steps towards a "protected" democracy can be taken.

The process of liberalization becomes even more difficult to accept for the Right, given the tremendous confusion into which it falls after the unexpected failure of the neo-conservative economic model. The "explanations" for the failure given by the Chicago technocrats are not convincing. Businessmen begin looking for alternative economic schemes. One that seems attractive to a private sector in crisis is that represented by the Gaullist model. Current economic policies in Chile follow roughly this pattern.[11] This model—close cooperation between government and largest firms—has the advantage of permitting the Right to recover from the losses caused by the economic crisis, while allowing it to gain time in order to position itself within any new democratic institutionalization designed from above by the state.

Perhaps the most promising tendency in the political spectrum of Chile, however, is that of a widely based, center-left coalition, such as Alianza democrática. But, even this type of coalition will be faced with some considerable challenges: a need to overcome the competition for ideological-programmatic differentiation among the principal components of the coalition; a need for improved interaction with and representation of corporatist organizations (especially labor organizations); the necessity to redirect each group's maximization of short-term political interests toward long-term cooperation; and the need to enhance the capacity to respond more to society's real demands than to those of its political and intellectual elites.

We conclude by going back to a central theme throughout this paper: that the structural weakness of the Chilean economy, the errors of pre-authoritarian policies, and the deficiencies in political institutions are only partial explanations of Chile's inability to sustain a democracy and of the military's lengthy stay in power. To some extent, the crisis of the democratic regime in Chile is also related to the constitution of a self-sufficient political class which exacerbated its own interests and radicalized itself under the influence of important intellectual groups that ended up rather removed from the "real agenda" of society's problems.

Perhaps a fundamental first step towards the reconstruction of a truly democratic and durable political system in Chile should be the critical self-examination by these actors—politicians and intellectuals alike—of the role they played in Chile's recent past.

NOTES

1. This paper was prepared for the conference on "Economic Development and Democracy," in honor of Albert Hirschman, sponsored by the Kellogg Institute of the University of Notre Dame, April 1984. The author wishes to thank various colleagues from CIEPLAN and Paul Drake, Albert Hirschman, Guillermo O'Donnell, and Alex Wilde for their helpful comments. The translation from Spanish was done by J. Kennedy and the editing by G. Steege. Their help is greatly appreciated.

2. Using Hirschman's expression: "Everything has to change before any improvement at all can be introduced."

3. The expression belongs to Flaubert and is quoted from Hirschman (1963).

4. The French Socialist party solved the same dilemma during Mit-

terrand's successful presidential campaign, by proposing that self-management be applied as a principle in social interaction (promoting the free association of citizens in autonomous bodies) but not to be applied in the production sphere.

5. For instance, under the first version of the theory, the public was told that money supply was the key instrument for price stabilization. But later the same economists were saying that money supply was totally irrelevant, because now the economy was working under the principle of global monetarism, where money supply is "endogenous."

6. A state of siege was imposed, starting in November 1984.

7. For definitions, see Schmitter (1982)

8. The expression is Schmitter's.

9. The data in the first column include the ninety-one firms and fourteen banks originally considered in the Popular Unity government's expropriation program. The last column provides similar information about those firms intervened by the Pinochet government, after the insolvency crisis of the main economic conglomerates which were formed during the period of laisse-faire economics reigning in Chile since 1973.

10. It corresponds to the pattern observed during the Unidad Popular government, 1970–1973.

11. "Current" refers to the date at which this paper is being revised, February 1985.

REFERENCES

Bitar, S. 1979. *Transición y Socialismo.*

Castles, F. 1978. *The Social Democratic Image of Society.* London: Routledge and Kegan Paul.

Cavarozzi, M. 1975. "The Government and the Industrial Bourgeoisie in Chile, 1938–1964." Dissertation, University of California, Berkeley.

Dahl, R. 1982. *Dilemmas of Pluralist Democracy.* New Haven: Yale University Press.

Dos Santos, M., and M. Grossi. 1983. "La concertación social: una perspectiva sobre instrumentos de regulación económica en procesos de democratización," in *Crítica y utopía,* (Buenos Aires).

Flanagan, R., D. Soskice, and L. Ullman. 1983. *Unionism, Economic Stabilization and Incomes Policies: the European Experience.* Washington, D.C.: Brookings Institution.

Foxley, A., ed. 1971. *Chile, búsqueda de un nuevo socialismo.* Santiago: Nueva Universidad.

Foxley, A. 1983a. *Latin American Experiments in Neo-Conservative Economics.* Berkeley: University of California Press.

_____. 1983b. "Después del monetarismo." In CIEPLAN, *Reconstrucción económica para la democracia*. Santiago: Editorial Aconcagua.

Garretón, M. A. 1983. *El proceso político chileno*. Santiago: FLACSO.

Hirschman, A. 1963. "Journeys toward Progress." New York: Twentieth Century Fund.

_____. 1981a. "The Turn to Authoritarianism in Latin America." In A. Hirschman, *Essays in Trespassing*. Cambridge: Cambridge University Press.

_____. 1981b. "The Rise and Decline of Development Economics." In A. Hirschman, *Essays in Trespassing*. Cambridge: Cambridge University Press.

_____. 1984. "La confesión de un disidente." *El Trimestre económico*, no. 201.

Kaufman, R. 1980. "Liberalization and Democratization in the Context of B-A Rule." Washington, D.C.: Wilson Center (mimeo).

Lehmbruch, G. 1982. "Changing Relationships between Labor and the State in Italy." In G. Lehmbruch and P. Schmitter, *Patterns of Corporatist Policy-Making*. Beverly Hills, Cal.: Sage.

Linz, J. 1981. "A Century of Politics and Interests in Spain." In S. Berger, ed., *Organizing Interests in Western Europe*. Cambridge: Cambridge University Press.

Moulian, T. 1983. *Democracia y socialismo en Chile*. Santiago: FLACSO.

O'Donnell, G. 1983. *El estado burocrático autoritario*. Buenos Aires: Editorial Belgrano.

O'Donnell, G., and P. Schmitter. 1984. "Political Life after Authoritarian Rule: Tentative Conclusions about Uncertain Transitions." Notre Dame, Ind.: Kellogg Institute, University of Notre Dame (mimeo).

Pinto, A. 1983. *Chile, un caso de desarrollo frustrado*. Ed. Universitaria.

_____. 1983. "Consensos y disensos en el espacio democrático popular." *Colección Estudios CIEPLAN*, no. 10.

Przeworski, A. 1984. "Democracy as a Contingent Outcome." Notre Dame, Ind.: Kellogg Institute, University of Notre Dame (mimeo).

Przeworski, A., and Wallerstein. 1982. "Capitalismo y democracia: una reflexión desde la macroeconomía." *Crítica y utopía*, no. 8. Buenos Aires.

Regini, M. 1982. "Changing Relationships between Labor and the State in Italy." In G. Lehmbruch, and P. Schmitter, *Patterns of Corporatist Policy-Making*. Beverly Hills, Cal.: Sage.

Schmitter, P. 1982. "Reflections on Where the Theory of Neo-Corporatism Has Gone." In G. Lehmbruch and P. Schmitter, *Patterns of Corporatist Policy-Making*, Beverly Hills, Cal.: Sage.

_____. 1984. "Democratic Theory and Neo-Corporatist Practice." In *Social Research*. Forthcoming.

_____. 1979. "Still the Century of Corporatism." In P. Schmitter and G. Lehmbruch, *Trends towards Corporatist Intermediation*. Beverly Hills, Cal.: Sage.

Stephens, J. 1979. *The Transition from Capitalism to Socialism*. London: Macmillan Press.

Stevenson, J. 1942. *The Chilean Popular Front.* Westport, Conn.: Greenwood Press, Westport.

Touraine, A. 1983. In Prefacio a M.A. Garretón *El proceso político chileno.* Santiago: FLASCO.

Valenzuela, A. 1978. "The Breakdown of Democratic Regimes: Chile." in J. Linz and A. Stepan, eds. *The Breakdown of Democratic Regimes.* Baltimore, Md.: John Hopkins Press.

Vial, G. 1981. *Historia de Chile, 1891–1973.*

Wilde, A. 1982. *Conversaciones de caballeros: la quiebra de la democracia en Colombia.* Bogotá, Colombia: Ediciones Tercer Mundo.

Problems of Social Learning and Social Control

Strategies for Change in View of Societal Learning Processes

Michel Crozier

As the only sociologist and the only Frenchman to attend the conference in honor of Albert O. Hirschman, I felt especially sorry to add to my marginal status by presenting a very speculative paper with a high-sounding title, the ambition of which I am unable to fulfill at this point. I only dared rise to the challenge because I have known Albert Hirschman for a long time and therefore I am familiar with his special indulgence for "trespassing" kinds of reasoning, and this especially from his French friends and admirers.

So let me try to insert into the debate some various and sundry thoughts inspired by Albert's seminal contribution which have stimulated me most recently.

I

I will begin with Albert's wonderful twisting of the old paradigm of the hidden hand into a much more active paradigm of the hiding hand.[1] In many of the projects and endeavors that we begin, if not most of them, Albert tells us, we systematically underestimate the costs and overestimate the results. These biases and the errors that ensue, according to Albert, are not necessarily damaging. Indeed they may be considered as functional. By hiding reality, by biasing our calculations in favor of action, we make the latter feasible whereas we would have otherwise rejected action because it seemed either unfeasible or unrewarding. We succeed because in the dynamic process of action, we discover new resources which we may—with a little luck—mobilize for our goals. And last but not least, we can learn from the experience.

Problems do stimulate individuals. People, in turn, are capable of learning and thus of growing. It is dangerous to calculate everything in terms that are too narrow. Neither change nor growth would be possible without the capacity to dream and take risks in a spirit of optimism.

I have always been attracted by this more humane mode of reasoning which is also more realistic than narrow cost-benefit analysis. At the same time, I have often wondered about the limits of this penchant for first dreaming and second acting. After all, many individuals, businessmen and even, at times, governments launch new ventures, few of which really succeed and many—too many—of which ultimately fail, some of them at disastrous costs. Admittedly one cannot reject economic calculus every time one feels strongly that some new scheme appears to be, in principle, very promising. Where does one stop, therefore, in the ability or inability to trespass?

Once the problem is set in such a way, there is no guidance either from philosophical principles or from common sense. Only intuition will work, with the aura of charisma it brings to those who are daring enough to take risks and lucky enough to succeed. If there is no guidance, however, from precise positivistic measurement, I will contend that it becomes possible now to delineate the problems to be solved and to get a much better qualitative and holistic view of them that can in turn help intuition and make it much less perilous. These are, in fact, very simple empirical problems. Here below are some of the issues which I will formulate as questions:

• Are there existing human and/or societal resources that can be tapped?

• May we mobilize them for our purposes and how is this to be done?

• Do the specific human groups which are concerned possess learning capacities?

Any strategy for change must be developed from the answers to these questions. I believe that this could be the decisive contribution of social sciences to action. Social psychology, for example, has made it possible to have a qualitative appreciation of the resources and capacities of individuals. But social psychology may not be enough since resources and learning capacities depend on more than the individual dimension. It is the collective capacity or, better still, the ability of the relevant social system to act, to learn and to develop throughout the course of its history that matters. Sociology, political science and history will give further cues.

Finally, resources and learning capacities should be viewed not only from the perspective of the objectives to be reached. Instead of searching for the resources to solve a problem, it may prove more rewarding to solve the problem for which resources are available. This will lead to new concepts for action and change.

If we return to Hirschman's "hiding hand" paradigm, the reasons why errors of appreciation could bring forth good solutions may be due not only to a sharper intuition of the available resources but also to greater flexibility about the goals to be pursued. In a way, this is the best answer to the second questions, that is, how to mobilize resources and/or to choose goals in order to mobilize resources.

II

The problem can be analyzed much more clearly and with empirical evidence at the microdecision level, where one can already find the complexity and contradictions of human groups. More specifically, I mean organizations and small systems.[2] Therefore, if I am allowed to change the level of discussion, I would like to take an example from my main field of enquiry: organizations and organizational systems.

From 1978 to 1980 we studied and analyzed in relative depth a dozen significant recent organizational innovations in France which led to new modes of human and social relationships between customers, company personnel and management. In each of these cases the outcome could not be predicted from a normal cost-benefit analysis. The key decisions were dependent on appreciation of the resources and growth possibilities from experience. All of the concerned innovators were very shrewd in making appreciations. They had also taken a calculated risk in choosing the best goals and areas of endeavor in view of the possibilities at hand, while at the same time taking into account the specific constraints of such areas.[3]

One case was especially striking. A young man, after leaving the Resistance in 1945,[4] had been struck by the formidable capacities of small groups of young fighters (one of which he was part of) to collectively achieve first-rate results because of their ability to work together, freely and openly. This was the resource that he wanted to build upon. Such a human fraternity, it seemed to him, should continue to be utilized because of the extraordinary rewards to its members and at the same time its great efficiency. The problem, however, was to find a field in which to exercise these talents and to define objectives. Initially they had the connections and technical skills to work in the area of Alpine sports. Several projects were attempted but they discovered quickly enough that in this area the field was already very well structured. Ski resorts offered great promise, and a bright future; in fact there was an up-and-coming boom. On the other hand the instructors and the sports clubs were already tightly organized. They were often tied to local interests, outsiders were rejected; it was in many ways a closed shop. Thus former Resistance fighters did not have much of a chance to bring about something new and revolutionary in such a system. Once the leader understood that the field itself was not crucial, he proposed to try to do the same thing in a field in which they had no previous experience—sailing sports. At the time in France the area of sailing was much less developed than Alpine sports. It was an open game. They did not have expertise but expertise could be developed, namely through the process of building a sailing club and a sailing school. The fraternal group of the Resistance gave birth to new social relationships and to new training methods. The enterprise has remained a nonprofit association but it has been a great success since, among other things, it has contributed greatly to bringing sailing into the realm of masses of young people of moderate incomes. The leader, himself, has retained a strong charismatic influence on the enterprise but has at the same time attempted several other ventures, some of them highly successful.

Such innovators may be more numerous than one might think even in societies that, at first glance, seem conservative. These individuals may be hampered in traditional business or government ventures by the unsophisticated belief in the virtue of cost-benefit analysis. At the same time one cannot simply discount the progress made by applying more sophisticated reasoning to the planning of human enterprise. May I suggest another way to conceptualize the difficulties. We are overwhelmed by a sort of institutionalized imbalance: on the one hand an avalanche of narrow rationalistic data and on the other the real vagueness or fuzziness of our knowledge of human problems. Successful innovators are dreamers and poets, but at the same time they are shrewd calculators. They intuitively know that things that cannot simply be measured in statistical terms may be, and often are, much more important than those whose precise measurement gives an illusion of certainty.

Indeed it would be great progress if we could therefore guide the hiding hand to help us to be more entrepreneurial and innovative. Fresh and more operational research grappling with the issues related to the complex network of human activities could make a great deal of difference if at least it allowed the community to accept a better balance between quantity and quality.

III

I shall now move one step further and consider two broader issues more central to the conference debate: first, the question of economic development as it has been set forth here once again by Albert Hirschman in his concept of generalized linkages, and second, the problem of political development in the current debate on pluralism and antagonistic growth.

Linkages

In his insightful essay on petrochemical development in Brazil, Peter Evans gives a persuasive demonstration of the heuristic value of Albert's concept of linkages.[5] I was especially struck by his emphasis on the two Hirchmanian consequences he uses as illustrations of Albert's imaginative formulation of the linkage idea. He first gives fresh importance to the organizational aspect in the chances of success of the forward/backward linkages he analyzes. It is the capacity of the "organizational structures to create or at least modify the linkages that connect investment in one activity with investment in another" that makes the difference. What are the origins of this capacity and where does it emerge? I will suggest that it emerges not only from organizational slack[6] but also from a completely non-economic variable, that is, organizational learning capacities to be initially assessed through analysis and then improved by appropriate guidance.[7]

Micro-Marxism is the second Hirschman concept utilized by Peter Evans. This concept helps us to understand the various propositions inherent in the notion of politization and power crucial to the success of the generalized linkage approach. Linkages will work only if they are attuned to the specific patterns of activities and/or power relationships that are characteristic of the relevant context for social change to occur. It is neither the invisible hand of the market nor merely abstract economic variables that will operate but a much more complex set of factors where human inventiveness and concern may indeed play the major role.

It seems to me that Evans's paper and his use of Albert's concepts demonstrate very clearly the central importance of the learning skill concept as a tool to implement action and change, if one accepts the extension of this concept to organizations and social systems. This is still, of course, a very vague notion and I shall try further to define what I mean in the course of this paper. To begin with, what if we were to translate it into normative advice intended for a "reform monger." It immediately makes more sense.

Clearly one must fight the tendency to give support immediately to those actions that at first glance seem fine, lofty or fundamental but that are too often based more on enthusiasm than on foresight. But it is as incorrect to work only for short-term cost-benefit results. While respecting constraints within the limits of common sense, as many efforts as possible should be oriented in directions where people's energies will be increasingly mobilized to induce learning skills. There is a caveat: one must exercise real care and pay as much (or more) attention to the collective entities as to individuals.

To illustrate these points, I shall take two recent examples of counterproductive policies from France that I was able to follow closely. Two years ago, the recently appointed Minister for Research and Industry, Jean-Pierre Chevènement, and his staff discovered a new idea which, from their point of view, was close to the idea of linkages. Their term was *"stratégie de filières."* Although this is difficult to translate into English, its particular connotation of linkage implies a sort of teleological, goal-oriented direction. Thus, to take a few concrete examples, in order to produce furniture a chain including a great variety of specialists, from wood-growers, sawmill workers, to plywood- and furniture-makers, engages in a step-by-step pattern toward production of a final product. The chain for producing cars would include everybody from steel producers, manufacturers of composite metals, and glass producers to all the different subcontractors for diverse appliances.

To gain a real understanding of growth, Chevènement and his colleagues maintained, one must perceive the complex relationship of the successive operations to be found in the industrial or manufacturing process. On the international scale, so they claimed, one can gain more profit by rationalizing these steps than by trying to specialize in one *créneau* (an industrial niche) where one excels. A domestic strategy of *filières*, also good for employment, was to replace the former capitalistic strategy of *créneaux*.[8] Chevènement and his advisers claimed that the conventional wisdom arguing for specialization in a few French products that would make France apparently more competitive was wrong. He therefore proposed that the best strategy was to encourage domestic *filières* relationships, in order to find a way to ensure that French companies would succeed in having a better share of the market.

Such arguments may have had some small local relevance, although only up to a certain point. Fundamentally, however, there was a complete misunderstanding of the linkage concept. Focusing on linkages may prove to be extremely rewarding to inducing new activities but only with the proper conditions that allow for learning to take place. If this is viewed from a strictly economic perspective it will not pay off. Above all, it will simply mean reverting to the old concept of industrial integration of the twenties: both the basic philosophy of German concerns and American captive industries resulted in long-lasting and damaging consequences.

As a matter of fact, the whole program never really took off because the ultimate stakes were not understood. By focusing on grand schemes to promote employment without caring enough to discover real opportunities for those concerned to increase innovative drive and learn, sizable sums of money were spent to virtually no avail while potentially rich opportunities were lost.

My second example concerns the machine tool industry whose poor results seem to be a perennial problem in France—at least for the last thirty years. Past governments had already invested a great deal in order to support, foster and develop the machine tool industry, which is supposed to be a key linkage in a number of "strategic industries." When the Socialists came into power they argued they could do better. Yet within a short time, like their predecessors, they too had to throw in the towel. At that point the experts and politicians, not surprisingly, used cultural and political reasons to explain their failure. Since putting the blame on an international capitalist conspiracy had become somewhat ridiculous, the lack of civic responsibility and entrepreneurial spirit of the French capitalist class was often heard in its place as the cause of failure. As I listened to many responsible officials lament over how the French lacked talent and technological expertise, it seemed peculiar to realize not only that France was in the forefront of this field in the nineteenth century but also that the Italians, who are in a comparable situation and are culturally not very different, have succeeded with their machine tool industry. It became clear after a brief schematic analysis that in this area the most fruitful linkage, or at least the one to be tapped and developed in France, was that of the powerful and prestigious system constituted by the French engineering schools.[9] One of the major reasons for the decline of the machine tool industry was the declining prestige of training in mechanical engineering with its diminishing reward system and, conversely, the promotion of scientific management skills. In addition to these changes the transformation of the managerial composition of companies and the lack of opportunity inside and outside the firms gradually dried up any influx of fresh talent.

Not only should the most promising objectives be chosen with emphasis on those areas conducive to learning but, almost as important, a much better specialized knowledge of all possible linkages, and especially the non-economic ones, should be developed.

Pluralism and Antagonistic Growth

I would now like to address another debated question which was also central to this conference. I shall call this problem political development. Michael McPherson and Alejandro Foxley, among others, have discussed on a theoretical basis and from a Latin American point of view the concepts of pluralism and of antagonistic growth that are pervasive in much of Albert's work.[10] Here again we confront the problems of limits—or to put it in Hirschman-like terms, the ability or inability to trespass. We may discard the monomaniac ideas of utilitarian or Marxist theoreticians who cannot really accept the idea of pluralism. Yet beyond a certain point antagonistic growth is no longer possible; it will lead to an explosion. To understand where to put the limit, i.e., at which point we can accept unrestrained pluralism and at which point we ought to intervene, we have to turn to social analysis. Here I would like to suggest its potentially rich contributions on three points.

First of all, the concept of a group or community of fragmented alliances should be made much more empirical by in-depth field research. We often don't even know what constitutes a group. There are so many groups which we take virtually for granted, and which, in fact, hardly exist. Differences, in any case, are extraordinary between the constitution, cohesion and capacity to act of any and all groups, and yet we still tend to discuss them as if they were similar entities. Moreover, groups crisscross each other. Multiple allegiances can paralyze them or restrain them from functioning in certain ways. Understanding the reality of pluralism and acting upon it requires a much deeper and more practical knowledge of the relevant groups.

Second, our views of power relationships between classes, groups and categories have been confused and distorted by widespread utilization of a narrow and rigid kind of Marxism. Marx's major contribution in the sociological area was to force people to understand that behind ideological smoke screens and the quarrels of persons, there are power relationships over real interests. But power relationships are much more complex than the simple class alignments and *rapports de forces* that tend to be substituted for reality. I would suggest that a conversion should be brought about in this domain very similar to the one suggested by Albert as micro-Marxism with regard to the context. Both conversions are complementary. Power is not merely a *rapport de forces*, it is a bargaining relationship in which sheer material force may be very important but never the only variable. Power develops within a certain context in relationships with material force and independently of it. Of course, people are concerned and indeed care about many matters other than those that are related to politics or economics. But more basically one of their first priorities, for economic, social and political matters, is freedom, which is also a major element in playing the power game. The volatile aspect of group antagonisms can be better understood with more realistic analyses of group existence and power relationships. Successful implementation of action in favor of political development will depend on this understanding.

IV

The real problem of political development is to achieve the gradual opening up of the small social systems which are the relevant context from a micro-Marxist point of view and of the broader societal systems which condition them. More open systems require different games between people, which are at the same time more rewarding but also more risky—they require better communications or, in other terms, a greater capacity on the part of the individual to deal effectively with others, and finally to accept ruthless criticism and to face the truth and accept responsibility. Training people is as important, if not in a way more important, than changes in the balances of power.

The opening up of the complex power relationships within the groups themselves is of special importance for these changes to occur. This is associated with the classic problem of the intermediary; intermediaries are indispensable but while they can be a necessary link in communication, they often tend to obscure, bias or even raise more barriers to communication. Militants in political parties and trade unions are likely to succumb to this natural drift which brings in turn passivity and decline in the organization, or alternatively, aggressive behavior and explosive crises. New, more open games are indispensable to develop a dynamic pluralist society.

V

The above remarks may help us broaden our angle. We may also try to view the issues from the stance of the development of societal learning as well as of reforms at the appropriate levels. Our Latin American colleagues who attended the conference sounded especially hopeful that more promising political changes are about to take place in their countries. Not only are they asking for fresh ideas to ensure successful transition and hasten constructive political development but some are suggesting new avenues, in fact, to achieve these goals. And indeed these stimulating papers provoked me to try out this mode of reasoning on our recent European history, whose common tidal flow seems to me virtually to call for comparative examination.

Contrary to the dismal rhetoric of the prophets of doom who, in the wake of World War II, heralded the demise of the countries of Western Europe, our countries quickly moved from social turmoil to a system of reasonably peaceful pluralism. This was accomplished in spite of explosive antagonisms inside each country as well as great pressure from the international scene. This present state of peaceful pluralism has tolerance as a principal virtue; tension often serves as a prop rather than an obstacle and assists social progress and economic growth.

But what seems like an attractive model at the present moment should not let us forget that in the aftermath of World War II few experts would have predicted that this Western European model of growth had any reasonable chance of success. Although today one often hears the story of the "miraculous" economic success of Europe, this is only the tip of the iceberg. Initiatives had to be taken, creative, constructive compromises had to be reached, taking into account the multiple changes in the social and political arena. The capacity for learning from past experience and from the consequences of specific courses of action was crucial.

European societies whose fate, half century ago, seemed precarious if not doomed have radically changed in the interim. A great deal has been learned from the traumatic years of upheaval resulting from political wars. The experience of rebuilding societies and economies has been rich and rewarding. And, increasingly, in the last decades these societies have seized many opportunities to develop in a more dynamic manner. Europeans have become more expansive and more open to the outside world. Even more deeply, they have learned new ways to communicate and cooperate. The real story behind this western model of growth has still not been told. Perhaps it is even more important than the ups and downs of the political game or even the successive spurts and stops of economic growth. The independent, active citizens' groups for ecology and for cultural initiatives of all sorts, the boom in association building (in France, the independent activity of parents on school issues is one recent illustration) are stark contrasts to the drift towards politicized violent conflict that was the mark of the thirties. This ongoing peaceful revolution makes it possible to resist new tensions from the outside environment, including economic crisis and military threats.

There has been too much insistence on the differences between the cultural and social fabric of these European societies. Admittedly there are differences; yet, by and large, each has moved in similar directions, and results have been on the whole positive. We can say, of course, that there are differences in degree—for example, tolerance and democratic pluralism have increased more in Germany and France than in the United Kingdom. But a country such as Sweden that seemed for a moment to be a paradise of democratic pluralism appears in retrospect to have been only somewhat ahead of its time.[11]

Strategies for Change

Strategies for change should, of course, take into account the problems plaguing society. But often it is not the spectacular initiatives that are the most significant ones. Both partisans of order and partisans of change must pay more attention to the workings of the social system and to its resources, capacities and constraints—to be searched for and discovered. Finding the opportunities for these resources to commit themselves is much more important finally than providing allegedly correct solutions to economic problems. The comparison between France and England comes to mind. In the late forties, the United Kingdom's policy of austerity seemed to be much more correct both rationally and morally than the sloppy muddling through of the French leadership. But France succeeded and the United Kingdom lagged behind. It was the French leadership that launched the Common Market which opened up many opportunities for all of Europe.[12]

Widening the space for opportunity, however, should not be an excuse for proposing seemingly visionary projects whose implementation is simply not feasible. With this in mind let me take a last example from France which helps clarify the above. This is the case of a major attempt in 1983 drastically to reform the organization of French hospitals and medical schools.[13] At first glance, this reform would appear to be very progressive. Its aims were worthy, namely to modernize and democratize the medical sector, which is widely considered to be too elitist. The "reform-mongers" considered these elites to be a large part of the reason for spiraling health costs. A new model of organization was to be imposed on the hospitals. This had been elaborated along the lines of United States and Swiss models which were then in fashion. Thus the medical schools were to be reformed in order to get rid of the numerous barriers between the professional elites and the rank and file (young doctors, students, nurses). Finally, it was intended that each hospital unit would be made more autonomous; hospital departments would consequently be created with separate budgets.

This apparently superlative policy however had several drawbacks which the reformers had not cared to think about in advance. First, it did not take into account the sharp differences between hospital units and the complexity of the multifarious contexts in which these units operated. It was intended that this reform be applied uniformly. Second, and even more important, the reformers, or reform-mongers, explained the problem by arguing that the villains were the medical elites. And it certainly seemed as if the reform was aimed at changing the balance of power, or at least at diminishing the power of the top doctors if not the medical profession on the whole, while giving more power to the administrators. A frontal attack was launched without paying attention to the power systems in the medical sector. To the great surprise of the reformers, they were confronted, in turn, by a united front of all the different catagories of the medical profession. (It was the first time in France that top doctors and medical students united in public demonstrations.) The reformers had counted on the wide diversity of interest between these groups; instead they were confronted with a solid front composed of elites and rank and file.

The massive strike that was launched was, to the government's dismay, generally supported by the public. A compromise was finally accepted which considerably weakened a part of the reform, postponed other parts and in general made reform much more vulnerable in the future since it had become somewhat of a political issue.[14]

Here we can well see the very negative or unintended consequences of overreliance on theoretical schemes, however worthy and democratic-seeming they may appear at the outset. It is more often than not extremely perilous to indulge in loud denunciations against the old order and elitist groups since their cooperation will certainly be subsequently required. Investment in learning skills of the sort required to understand realistic backward-forward linkages would be a constructive beginning for any reform-monger. Such an investment could allow reform more attuned to people's problems and serve as a guide to productive implementation.

Recent Latin American history is only one illustration of the great complexity of the network of groups, interests and categories, which any micro-Marxist analysis would reveal. It is my hunch that this complexity has increased and continues to do so with the advent of democratic regimes. This has made and will make life especially miserable for do-gooders who would like to reach clearcut decisions and get rid of the bad guys forever. Real chances do exist to promote a more open, pluralistic system. But as I have implied all along in this paper, in order to rise to the opportunity, reformers should break away from the perilous temptation of pushing through abstract theoretical schemes. Moderation in politics is not enough, nor is pragmatism. Viewed in this light, a new understanding is called for, whereby opportunities for trust and easy exchange between all concerned parties not only are to be encouraged but are to be designated a top priority.

NOTES

1. See Albert O. Hirschman, *Development Projects Observed* (Washington: Brookings Institution, 1967).

2. It could also be discussed, of course, at the individual level in problems such as career choices and marriage, to name but two. However, this would divert us from the present debate.

3. Jacques Guyaz, *Les innovateurs et leurs innovations: Trente ans de création d'entreprises dans le secteur des services* (Thèse de Doctorat de IIIe Cycle, 1981).

4. It is not reviewed in Guyaz' thesis.

5. See Evans's essay in this volume.

6. Albert O. Hirschman, *Exit, Voice and Loyalty, Responses to Decline in Firms, Organizations and States* (Cambridge: Harvard University Press, 1970).

7. This is discussed in Peter Evans, *Actors and Systems: The Politics of Collective Action* (Chicago: The University of Chicago Press, 1980), Part V, "Reflections on Change," 211–59.

8. On this point it is extremely stimulating to read Albert's discussion of inside versus outside linkage categories with their balance of advantages and disadvantages. See *Essays in Trespassing: Economics to Politics and Beyond* (Cambridge: Cambridge University Press, 1981), especially 75–83.

9. Here in this second example, once again, the crucial question of cooperation between the *"grand écoles,"* which are in France the top profes-

sional schools, and the industrial community is a vital non-economic linkage issue.

10. See Michael S. McPherson, *Pluralism and Community and Economic Development* and Alejandro Foxley's essay in this volume ("After Authoritarianism: Political Alternatives").

11. We should remember that Sweden had been a country prone to violence in the twenties and early thirties and might have reverted once again to violence in the early fifties except for the wise leadership of the two leading parties in the compromise between big business and the Social Democratic trade unions.

12. One person, Jean Monnet, played a major role, but there was in France and Germany a broad support he could not find in England.

13. In France the medical schools which are part of the public education sector and part of the national university system are dependent on the state bureaucracy and can therefore only be reformed through governmental fiats. This applies to most of the hospitals as well, for they are mostly in the public sector.

14. The trajectory of the theoretically sweeping decentralization reforms of 1982 are in many ways comparable to this medical example. See Michael Crozier, *Strategies for Change,* English translation (Cambridge: MIT Press, 1982), 79–102.

Against Backsliding

T. C. Schelling

Albert Hirschman observed some years ago that countries that are technically backward are far better at maintaining airlines than maintaining roadbeds. The point had to do with incentives: you can patch the road surface cheaply and over the years let the roadbed invisibly go to ruin, but airplanes don't go to ruin invisibly. Had he been an observer of urban economies in advanced countries he might have made the same point about fire engines and sewers in New York. Individuals display similar behavior: in a hurry, a man will shave rather than brush his teeth.

This is an essay on the theory and practice of backsliding. As a phenomenon and as a problem, backsliding concerns individuals, groups, and even governments. Not only is backsliding in general characteristic of both families and governments, but some specific kinds have counterparts at both those levels of aggregation. The federal government's statutory debt ceiling, so regularly and so easily elevated, and the proposed balanced-budget amendment to the Constitution, must be among the most widely understood self-denying legislative acts and proposals because so many families poignantly share the problem. Cruel and unusual punishment has tempted most parents at one time or another. White lies and small secrets can accumulate like some environmental poison, for husbands and presidents. And gamblers who know and even repeat the maxim, "Don't throw good money after bad," are notoriously unable to heed it in the casino, in repairing an automobile, or in Vietnam. "Lest we forget," we build monuments to men and women, dead and alive, who risked and sometimes gave their lives. Still we forget, as a nation, or as close buddies who shared an "unforgettable" experience and want to celebrate an anniversary a decade from now. Building a preference for veterans in a state or federal civil service system is something of a safeguard against the inevitable decline in how much we care, saving for them a modest privilege that, thirty years later, they probably could not successfully claim.

Collective self-binding is richer in its dimensionality than individual attempts to resolve now for the future and to bind oneself. Collectively there are more kinds of mistrust.

Each of us—to identify one way—may doubt the steadfastness of his own resolve, be concerned only with his own resolve, and join in collectively requiring daily exercise or banishing dessert. This would be *using* some collective authority—typically not the kind of authority we think of as "government"—to make ourselves behave as we now resolve to behave, converting what is sometimes called "self-paternalism" into genuine paternalism, the authority making each of us do what it (we) thinks is good for us. That is not the situation that Hirschman had in mind, but once we are on the subject we may as well sort out the different motives and situations.

A second motivation for collectively binding ourselves, one that is especially pertinent to government, is the incentive structure that in the last couple of decades has become widely known as the many-person Prisoners' Dilemma. These are the situations in which each individual wants all the others to perform or abstain, but everybody would prefer to be a free rider and knows that everybody else would. All will be better off with an enforceable contract, and the authority of government can be invoked in lieu of contract. This is the commonest motive for collectively binding ourselves through statute and ordinance, but it is so common and so well understood that it altogether lacks the paradoxical quality of anti-backsliding measures. It could, though, be pertinent to Hirschman's airlines and roads, if the roads are mainly worn out by people who use and depend on them but who drive overweight vehicles or park on the shoulders or otherwise do what is cheap or convenient, aware that others do too and that this is what is ruining the roads, sorry that the rules can't be enforced. But this is not backsliding, and I mention it only to lay it aside.

There is the important possibility that we do not doubt the durability of our own conscientiousness and concern but are not altogether sure of each other. We have identified some temptations that we have resolved to resist, having just hanged an innocent man or been almost defeated by a surprise attack, and I know that I'll never forget this stunning lesson and never again get carried away but some of you look to me like the kind of people who could do it again. (University departments often find themselves to have succumbed to a temptation to lower their standards—examinations, admissions, appointments, discipline—and everybody agrees that "they" will go and do it again sometime in the future unless "we" find some preclusive measure to forbid it.)

A less symmetrical motivation is that we are a system of individuals who interact together. I can trust myself as long as those about me are not losing their heads or their tempers or their resistance to temptation; I can drive slowly or keep my temper or do without dessert or maintain grading standards or leave promptly when the fire alarm rings as long as the rest of you do. But my resolve, like yours, gets demoralized when the whole system relaxes. The backsliding of each of us affects the backsliding of others, and we need protection against our common tendency to undermine each other's morale as we lose our own.

The interest in this case can be joint or several. It can be attendance, say, at a department meeting or a legislative session, each of us acknowledging a share in that weakness that would ultimately lead to empty chambers, to the detriment of our collective interest. Or it could be an attempt to quit smoking, each of us solely concerned with his own success but each being part of the other's environment where smoking is concerned, supportive or erosive according to how well we abstain, our several personal interests coming together in a no-smoking rule while we work together.

Sometimes when this interactive feedback has the right bias, just forming a collectivity reinforces everyone's resolve: four people who jog together three times a week at lunch hour may go on for years as a team; jogging separately on different days they all might have been early dropouts. S. L. A. Marshall in *Men Against Fire* (Magnolia, Mass: Peter Smith, rpt. 1985) discussed the phenomenon that in all armies in World War II most individual soldiers never fired their rifles—no matter how long a battle lasted, how brave they were, or what targets presented themselves—while weapons that required joint action by two or three soldiers, like feeding a belt of ammunition into a machine gun or loading and aiming an artillery piece, were regularly fired as intended.

Often the collective self-binding appears oriented not so much toward the loss of resolve or control that can occur when the members of the collectivity pass through a disturbing episode or forget, or grow older and change their values with age, as toward successor members of the collectivity. We want to bind later generations to our current values. These can be generations in the literal demographic sense, or the people who replace us when we retire or are voted out of office. The First Amendment was undoubtedly less intended by those in the Congress to keep themselves as individuals from turning around, contrary to their own sentiments at the time the amendment was passed, and establishing a religion or abridging speech, than to guard against unconsidered actions of later generations who would not have fresh in mind the experience of colonial subordination or the intense exposure to constitutional debate.

Again there is a comparison with individuals, couples, or extended families. In the days when life insurance and retirement annuities were more sexually asymmetrical it used to be proposed that husbands might wish to structure benefits so that a surviving wife could not spend her resources impetuously or invest them unwisely. But sometimes even the husband, contemplating retirement, was advised to guard against his own spendthriftiness by tying up his resources in a life annuity, even setting something aside for burial expenses or modest bequests for his grandchildren. An occasional feature of primogeniture was that an inheriting scion could legally allow *his* successor to dispose of the land and property but could not convert it to cash himself, the expectation being that each would preserve the restriction on his successor. It sounds a little like the principle, sometimes expressed in legislation, that a pay increase for the members of a legislature shall take effect only after the next election.

Among techniques one is simply delay. Delay can be imposed by rules that specify delay, if the rules themselves are subject to the same delay or have a constitutional status that requires a greater majority to change them than is required for ordinary legislation. Some parliaments have a constitutional rule that a bill must have a second or even a third "reading" before enactment. Certain proscriptions, like the delay rules, can themselves have constitutional status, requiring greater majorities or some further ratification, such as by three-quarters of the states in the United States. The balanced-budget amendment, in contrast to the merely statutory debt ceiling, is an effort to take advantage of the extreme difficulty of repealing an amendment, and the failure to date of that amendment reflects the success of the Founding Fathers in making such amendments rare and difficult. Faculties often impose "constitutional" restraints, including delay, to guard against their own impetuosity or the decay of their standards, or to be more immune to coercion. Individuals even use mandatory delay, successfully at least sometimes, to guard against backsliding where cigarettes, food, or alcohol may momentarily become so tempting that one forgets what is so wrong with just one cigarette after dinner. The rule that you may change your mind any time you want to and go ahead and smoke a cigarette but not until twenty-four hours have elapsed, with the change of mind subject to rescission during the interim, has, when it works, some of the qualities of an unwritten constitution—the reason why "just one cigarette after dinner" is so damaging now is that it violates and threatens the former smoker's own constitution.

Precautions against backsliding are typically non-discriminatory or undiscriminating. A constitutional provision that states may not deny due process applies to all the states, without regard to whether some of them may need the restraint more than others. Bicameral legislatures often have, by design or by tradition and evolution, somewhat different safeguards against backsliding in the two houses. The Senate's six-year overlapping terms can make that body more immune to momentary popular passions than the two-year coincident terms in the House, and where backsliding takes the form of action rather than inaction there needs to be only one steadfast chamber.

But when we use some governing body for self-paternal reasons, to guard ourselves as individuals against our own backsliding, the motive is potentially discriminating. I may be desperately willing to subscribe to rules that will keep me from gambling or squandering my inheritance, driving too fast after drinking, smoking or neglecting to exercise, or even talking too much in a heated meeting, but not care whether you smoke or squander your money, or, if you don't attend the same meetings I attend, waste other people's time. Furthermore, some of these constraints may be feasible while discriminating and others capable only of uniform enforcement. I may want to ban high-calorie desserts in my faculty dining room because just knowing they are available, especially seeing them, destroys my resolve, but if we can have two dining rooms and my resolve against dessert is all right at the time that I choose between rooms and only dissolves as dessert time approaches, we can let the ban on dessert apply only to volunteers. I might have license plates that waived my right to refuse a breatholator test or subjected me to lower speed limits than other drivers. There are some modern technologies that might permit some of us to submit to curfews or that could put drinking places off limits, by monitoring the signalling devices that had been irremovably implanted in or attached to us. We have to be careful: it is constitutional for my state to forbid the sale or serving of alcoholic drinks, but not to keep me home on weekends or out of bars that are open to the public, even if I have volunteered the authority to them, because some of my rights are not alienable, even by myself.

I have spoken about legislative safeguards against backsliding. Executives and departments of government, military services, schools, the courts and even such estates as the media and the churches need ways to police themselves against backsliding. For some governments a most demanding issue is how to keep from being taken militarily by surprise again, as the United States was at Pearl Harbor or the Israeli government on Yom Kippur. Apparently what does not work is *routines* designed to avoid surprise. In the school where I teach we have had uncommonly numerous false fire alarms in the past five years; most of us are remarkably good at stopping in mid-sentence and insisting that we all head instantly for the exits. Possibly it's because we have had enough false alarms to keep the question of appropriate behavior on our minds, but not so many as to make us disregardful. I also notice, in the same school, that the signs saying "no food or beverages in the classroom" are regularly disregarded although the faculty supported that prohibition when it went into effect.

What Irving Janis has called "groupthink" is a malady for which it is hard to find an antidote even among people who acknowledge together that they are collectively susceptible to it. *(Groupthink,* Boston: Houghton Mifflin, 1983). Members of an athletic team have trouble effectively reminding themselves not to become overconfident. I have attended many senior department meetings that spent an hour and forty-five minutes clearing away the trivia in order to get down to some serious business, like a new tenured appointment, only to discover that there was no time left even to get started, remembering that that was exactly what happened at the preceding meeting, and the one before that, trying to resolve next time to leave the trivia for the end of the meeting, recognizing with some sense of futility that it is characteristic of trivia that it always looks like something that can be disposed of promptly

Agencies like people, worry about growing old and conservative, losing the capacity for adventure, initiative, innovation. Agencies, like people, worry about becoming too large, about becoming too susceptible to habit. And agencies, like people, should worry, if they do not, about how to make a graceful exit when life's work is done and it is time to expire.

Suffering from Success

Paul Streeten

Reviewing the course of our thinking about development, we become aware of the numerous apparent errors, false starts, and dead ends. It is claimed that we have been wrong in stressing industrialization, capital accumulation, government planning, import substitution and many other policies. There are critics who say that our objectives of economic growth, redistribution, employment creation, meeting basic needs were all misguided. Some critics say that our very concepts of income, savings, investment, employment, are inappropriate for underdeveloped countries. In accounting for these errors (as well as for the true insights), there are Keynesians and Marxians. In a much-quoted passage Keynes wrote that

> the ideas of economists and political philosophers, both when they are right and when they are wrong, are more powerful than is commonly understood. Indeed the world is ruled by little else. Practical men, who believe themselves to be quite exempt from any intellectual influences, are usually the slaves of some defunct economist. Madmen in authority, who hear voices in the air, are distilling their frenzy from some academic scribbler of a few years back. I am sure that the power of vested interests is vastly exaggerated compared with the gradual encroachment of ideas. Not, indeed, immediately, but after a certain interval; for in the field of economic and political philosophy there are not many who are influenced by new theories after they are twenty-five or thirty years of age, so that the ideas which civil servants and politicians and even agitators apply to current events are not likely to be the newest. But, soon or late, it is ideas, not vested interests, which are dangerous for good or evil.[1]

According to this interpretation it was the mistaken doctrines of Nurkse, Prebisch, Singer and Rosenstein-Rodan that led governments to adopt numerous interventions, to subsidize industrial capital equipment, to support high urban wages, to overvalue exchange rates, to raise the costs of farm inputs by protecting domestic industry, to keep the prices of farm outputs low, and generally to neglect, discriminate against or exploit exporters, farmers and the rural poor.

A. K. Sen has shown that some of the major strategic recommendations of the development pioneers, though they have been subjected to much criticism, have turned out to be quite sound. Among them are an emphasis on (1) industrialization, (2) rapid capital accumulation, (3) the mobilization of underutilized manpower, and (4) planning and an economically active state.[2] But, according to Sen, the same pioneers have been less successful in characterizing economic development, because they selected economic growth, with its emphasis on goods produced and consumed, as the main performance test of development.

If Keynes believed that it is "ideas, not vested interests, which are dangerous for good or evil,"[3] Marx believed that it is the power of class interests that is reflected in ideas. The doctrines mentioned above, in the Marxian view, are merely an ideological superstructure, reflecting the powerful vested interests of the ruling class, or, by a modification of Marxist analysis, of the urban industrialists and the labor aristocracy who benefit from expansion of the organized industrial urban sector.

A third view of the relation between the power of ideas and policies is that it is neither ideas nor class or vested interests that shape our notions and policies, but that they grow out of praxis and experience. Solutions to economic and social problems are worked out by men and women going about their daily work, by politicians and party officials, farmers, businessmen, union organizers, administrators, teachers, extension workers. The grand theories only distill these practical experiences, or spin a theology above the real day-to-day tasks, mistakes and achievements.

A more subtle analysis of the respective influence of interests and ideas was presented by Max Weber. "Interests (material and ideal), not ideas, dominate directly the actions of men. Yet the 'images of the world' created by these ideas have often served as switches determining the track on which the dynamism of interests kept the action going."[4]

There is a Hydra-like aspect to development (and perhaps to all human endeavor). Many of the difficulties encountered in the path of development are neither the result of ideological errors, nor attributable to vested interests, but are the offspring of the successful solution of previous problems. Scientific confidence asserts that there is a solution to every problem, but experience teaches us that there is a problem to every solution, and often more than one.

Consider the change from the emphasis on industrialization to agriculture and rural development. The Keynesian explanation of those who consider this emphasis wrong would be that it is the result of the misleading writings of the pioneers of development, who thought that industry is the key to accelerated economic growth. The (modified) Marxians, on the other hand, would attribute it to the protected vested interests of the urban industrialists, who stood to lose from more resources going to agriculture and rural development. But the sequence can be better understood as the result of the solution of one problem, which has created a series of new ones. Success in manufacturing industry combined with the successful reduction in mortality that has led to population growth have brought out the lag in agriculture. The need to expand food production for domestic consumption became so acute partly because of the remarkable, unexpected, unprecedented growth of industrial output and population.

Similarly, the seed-fertilizer revolution has spawned a collection of new problems about plant diseases, inequality, unemployment and the other so-called second-generation problems of the Green Revolution. The need for population and birth control arose from the successful attack on mortality through cheap and efficient methods of death control. It was the welcome introduction of modern death rates into societies with primitive birth rates that caused the population explosion. Growing unemployment is (partly) the result of high productivity and growth in manufacturing investment. Education raises aspirations and contributes to the movement to the cities and the consequent unemployment of the educated. Successful higher educational efforts in developing countries have also contributed to the brain drain of professional manpower to the industrial countries of the North. The success and attractions of urban development have shown up the need to accelerate rural development, which, by the turmoil it creates, may further accelerate the migration to the cities.

The successful pursuit of outward-looking trade and industrialization strategies has not been the result of a simple rejection of old faulty inward-looking policies, but it was precisely these policies that provided the basis in infrastructure, and industrial and technological capacity, for the subsequent outward turn. Latin America during the Depression and World War II was forced to turn inward and laid the foundations for benefiting from the world trading and financial system.[5] The People's Republic of China, India and Turkey similarly alternated phases of high protection with liberalization in trade and other policies.

The import-substituting form of industrialization has come under particularly heavy attack. Yet, some of these industries have now become very successful exporters, such as Volkswagen Brazil and Bharat Heavy Electrical Industries in India. Clearly this does not mean that India should not also have made greater efforts to export, or that the implicit time discount rate that might justify some early white elephants is not extremely low, or possibly negative. But it does mean that some of the critics have underestimated the ability to learn, even from past mistakes, and underestimated the prospects of lowering production costs after this learning period.

Successful warnings are often mistaken for errors. Prophecy is not the same as forecasting, though the prophet Jonah failed to see the difference. He was told by God to predict the destruction of Nineveh. But this was intended as a warning: God would destroy Nineveh unless its people mended their ways. Mistaking the prophecy for a forecast, he thought that God had let him down when the people of Nineveh did mend their ways and God spared them. Many self-falsifying forecasts are of this kind. The prophecy's function is to warn and teach and, as a result of the learning process, change the forecast. Some of the gloomy prophecies of Malthusians that population will outrun food supply, of postwar mass unemployment, of the dollar shortage, the energy crisis, or environmental disasters, are of this kind.

In the twenty-five years after the War, investment was determined largely by demand and we experienced the longest period of prosperity. But it was this boom that bred the accelerating inflation, the response to which was a return to an emphasis on interest rates and rates of return on investment as the determinants of investment. What to a superficial view looks like a complete reversal of doctrines (from emphasis on fiscal to monetary policy, from demand management to supply management, from the accelerator to interest rates, from fixed to flexible exchange rates), can be seen to be the response to the successful solution of one set of problems.

Can the current revulsion against government be analyzed along the same lines? Those who believe that governmental organizations do not solve problems, but are the problem, have failed to see that it is sometimes the success of government action which undermines itself. It was the spectacular success in the quarter century after World War II of Keynesian demand management and international cooperation (though some would deny that these were responsible for the success) that carried the seeds of the Keynesian counter-revolution.

A sequence in which one set of solutions throws up new problems and pressures to apply intellectual efforts to their solution is a process analogous to Albert Hirschman's unbalanced growth. If all problems were fully anticipated and solved, and no new problems were to arise from this solution, we might be approaching a kind of intellectual entropy death. Only the stimulus of unexpected new challenges keeps us moving on. As in the doctrine of unbalanced growth, this mechanism cannot be used to justify or legitimize errors in development thinking and policy. Of these there were plenty. But not all difficulties, tensions, and contradictions are the result of past mistakes. In many cases we suffer from our very successes.

"Hydra" is perhaps the wrong metaphor, for it suggests hopelessness. "Second generation problems," on the other hand, may be too optimistic a term. The question is, whether, in spite of the subsequent emergence of new problems, progress is registered. Some solutions present us with a situation worse than the initial problem. Examples would be salination resulting from irrigation, or deforestation from the use of wood for fuel. Other solutions represent progress, such as those mentioned above. Nor are solutions readily transferable between places and periods. Import substitution can be a success in South Korea and a failure in the Philippines. But it is consistent not only with Albert Hirschman's bias for hope and love of paradox, but also with the facts, to interpret some of our difficulties as the result of success.[6]

A discussion of the doctrines of the primacy of ideas versus interests versus *praxis* raises the wider question of the relationship between thinkers and doers. There is a wide and much deplored gap between thinkers and doers, between scholars and academic economists on the one hand, and administrators, officials, and politicians on the other. Administrators have normally a quite different cast of mind from that of economists, especially those fresh from universities. Whether by endowment and temperament or whether from the pressure of events and institutions, administrators lay great store in "judgment." They dismiss subtle distinctions as academic and analysis in depth as a waste of time. Their purpose is to serve those who must quickly reach agreement on a course of action, and such agreement can normally be reached only after blurring distinctions and avoiding subtlety in order to reach an agreed formulation. This is particularly true of value premises. Academic economists, on the other hand, do not have to agree, or help others to agree, on a course of action. Agreement among them, on the contrary, is reached by clarifying concepts, and by drawing finer and sharper distinctions. They shun agreed formulae. Indeed, they reach agreement by bringing out explicitly what it is they disagree about.

It has often been observed that the official, the practical man in authority, does not work without a theory, but that his theory is often implicit and fairly crude. The scholar's model is by contrast explicit and, though crude compared with the complexity of reality, complex compared with the official's implicit model. When a civil servant or politician has said something thrice he believes it to be true; when a scholar says something twice, he ceases to believe that it is true. It has lost the blush of freshness, the shock of original recognition.

The scholar believes that, with adequate time, every problem has a solution. The administrator, by nature conservative, believes, like the above-discussed commonsensical interpretation of Hegel, that every solution has at least one problem. The scholar is not accustomed to working under the pressure of deadlines, the official is in a hurry, always ready to sacrifice the important to the urgent. When he asks what to do next, the scholar replies, you are trying to change the world, the point is first to understand it. Albert Hirschman has illuminated the problems that arise when there is a discrepancy between our desire to change the world and our correct interpretation and understanding.[7]

In spite of some limited movement between the two groups, more in the United States than in Britain, and more now than in the past, each, more or less secretly, rather despises the other. Academics regard administrators as mindless, or at best second-class, or "non-alpha" minds, and administrators dismiss academics as—well—academic: as long-haired boys, usually to be found up above the clouds, stargazing from an armchair at the top of an ivory tower.

It is therefore exceedingly rare that an economist straddles both worlds and is regarded by each group as being in the top flight. If he succeeds in acquiring a high reputation in each group it is because of an element of schizophrenia in his mental makeup, as well as because of outstanding intelligence. For the direct application of economic theories to economic advice is bound to be wrong or seriously misleading; and while practical experience obviously can illuminate theoretical work, it can also blunt the cutting edge of pure reasoning. This is why so many good academic economists give indifferent advice to officials, and why so many highly respected government economists and officials appear so dull and unoriginal in an academic seminar or at the lectern.

Since the doers are better at foreseeing some of the practical difficulties that might arise from the solution of a problem, are they therefore better at forecasting the problems that rise from success? This may be true of some academic solutions, based on gimmicks or simple tricks, to which some academic minds, inclined to abstractions, are prone. But the temperamental resistance to change and innovation of the doers is not so much the result of imaginative analysis of all implications as of conservatism. They have got to know the workings of the existing system so thoroughly that they have acquired an emotional vested interest in the *status quo*. The scholarly imagination can leap ahead and envisage orders of things quite different from the existing ones, but in its flight may ignore some of the practical obstacles. "This may be alright in theory but won't work in practice" gives expression to this conflict between thinkers and doers. A marriage of the two approaches would contribute to the creation of what the sociologist Peter Berger called pedantic utopians or utopian pedants: people who apply careful detailed analysis to a radically different social system, who use informed fantasy to envisage change and innovation.

NOTES

1. J. M. Keynes, *General Theory of Employment, Interest and Money* (Macmillan, 1942), 383–84.
2. A. K. Sen, "Development: which way now?" *Economic Journal* (December 1983).
3. Keynes, 384.
4. From Max Weber, *Essays in Sociology* (New York: Oxford University Press, 1947), 280.
5. Albert O. Hirschman, "The Rise and Decline of Development Economics," in *Essays in Trespassing* (New York: Cambridge University Press, 1981, 17.
6. Michael McPherson drew my attention to John Dewey's *Human Nature and Conduct*. In commenting on an earlier draft of this paper, he wrote: "One observation I have, for what it is worth, is that the picture of history as a succession of problem solutions generating new problems is very much in line with what I understand to be John Dewey's philosophy of history. Dewey thought of this standpoint as a way of bringing Hegel's dialectic down to earth." The passages most nearly expressing this view are the following:
"No matter what the present success in straightening out difficulties and harmonizing conflicts, it is certain that problems will recur in the future in a new form or on a different plane. Indeed every genuine accomplishment instead of winding up an affair and enclosing it as a jewel in a casket for future contemplation, complicates the practical situation. It effects a new

distribution of energies which have henceforth to be employed in ways for which past experience gives no exact instruction. Every important satisfaction of an old want creates a new one; and this new one has to enter upon an experimental adventure to find its satisfaction. From the side of what has gone before achievement settles something. From the side of what comes after, it complicates, introducing new problems, unsettling factors. There is something pitifully juvenile in the idea that 'evolution,' progress, means a definite sum of accomplishment which will forever stay done, and which by an exact amount lessens the amount still to be done, disposing once and for all of just so many perplexities and advancing us just so far on our road to a final stable and unperplexed goal."

"Adherents of the idea that betterment, growth in goodness, consists in approximation to an exhaustive, stable, immutable end or good, have been compelled to recognize the truth that in fact we envisage the good in specific terms that are relative to existing needs, and that the attainment of every specific good merges insensibly into a new condition of maladjustment with its need of a new end and a renewed effort."

7. Albert O. Hirschman, *Journeys Toward Progress* (New York: Twentieth Century Fund, 1963), 237–38.

PART III

Exit, Voice, and Loyalty

On the Fruitful Convergences of Hirschman's *Exit, Voice, and Loyalty* and *Shifting Involvements:* Reflections from the Recent Argentine Experience

Guillermo O'Donnell

I

As this volume abundantly, albeit partially, shows, the works that Albert Hirschman has addressed to the economic and political development of Latin America have had enormous impact on the students (and often on the social and political leaders) of the region. Hirschman's influence on Latin America, however, goes well beyond those writings: his more general or theoretical publications, including those that were written more with the developed world in mind, have been extremely useful to many Latin Americanists from various disciplines. In the present chapter, I will use some of the ideas developed by Hirschman in *Exit, Voice, and Loyalty, (EVL)*,[1] and in *Shifting Involvements, (SI)*,[2] which I found illuminating for the study of some issues raised by the hectic and violent politics of my country, Argentina. By "transplanting" those ideas to a deeply repressive and authoritarian context, I hope to show that they can be further extended in ways that enhance their comparative and theoretical import.

II

The coups that implanted bureaucratic-authoritarian regimes in South America in the 1960s and 1970s occurred after, and to a large extent as a consequence of, serious economic crises, great waves of popular mobilization, widespread politization, and—quite often—high and increasing levels of violence.[3] In most cases, however, as happened with the emergence of fascism in Europe, those phenomena had already peaked before the respective military coups. This was certainly the case in Argentina before the 1976 coup: the massive mobilizations, the extensive and intense politization of many individuals from practically all social sectors, and even the challenges posed by urban guerrillas, had been declining for approximately two years before the coup. Although relevant data is sparse, it is clear that many individuals, tired of intense political involvement and threatened by the chaotic violence that characterized the post–1969 period in Argentina,[4] had quite eagerly returned to private pursuits before the 1976 coup.

In *SI* Hirschman persuasively discusses the factors that seem to account for the cycles of (to use terms which are equivalent to Hirschman's but which are more appropriate for my purposes here) politization and privatization observable in many countries. As Hirschman points out in *SI,* there are important differences in these cycles depending on whether or not the general political context is democratic. Pursuing this distinction further, we may note that when individuals opt for privatization in a democratic context, they are not haunted by the possibility of being victimized for whatever political reason. Furthermore, in those circumstances, the regime and, in general, the rules that regulate events in the public sphere remain unchanged, except for the lowered political participation entailed by the turn of many individuals to their private pursuits. On the other hand, when a new wave of politization occurs, the costs eventually incurred by each individual are those resulting from his/her changed allocation of time and efforts. A quite different matter are the additional (and eventually much more important) costs that may result from the actions of a government determined to prevent and, if necessary, repress such repolitization. As we shall see, both *SI* and *EVL* are useful for studying some processes that occur under bureaucratic-authoritarian rule, but further specification of the contextual assumptions of those works is needed: first, those regimes were committed to preventing the repolitization of their subjects and were ready to apply extremely harsh repression for that purpose; and second, even while living very privatized lives, many individuals had reason to fear reprisals motivated by their former politization.

In such situations, in Argentina as well as in Chile and Uruguay, many persons exited: they went into exile, some literally to save their lives, some because they could not stand the existing climate of pervasive fear and uncertainty. But many had not, or thought they had not, such an option. Their main alternative was the antonym of voice—silence—which is not discussed in detail under the contextual assumptions of *EVL* and *SI*. Silence and, as we shall see, "oblique voice" are, however, prime alternatives when the exit option is fore-closed and one is subjected to a repressive power.[5]

A situation such as the one I have sketched entails a sharp reduction of voice in at least two senses: first, in respect to the kind and number of individuals who can address the rulers without serious personal risk and, second, in what pertains to the permissible content and style of whatever voice is allowed to remain. Notice that I have referred to the type of voice that Hirschman analyzes in *EVL* and in the papers subsequently published in *Essays on Trespassing*.[6] This voice is addressed to the "top," by customers or citizens, toward managers or governments. This is what I shall call "vertical voice." This kind of voice is indeed crucial, but I shall argue that there is another type of voice that is no less important, and in some senses even more important, since it is a necessary condition for the exercise of vertical voice. This other kind of voice I shall call "horizontal."

In a democratic context, we assume that we have the right to address others, without fear of sanctions, on the basis of the belief that those others are "like me" in some dimension that at least I consider relevant. If we actually recognize ourselves as a "we" (for example, as workers who have the right to unionize), we have taken a necessary, and at times sufficient, step towards the formation of a collective identity. Such an identity entails not only that we share some basic (if often fuzzy) ideas about what it is that makes us a "we," but also that we share some ideal and/or material interests, the pursuit of which supposedly will guide our collective action.[7] When I am addressing others, or others are addressing me, claiming that we share some relevant characteristics, we are using horizontal voice.

Horizontal voice may or may not lead to the use of vertical voice. There exist collective identities which are not interested in addressing those "in power." On its part, vertical voice may be in-dividual, such as when a customer writes to management or a citizen to a member of parliament or when an entrepreneur enjoys direct access to a public agency. This may be the usual mode of vertical voice in business organizations, but in politics—particularly in demo-cratic politics—the more important mode of vertical voice is collective. Collective vertical voice at times is used directly, such as when in-dividuals take to the street together to express their grievances. But the more frequent mode of collective vertical voice is indirect, particu-larly in the densely organized world of contemporary societies: i.e., when some individuals speak to the authorities claiming that they are doing so in representation of some reasonably ascertainable con-stellation of individuals.

Whether in its direct or indirect modes, collective vertical voice at least if it has reasonable hope of being heard, must be based on the plausible existence of a constellation of individuals whose ideal or material interests it invokes. This usually means that some process of collective identity formation has occurred. Horizontal voice is one of the mechanisms that lead to such identity formation. Certainly, collective identities may be created or reproduced by the discourse of those "on top" toward their subjects. But the possibility of using horizontal voice without serious restrictions or dangers is a constitutive feature for a democratic (or, more generically, a non-repressive) context. Horizontal voice is a necessary condition for the existence of the kind of collective vertical voice that is reasonably autonomous from those "on top." This, in turn, is a necessary condition for the existence of a democratic context.

Notice that I am not referring to all sorts of social communication. Even though the analytical boundaries are fuzzy, here I want to confine myself to collective identities that are political in a rather narrow sense: those that somehow wish to address themselves to the existing governmental authorities, or those that for whatever reasons want to change those authorities. An important case (important at least in regard to the intensity with which it is likely to be felt) of political collective identity is that of those who oppose a repressive regime and who, even though they may disagree in other important respects, converge in the common purpose of terminating such a regime. I shall argue that this kind of situation demonstrates the importance of horizontal voice and, consequently, the convenience of extending Hirschman's framework to include the former.

III

Now I must briefly tell a story about which I have given more details in recent works.[8] The origin of this story is that, for reasons that are of no interest here, I chose to remain in Argentina after the March 1976 coup until December 1979, i.e., during the most repressive years of a very repressive regime. In 1978, my wife, Cecilia Galli, and I decided to investigate in others the fear that many of us had of being abducted, tortured, and murdered, alledgedly for political reasons. We also hoped to find the sharp opposition to the regime that we supposed many concealed behind a very privatized life. Thus, we undertook to interview as many persons as we could; we tried only with persons we had known before, or those who were referred to us by previous interviewees who could reasonably guarantee them, and us, that neither we nor they were police informers. The result was surely the most unrepresentative sample in the history of the social sciences. In addition, we kept something like an ethnographic diary. In it we registered the many events in which, inspired both by our professional training and the paranoia we developed under such conditions, we saw pervasive fear and uncertainty. Furthermore, aided by a world that became more *machista* than ever, as well as by her foreign accent (she is Brazilian), Cecilia asked the manifold *personae* one finds in a big city like Buenos Aires some "naive" questions about the regime and the changes in their lives after March 1976. This is the limited and biased data that our neurotic behavior led us to gather. (Only after having left Argentina did we realize that obsessively doing what we were trained to do was our way of displacing and to some extent exorcising our own fear.) But since I doubt that under similar circumstances anyone could do much better than that, I shall make use of this research in illustrating the arguments that follow.

First, however, some minimal background is needed for those who are not acquainted with contemporary Argentine history. At least since 1969 we Argentines inflicted upon ourselves the following: an extraordinarily pervasive and chaotic violence, where various so-called "public security agencies," guerrilla groups, and bands organized by some unions and business groups killed each other and many unarmed persons; the plain fact that almost literally nobody could feel safe from that violence; massive and recurrent demonstrations, often violent, which expressed and reinforced widespread politization in streets, factories, and schools; an economic crisis that may be synthesized by noting that, according to the (artificially low) official prices, in the months before the March 1976 coup inflation ran at about 1,200% per year; and a government, that of Isabel Perón, whose irrationality and talent for the grotesque only the imagination of García Márquez, Carpentier, and Roa Bastos had dreamed of.

Then the 1976 coup took place. For reasons I cannot discuss here, but which are in part (but only in part) accounted for by what I have just described, the regime implanted by that coup was, plainly, terroristic. Not only did it apply severe and cruel repression to many individuals, it did so in a decentralized, largely unpredictable, and usually clandestine way. That this was so is sufficiently well-known today, so I do not need to go into details here. I must only stress that the risks were as high as they were difficult to gauge: almost anyone (because he/she had been politically active in the past, or simply because he/she knew somebody whom some repressive agency suspected of "subversion") could be abducted, tortured, and murdered without even knowing the "reasons." Furthermore, since in keeping with its terroristic nature the regime refused to issue any clear rules about what was and was not punishable, it was practically impossible to feel safe—in our melancholic encounters with Chilean and Uruguayan friends we found ourselves envying them because of their no less repressive but more bureaucratized, and hence more predictable, regimes.

IV

There was, however, one major prohibition that was clear, not because somebody decided to make it explicit but because it is inherent in the very nature of repressive, deeply authoritarian rule—not only at the level of the national-state but also, with a logic that reverberates through all social contexts, down to the more micro levels. That logic means that occasionally one may address the rulers, on some issues and in the forms that they determine and may modify at their whim; but what one should never do is to address other subjects of the rulers in terms of the shared condition as such subjects. This is the logic of *divide et impera,* not only as a useful strategy for maximizing power but as the very core of authoritiarian domination, made nakedly explicit at its more repressive limits.

Accordingly, during those years in my country, with some risks and slight chances of success, one could think of using some vertical voice (i.e., "respectfully petition the authorities" on some thoroughly depoliticized issues), but what meant almost certain death was any attempt to use horizontal voice. Individuals had to be isolated, obedient subjects of the regime, happy to devote themselves to their private pursuits—work and family—avoiding the dangerous world of public affairs, of which the rulers claimed they were taking good care. Any attempt to keep alive former collective identities (such as those of members of a political party, or workers who had conquered certain rights, or students who could ask questions) was a sure signal of "subversive contamination." Even apparently innocuous activites (such as being part of a music or theater group, or participating in a study group on whatever theme, or simply joining other persons chatting in the street) were suspect and, therefore, dangerous.[9] Getting together, in any of the manifold forms of sociability one takes for granted in more benign contexts, was suspect precisely because it meant getting together. Since it was potentially even more subversive to address relevant others beyond face-to-face relationships, by perverse mechanisms that it is not the occasion to narrate here, the media were strictly controlled. This was not only with respect to overtly political messages which anyway nobody except the rulers and their propagandists would have dared to convey through the media. Controls were also applied—as a linguist at the service of the regime told a theater director we interviewed—to messages that "even if apparently apolitical, could trigger semantic series of subversive potential."

It goes without saying that attempts to extend mutual recognition as opponents to the regime—the, under the circumstances, crucial type of horizontal voice at stake—were especially dangerous. We shall see, however, that this kind of voice was not entirely suppressed, and I shall argue that, in contrast with what a repressive regime can do, at least for a time, with vertical voice, not even the most efficiently terroristic regime could ever completely suppress horizontal voice. But before making this argument we must undertake a digression.

V

Even though I cannot report our research in detail here (this is the subject matter of a book which until now we have been unable to write), I must mention some relevant findings. We found, indeed, fear in our interviews, in many cases repressed and displaced toward other objects. This was a major, if ultimately precarious, ideological victory of the regime. In spite of the fact that during the second half of the interviews some of those persons began to convey to us a deep feeling of loss because of the extremely privatized lives they were living, many of them agreed with the messages with which the regime bombarded them everyday. First, nothing could be worse than the generalized chaos of the preceding period; even the peculiar "order" that the regime offered—an order in which violence came from only one side, its own—was preferable to the former chaos. Second, at the roots of the country's problems was the "irresponsible demagoguery," and the easy chances it offered for the "subversion" that had characterized the widespread politization of the pre-coup period. Third, the economy seemed to be under control, even if at the cost of a brutal redistribution of income. Fourth, the duty of every good Argentine was to work hard and enjoy the benefits of the upcoming "economic modernization" of the country and to take good care that the ever-present danger of subversion would not again raise its head in the family, the school, the workplace and the streets.

In other words, the repression that the regime applied for achieving the depolitization of its subjects was successful for some time. Such success was based not only on the fear raised among those who disagreed but also—at least in our sample—on the fact that there were many who, even before the emergence of that regime, were in full swing away from the politicized pole of the Hirschmanian cycle of involvements. In the often repeated words of those interviewees, the previous period had been "too much"—crazy years in which they had been "intoxicated" with politics, when they had believed, and at times done, things that now lingered on dangerously in their lives. Thus, even though, as mentioned, after talking to us for a while some sadly recognized that they had lost something important in the shift toward their profoundly privatized lives, those respondents felt that they had become "more realistic and mature." After all, what life was about was work and family and, eventually, with some luck, the purchase of the imported junk that the regime at the time was making available as the *panem* for its subjects. The *circus* was a one-shot event: the vicarious (but practically unanimous) experience of politically sanitized (but ecstatic) participation manipulated by the regime after the victory of the Argentine team in the world soccer cup of 1978.

Furthermore, many of those respondents seemed to agree so fully with the already-mentioned injunctions of the regime that they declared that, for reasons that in most cases they could not articulate, they had also drastically reduced other forms of apolitical sociability. But those reasons became clear when they talked about their children, or when we interviewed adolescents' psychologists and psychoanalysts. Any form of sociability that could not be controlled by the family or by the school (which, of course, became more authoritarian than ever) was inherently dangerous: "bad influences" could operate or, even if such were not the case, the son or the daughter could be linked to someone that the government (rather, the various groups that abducted and killed as part of the terroristic strategy of the regime) could at any time, and without possible appeal, define as "subversive."

These data have many implications, both political and psychological, which I cannot deal with here. But I hope that the underlying argument of this section is plausible: that it may be illogical but it is not existentially impossible that those individuals felt two very different things at the same time. On the one hand, they agreed with the regime that they should live thoroughly privatized lives and that they should do whatever they could to prevent their family members from transgressing that norm. On the other hand, at a less immediately conscious level, they felt something of which, as some of them put it, they only became aware by talking to us about some public issues they had been striving to ignore: that, by so extensively privatizing their lives, they had lost something very important. They seemed to feel as if they had amputated an important dimension of their lives and that this loss was not only the suppression of their rights *qua* citizens, but also something that impoverished them in very intimate dimensions. Thus, many of our interviewees, at least at the level of their superficial beliefs, agreed with the regime about what was meant by a "good Argentine": half-time *homo economicus,* half-time jealous and authoritarian parent, and all the time an obedient subject of threatening powers.

In *SI* and further works, Hirschman, in a cogent critique of the usual assumptions of economic theory about stable and transitive individual preferences, makes the argument that, as illustrated among other things by the shifts between public and private involvements, "men and women have the ability to step back from their 'revealed' wants, volitions, and preferences and consequently to form meta-preferences that may differ from their preferences."[10] The fact that many of our interviewees behaved as I have described but that, at the same time, they felt a deep sense of loss, supports Hirschman's argument. Our interviews suggest that, at least in cultures that share a common root in classical Greece, the idea that many of us have of a "well-rounded," properly self-esteeming individual includes both an active public life and an intense involvement in private concerns. But we cannot have both at the same time—not to the degree that our more or less conscious normative images demand. So we tend to shift from one kind of involvement to the other. Thus, while we have chosen one kind of involvement over the other (and have dressed such choice with the remarkable talent we have for giving ourselves good reasons for our preferences), at a less conscious level we may be nostalgic for that "other world" which, at least for the time being, we have abandoned. *Angst,* omnipotence, denial of death, *hubris* and innumerable related terms point to a much more inherently dissatisfied and tense animal than the chooser between two or more preferences that mainstream economics—and, to a large extent, political science—present to us.

That the interplay between public and private impulses may be an unsolvable tension is suggested by the negative connotations that in our cultures evoke persons who give the impression of being entirely devoted to public or to privatized concerns. An entirely public man (not to say anything about the "public woman," as Hirschman reminds us in *SI,* that euphemism for prostitution which, in the sense I am discussing here, is not too different from the connotations of an "excessively public man") is suspected of having nothing behind the mask he wears, just shallow, "de-humanized" emptiness. This may be why the ultimate public persons, the politicians, find it useful to show that, in spite of their heavy public obligations, they have a beautiful, intense family life. On the other hand, a person entirely dedicated to his private concerns (his, because women are supposed to be so dedicated, which means, precisely, that in an important sense they are "less" than men) raises connotations of selfishness and pettiness, of a life which is "too small" and without a dignified purpose. This may be why, when they have been successful in the very private pursuit of earning money, some rich persons feel obliged to show their "public consciousness." One way or the other, the language we use, as well as the innumerable portraits that the literary imagination has drawn of the manifold variations of these archetypes, express the feeling that a person "excessively" immersed in a public or a private life is less than "fully" or "truly" human.

If, as I am suggesting, a shift toward a very politicized or privatized life is deeply conflictive and leads to guilt feelings that we usually repress from our consciousness, it follows that the strength of the "rebound effects" from private to public involvements that *SI* discusses, is dependent upon the general contextual situation. In a democratic setting, the decision to live a very private life is, in principle a free one; if afterwards I decide to involve myself politically and then I look negatively at my "excessively privatized" previous period, short of acute neurosis I cannot but criticize myself. The situation is different in repressive contexts. As we saw, our interviewees were living extremely privatized lives for reasons more complicated than the coercion that the government was applying. But when, as we shall see, a new cycle of politization occurred, those persons could project upon an obvious target all the blame for what they now recognized as deep losses during the period through which they had just lived. That target was the authoritarian regime. The availability of such an external (and, of course, in many senses, very appropriate) target exempted those persons from self-criticism and, thus, unleashed the full intensity of their guilt-feelings and grievances against the authoritarian regime. This is why Hirschman's "rebound effects" are likely to be stronger when a politicized cycle occurs after a period of privatization that has been backed by a repressive power. This strengthened rebound effect, even if not particularly useful in terms of the self-knowledge of the individuals concerned, is a powerful weapon against authoritarian rule. Through it we may understand another theme often tackled by the literary imagination: the scenes of liberation from authoritarian rule, where those who have fought against it are the more serene, while those who have been passive or in some senses collaborated are the more cruel and vengeful. But for this enhanced rebound effect to occur, some horizontal voice must have reappeared. This theme will occupy us in the following pages.

VI

The remarks of the preceding section can now be put in a different way: at its limit, the logic of authoritarian domination tends to exercise full control of the collective identities of its subjects (as we saw, in our case, the constellation of attributes connoted by the idea of "a good Argentine"). This is a monologal structure: those "on top" address their subjects and allow very little, and strictly controlled, vertical voice; furthermore, they forbid the dialogical structure entailed by horizontal voice. This results not only in the suppression of the specifically public dimension of the subjects, but also in severe loss of their sociability. The themes of loneliness, of cold as opposed to the warmth of spontaneous sociability, and of darkness as the expression of the cognitive difficulties resulting from the suppression of most channels of free communication, are recurrent in literature, psychology and history (as they were in our own feelings and in those conveyed to us by our interviewees) in the depiction of the experience of repressive rule. He who must listen but cannot speak is the infant in the authoritarian family. Such an infant cannot possibly know what is good for him, much less for others; he must be told who he is: with whom, how, and why he should identify.

In a nation-state (as well as, I surmise, in many organizations) the obliteration of horizontal voice has some crucial consequences. First, it is a sufficient condition for the severe decay of vertical voice. Even if an authoritarian regime would leave unobstructed the preexisting channels for the use of vertical voice, the suppression of horizontal voice entails that such information as does get through to the top consists exclusively of individual—and in a sense perversely privatized—messages. This means that collective vertical voice (which, as we saw, presupposes collective identities which in turn presuppose the use of horizontal voice) is suppressed. Furthermore, the obliteration of horizontal voice means that those social sectors whose mode of voicing cannot but be collective, are condemned to silence;

consequently, as we descend the ladder of social stratification a deeper silence is imposed. Thus, whatever vertical voice remains is not only drastically diminished, it is also inherently biased. A second consequence is that, since all sources of collective identity not monopolized by the authoritarian rulers are prohibited, they place extraordinarily jealous demands on another theme of *EVL:* loyalty, in this case the loyalty due to the collective identity that those rulers wish to impose. This is a jealous demand, because it pretends to exclude all others and, thus, it defines *a contrario* that most dangerous of categories to be placed in, all the way from repressive regimes to street gangs: those who do not "truly deserve" to be considered members. A third consequence is that the more repressive a regime is, the more exclusive and paranoid it becomes toward autonomous sources of voice. The resulting closure to potentially relevant information entails the lack of the "corrective mechanisms" discussed in *EVL*[11] and, at the limit, is equivalent to the clinical definition of madness— this is why these systems are disaster-prone, as was superbly illustrated by the Malvinas/Falklands fiasco of the Argentine regime.

Another consequence of the suppression of horizontal voice— already suggested—has to do with the subjects of repressive rule: the atomized life they are forced to live, the extreme privatization of their concerns, and the caution and mistrust with which the few remaining occasions of sociability must be approached. These restrictions entail a sharp impoverishment, as our interviews and observations in Argentina showed, even of very personal and not at all political dimensions of human life. As research on political culture shows, in all countries there are many who never use vertical voice, probably do not feel the tensions between the public and private discussed above, and still may be quite happy human beings. But life with horizontal voice severely repressed is plainly awful. If I have not become a perfect *idiotes* and, thus, if I have opinions about the politics and economics of my country, I need others, who even if they disagree, confirm that my opinions and beliefs are not senseless. Without the emotional and cognitive anchoring that such communications furnish to my personal and social identities, the very assumptions about what is real and valuable may enter into flux. Short of the psychological disintegration of the individual—of which our interviews with various sorts of psychological therapists gave sad and quite extensive evidence—the resulting tendency converges with the purposes of the authoritarian regime: to take refuge in an extremely privatized life, "forgetting" the dangerous and cognitively uncertain "outside world." On the other hand, if in such situations one still tries to use horizontal voice, some interesting things happen. This will occupy us in the following section.

VII

It is conceivable that an extremely repressive regime could, at least for a time, entirely suppress vertical voice. But the trick with horizontal voice is that, even if such a regime might get quite close to it, it can never completely suppress or control it. Not only through personal experience in Argentina but also in a comparative study of authoritarian rule[12] that I undertook with a group of colleagues, the importance of what I shall call "oblique voice" became evident. This is a particular kind of horizontal voice. It intends to be understood by "others like me" in our opposition to a repressive regime and, at the same time, it hopes not to be perceived by the agents of the latter. After the March 1976 coup there was not much horizontal voice in Argentina but there was something, enough for not falling into utter despair. Certain unconventional (slightly so, there was not room for more that that) ways of dressing, clapping hands with excessive enthusiasm in front of the public authorities, going to the recitals of singers or musicians who were known to disagree with the regime, some quick glances in the streets and other public spaces—these were some of the ways with which, in this most fertile area of human imagination, one could recognize and be recognized by others as opponents to the regime. Notice that such signals did not intend other behavioral consequences, such as the ones that members of a resistance movement ready to enter in action might exchange. Notice also that there were no instrumental rewards expected, and that oblique voice always entailed some degree of risk. But these signals had great emotional and cognitive import, as the way to recognize that each one was not entirely alone in his/her opposition to the regime. This was the untransposable limit of the violence of the regime, that residue of oblique, non-verbal horizontal voice which one could still exercise when all other forms of voice had been suppressed. As Hirschman notes in *SI* and other works,[13] there are some activities that gratify because of the very fact that they are undertaken; this is why some forms and moments of political participation cannot be reduced to a utilitarian calculus nor, consequently, are subject to the free-rider problem.[14] This is suggested by oblique voice, that irreducible core of political involvement: by exercising it one obtained the crucial cognitive gratification of confirming a shared collective identity, as well as the no less crucial emotional benefit of asserting one's self-respect as a non-*idiotes*. Notice, finally, that even though oblique voice is practiced in an apparently depoliticized context, it has an intrinsic reference to a very public involvement. It is this capacity of linking the most personal with the most public, not only of oblique but also of all sorts of horizontal voice, that makes it so important politically.

This argument can be further illustrated *a contrario* with another piece of the story I began to narrate above. I was living in Brazil when the Argentine government launched the invasion of the Malvinas/Falklands. As soon as it happened, I felt a strong urge to go to Buenos Aires, hoping that I could find others who shared my unconditional rejection of such an adventure and of the war it would predictably trigger. But I was immensely distressed to find that an overwhelming majority of my acquaintances, including many of those who opposed the regime, enthusiastically supported the invasion and, later on, the war. "Before anything else we are Argentines" was the argument I heard *ad nauseam*. Until appalling defeat occurred, the regime was enormously successful in establishing a hyper-nationalistic collective identity that practically erased all others. Even oblique voice almost disappeared; almost everyone was trying to "help the country" win the war. This led me into quite a few painful discussions in which even opponents of the regime accused me of "thinking like a foreigner," if not worse. The rather lonely reflections with which I tried to stand fast to my opinions and values were not enough, not even when I recognized in myself a well-known psychological problem: the immense difficulty of holding on to values and even to elementary factual opinions when most social interactions refute them. This had been quite easy to do before the war, while some oblique voice existed. But it became immensely difficult when even oblique voice was practically obliterated during those awful days. Then, faced with the arguments of most relevant others that I was at best misinterpreting everything, I realized I was losing the social support—cognitive and affective—needed in order to stick to basic opinions and values;[15] even what was and was not real became doubtful. Afterwards, chatting with persons who had shared my views during those days, they told me that they had suffered similar problems; some of them had ended up by supporting the war. (My own part of the story is that, in despair, in the midst of those events I exited to Brazil, where, even in a deeply polemical *milieu* with fellow Argentines, I found enough supportive interactions to enable me to stick to my opinions and values.)

VIII

As is well-known, the Malvinas/Falkland adventure ended in the complete defeat of the Argentine troops. It soon became evident to the population that the government had lied outrageously about the developments of the war, and that the behavior of many officers of the armed forces had been remarkably inept and cowardly. The regime thus entered into collapse, eroded by its internal conflicts and recriminations, and pushed by the rage with which suddenly many demanded rapid democratization. The atrocities that the regime had committed in the previous years began to be publicly exposed, jointly with the abysmal corruption of most of the rulers. These facts, which many had refused to acknowledge or had until recently justified, fed still further the moral indignation with which most Argentines suddenly found themselves agreeing in their demand for democratization.

Even though the circumstances made this process particularly rapid and intense in Argentina, in the already mentioned study on transitions from authoritarian rule, we found that this "resurrection of civil society," as Schmitter and I call it,[16] is a typical occurrence. At some moment, and for reasons too varied to be discussed here, many individuals who have been formerly passive, depoliticized, acquiescent or simply too afraid to do anything, converge in a broadly-shared (and often daring) demand for the termination of the authoritarian regime. Whether successful or not in the achievement of its goals, such a convergence is a powerful driving force in the transition.

As I suggested above, the mechanisms that lead to this—for the actors, at least—surprising emergence, are more complex than the existence, under the *aegis* of the authoritarian regime, of many individuals who purposely conceal their opposition until the situation becomes ripe for acting. Undoubtedly there are such individuals but, if the lesson from the Argentine case has any value, there are also many who are at best politically passive or indifferent during that period, but who as the contextual conditions begin to change, quite suddenly repoliticize in determined opposition to the authoritarian regime. When the regime in Argentina was already collapsing, in a rather perverse move—with the pretext that we had lost the transcript of their former interviews and needed their help for reconstructing them—we reinterviewed some of the more depoliticized and acquiescent individuals in our sample. On this second occasion, most of them were full of rage against the regime, the armed forces, its behavior in the war, and the atrocities it had committed in the country. Furthermore, some of those respondents had again become politically active. All of them "remembered" what they had told us before in a way that sharply contrasted with what they had actually told us. They were wrong, but evidently sincere, as they had been sincere before, in telling us, in the reinterviews, that they had always strongly opposed the regime and had never accepted its injunctions. In the first interviews those respondents had given distressing responses to our probings concerning the abductions, tortures and murders that were going on: these were only "rumors" or "exaggerations" and, at any event, "there must be some reason" why some persons were so victimized. Refusal to know, and in some worse cases, identification with the aggressor and blaming the victim, were ugly mechanisms about which we had read in studies on Nazi Germany. To our deep sadness because, quite naively, we had not expected these mechanisms to operate in so many of our interviewees, we had to recognize them during our research; most of those persons told us on the second occasion that "only now" had they become aware of those atrocities and that, "of course," they energetically condemned them.[17]

The persons we reinterviewed gave us the impression that they had just "discovered" what they subconsciously felt they should have believed during the years of harsh repression. As a consequence, they had rewritten their memories to fit that discovery. The sense of continuity of their personal identity was preserved and, thus, they could look at the past without conscious guilt or shame: they had had "nothing to do" with the atrocities perpetrated by the regime (which was true in the real but partial sense that they had not personally participated in repression), and had known little or nothing of those atrocities. It is my impression that these important although unacknowledged changes were closely related to the previous obliteration of most forms of horizontal voice and, at the moment of the reinterviews, to the rapid recuperation of all sorts of voice that was taking place.

During our first round of interviews, trying to find a not entirely dark side to our data, we told ourselves that the refusal of many interviewees to recognize what was going on was a defense mechanism that preserved them for better times. Given the extremely repressive conditions, short of conscious identification with the regime and, consequently and necessarily, with its atrocities, the actual alternative for such persons was to plunge into an absorbed private life, and to refuse to know what was going on "outside." This, at least, preserved them (more specifically, their self-esteem) for the moment when it eventually would become not too dangerous to "know" and, thus, to become indignant about what had happened. Imagining that they had "always" been opposed to the regime and only coming to terms with reality after the regime had begun to collapse are expressions of well-known defenses such as psychological rationalization, selective memory, and cognitive dissonance. The aspect of these complex phenomena that interests me here is how their occurrence may be triggered by changes in the political context.

As we found in the already mentioned study of transitions, there are—generalizing beyond the Argentine case—circumstances that lead to the collapse or, less dramatically, to the obvious decay of repressive rule. There are, then, some noble individuals who have the courage to say that the emperor is naked (some of them even had the courage to say it before, but then very few listened). There are, also, other no less noble individuals who dare to spread such, shortly before, unimaginable opinions. The exemplary character of those statements leads others, and then others, to address others saying that what really matters is to act together for the purpose of getting rid of authoritarian rule. In other words, civil society has resurrected, horizontal voice has reemerged, its "subversive" implications operate again, oblique voice becomes unnecessary, and—as a consequence—vertical voice aimed at changing those who are "on top" is heard. In the first stages of this process, repression by the crumbling authoritarian regime may be and usually is harsh, but it tends to be erratic and, above all, few believe that it can restore the hold the regime previously had on individual lives.[18] In such circumstances, horizontal voice again appeals to the "public self" of individuals, in ways that allow them to recover a feeling of integrity: now they can demand the rights that pertain to them as citizens, and they again have moral standards with which to take a stand against the authoritarian regime. This is why the rebound effects toward public involvement are so widespread and intense in these cases: many repoliticize themselves, electoral campaigns draw big crowds, attempted authoritarian reversions are usually defeated with the support of an active and mobilized public opinion, and electoral participation in the founding elections of a more or less democratic regime is unusually high. Whatever free riding may exist does not weigh enough to weaken such processes, and there seems to be nothing like the perception of the "paradox of voting": on the contrary, participating in the demise of authoritarian rule and voting (the very act of symbolic and, to a significant extent, also practical negation of authoritarian rule, which constitutes not only the democratic authorities but also the voter *qua* citizen) are undertaken, as Hirschman argues, because those activities are felt as extremely rewarding in themselves.

What is clear in the admittedly exceptional circumstances of the demise of authoritarian rule, may well also be true—although less intense and, thus, more difficult to perceive—of many forms of political participation and repolitization occurring in more normal circumstances. The sense of personal worth and self-respect, the feeling that one is not an *idiotes,* the hope of achieving valued goals by means of collective action, the motivation of overcoming the "coldness" and "darkness" of an isolated life through the emotional warmth of sociability and collective identity, and the cognitive reassurance that comes from the public sharing of values and opinions with many others—all these are crucial phenomena of political life, even if often they fade away and then, again and again, reappear under old or new faces. These phenomena cannot be accounted for on utilitarian grounds, so we should not expect that they will be subject to (or, at least, that they should be dominated by) the dilemmas and paradoxes of the kinds of social action for which utilitarian assumptions are reasonably realistic. Horizontal voice has crucial importance for the emergence and reproduction of such phenomena, as well as for the very existence of a democratic context.

NOTES

1. Albert O. Hirschman, *Exit, Voice, and Loyalty: Responses to Decline, Organizations, and States* (Cambridge: Harvard University Press, 1970).

2. Albert O. Hirschman, *Shifting Involvements: Private Interest and Public Action* (Princeton: Princeton University Press, 1979).

3. See esp. David Collier, ed., *The New Authoritarianism in Latin America* (Princeton: Princeton University Press, 1979).

4. These processes are analyzed in Guillermo O'Donnell, *El Estado Burocrático-Autoritario. Argentina 1966–1973* (Buenos Aires: Editorial de Belgrado, 1982; English edition, The University of California Press, forthcoming).

5. For a similar argument, Jean Laponce, "Hirschman's Voice and Exit Model as a Spatial Archetype," *Social Science Information* 13, no. 3 (June 1974), 67–81.

6. Albert O. Hirschman, *Essays in Trespassing: Economics to Politics and Beyond* (Cambridge: Cambridge University Press, 1981).

7. On this point, Alessandro Pizzorno, "Political Exchange and Col-

lective Identity in Industrial Conflict," in Colin Crouch and Alessandro Pizzorno, eds., *The Resurgence of Class Conflict in Western Europe since 1968*
(London: Macmillan Press, 1978), Vol. 2, 277–97.

8. Guillermo O'Donnell, "Democracia en la Argentina: Micro y Macro,"
in Oscar Oszlak, ed., *'Proceso,' Crisis y Transición Democrática* (Buenos
Aires: Centro Editor de América Latina, 1984), Vol. I, 13–30.

9. It even became dangerous to participate in psychological therapy
groups: the repressors soon discovered that if appropriately pressured or
tortured, members of such groups were excellent informants about any other
members whom they suspected. Many psychologists and psychoanalysts
stopped working with groups. As it often happens, this high uncertainty and
risk has been better expressed in literary works; see, e.g., Humberto Con-
stantini, *De Dioses, Hombrecitos y Policías* (Buenos Aires: Editorial Bruguera,
1984).

10. Albert O. Hirschman, "Against Parsimony: Three Easy Ways of
Complicating Some Categories of Economic Discourse," in *American Economic Review* 74 (2), May 1984.

11. The tendency of authoritarian regimes to close themselves to crucial
information and the destructive consequences that follow from this, are
cogently discussed in David Apter, *Choice and the Politics of Allocation* (New
Haven: Yale University Press, 1973).

12. Guillermo O'Donnell, Philippe Schmitter and Laurence Whitehead,
eds., *Transitions from Authoritarian Rule: Latin America and Southern Europe*
(Baltimore: The John Hopkins University Press, forthcoming). These processes
are discussed in Guillermo O'Donnell and Philippe Schmitter, "Political Life
after Authoritarian Rule: Tentative Conclusions about Uncertain Transitions,"
Vol. IV of *Transitions*.

13. Esp. "Against Parsimony: Three Easy Ways of Complicating Some
Categories of Economic Discourse."

14. As we shall see below, this is why Brian Barry's critique of *Exit,
Voice, and Loyalty* to the effect that this work fails to take into account free
riding and its consequences for political action, misses the target at least with
respect to some, often very important, forms of collective action; Brian Barry,
"Review Article: 'Exit, Voice, and Loyalty,' " *British Journal of Political
Science* (4 February 1974), 79–107. Of course, the reference to "free riding"
is to the *locus classicus* of Mancur Olson, *The Logic of Collective Action*
(Cambridge: Harvard University Press, 1965).

15. Some readers may find interesting to know that, in those circum-
stances, it was helpful to me to remember the classic experiment of S. E.
Asch, which had fascinated me when I studied in Graduate School. See S.
E. Asch, "Effects of Group Pressure on the Modification and Distortion of
Judgments." First printed in H. S. Guetzkow, ed., *Groups, Leadership and
Men: Research in Human Relations* (Pittsburgh: Carnegie Press, 1951); re-
printed in H. Proshansky and B. Seidenberg, eds., *Basic Studies in Social
Psychology* (New York: Holt, Rinehart and Winston, 1965), 393–401.

16. O'Donnell, Schmitter, and Whitehead, *Transitions*.

17. An obvious question that we posed ourselves from the beginning of our research was whether the respondents concealed from us their true opinions due to fear and mistrust. We are sure this was not the case because practically all the interviews, after an uptight beginning, became very emotional. Often our respondents cried and gave other unmistakable signals of the deep emotions they were feeling as they talked to us about themes related to the public sphere and/or their own past that—as some of them insisted—they had "forgotten." Both factually and emotionally the more difficult moment for us was not to begin but to end the interviews. In no less than half of the cases the respondents asked us to continue (after an average of two hours and a half of interview) or to make another appointment with them, arguing that the very fact of talking to us was very important for them.

18. These processes are discussed in O'Donnell, Schmitter, and Whitehead, *Transitions*.

Dismantling Repressive Systems: The Abolition of Slavery in Cuba as a Case Study

Rebecca J. Scott

This essay will examine the dismantling of a specific coercive economic system—the Cuban slave system—and analyze the varied responses of those within it and the factors that determined the pace and character of its decline. Of special interest will be a feature of this system that it shares with certain other highly repressive systems: an *interdependence* of its component parts that makes it particularly vulnerable both to certain kinds of challenges from below and to the consequences of efforts at internal reform. I hope the examination of a complex and completed instance of the dismantling of a repressive system in the past will make possible some parallels with complex and *un*completed cases of dismantling in the present, though I shall also point out some of the special features of colonial slavery which contrast with modern repression.

In adapting Albert O. Hirschman's concepts of exit, voice, and loyalty to the institution of slavery I am pressing these notions into service in a situation that is, surely, a limiting case. For the slave, exit from slavery was extraordinarily difficult, voice was likely to be ignored, and loyalty was implausible. This does not mean, however, that the alternatives were inevitably acquiescence or rebellion. Slaves' responses to their situations were multifaceted, drawing on the fragments of exit and voice available to them. Moreover, as the system of slavery entered into decline, these options increased markedly, and the nature of slave initiatives evolved, further accelerating that decline. The responses of masters were similarly complex as they sought to resist change, forestall what they could not prevent, or adapt to an emerging system of labor control through other means. Analyzing these behaviors in historical terms may thus give us some idea of how the categories of exit, voice, and loyalty function in the context of a thoroughly repressive system, and may suggest ways in which they might be modified.

Slavery and Abolition

Slavery in Cuba in the mid-nineteenth century was both the material foundation of a prosperous export economy based on sugar, and the dominating social fact determining the character of class relations and race relations in the countryside. The labor of hundreds of thousands of African and Afro-Cuban slaves had enabled Cuba to become the world's largest exporter of sugar. At the same time, the continued existence of slavery had helped to lock Cuba into its colonial status, for its elite feared the social unrest that might accompany an anti-colonial rebellion, and the metropolitan government feared the loss of revenue that would follow from ending colonial domination over so wealthy an outpost. Slavery thus continued in the island into the 1860s and 1870s, after it had been eliminated in much of the rest of the New World.[1]

Though some modern scholars, and a few nineteenth-century observers, have viewed the persistence of slavery in Cuba as a brake on the island's technological advancement, as a practical matter major Cuban planters managed to adopt sophisticated processing equipment while maintaining substantial portions of their work force in bondage. They made use of a stratified and segmented labor market to permit the introduction of new workers without relinquishing power over the old. The "contradiction" between slavery and technological advance, if indeed there was one, did not incline most planters to support abolition in pursuit of economic modernization. They chose instead a path of gradual substitution and adaptation.[2]

A series of internal and external factors nonetheless served to force the decline of slavery. The effective British interdiction of the contraband slave trade to Cuba in the 1860s, combined with the Northern victory in the U.S. Civil War, set limits to Cuban slavery. A racially-based slave system with a negative natural rate of increase among its slaves could not endure indefinitely once the supply of new slaves had been terminated. At the same time, a domestic challenge to the reliance on slave labor began to emerge. In 1868, anti-colonial rebels led by small-scale sugar producers and professionals in the eastern end of the island rose up in revolt against Spanish domination, and included among their demands the eventual indemnified abolition of slavery. As the social base of their rebellion expanded, the insurgents found themselves under pressure to take the more direct step of ending slavery in regions under their control.[3] This formal declaration of abolition, though qualified in its definition of "freedom," raised slave expectations and, in conjunction with the recruitment of slaves into the rebel forces, led to the rapid breakdown of the social relations of slavery in insurgent controlled zones.[4]

In an attempt to recapture the political initiative, while maintaining the support of sugar planters, the Spanish parliament in 1870 began the abolition of slavery in areas under metropolitan control, but with a law so cautious and partial that its effects on the rural slave work force were negligible. (The government freed newborn slave infants and slaves over the age of sixty.) In 1878 the war against Spanish domination ended in defeat for the rebels, but slaves who had taken up arms on each side were granted freedom in the peace treaty—a practical necessity, from the Spanish point of view, if pacification was to be achieved. This concession, however, served to provoke further unrest among slaves in the east, who demanded their freedom *"como los convenidos,"* like those covered by the peace treaty. Fearful of the consequences of further temporizing, the Spanish parliament in 1880 took another cautious step, and declared that all slaves in Cuba were now free, but were to remain as "apprentices" under the tutelage of their masters for another eight years. This intermediate institution of the *patronato,* as it was called, stalled full emancipation, but was not in itself a stable state. Apprentices, both as individuals and in groups, made use of a variety of legal and extralegal mechanisms to hasten their own freedom. Moreover, masters were uncertain whether to attempt to maintain all the control the law allowed over their bondsmen, or whether to shift more decisively to free labor, and competition and uncertainty among them accelerated the pace of change. In 1886, as the number of remaining *patrocinados* declined rapidly, the Spanish parliament terminated the *patronato,* and slavery was finally over in Cuba.[5]

Exit, Voice, and Loyalty: The Responses of Slaves and Masters

While the terms exit, voice, and loyalty suggest clear categories, both the Hirschman volume and this case study find multiple hybrids of the three at every turn. The variants and recombinations in this instance reflect not only the inherent complexity of human responses to change, but also the peculiar dynamics involved in dismantling this particular repressive system.

Sugar planters in Cuba had long relied on slavery for their prosperity, had for decades fought a largely successful battle against the repression of the transatlantic slave trade, and had inhibited discussion of even the possibility of abolition. It may therefore come as a surprise that the Hirschman model, which is premised on dissatisfaction with some state of affairs, should be applicable to masters. But by the 1870s and 1880s the system on which slaveholders had long relied came to face a range of problems, and they had to figure out how to respond.

Some chose the path of loyalty to the institution of slavery. Committed to the social relations of slavery, they refused to bend to the reformist legislation emanating from Madrid. They attempted to block their slaves from communication with outsiders; they stalled or refused to pay the stipends called for in the 1880 legislation; they persisted in corporal punishment. Their intransigence posed a serious problem for governmental authorities. Some conformity with reformist legislation was necessary if the gradualist scheme was to have any credibility at all. Spanish officials thus urged slaveholders to observe the laws. On the other hand, *punishing* a slaveholder for breaking these laws, and granting his slaves freedom as called for in the regulations, threatened still further disruption. In a recently pacified colony, no governor wanted to contend with a seriously embittered elite or with former slaves who sensed their own power. Because of the halfheartedness of the reforms, and the reluctance of authorities to enforce them, masters who chose to remain loyal to the old order of things were thus able to maintain a certain continuity of labor and of discipline. This strategy, however, could only be a short-term one.

For large planters concerned with the overall evolution of labor relations on the island, voice was a more promising alternative. Slaveholders like the Conde de Casa Moré, or Julián Zulueta, bastions of Spanish conservatism and owners of hundreds of slaves, sought to influence policy directly. They petitioned the Spanish government to redefine key terms in the reform legislation and to modify the regulations through which the legislation would be enforced. In these efforts they were very largely successful, stalling and modifying the terms of what were already quite timid efforts at change. Moreover, they participated directly in the enforcement of the laws as members of the Juntas Protectoras de Libertos, by shaping the interpretation of the legislation and by ruling on slave petitions. As the process of decline of slavery accelerated, figures like the Conde de Casa Moré turned their attention to the encouragement of immigration, attempting to smooth the transition from slavery to free labor.[6]

Exit, of course, was also a possibility. Some slaveowners chose to abandon the institution altogether, and to move quickly toward wage labor. There were various ways of doing this. Some struck private bargains with their slaves on the terms of freedom, received payments from the slaves in return, and rehired them along with other workers. A few masters simply freed their slaves, though this appears to have been most common not on the plantations but in urban areas, where selective manumission of domestic servants had long been a gesture of paternalistic benevolence—and an incentive to faithful labor. Others sought to build up their work forces through the attraction of *patrocinados* and others as wage laborers, and were willing to assist *patrocinados* in suits for freedom.

The effects of these varied patterns of response by masters were contradictory. Loyalty on their part tended to stall the exercise of freedom by slaves, though when it became utterly intransigent it invited more overt challenge, which in turn could accelerate change. The use of voice generally postponed the transition, as planters shaped the process of emancipation to minimize substantive change. Exit clearly sped up the process of change, for the rift in the employing class engendered by such overt competition for the labor of *patrocinados* undermined the social relations upon which the system relied.

As one turns to the reactions of slaves, the picture becomes even more complex. Historians' discussions of slave personality and behavior centered for a time on concepts like accommodation and resistance, which seem in retrospect to be far too dichotomous to encompass the multiple responses of individuals to coercion and lack of autonomy. Exit, voice, and loyalty, as categories, are somewhat more promising, in part because they do not carry the powerful moral and emotional overtones of accommodation and resistance, and in part because they invite examination of mixtures of behavior at different times.

In the Cuban case, loyalty on the part of slaves to the institution of slavery seems by the 1870s and 1880s to have been a response so infrequent as to be hardly worthy of note. The notion may nonetheless be of some use, if we look at what one might call "loyalty in pursuit of exit." Take the following example: during the *patronato* (1880–1886) apprentices *(patrocinados)* were permitted by law to purchase their full freedom for a specified and gradually diminishing amount. In the early years, the amount remained high in comparison with the derisory stipends paid to apprentices. As time went on, however, more and more *patrocinados* found ways to put together their purchase price, combining stipends with earnings from the sale of goods grown on their provision grounds, pooling resources within a family, bargaining with their masters. Their behavior was, in the terms of the law, loyal. They had violated no regulation, challenged no authority. But their aim was clearly to hasten the end of enslavement for themselves and their kinfolk, and in doing so they helped to shift the balance of bound and free labor on estates, and thus accelerated the decline of the institution as a whole.

Slaves also exhibited what might be called "voice in pursuit of exit." Under the regulations governing the *patronato,* an apprentice could bring a charge against his master before a Junta de Patronato for any violation of the basic regulations governing the provision of food, maintenance, and payment. If the master were convicted, the apprentice would go free. The system of appeals was set up to minimize the likelihood of successful complaints: the boards that ruled on them were composed of members of the elite, and were reputed to be anti-abolitionist in their sympathies. But apprentices appear not to have been deterred. They brought charges for gross and for small violations of the rules; they allied with free blacks and with abolitionists to pursue cases up through the process of appeal. And despite all obstacles, over 7,000 *patrocinados* obtained freedom in this way. The point here is not that abuses of apprentices were effectively curbed, which they were not, or that all abused apprentices could gain freedom, which they could not, but rather that the mechanism of complaint, by providing an avenue of voice where there had previously been almost none, widened the range of possible responses by slaves.

Indeed, the process of emancipation was characterized by a striking degree of what Guillermo O'Donnell has labelled "horizontal voice." Groups of slaves, particularly in the countryside, would join together to make an appeal to the Junta; kinfolk would pursue the appeals of family members remaining in slavery; free blacks would assist slaves. Indeed, some of the adaptations undertaken by masters had increased the range of possible alliances: by introducing Asian contract laborers who later formed unions with slave women, for example, they had inadvertently created a shared interest on the part of a free and a slave worker in the freedom of a resulting child.

Finally, one finds pure exit. In the war-torn east and center of the island in particular, slaves and apprentices were on occasion able to depart the plantation and join the insurgent forces, or move into the hills. Elsewhere, the death of a master might provide an occasion for flight. With much of the repressive apparatus of the state still devoted to the maintenance of slavery, however, flight was not an easy option. Individual Afro-Cubans who could not prove themselves free were routinely incarcerated while notices were run in the local press in an attempt to locate their masters. When entire groups of apprentices attempted to challenge their owners, troops were brought in to suppress what was viewed as "mutiny." It was consistent with the logic of the limited reforms undertaken between 1870 and 1886 that voluntary exit from slavery remain prohibited.

The categorization of slave and apprentice behavior in terms of exit, voice, and loyalty helps one to see its component parts, but perhaps the most striking feature of that behavior is its flexibility. One finds apprentices bringing suits for freedom against their masters—while making a down payment on their purchase price for good measure. Others would file a complaint, and when the process became hopelessly prolonged, vanish into the city or the countryside. They had been drawn part way into the legal culture of procedural appeal, but only part way.

Slave behavior also reveals some of the ambiguities contained within the concepts of exit, voice, and loyalty. The character of exit, for example, depends in part on what follows it. Exit could be either a personal solution, or part of a larger family or collective effort to reduce the hold of slavery. Those who fled slavery into anonymity in the city were in that sense very different from those who used their freedom to assist other slaves in making claims or those who fled to the hills and joined the insurrection. Similarly, voice could involve using existing channels to enforce specific regulations, which can be seen as a partial acceptance of existing arrangements. This, however, might intentionally or unintentionally undermine the pattern of authority on which those arrangements depended. Charging one's master with failure to pay stipends on time in effect acknowledged his claim over one's labor, but reduced his freedom of action in exercising that claim. And loyalty could involve either actual allegiance to a system, or apparent allegiance while one sought recourse elsewhere. In the context of highly repressive systems, where voice and exit are choked off, and loyalty is exacted, each of these responses can evolve into a kind of sabotage.

Virtually all of the behaviors in pursuit of exit of Cuban slaves and apprentices tended to hasten the decline of slavery, either by lowering the number enslaved or by raising the cost of maintaining authority. The process, moreover, had an internal logic that tended toward acceleration. Newly freed slaves were potential allies for those still enslaved; the increasing numbers of legitimately free Afro-Cubans made it more difficult to detect runaways; the departure of former slaves from estates made their former owners more likely to seek out new wage laborers, shifting the balance away from slavery.

The Dynamics of Decline

What general observations about the process of dismantling repressive systems might one draw from this case history? I would emphasize two patterns that emerge from the Cuban experience:

(1) The Interdependent Character of This Particular Coercive System

Slavery as an economic system required a high degree of repression in the larger society, in part because control over slaves depended on the maintenance of a social order that blocked effective mobility and discouraged slave initiatives. Legalized racial hierarchy and limitations on freedom of expression, association, and movement contributed to sustaining a specific kind of labor exaction, as well as to sustaining colonial rule. While such rigid structures had helped to preserve slavery, they also carried with them a certain vulnerability, for attacks on separate component parts could have repercussions throughout the system. Even a genteel, white-led moderate abolitionist movement could break the monopoly of information to slaves and threaten social order. Alliances between otherwise relatively powerless individuals—such as *patrocinados* and free persons of color—could break the physical isolation of the plantation and permit challenges that undermined the economic and racial order.

Slaveowners' authority also depended on their ability to dominate small as well as large aspects of their slaves' lives. Control over the use of time, over communication with others, and over patterns of movement were part of control over labor power. Reforms that limited masters' absolute authority over details of life could—in a situation where challenges to the entire system already existed—undermine essential aspects of that control. Slavery as a system of production required specific constraints on slaves' rights within civil society. When an apprentice could take his master to court for failing to supply sufficient food, the monopoly of power had been threatened, however cautious the law on which the appeal had been based.

Slaveholders, moreover, relied on implicit powers of coercion, and were not necessarily capable of effectively wielding that power if challenged. Though masters might call in troops to guarantee order in the short run, they could not rely indefinitely on the direct applica-tion of force. When the background of social order was threatened—as in the eastern end of the island during the Ten Years' War—slaveowners might have to compromise rather than risk triggering mass desertions.

(2) The Contradictions of Reforming a Repressive System

Attempting to maintain an overtly repressive system in an inter-national climate of hostility to the specific forms of repression that system entailed, Spanish authorities faced frequent pressure for the elimination or modification of Cuban slavery. Reforms undertaken under such circumstances are characteristically opportunistic, intended to wed some fragment of the ideology of the opposition to the continu-ing repression. Freedom, or civil rights, or wage labor are defined in such a way as to make them compatible with continued coercion. This is hardly surprising. What is notable in the Cuban case is the extent of the consequences of such opportunism. The granting to slaves of partial rights and partial access to redress was intended by many in the Spanish parliament in 1870 and 1880 as a means of mitigating domestic and international criticism of Cuban slavery. "Gradualism" was more a mechanism for stalling real change than for promoting it. It is possible that in a smoothly functioning system, these limited and legalistic concessions might have been incorporated into the existing order and further legitimated the status quo. But under circumstances of domestic and international pressure, and in a system like that of chattel slavery where the monopoly of authority of the master was essential for the maintenance of order, even partial concessions that involved appeals to an outside authority were dan-gerous to the social order. Bringing a magistrate to an estate to investigate a claim of inadequate food could unleash further com-plaints, and an order to the master to comply with a specific regulation could, if known to the slaves and ignored by the master, provide the occasion for mutiny.[7]

This apparent logic in favor of freedom was in part conditioned by the political circumstances of the island. Obliged by international pressure to find some substitute for slavery, planters and the state did not have the option of reversing emancipation through brute force. The numbers over whom they would thereby regain control were inexorably declining, and the free immigrants they sought to attract as substitutes would likely shun the island if full slavery were reimposed. Moreover, the highest priority of the Spanish state was the maintenance of the colonial tie, and metropolitan authorities did not wish to provoke a new rebellion. Finally, we are dealing here with the nineteenth century, and with repressive mechanisms of a limited sophistication. There were hints already that some planters sought to adopt more modern means of control—as in the case of the Cuban slaveowner who proposed to photograph all of his slaves for better identification in case of flight.[8] But the impecunious Spanish government was constrained by the limitations of long-distance, low-budget repression. In this respect, our case history differs greatly from twentieth-century instances of wide-scale coercion.

The ideological dimension of the process of defensive reform is also complex. The assault on slavery as a backward economic system had affected the perceptions of those who were otherwise committed to its continued maintenance. The belief that economic development would *eventually* require a shift to free labor, combined with the relative unavailability of new slave laborers, encouraged masters to add free workers to their slave work forces and stimulated government and planter efforts to attract immigrants. In contrast to most planters in the American South, Cuban slaveowners acknowledged the wisdom of one day shifting to wage labor, though they generally sought an indefinite postponement of that day. Thus although they seem not to have been directly motivated by declining profitability to seek an end to slavery, planters were affected by the *claim* that their profits would decline and that they should shift to wage labor.

The attack on slavery as immoral had a similarly indirect effect on planter behavior. It was met in part by a counterclaim that Cuban slavery was paternalistic and benevolent, a claim parallel to the "positive good" argument advanced by Southern slaveholders. But the growing belief that slavery was *"una institución que el siglo rechaza"* (an institution rejected by the century), in the words of one policymaker, modified this self-defense. It is probably too much to impute to Cuban slaveholders a substantial guilty conscience, but one can infer by the 1870s and 1880s a certain lack of self-confidence. Both planters and policy-makers were thus obliged to contemplate reforms that would indicate a general willingness to move away from a system that now engendered such opprobrium. And these reforms in turn undermined their efforts at controlling change.

Conclusion

While I have thus far emphasized elements of vulnerability within slavery as a repressive system, and the accelerating dynamic of decline, there are also notable characteristics of resiliency in such systems. Many of these are very familiar, and include such maneuvers by the state and the elite as changing the name of a specific institution, or placing certain individual rights on the books while blocking access to the procedures that would make these rights operable. In the case of Cuba, "slavery" could be replaced by "apprenticeship," and intimidation on the estates could vitiate concessions granted by the government under pressure from reformists. But perhaps more interesting than such obviously manipulative maneuvers are the kinds of redirection that take place when key elements of the old system of repression appear to be on their way out.

Slavery as an economic and social system involved a high degree of direct personal control over laborers, and it was precisely that legal personalized control and its attendant immobility of labor that would eventually have to be relinquished. Once planters had realized the inevitability of the abolition of the system called slavery, however, they turned their attention to a search for ways to retain elements of its essence. Legalized chattel slavery had combined racial subordination, guarantee by the state of a specific social order, a high degree of control by masters over work rhythms, and so forth. Not all of these could be maintained without the structure of slavery, but some could be modified or substituted. Formal abolition was thus not a simple defeat for masters, but a moment of truth for both sides. Slaves who had sought their legal freedom as individuals or as groups had been striving for many things, including a measure of participation in their own destiny. Masters who had attempted to block that freedom also had a variety of goals. Once the battle for the maintenance of a specific form of repression had been lost, the battle to define the terms of the new order began.[9]

It is at this point in the analysis that we must move beyond the categories of exit, voice, and loyalty. These categories are defined in relation to specific, continuing institutions, whether they be firms or states. But once decline turns into collapse, new options emerge, and decisions must be made based on underlying values and goals as well as the distribution of power. Sugar planters had no other choices than to attract new workers and persuade former slaves to labor for wages, or to retire from export production. Former slaves had no choice but to seek wage employment, to find land for subsistence, or to combine the two. Responses by both groups continued to be mixed, with most planters abandoning sugar processing but continuing cane growing, and most rural slaves undertaking agricultural wage labor, but attempting to limit their dependence on specific plantations.[10]

In the reorganization of production that followed emancipation, estates moved from reliance on slave labor to reliance on a shifting, mobile population of wage laborers (former slaves, former smallholders, immigrants, and others), complemented by *colonos* (cane farmers) who took responsibility for providing cane to the expanded mills. Overall production of sugar climbed, breaking the one million ton mark in 1892.[11] But the world of the plantation was drastically altered, and control by planters over the behavior of their workers was diminished. The estate was both more productive and more vulnerable, more efficient and more penetrable.[12]

The direct authority of masters over slaves was gone, and the role of extra-economic coercion in the labor market was sharply diminished. But planters' desire for prosperity and rural Cubans' desire for subsistence and autonomy remained unfulfilled. Once again, the choices of exit, voice, and loyalty emerged—only this time the institution in question was not just the labor system but the colonial state itself. In 1895 the final war against Spanish domination broke out, drawing support from a wide range of regions and classes. The elimination of one aspect of repression had created the preconditions for a successful attack on another.

The ideology of the new insurgency was more far-reaching than that of the 1868–78 uprising. Under the leadership of José Martí, Máximo Gómez, and Antonio Maceo, the Cuban Revolutionary Party rejected not only colonial rule by Spain but also the racism and hierarchical relations that came with it. In the more fluid environment of the postemancipation countryside, they communicated with and mobilized support from the rural population, effectively attacking both the Spanish military and the sugar estates themselves.

It is difficult in retrospect to evaluate the precise roles played in this movement by, on the one hand, nationalism and, on the other, socially radical goals and actions. This was clearly something more than a war for political independence, but how it might have evolved after achieving that independence is uncertain. The U.S. intervention of 1898 abruptly blocked its forward motion and undercut any potential for more thoroughgoing social change.[13] To attempt to analyze the character and consequences of the repeated U.S. interventions in Cuba would take us well beyond the scope of this essay. We might nonetheless conclude with the observation that the task of dismantling repressive systems must have begun to seem to many Cubans, as it seems to us today, one that is virtually endless.

NOTES

1. The major analyses of slavery in Cuba in this period are Franklin Knight, *Slave Society in Cuba during the Nineteenth Century* (Madison: University of Wisconsin Press, 1970), and Manuel Moreno Fraginals, *El ingenio. Complejo económico social cubano del azúcar,* 3 vols. (Havana: Editorial de Ciencias Sociales, 1978).

2. This argument is made in greater detail in Rebecca J. Scott, "Explaining Abolition: Contradiction, Adaptation, and Challenge in Cuban Slave Society, 1860–1886," *Comparative Studies in Society and History* 26 (January 1984): 83–111.

3. See Raúl Cepero Bonilla, *Azúcar y abolición* (Havana: Editorial Cenit, 1948) for a discussion of the ideology of the rebel leadership.

4. On social relations in the rebel zones of the east and center, see the captured insurgent documents in the files of the Colección Fernández Duro, Biblioteca de la Real Academia de Historia, Madrid.

5. For a full discussion of this process, see Rebecca J. Scott, *Slave Emancipation in Cuba: The Transition to Free Labor, 1860–1899* (Princeton: Princeton University Press, 1985).

6. For planters' petitions, see Archivo Histórico Nacional, Madrid, Sección de Ultramar (hereinafter AHN, Ultramar), legajo 4884, tomo 8, expedientes 134 and 135 and leg. 4883, tomo 5, exp. 65.

7. For such a case, see AHN, Ultramar, leg. 4884, exp. 101, and Rafael M. de Labra, *Mi campaña en las Cortes españolas de 1881 a 1883* (Madrid: Imprenta de Aurelio J. Alaria, 1885), 301.

8. The owner was Tomás Terry, and the technique is recorded in *El Sagua* (Sagua la Grande, Cuba), June 9, 1872.

9. For a perceptive discussion of the ideological dimension of this battle, see Thomas C. Holt, "'An Empire over the Mind': Emancipation, Race, and Ideology in the British West Indies and the American South," in J. Morgan Kousser and James M. McPherson, eds., *Region, Race, and Reconstruction: Essays in Honor of C. Vann Woodward* (New York: Oxford University Press, 1982), 283–313.

10. Adaptions by slaves and masters to emancipation are described in chapters 9–11 of Scott, *Slave Emancipation.* A major source for understanding the aftermath of abolition is the U.S.-supervised census of 1899: U.S. War Department, *Report on the Census of Cuba, 1899* (Washington: Government Printing Office, 1900).

11. For figures on sugar production, see Moreno, *El ingenio,* 3: 36–38.

12. For a discussion of the consequences of this penetrability, see Rebecca J. Scott, "Class Relations in Sugar and Political Mobilization in Cuba, 1868–1899," *Cuban Studies/Estudios Cubanos,* forthcoming.

13. For an excellent discussion of the ideologies and groups within the 1895–98 revolutionary forces, and of the impact of U.S. intervention, see Louis A. Pérez, Jr., *Cuba between Empires, 1878–1902* (Pittsburgh: University of Pittsburgh Press, 1983).

Exit-Voice Dilemmas in Adolescent Development[1]

Carol Gilligan

In *Exit, Voice, and Loyalty* Albert Hirschman contrasts two modes of response to decline in social organizations—the options of exit and voice. Exit, central to the operation of the classical market economy, is exemplified by the customer who, dissatisfied with the product of company A, switches to the product of company B. In comparison to this neat and impersonal mechanism that operates "by courtesy of the Invisible Hand," voice—the attempt to change rather than escape from an objectionable situation—is messy, cumbersome and direct. "Graduated all the way from faint grumbling to violent protest," voice is political action par excellence, carrying with it the potential for "heartbreak" by substituting the personal and public articulation of critical opinions for the private, secret vote. Introducing exit and voice as the two principal actors in his drama of societal health, Hirschman puts forth a theory of loyalty to explain the conditions for their optimal collaboration. Loyalty, the seemingly irrational commitment of "the member who cares," activates voice by holding exit at bay, while sustaining in the implication of disloyalty the possibility of exit as the option of last resort.[2]

To the economist's view of the individual as motivated by the desire for profit and to the political theorist's view of the person as seeking power in social organizations, Hirschman thus adds a new dimension—an image of the person as motivated by loyalty or attachment to stem decline and promote recuperation. Demonstrating the power of attachment to influence action and shift the parameters of choice, Hirschman illustrates across a wide range of situations how the presence of loyalty holds exit and voice in tension and thus changes the meaning of both leaving and speaking. The psychological acuity of Hirschman's analysis of exit and voice is matched by the transformation implied by bringing the psychology of attachment to the center of developmental consideration.

In honoring Hirschman's contribution I wish to illuminate the psychological dimensions of his conception by extending it to the seemingly remote domain of adolescent development. Here it is possible to see not only the interplay of exit and voice that Hirschman describes but also the dilemmas posed by loyalty at a time of transition in human life. The central themes of Hirschman's work—the importance of values and ideas in the developmental process, the connection between passions and interests, the reflection on historical periods of development—will be addressed here in the context of the life cycle. But following Hirschman's example of trespass, I will suggest that the analysis of loyalty in family relationships speaks across disciplinary boundaries to the problems of interdependence that face contemporary civilization.

Hirschman's focus on loyalty is in part a correction to the more popular view of the exit option as uniquely powerful in effecting change. In challenging this view, he underscores the problems of attachment which arise in modern societies—problems which have taken on an added intensity and urgency in an age of nuclear threat. This threat which signals the possibility for an irredeemable failure of care also calls attention to the limits of exit as a solution to conflicts in social relationships. Yet "the preference for the neatness of exit over the messiness and heartbreak of voice"[3] which Hirschman finds in classical economics as well as in the American tradition extends through the study of human development, emerging most clearly in the psychology of adolescence. This paradigm of problem-solving, based on an assumption of independence and competition, obscures the reality of interdependence and masks the possibilities for cooperation. Thus the need to reassess the interpretive schemes on which we rely, the need to correct a "defective representation of the real world"[4] in which our actions take place, extends across the realm of economics to the psychological domain, calling attention to shared assumptions about the nature of development and the process of change.

This parallel is forcefully evoked by the easy transfer of the characters from Hirschman's drama to the adolescent scene where puberty signals the decline of the childhood world of relations and exit and voice enter as modes of response and recuperation. The growth to full stature at puberty releases the child from dependence on parents for protection and heightens the possibility of exit as a solution to conflicts in family relationships. At the same time, the sexual maturation of puberty—the intensification of sexual feelings and the advent of reproductive capability—impels departure from the family, given the incest taboo. The heightened availability of and impetus toward exit in adolescence, however, can stimulate the development of voice—a development enhanced by the cognitive changes of puberty, the growth of reflective thinking and the discovery of the subjective self. Seeing the possibility of leaving, the adolescent may become freer in speaking, more willing to assert perspectives and voice opinions that diverge from accepted family truths. But if the transformations of puberty heighten the potential for both exit and voice, the experience of adolescence also changes the meaning of leaving and speaking by creating dilemmas of loyalty and rendering choice itself more self-conscious and reflective.

Thus the adolescent, striving to integrate a new image of self and new experiences of relationship, struggles to span the discontinuity of puberty and renegotiate a series of social connections. This effort at renegotiation engages the adolescent voice in the process of identity formation and moral growth. But this development of voice depends on the presence of loyalty for its continuation. Hirschman, pointing out that the availability of the exit option tends "to atrophy the development of the art of voice,"[5] but also noting that the threat of exit can strengthen voice's effective use, observes that the decision of whether to exit will often be made in light of the prospects for the efficacy of voice. Development in adolescence thus hinges on loyalty between adolescents and adults, and the challenge to society, families and schools is how to engage that loyalty and how to educate the voice of the future generation.

In the life cycle the adolescent is the truth-teller, like the fool in the Renaissance play,[6] exposing hypocrisy and revealing truths about human relationships. These truths pertain to justice and care, the moral coordinates of human connection, heightened for the adolescent who stands between the innocence of childhood and the responsibility of adults. Looking back on the childhood experiences of inequality and attachment, feeling again the powerlessness and vulnerability which these experiences initially evoked, the adolescent identifies with the child and constructs a world that offers protection. This ideal or utopian vision, laid out along the coordinates of justice and care, depicts a world where self and other will be treated as of equal worth, where despite differences in power things will be fair; a world where everyone will be included, where no one will be left alone or hurt. In the ability to construct this ideal moral vision lies the potential for nihilism and despair as well as the possibility for societal renewal which the adolescent symbolizes and represents. Given the engagement of the adolescent's passion for morality and truth with the realities of social justice and care, adolescents are the group whose problems of development mirror society's problems with regeneration.

In analyzing these problems I will distinguish two moral voices that define two intersecting lines of development—one arising from the child's experience of inequality, one from the child's experience of attachment. Although the experiences of inequality and attachment initially are concurrent in the relationship of parent and child, they point to different dimensions of relationship—the dimension of inequality/equality and of attachment/detachment. The moral visions of justice and care reflect these different dimensions of relationships and the injunctions to which the experiences of inequality and attachment give rise. But these experiences also inform different ways of experiencing and defining the self in relation to others and lend different meanings to separation. These different conceptions of self and morality[7] have been obscured by current stage theories of psychological development that present single linear representation, fusing inequality with attachment and linking development to separation. But the problems in this portrayal are clarified by noting how the axis of development shifts when dependence, which connotes the experience of connection, is contrasted with isolation rather than opposed to independence.

To trace this shift and consider its implications for the understanding of progress and growth, I will begin with theories of identity and moral development that focus on the dimension of inequality/equality, noting that these theories have been derived primarily or exclusively from research on males.[8] Then I will turn to research on females to focus the dimension of attachment/detachment and delineate a different conception of morality and self. Although these two dimensions of relationship may be differentially salient in the thinking of women and men, both inequality and attachment are embedded in the cycle of life, universal in human experience because inherent in the relation of parent and child. By representing both dimensions of relationships it becomes possible to see how they combine to create dilemmas of loyalty in adolescence and to discern how different conceptions of loyalty give rise to different modalities of exit and voice.

Current Theories of Adolescent Development

The theories that currently provide the conceptual underpinning for the description of adolescent development trace a progression toward equality and autonomy in the conception of morality and self. All of these theories follow William James in distinguishing the once-from the twice-born self[9] and tie that distinction to the contrast between conventional and reflective moral thought. This differentiation separates those youth who adopt the conventions of their childhood society as their own, defining themselves more by ascription than choice, from those who reject societal conventions by questioning the norms and values that provide their justification. The distinction between two roads to maturity and the clear implication that the second leads far beyond the first appears in Erikson's division between the "technocrats" or "compact majority" and the neo-humanists[10] as well as in Kohlberg's division of moral development into preconventional, conventional and principled thought.[11]

This dual or tripartite division of identity formation and moral growth generates a description of adolescent development that centers on two major separations—the first from parental authority, the second from the authority of societal conventions. In this context, loyalty, the virtue of fidelity that Erikson[12] cites as the strength of adolescence, takes on an ideological cast, denoting a shift in the locus of authority from persons to principles—a move toward abstraction that justifies separation and renders the self autonomous. Key to this vision of the self as separate and constant is the promise of equality built in to the cycle of life, the promise of development that in time the child will become the adult.

The tracing of development as a move from inequality to equality marks adolescence as a critical time for the renegotiation of authority relationships and ties development in adolescence to a series of power confrontations. To emerge victorious the adolescent must overcome the constraint of parental authority through a process of "detachment" described by Freud as "one of the most significant, but also one of the most painful, psychical accomplishments of the pubertal period . . . a process that alone makes possible the opposition, which is so important for the progress of civilization, between the new generation and the old."[13] This equation of progress with detachment and opposition leads problems in adolescence to be cast as problems of exit or of separation. Observing that as "at every stage in the course of development through which all human beings ought by rights to pass, a certain number are held back; so there are some who have never got over their parents' authority and have withdrawn their affection from them either very incompletely or not at all," Freud concludes that this failure of development in adolescence is one that occurs mostly in girls.[14]

Thus exit, in resolving the childhood drama of inequality, symbolized for Freud by the Oedipal dilemma, becomes emblematic of adolescent growth. Yet the option of exit, as Hirschman observes, leaves a problem of loyalty in its wake, a problem which if not addressed can lead to the decline of care and commitment in social relationships.[15] In this light adolescent girls who demonstrate a reluctance to exit, may articulate a different voice—a voice that speaks of loyalty to persons and identifies detachment as morally problematic. To represent this perspective on loyalty changes the depiction of adolescent growth by delineating a mode of development that relies not on detachment but on a change in the form of attachment—a change that must be negotiated by voice.

Yet the preference for the neatness of exit over the messiness and heartbreak of voice, the focus on inequality rather than attachment in human relations, and the reliance on male experience in building the model of human growth have combined to silence the female voice. This silence contributes to the problems observed in adolescent girls, particularly if these problems are seen to reflect a failure of engagement rather than a failure of separation. But this silence and the implicit disparagement of female experience also creates problems in the account of human development—a failure to trace the growth of attachment and the capacity for care and loyalty in relationship.

The omission of female experience from the literature on adolescent development was noted by Bruno Bettelheim in 1961,[16] and the significance of this omission was underlined by Joseph Adelson who edited the *Handbook of Adolescent Psychology,* published in 1981. Adelson had asked a leading scholar to write a chapter for the handbook on female adolescent development, but after surveying the literature she concluded that there was not enough good material to warrant a separate chapter. Observing that "to read the psychological literature on adolescence has, until very recently, meant reading about the psychodynamics of the male youngster writ large,"[17] Adelson and Marjery Doehrman end their chapter on psychodynamics by noting that "the inattention to girls and to the processes of feminine development in adolescence has meant undue attention to such problems as impulse control, rebelliousness, superego struggles, ideology and achievement, along with a corresponding neglect of such issues as intimacy, nurturance and affiliation."[18] They found particularly troubling the fact that current biases in the literature reinforce each other, with the result that "the separate, though interacting emphases on pathology, on the more ideologized, least conformist social strata, and on males has produced a psychodynamic theory of adolescence that is both one-sided and distorted."[19]

At the same time girls, the group left out in the critical theory-building studies of adolescent psychology, the group repeatedly observed to have problems in adolescence with separation, emerge as the group whose experience may best inform an expanded theory of growth. In girls' accounts of their experience in the adolescent years, problems of attachment and detachment emerge as a central focus of consideration, and this shift in attention provides a new lens on the adolescent's experience of self and relationships.

The Missing Line of Adolescent Development

In adolescence, the renegotiation of attachment centers on the inclusion of sexuality and perspective in relationships—each introducing a new level of complication and depth to human connection. Conflicts of attachment that arise at this time are exemplified by the problems that girls describe when including themselves—their views and their wishes—is perceived as hurting their parents and including their parents implies excluding themselves. This revival of the triangular conflicts of the Oedipal years demonstrates how that drama tends to be recast in the experience of girls as a drama of inclusion and exclusion rather than of dominance and subordination. If the Oedipal wish is conceived as the wish to be included in the parents' relationship—to be a "member of the wedding" in Carson McCuller's phrase—then the Oedipal threat is the threat of exclusion, experienced as endangering the integrity of the connected self.

But adolescents, gaining the power to form family relationships on their own, confront the implications of excluding their parents as they remember their own experience of having been excluded by them. Construed as an issue of justice, this exclusion seems eminently fair, a matter of simple reciprocity. Construed as an issue of care, it seems instead morally problematic, given the association of exclusion with hurt. In resisting detachment and criticizing exclusion, adolescent girls hold to the view that change can be negotiated through voice and that voice is the way to sustain attachment across the leavings of adolescence.

Thus adolescents, aware of new dimensions to human connection, experiment in a variety of ways as they seek to discover what constitutes attachment and how problems in relationships can be solved. Girls in particular, given their interest in relationships and their attention to the ways in which connection between people can be formed and maintained, observe that relationships in which voice is silenced are not relationships in any meaningful sense. This understanding that voice has to be expressed in relationships to solve rather than escape the dilemmas of adolescence calls attention not only to the limitations of exit but also to the problems that arise when voice is silenced. In sum, adolescent girls who resist exit may be holding on to the position that solutions to dilemmas of attachment in adolescence must be forged by voice and that exit alone is no solution but an admission of defeat. Thus, their resistance may signify a refusal to leave before they can speak.

Hirschman, describing how the high price of exit and the presence of loyalty in family relationships encourages the option of voice, also indicates that resort to voice will be undertaken in a conflict situation when the outcome is visualized as either possible victory or possible accord. But adolescents in their conflicts with their parents cannot readily visualize victory, nor can they visualize full accord for, given the closeness of the relationship, a meeting of minds would suggest a meeting of bodies which is precluded by the incest taboo. Therefore, exit must be part of the solution, and some accommodation must be found, some mixture of leaving and speaking which typically may occur in different proportions for boys and girls.

The focus on leaving in the psychology of adolescence, manifest by the equation of development with separation, may be an accurate rendition of male experience, at least within certain cultures, since the more explosive potential of the tensions between adolescent sons and parents highlights the opposition between dependence and independence which renders exit appealing. In contrast, the propensity toward staying, noted as the problem in female development, may reflect the different nature of the attachment between daughters and parents and the greater salience for girls of the opposition between dependence and isolation. In this way, the two opposites of the word dependence—isolation and independence—catch the shift in the valence of relationships that occurs when connection with others can be experienced both as an impediment to autonomy and as a protection against isolation and source of empowerment. This ambivalence of human connection creates an ongoing ethical tension, manifest in the problems that rise sharply in adolescence.

The ways in which adolescents consider decisions about staying and leaving, silence and speaking, illustrate the interplay of exit, voice and loyalty that Hirschman describes. But the dilemmas of adolescence become most intense when they involve conflicts of loyalty, especially in situations where attachment to persons vies with adherence to principles. Psychological theorists typically have given priority to principles as the anchor of personal integrity and focused their attention on the necessity and the justification for leaving. But in doing so, they have tended to overlook the costs of detachment—its consequences both to personal integrity and to societal functioning. Since adolescent girls tend to resist detachment and highlight its costs to others and self, we may learn about ways of solving problems through voice within the context of ongoing relationships by observing the way that they struggle with conflicts of loyalty and exit-voice decisions.

In a series of studies, concerns about detachment have emerged saliently in girls' and women's moral thinking, pointing to an ethic of care that enjoins responsibility and responsiveness in relationships. These concerns were so insistent in an ongoing study of girls in the high school years, and focused so specifically on problems of speaking and listening, that it seemed interesting to inquire directly about situations in which voice failed and to explore empirically the conceptual distinction between problems of inequality and problems of detachment. Thus two questions were added to the interview schedule in the second year of the study—one pertaining to incidents of unfairness, one to incidents of not listening. Asked to describe a situation in which someone was not being listened to, girls spoke about a wide variety of problems that ranged across the divide between interpersonal and international relations. "The Nicaraguan people," one girl explained, "are not being listened to by President Reagan." Asked how she knew, she said that Mr. Reagan, in explaining his own position, did not respond to the issues raised by the Nicaraguans and thus appeared to discount their view of their situation. The absence of response as it indicated not listening was acutely observed by girls in a wide range of settings and interpreted as a sign of not caring. The willingness to test the extent of detachment, to ascertain whether not listening signified a transitory distraction or a more deeply rooted indifference, appeared critical to the decisions girls made about silence and speaking.

The moral outrage and passion that infused girls' descriptions of not listening were also apparent in their accounts of unfairness. Yet over the high school years, concerns about listening tended increasingly to temper judgments about fairness, reflecting a growing awareness of differences in perspective and of problems in communication. The amount of energy devoted to solving these problems, the intensity of the search for ways to make connection and achieve understanding, led girls to express immense frustration in situations where voice failed. When others did not listen and seemed not to care, they spoke of "coming up against a wall." This image of a wall had as its counterpart the search for an opening through which one

could speak. The nature of this search together with the intensity of
its frustration are conveyed in the following description of a girl's
attempt to reestablish communication with her mother without abandoning her own perspective:

> I called my mother up and said, "Why can't I talk to you
> anymore?" And I ended up crying and hanging up on her because
> she wouldn't listen to me. . . . She had her own opinion about
> what was truth and what was reality, and she gave me no
> opening. . . . And, you know, I kept saying, "Well, you hurt me."
> And she said, "No, I didn't." And I said, "Well, why am I hurt?"
> you know. And she is just denying my feelings as if they didn't
> exist and as if I had no right to feel them, even though they
> were. . . I guess until she calls me up or writes me a letter saying
> I want to talk instead of saying, well, this and this happened,
> and I don't understand what is going on with you, and I don't
> understand why you are denying the truth. . . until she says, I
> want to talk, I can't, I just can't.

Simone Weil in a beautifully evocative and paradoxical statement
defines morality as the silence in which one can hear the unheard
voices.[20] This rendering of morality in terms of attention and perception is central to Iris Murdoch's vision[21] and appears as well in
Hannah Arendt's question as to whether the activity of thinking as
such, "the habit of examining whatever happens to come to pass or
to attract attention, regardless of results and specific content," can be
considered a moral act.[22] The visions of these women philosophers
illuminate the activities of care that high school girls describe, their
equation of care with the willingness "to be there," "to listen," and
"to understand." Through the association with choice, these activities
of care take on a moral dimension, and the willingness and the ability
to care become a source of empowerment and a standard of self-
evaluation. Detachment then signifies not only not caring in the sense
of choosing to stand apart but also not being able to care, given that
in the absence of connection, one would not know how to respond.
This portrayal of care reveals its cognitive as well as affective dimensions, its foundation in the ability to perceive people in their own
terms and to respond to need. As this knowledge generates the power
not only to help but also to hurt, the uses of this power become the
measure of responsibility in relationships.

In adolescence when both wanting and knowing take on new
meanings, given the intensity of sexual feelings and the discovery of
subjectivity, conflicts of responsibility assume new dimensions of

complexity. The experience of coming into a relationship with oneself and the increasing responsibility for taking care of oneself are premised in this context not on detachment from others but on a change in the form of attachment to them. These changes in the experience of connection both with others and with oneself set the parameters of the moral conflicts that girls describe when responsibility to themselves conflicts with responsibility to others. Seeking to perceive and respond to their own as well as to others' feelings and thoughts, girls ask if they can be responsive to themselves without losing connection with others and whether they can respond to others without abandoning themselves.

This search for an inclusive solution to dilemmas of conflicting loyalties vies with the tendency toward exclusion expressed in the moral opposition between "selfish" and "selfless" choice—an opposition where selfishness connotes the exclusion of others and selflessness the exclusion of self. This opposition emerges repeatedly in the moral judgements of adolescent girls and women. But the conventional norms of feminine virtue, which hold up selflessness as an ideal, conflict with an understanding of relationships derived from the experience of attachment. Since the exclusion of self as well as of others dissolves the fabric of connection, both exclusions create problems in relationships, diminishing the capacity for care and reducing the efficacy of the self as a moral agent.

The bias toward voice in girls' moral thinking contains this recognition and directs attention toward the ways that attachments can be transformed and sustained. "There is not a wall between us," one adolescent explains in describing her relationship with her parents, "but there is a sort of strain or a sieve." And this metaphor of connection continuing through a barrier to complete attachment conveys a solution to problems in family relationships that avoids detachment while recognizing the need for distance that arises in adolescence. The following examples further illustrate the mixture of exit and voice in adolescent girls' thinking, indicating the value placed on loyalty or continuing attachment. In addition they suggest how attachments can be sustained across separation and how relationships can expand without detachment.

> I have been very close to my parents mentally. . . . We have a very strong relationship, but yet it is not a physical thing that you can see. . . . In my family we are more independent of each other, but yet we have this strong love.

> All the boyfriends that I have ever really cared about, they are

still with me . . . in mind, not in body, because we are separated by miles. But they will always be with me. Any relationship that I have ever had has been important to me. Otherwise I wouldn't have had it.

These evocations of the mind-body problem of adolescence convey a view of continuing attachment as consonant with autonomy and growth. Given this view, dependence and independence are not opposed but are seen instead to commingle, as exemplified by the following description of a relationship between close friends:

I would say we depend on each other in a way that we are both independent, and I would say that we are very independent, but as far as our friendship goes, we are dependent on each other because we know that both of us realize that whenever we need something, the other person will always be there.

In this way, the capacity to care for others and to receive care from them becomes a part of rather than antithetical to self-definition.

Defined in this context of relationships, identity is formed through the gaining of perspective and known through the experience of engagement with different points of view. Over the high school years, girls displayed an increasing recognition that attachment does imply agreement and that differences constitute the life of relationships rather than a threat to their continuation. The ability to act on this recognition generated a more empirical approach to conflict resolution, an approach which often led to the discovery of creative solutions to disputes. Hirschman describes how the willingness to trade off the certainty of exit for the uncertainty of improvement via voice can spur the "creativity-requiring course of action" from which people would otherwise recoil and thus how loyalty performs "a function similar to the underestimate of the prospective tasks's difficulties."[23] The observation of girls' persistence in seeking solutions to problems of attachment even in the face of seemingly insurmountable obstacles extends this point and indicates further how attachment to persons rather than adherence to principles may enhance the possibility for arriving at creative forms of conflict resolution.

Yet the vulnerability of voice to exclusion underscores how easily this process can fail, when the search for victory or domination defeats efforts at reaching accord. "If people are thinking on two different planes," one girl explains, then "you can't understand." Asked whether people on different planes can communicate, she describes how voice depends on relationship while exit can be executed in isolation.

Well, they can try, maybe they can . . . if they were both trying to communicate. But if one person is trying to block the other out totally, that person in going to win and not hear a thing that the other person is saying. If that is what they are trying to do, then they will accomplish their objective: to totally disregard the other person.

This vulnerability of voice to detachment and indifference becomes a major problem for girls in adolescence, especially when they recognize a difference between their own perspectives and commonly held points of view. Given a relational construction of loyalty, the drama of exit and voice may shift to the tension between silence and speaking, where silence signifies exit and voice implies conflict and change in relationships. Then development hinges on the contrast between loyalty and blind faith, since loyalty implies the willingness to risk disloyalty by including the voice of the self. This effort to bring the subjectively known self into connection with others signifies an attempt to change the form of connection and relies on a process of communication, not only to discover the truth about others but also to reveal the truth about oneself.

"If I could only let my mother know the list (that I had grown inside me . . . of over two hundred things that I had to tell my mother so that she would know the true things about me and to stop the pain in my throat) she—and the world—would become more like me, and I would never be alone again."[23] So the heroine of Maxine Hong Kingston's autobiographical novel, *The Woman Warrior,* defines the parameters of adolescent development that extend through the contrast between silence and voice. The silence that surrounds the discovery of the secret, subjectively known self protects its integrity in the face of disconfirmation but at the expense of isolation. In contrast, voice, the attempt to change rather than escape from an objectionable situation, contains the potential for transformation by bringing the self into connection with others.

Thus the contrast between selfish and selfless behavior around which the problem of exclusion turns is countered by the wish for inclusion, a wish that is enacted through voice. In recent years, the exit option has become increasingly popular as a solution to conflicts in relationships as the incidence of divorce attests. Yet the meaning of leaving, although commonly interpreted as a move toward separation and independence, is more complex. For example, the more unencumbered access to exit from marriage can spur the exercise of voice in marriage, which in turn can lead to the discovery of the truth about attachment. When the costs of divorce are high, this investigation may not be risked. But where the exit option is tenable and voice consistently fails, then the wish for attachment may be enacted through exit from marriage.

The distinction between true and false attachment, between relationships where voice is engaged and relationships where voice is silenced, often becomes critical to exit decisions both for women considering divorce and for adolescent girls. Given the tendency for girls and women to define loyalty as attachment to persons, the implication of disloyalty holds out exit as an alternative to silence in situations where voice has failed. Thus the recognition of the costs of detachment not only from others but also from oneself becomes key to girls' development in adolescence since it encourages voice while sustaining exit as the option of last resort.

The wish to be able to disagree, to be different without losing connection with others, leads outward in girls' experience from family relationships to relationships with the world. The adolescent girl who seeks to affirm the truths about herself by joining these truths with her mother's experience aspires through this connection to validate her own perceptions, to see herself as part of the world rather than as all alone, But the difficulty for girls in feeling connected both to their mothers and to the world is compounded when the world is defined in terms of male experience and thus disconnected both from their mothers and from themselves.

Consequently, the problems of attachment in adolescent development are inseparable from the problem of interpretation, since the ability to establish connection with others hinges on the ability to render one's story coherent. Given the failure of interpretive schemes to reflect female experience and given the distortion of this experience in common understandings of care and attachment, development for girls in adolescence hinges not only on their willingness to risk disagreement with others but also on the courage to challenge two equations: the equation of human with male and the equation of care with self-sacrifice. Together these equations create a self-perpetuating system that sustains a limited conception of human development and a problematic representation of human relationships.

By attending to female voices and including these voices in the psychological schemes through which we have come to know ourselves, we arrive at a correction of currently defective modes of interpretation. As the understanding of morality expands to include both justice and care, as identity loses its Platonic cast and the experience of attachment to others becomes part of the definition of self, as relationships are imagined not only as hierarchies of inequality but also as webs of protection, the representation of development shifts from a progress toward separation to a chronicle of expanding connection.

Adolescent Development in the Contemporary Context

The student protest movements of the late 1960s focused on the consequences of social inequality and held up against existing unfairness the ideals of justice and rights. But these movements contained as a countercultural theme a challenge to the existing state of relationships, articulated by a generation of "flower children" that included a large female representation. With the disillusionment of the 1970s, these movements for change degenerated into privatism and retreat, as concerns with both justice and care focused increasingly on the self. But the growing awareness of global pollution and the escalation of the nuclear threat underline the illusory nature of the exit solution and call attention to the reality of interdependence. The need to develop the art of voice then becomes a pressing agenda for education. The popularity of psychotherapy may reveal the extent to which voice has been neglected in a society that has come increasingly to rely on exit solutions and to prefer neat, impersonal, and often secret forms of communication.

As youth of both sexes currently oscillate between moral nihilism and moral indignation, given the impending potential for an irretrievable failure of care on the part of the older generation, the relativism that has diluted the engagement between adolescents and adults gives way to a recognition of the moral challenges which they commonly face—the challenge of fairness, that coming generations be allowed their chance to reach maturity; the challenge of care that the cycle of violence be replaced by an ecology of care[25] that sustains the attachments necessary to life.

When Erikson pointed to adolescence as the time in the life cycle when the intersection of life history and history becomes more acute, he called attention to the relationship between the problems of society and the crises of youth.[26] In this light, the current increase of problems among adolescent girls, the startling rise of eating disorders among the high school and college population,[27] reveals a society that is having problems with survival and regeneration. The anorexic girl, described in literature as not wishing to grow up, may more accurately be seen as dramatizing the life-threatening split between female and adult.[28] This tragic choice calls attention to the extent that care and dependence have been doubly disparaged by their association with women and children rather than seen as part of the human condition—as literally facts of life. To heal the division between adult and female thus requires a revisioning of both images, and this revision retrieves the line that has been missing from the description of human development.

The unleashed power of the atom, Einstein warned, has changed everything except our way of thinking, implying that a change in thinking is necessary for survival in a nuclear age. Our indebtedness to Hirschman is that he charts the direction for a change that also carries with it the implication of a change of heart. By describing modes of conflict resolution that do not entail detachment or exclusion, he aligns the process of change with presence of loyalty or strong attachment. Thus he offers an alternative to the either/or, win/lose framework of the prisoner's dilemma, which has become, in this nuclear age, a most dangerous game. In this paper I have tried to extend the optimism of Hirschman's conception by demonstrating the potential for care and attachment that inheres in the structure of human experience. By describing development around a central and ongoing ethical tension between problems of inequality and problems of detachment, I have called attention to dilemmas of loyalty as moments when attachment is at stake. The importance at present of expanding attachment across the barriers of what Erikson called "subspeciation" brings problems of loyalty to the center of our public life. As the contemporary reality of global interdependence impels the search for new maps of development, the exploration of attachment may provide the psychological grounding for new visions of progress and growth.

NOTES

1. I wish to thank the Geraldine Rockefeller Dodge Foundation for supporting the study of adolescent girls, Scott McVay and Valerie Peed of the Dodge Foundation for their interest in this work; Robert Parker and Trudy Hanmer of the Emma Willard School for initiating and collaborating in this project, and Nona Lyons and Sharry Langdale of the Harvard Graduate School of Education—my colleagues in this research. I am also grateful to the Carnegie Corporation for a Faculty Fellowship which has enabled me to spend this year at the Bunting Institute of Radcliffe College and to Susan Pollack and Catherine Steiner-Adair for their helpful comments on previous drafts of this paper.

2. Albert O. Hirschman, *Exit, Voice, and Loyalty: Responses to Decline in Firms, Organizations, and States* (Cambridge: Harvard University Press, 1970), 16, 30, 37, 78, 83.

3. Ibid., 107.

4. Ibid., 2.

5. Ibid., 43, 37.

6. For this analogy, I am grateful to Jamie Bidwell, a student at the Harvard Graduate School of Education.

7. Carol Gilligan, *In a Different Voice: Psychological Theories and Women's Development* (Cambridge: Harvard University Press, 1982), Chap. 2.

8. Kohlberg's six stages of moral development were defined on the basis of his longitudinal research on seventy-two white American males, originally age 10–16. L. Kohlberg, "The Development of Modes of Thinking and Choices in Years 10–16," (diss., University of Chicago, 1958); see also his *The Psychology of Moral Development* (New York: Harper and Row, 1983). Erikson has drawn almost exclusively on the lives of men in tracing the crises of identity and the cycle of life (see *Childhood and Society*, W. W. Norton, 1950; *Young Man Luther*, W. W. Norton, 1958; *Gandhi's Truth*, W. W. Norton, 1968; and "Reflections on Dr. Borg's Life Cycle," *Daedalus* 105, 1976, 1–29). Note also D. Offer, *The Psychological World of the Teenager: A Study of 175 Boys*, (New York: Basic Books, 1969) and D. Offer and J. Offer, *From Teenage to Young Manhood* (New York: Basic Books, 1975).

9. William James, *The Varieties of Religious Experience* (New York: Collier, 1961; orig. 1902).

10. Erik Erikson, *Identity: Youth and Crisis* (New York: W. W. Norton, 1968), 31–39.

11. Lawrence Kohlberg, *Essays on Moral Development*, vol. 1 of *The Philosophy of Moral Development* (San Francisco: Harper & Row, 1981).

12. Erik Erikson, *Insight and Responsibility* (New York: W. W. Norton, 1964), Chap. 4, "Human Strengths and the Cycle of Generations."

13. Sigmund Freud, *Three Essays on the Theory of Sexuality* (1905), vol. 7 of the Standard Edition of *The Complete Psychological Works of Sigmund Freud*, J. Strachey, ed. (London: Hogarth Press, 1953), 227.

14. Ibid., 227.

15. Hirschman, *Exit, Voice, and Loyalty*, 112.

16. Bruno Bettelheim, "The Problem of Generations," in E. Erikson, ed., *The Challenge of Youth* (New York: Doubleday, 1965), 105–6.

17. Joseph Adelson, ed., *Handbook of Adolescent Psychology* (New York: John Wiley & Sons, 1981).

18. Joseph Adelson and Margery J. Doehrman, "The Psychodynamic Approach to Adolescence," in J. Adelson, ed., *Handbook*, 114.

19. Ibid., 115.

20. Simone Weil, "Human Personality," in G. Panichas, ed., *The Simone Weil Reader* (New York: David McKay, 1977), 316.

21. Iris Murdoch, *The Sovereignty of Good* (London: Routledge & Kegan Paul, 1970).

22. Hannah Arendt, *The Life of the Mind,* vol. 1, *Thinking* (New York: Harcourt Brace Jovanovich, 1978), 5.

23. Albert Hirschman, *Exit, Voice, and Loyalty,* 80.

24. Maxine Hong Kingston, *The Woman Warrior: Memoirs of a Girlhood Among Ghosts* (New York: Alfred A. Knopf), 197–98.

25. For the phrase "the ecology of care" I am grateful to Scott McVay and Valerie Peed of the Geraldine R. Dodge Foundation, Morristown, New Jersey.

26. Erik Erikson, "Youth: Fidelity and Diversity," in Erikson, ed., *The Challenge of Youth* (New York: Anchor Books, 1965).

27. H. Bruch, *The Golden Cage* (Cambridge: Harvard University Press, 1978) and A. H. Crisp, R. L. Palmer, and R. S. Kalucy, "How Common is Anorexia Nervosa? A Prevalence Study," *British Journal of Psychiatry,* 128 (1976), 549–59.

28. Catherine Steiner-Adair, "The Body Politic: Normal Female Adolescent Development and the Development of Eating Disorders" (diss., Harvard University, 1984).

An Antinomy in the Notion of Collective Protest

Pierre Bourdieu

Deserting or protesting, *exit* or *voice,* appear as clear-cut alternatives only so long as one remains within the logic of individual action. The institutions specially designed to express demands, aspirations and protests provide a third way: the *spokesman* is an authorized voice speaking on behalf of a whole group. To stand up to an organization—a firm which sells shoddy goods or lays off its workers, or any other instituted power—the group puts forward its own organization, a party, union or association, charged, at least officially, with the collective defense of the individual interests of its members. Through the social technology of delegation which endows the official representative with *plena potentia agendi* (full power to act), the represented group becomes constituted as a collective person. Capable of acting and speaking "as one man," it can mobilize all the physical and, above all, symbolic strength that is potentially available to it. The impotent protest or insignificant desertion of the isolated individual—different forms of "serial" action, which as in elections or in the marketplace, act only through the blind and sometimes perverse mechanisms of statistical aggregation—gives way to a protest that is at once unitary and collective, coherent and powerful. So, at least, one would conclude from the equally mythical representations which the progressive tradition has constantly counterposed to the myth of the "invisible hand," and which are so many variants of the Rousseauistic figure of the "legislator" capable of embodying and expressing a "general will" that is irreducible to the "will of all" obtained by simple addition of individual wills.

The most radical questioning of the founding myth of delegated authorities comes from situations in which the antinomy of delegation is revealed: I cannot achieve powerful speech, a legitimate, known, recognized, authorized and authoritative voice, without running the risk of being dispossessed of my own voice, deprived of an expression

301

which specifically expresses myself, even finding the singularity of my experience and my specific interests denied and annulled, by the common voice, the *opinio communis* as produced and uttered by my accredited spokesmen. In such cases, the members of corporate bodies, particularly those that are specially designed to produce and express protest and dissent, such as political parties or trade unions, are themselves faced with a choice between desertion and protest, exit and voice, because of a discrepancy between what they have to say (which they may discover through that very discrepancy) and what is said on their behalf by the authorized speech of the spokesmen. And the only way they can escape from one form or another of serial impotence—individual exit or voice, or even the petition that aims to force the mandated spokesmen to change their speech and language—is by instituting a new organization, itself bound to provoke new protests and new heretical desertions inasmuch as it claims a monopoly of legitimate protest. Such is the antinomy of the reformed Church which, born of collective protest against the Catholic Church, makes its protest the basis of a new church which, as such, calls forth new protest.

Is this an insuperable antinomy, linked to the need to concentrate symbolic capital in a single person, or a small number of persons, so as to endow them with maximum strength? Or an inevitable effect of the unequal distribution of the means of production of speech, even (and especially) critical speech? At any rate, it cannot be denied that if the speech of the spokesman derives its legitimacy and strength essentially from the recognition that the group which he expresses grants him (if only though the forced plebiscite of silence), it owes part of this recognition to the fact that it is seen as the best, or least bad, transmutation of felt, implicit awareness into manifested, public, explicit utterance. Thus the simple cry of revolt or indignation becomes a voice that can get itself recognized as such—as having its share of universality and therefore of humanity.

PART IV

Essays on Method

The Social Scientist as Constructive Skeptic: On Hirschman's Role

Michael S. McPherson

It's hard to imagine that the definitive piece on Albert Hirschman's "method" will ever be written. Certainly that task won't be accomplished in his lifetime, if only because Hirschman's reading of the essay would be sure to cause him to think of some new approach or perspective he hadn't tried before, thus rendering that allegedly "definitive" characterization incomplete. Indeed this inclination of Hirschman's always to look for a fresh perspective or to uncover some neglected aspect of a phenomenon may be as close as we can come to finding a feature that defines his "method."

This inclination, which seems to be partly a matter of personality and partly one of conscious intellectual strategy for Hirschman, is worth a closer look. It sheds light, I will argue, on certain distinctive aspects of Hirschman's own role and career in social science. More tentatively, I will propose that reflection on this aspect of Hirschman's work also raises some interesting questions about current understandings in the philosophy and sociology of social science. But before exploring these larger issues I should say something more to characterize the particular feature of Hirschman's thought that I propose to focus on.

I

The closest thing Albert Hirschman has written to a description of his own approach to social science is the essay, "Political Economics and Possibilism," that introduces his collection *A Bias for Hope*.[1] The "possibilism" Hirschman describes there is tied up on the normative side with a hopeful attitude toward the prospects for constructive social change, but on the more purely intellectual side it is closely connected to the proposition that available social science explanations of events rarely, if ever, exhaust the interesting features of the events in question. There is generally something further to be discovered. "Possibilism" thus seeks "to widen the limits of what is or is perceived to be possible, be it at the cost of lowering our ability, real or imaginary, to discern the probable."[2] "Quite possibly," Hirschman observes, "all the successive theories and models in the social sciences, and the immense efforts that go into them, are motivated by the noble, if unconscious, desire to demonstrate the irreducibility of the social world to general laws!"[3] Hirschman characterizes his own work as a search for "novelty, creativity, and uniqueness."[4]

It is important that Hirschman never sets this search of his for "the unexplained phenomenon . . . the odd fact"[5] in opposition to the social scientific search for general laws. One could imagine such a nihilistic posture: a claim that since all putative general laws in social science are bound to fail, the search for them—the standard kind of social scientific activity—ought to stop. This would be quite foreign to Hirschman's purpose, which is to obtain "equal rights of citizenship in social science to the search for general laws and to the search for uniqueness."[6] The concession to the value of general laws is not mere tactical politeness—indeed Hirschman himself has more than once propounded social scientific "laws" of his own. Besides being useful in themselves, such general laws provide the necessary background against which the unique and the unexpected can stand out.

The feature of Hirschman's approach that I shall focus on can be described metaphorically as one of peering around the edges and through the cracks in social scientific laws, to find what's being over-looked. It's hard to think of a feature more pervasive in Hirschman's writing, from his early work on the virtues of unbalanced growth through his discovery of the "tunnel effect" by which the familiar emotion of envy is transmuted into pleasure at others' good fortune, and on into more recent work like his uncovering of unexpected arguments for capitalism as a device for "gentling" men's unruly passions. In Hirschman's most recent published work he argues "against parsimony" and for the need to recognize a variety of aspects of human conduct that are omitted from the usual characterizations of economic law.[7]

Even when Hirschman does express his findings in the form of law-like generalizations, these are typically couched in language that gently reminds us not to endow the "law" with too much finality and completeness. Thus in his recent book on cooperatives in Latin America he formulates the "Law of Conservation and Mutation of Social Energy" to describe the tendancy for those once involved in political or social action to find a way to return to it, often in another form.[8] The reference here to Newton's Laws serves both to capture an important finding in a memorable phase and, implicitly, to remind us how much more limited and context-dependent such a finding is compared to the laws of classical mechanics.

Hirschman's insistence on the complexities that embarrass economists' attempts at simple generalizations are often presented with humor and irony. An example is his observation in *Shifting Involvements* that Mancur Olson's celebrated book demonstrating the irrationality and hence unlikelihood of mass political action appeared on the eve of the era of Vietnam protest.[9] Hirschman's tone, here and elsewhere, is one of "serious playfulness," a questioning and amused attitude based on an awareness of our profound ignorance about the truth concerning social life, and hence of the pretentiousness of most claims to settled knowledge. Hirschman is, in that sense, a skeptic, but a skeptic of an essentially constructive rather than nihilistic variety. Our lack of certainty about how things work carries worrisome risks— but also hopeful possibilities.[10]

II

This persistent search for the new angle of vision, the overlooked phenomenon, illuminates some important aspects of Hirschman's unique place in contemporary social science.

One such aspect is the "unity and diversity" of Hirschman's work. Readers of Hirschman's work are aware of the exceptionally wide variety of topics, themes, and even structures of argument[11] his writings display. Yet, at the same time, almost all his writings share a highly distinctive, almost unmistakable, style of thought. A key element in this intellectual style, I would suggest, is precisely this "contrapuntal" quality of Hirchman's thought. What has been neglected or overlooked will vary according to subject matter or occasion—it may be an abstract logical symmetry or a recalcitrant historical fact. But the common thread is found in the desire to search it out and discover the hidden features of reality it reveals.

Second, this feature of Hirschman's thought helps us to understand why, despite his wide influence, he has never been the founder of a school. A school which numbered among its prime doctrines that of searching out what the doctrines overlooked would have something in common with an anarchists' convention. Of course, it is possible to imagine people doing work in the spirit I have identified as Hirschman's, and indeed some of these are among the authors of this volume. But they wouldn't, and don't, look much like disciples in the conventional sense.

In fact, this point can be pushed further. It would probably be impossible for Hirschman's work (or those aspects of it stressed here) to be the norm or standard or (to use Kuhn's term) the paradigm of a discipline.[12] For Hirschman's work is, in an important sense, *reactive* to the main lines of work being undertaken in the disciplines he takes up. The search for the overlooked must be guided by what is being focused on. The point is analogous to the observation that altruism cannot be everybody's prime motivation: there have to be some folks around who care substantially for their own satisfactions, so that the altruists have someone to help. Just so (to put it too mechanistically), somebody has to be promulgating the laws Hirschman finds the exceptions to.

It should follow that, when one of Hirschman's formulations becomes part of the prevailing wisdom, it becomes his task to peer around the edges of *that,* to see what it omits. And there are in fact in Hirschman's writings some interesting cases of this, several of which are elaborated in Hirschman's retrospective essay "A Dissenter's Confession"[13] and in a reflective essay on his early book *National Power and the Structure of Foreign Trade.*[14] But perhaps the most striking instance appears in Hirschman's less personal essay on the history of his specialty, "The Rise and Decline of Development Economics."[15]

In that remarkable piece, Hirschman examines the historically quite exceptional circumstances that gave birth to development economics, and shows how its optimistic assumptions about the benefits of economic development ran afoul of the unfolding of political disasters in many developing countries. The analysis thus uncovers a hidden or overlooked aspect of the relation between development economics and political outcomes, and thereby sheds light on many complexities in the recent evolution of development thought. The essay is indeed self-critical, since Hirschman plainly numbers himself among the development pioneers whose understanding of the relation between political and economic development has proven too naive. Yet this criticism of himself and his peers is, again, of a constructive rather than nihilistic sort. Hirschman recognizes the value of what development economists tried to, and in part did, achieve, and he employs his uncovering of the political limitations of development economics to enrich, rather than dispose of, the field.

The final aspect of Hirschman's own work that I shall touch on is his attention—unusual in contemporary social science—to history. In contemporary economics, history has come to be viewed largely as a laboratory for testing general economic laws.[16] For Hirschman, however, a principal purpose of historical study is to uncover the role of the exceptional or unpredictable in human affairs. A striking illustration, pointing to the normative as well as the explanatory value of such historical insight, appears in Hirschman's comment on a paper by S. N. Eisenstadt concerning theories of revolution.[17] Hirschman observes there that any attempt to identify probabilistic laws of revolution is bound to be pessimistic: few oppressed groups will be in a condition that makes a successful revolution likely. And in fact any path one can discern that leads from authoritarianism to pluralist democracy will appear both quite narrow and highly improbable.

"But," Hirschman argues, "such unlikely sounding combinations are the kind of stuff history is made of! It is a considerable paradox, but I believe it is true that the spelling out of such a priori quite unlikely *combinations* of needed favorable factors is less discouraging than the laying down of just *one* overriding precondition for redemocratization. The reason why the *less* probable turns out here to be subjectively *more* hopeful is, precisely, that the bringing together of various conditions conjures up the image of a conjunction of circumstances such as we are familiar with from history. The mere act of describing such a conjunction gives confidence that, even if this particular one cannot be translated into reality a second time, there must be quite a few other similarly far-fetched ones that history might have up its sleeve. For history is nothing if not far-fetched."[18]

These remarks concern study of the history of the phenomena an investigator deals with. Hirschman is also interested, for rather different reasons, in the history of thought about the subject matters he works on. A lively awareness of both the current state of thinking about a subject and the evolution of that state is essential to Hirschman's distinctive approach to social theory. For it is only *relative* to current understandings and their background that Hirschman can define neglected and overlooked aspects. A sensitive and broad-ranging awareness of the currents of thought in the social sciences is an essential characteristic of Hirschman's make-up; although it is plainly a natural part of his personality, it is also central to his distinctive way of working. Hirschman's introductory remarks about an essay of his entitled, "Morality and the Social Sciences: A Durable Tension" capture this outlook nicely: "If there is to be a fruitful reencounter of morality and social science, then the strength of the resistance against such an enterprise must be realistically appreciated. The essay thus explores the historical and epistemological reasons why the many well-meaning exhortations to build moral values into economic analysis have not been notably effective."[19]

Hirschman, it appears, sees his own writings as embedded in a particular historical and cultural context, and he allows his self-consciousness about that to shape his writings. This posture stands in revealing contrast to much contemporary writing in social science, whose ambition is to be context-free and universal, to aim (even if inevitably falling short) at general truths about society. It is time to ask whether this contrast tells us anything interesting about contemporary philosophy and sociology of social science.

III

The characteristic Hirschmanian activity of uncovering hidden aspects of phenomena fits rather uncomfortably with standard views of scientific practice. Literature in both the philosophy and the sociology of science leads us to conceive of scientists as engaging in three principal sorts of activities, which we might call accumulation, refutation, and replacement. Researchers are engaged either in elaborating and extending currently available theories, developing evidence to show the falsity of those theories, or proposing new theories to replace ones that have been found inadequate.

The awkward thing about Hirschman's approach, relative to this typology, is that while he is indeed concerned to show inadequacies in existing theories he is not typically concerned either to overthrow those theories or to replace them with a new alternative theory. The aim is rather to say, "Yes, there is something right about the existing theories, *and also* there is something over here, not noticed by those theories, which we should keep in mind as well."

One could try to argue that this sort of formulation really amounts to refutation and replacement. The earlier theory missed the "and-also" and so is wrong; the new theory, which is the old theory plus the "and-also," is superior. But this doesn't work because the new "theory" will not, in the case of Hirschman's characteristic arguments, be a full-fledged theory in the usual scientific sense, with law-like generalizations and testable hypotheses. It is more likely to consist of a narrative account of some instances where the theory breaks down, or some illustrations of aspects of reality the theory overlooks, or a collection of admittedly fragmentary theoretical insights. The new formulation doesn't claim to do the same job the old theory did, only better. It simply claims to notice some significant things the old theory missed.

Good illustrations are provided by Hirschman's arguments that what look like obstacles to development sometimes aren't, or that reliance on comparative advantage sometimes isn't a satisfactory strategy for growth. A full-fledged replacement to a theory of development obstacles would say when apparent obstacles are real and when they are not and would stipulate criteria and tests for determining which they are. And similarly for a modified theory of comparative advantage. Hirschman's arguments are not in general ambitious in that way.

The underlying rationale for this modest approach, I would suggest, is Hirschman's perception that anything approaching the "whole truth" about any interesting piece of social reality is bound to be much more complicated than our available attempts to grasp it. The theories we possess are inevitably partial, constrained by our limited point of view, our imperfect knowledge, and our finite imagination.[20] But we should not, on that account, be contemptuous of those available attempts at systematic theory—they give us whatever grasp we have. There is no point at our current (or forseeable) level of understanding in demanding or trying to produce a completely adequate view. Rather we have to find helpful ways of living with our ignorance.

It is not, from that perspective, particularly helpful simply to refute available theories—given their limits, that's liable to be both fairly easy and not very illuminating. It can, however, be helpful to be *reminded* of our ignorance, if that can be done in ways that encourage us to widen our vision, and to see possibilities we had overlooked.

Hirschman in fact expounds this viewpoint in closing his essay on applications of the "exit-voice" dichotomy to the problem of European integration: "The injection of exit-voice reasoning has not pretended to produce fundamental new solutions to some major puzzles of integration. What then is the point of the exercise? Perhaps that it sensitizes us to certain situations which can be effectively *reformulated* in terms of exit and voice. Such reformulations will not leave things exactly as they were: occasionally they will make us see the forces at work as well as possible options and outcomes in a new light. And that is about as much, I have come to think, as we can expect from social theory."[21] This statement is too one-sided to be entirely typical of Hirschman, laying stress on the limits of social theory almost to the exclusion of its more directly constructive contributions. However, it underlines an aspect of social theory's role which has been important to Hirschman's work and which is widely neglected.

The difference between Hirschman's outlook and that of standard

philosophy and sociology of science can be crystallized as follows:
The more traditional among those standard views regard competing
theories as candidates for *the* truth, while the currently more popular
relativist views (such as Kuhn's) see competing theories as surrogates
for the truth, imposing disciplined order on the beliefs and scientific
conduct of a particular generation, or at least as candidates for the
position of dominating the beliefs and conduct of a generation of
scientists. The traditional standpoint is clearest with the logical positivist philosophers of science and with Popper—who regards as viable
candidate theories those that are possibly true, because they have not
been shown to be false. Kuhn's more sociological standpoint winds
up identifying the main scientific activities as accumulation (in normal
science) and replacement (during scientific revolutions). In effect Kuhn
asserts that the scientific community of a given time and discipline
must, in order to function, *act as if* the dominant paradigm is true
until such time as it is replaced by a new one. Merton's sociology
leads similarly to a stress on universalism and impersonality as foremost characteristics of the scientific community.[22]

One could see Hirschman as responding to these related outlooks
in something like the following way. It is of course necessary that
researchers hold firmly to certain basic propositions and theories as
they try to advance knowledge; it is both understandable and useful
that they should evolve ways of enforcing agreement among themselves
in order to get on with the work. But, however useful for a certain
kind of theoretical work to put on blinders, at least in social science
we also have to *live* with those theories and their implications. Such
theories are not confined to the textbook or the laboratory. They help
guide our deliberations about social policy and our judgments about
the limits of social possibility. Indeed, in an era as "theory-soaked"
as our own (to borrow a phrase from Charles Taylor), social scientific
theories may importantly shape our own self-understanding as well.

We need, then, in conducting our lives, to draw on these theories
but also to learn to keep our distance from them, to retain a measure
of perplexity and puzzlement about the character of our social lives.
Kuhn has brought out strikingly that wearing blinders may be highly
functional for scientists seeking to advance their disciplinary understanding of society, but those same blinders may be quite disabling
for those seeking to conduct themselves intelligently in society, as
well as disastrous for the rest of us if they are worn by policy makers
equipped with executive energy and the means of coercion. And, of
course, the disability is all the greater if we forget we are wearing
blinders.

This suggests that there is a role to be played by some social thinkers in probing beyond the limits of available views, trying in a constructive fashion to remind us that there is indeed more to the story. There is no "method" to playing this role: what is needed is a broad knowledge of society, a good imagination, and something of an adventurous spirit. Thought in this vein should be tolerant of, indeed supportive of, more "single-minded" theorists (although not above poking fun at their exaggerated claims). And such thinkers would not aspire to lofty heights of abstraction and universality, but instead would see their work as deeply entangled with the particular needs and limits of social thought in their time and place.

Some such posture seems to me to characterize at least one important aspect of Hirschman's role in contemporary social science. If this analysis is at all persuasive, then it may prove interesting to note that it can be viewed as an application of some of Hirschman's own views about the development of societies to the development of social science. Hirschman helped pioneer the view that the policy process was best understood, not as a well-informed optimization process, but instead as a process of disjointed search for improvements and opportunities. In that context, he argued (along with Charles Lindblom) that putting too much faith in a systematic plan or an allegedly comprehensive theory could impede the process of effective search.

Hirschman wrote in 1958 that "development depends not so much on finding optimal combinations for given resources and factors of production as on calling forth and enlisting for development purposes resources and abilities that are hidden, scattered, or badly utilized." Perhaps improvements in social science sometimes depend not so much on advancing more encompassing theories as on uncovering ideas and possibilities that are hidden, scattered, or badly understood. Such, I suggest, has been Albert Hirschman's role.

NOTES

1. Albert O. Hirschman, "Introduction: Political Economics and Possibilism," *A Bias for Hope: Essays on Development and Latin America* (Yale University Press, 1971), 1–37.

2. Ibid., 28.

3. Ibid., 27.

4. Ibid., 28.

5. Ibid., 27.

6. Ibid., 28.

7. See Albert O. Hirschman, *The Strategy of Economic Development* (Yale University Press, 1958; The Norton Library, 1978); and "The Changing Tolerance for Income Inequality in the Course of Economic Development," *Quarterly Journal of Economics* 87, no. 4 (November 1973), 544–62; and *The Passions and the Interests: Political Arguments for Capitalism before Its Triumph* (Princeton University Press, 1977); and "Against Parsimony: Three Easy Ways of Complicating Some Categories of Economic Discourse," *Economics and Philosophy* 1, no. 1 (April 1985), 7–21.

8. Albert O. Hirschman, *Getting Ahead Collectively: Grass Roots Experiences in Latin America* (Pergamon Press, 1984).

9. Albert O. Hirschman, *Shifting Involvements: Private Interest and Public Action* (Princeton University Press, 1982); Olson's book referred to is Mancur Olson, *The Logic of Collective Action: Public Goods and the Theory of Groups* (Harvard University Press, 1971).

10. Perhaps the other contemporary social thinker who has made as much out of the limitations of our general knowledge about society is Friedrich Hayek. It is intriguing to note that from this similar starting point, two thinkers could derive such divergent views about the prospects for constructive social reform.

11. Compare, for example, the detailed historical narrative of *Journeys Toward Progress* with the essentially abstract argument of *Exit, Voice, and Loyalty* or the textual exegesis of *The Passions and the Interests*. Albert O. Hirschman, *Exit, Voice, and Loyalty: Responses to Decline in Firms, Organizations, and States* (Harvard University Press, 1970); and *Journeys Toward Progress: Studies of Economic Policy-Making in Latin America* (Twentieth Century Fund, 1963 and The Norton Library, 1973).

12. Thomas S. Kuhn, *The Structure of Scientific Revolutions* (University of Chicago Press, 1962).

13. Albert O. Hirschman, "A Dissenter's Confession: Revisiting The Strategy of Economic Development" in Gerald M. Meier and Dudley Seers, eds., *Pioneers of Development* (Oxford University Press, 1984).

14. Albert O. Hirschman, *National Power and the Structure of Foreign Trade* (University of California, 1945); "Beyond Asymmetry: Critical Notes on Myself and Some Other Old Friends," *Essays in Trespassing: Economics to Politics and Beyond* (Cambridge University Press, 1981), 27–33.

15. Albert O. Hirschman, "The Rise and Decline of Development Economics," *Essays in Trespassing*, 1–24.

16. For a searching critique of this standpoint, see Robert M. Solow, "Economic History and Economics," *American Economic Review* 75, no. 2 (May 1985), 328–37.

17. To be published in Italian in a volume honoring Gino Germani, and in English as "In Defense of Possibilism" in Hirschman, *Rival Views of Market Society and Other Recent Essays* (New York: Viking/Penguin, 1986).

18. Quoted from the English language manuscript of the comment, pp. 4-5.

19. Albert O. Hirschman, "Morality and the Social Sciences: A Durable Tension," *Essays in Trespassing*.

20. Indeed, as Dan Hausman has pointed out to me, the very idea that there exists a "whole truth" or "complete explanation" of a set of phenomena may be misguided, failing to recognize that events can be described and analyzed in indefinitely many ways.

21. Albert O. Hirschman, "Three Uses of Political Economy in Analyzing European Integration," *Essays in Tresspassing,* 284.

22. See especially Robert K. Merton, "The Normative Structure of Science" in *The Sociology of Science: Theoretical and Empirical Investigations* (University of Chicago Press, 1973).

23. Albert O. Hirschman and Charles E. Lindblom, "Economic Development, Research and Development, Policy-Making: Some Converging Views," *A Bias for Hope*.

24. Hirschman, *The Strategy of Economic Development*.

The Methodological Basis of Hirschman's Development Economics: Pattern Model vs. General Laws

Charles K. Wilber and Steven Francis

Over the past three decades, Albert O. Hirschman has shaped the direction and broadened the scope of economic development theory in a manner that is matched by only a few seminal thinkers. Hirschman's central insights have been incorporated so thoroughly into mainstream theory that today many development experts may recognize Hirschman's contributions, from backward and forward linkages[1] to the role of exit and voice in development processes,[2] without ever having read his original works.

What can be said about the truth value of explanations found in the work of Albert O. Hirschman? To discuss the truth value of propositions requires initially a consideration of models of explanation. Since Hirschman's method of explanation has developed, at least in part, in reaction to the inadequacies of mainstream economic theory to deal with development problems, the models of explanation underlying both mainstream economics and much of Hirschman's work must be analyzed and compared.

An examination of Hirschman's methodology will serve two purposes. First, it will allow us to discover certain features of Albert Hirschman's method of inquiry which differ significantly from that of mainstream economics. Second, it will allow us to show that Hirschman's methodological approach provides lessons and insights which, in some cases, better explain development experience than the explanations obtained by the methodology of mainstream economics.

Based on a thorough reading of Hirschman's development works, we contend that much of Hirschman's approach to explanation is best understood as a holistic pattern model. For the holist, explanation of reality cannot be had through the application of universal laws, with successful predictions the only form of verification. Rather, an event or action is explained by identifying its place in a pattern that characterizes the ongoing processes of change in the whole system. The formal models of mainstream economics, described below, cannot handle the range of variables, the specificity of institutions, and the nongenerality of behavior encountered in development. Before presenting a more detailed description of Hirschman's methodology, a brief description of the methodology of mainstream economics will help clarify how it differs from the method of the holistic pattern model.

Formalism, Positivism and Standard Economics

Standard economics has striven to become both formal and positive, where the former provides for logical deduction and the latter provides for empirical verification.

Formalism is a method that consists of a formal system of logical relationships abstracted from any empirical content it might have in the real world. For example, the theory of the firm in standard economics deals with the behavior of the firm involved in *any* process of production, using *any* inputs at *any* set of relative prices with *any* technology. It is characterized by the use of mathematics (at least implicitly) and by the development of an axiomatic, deductive structure. A set of postulates and definitions is derived by separating an empirical process into its obvious divisions and specifying the necessary or possible relations among them.

Once the definitions and postulates are established, the next step is to deduce the essential elements of the system. At this point in the formal method, the abstract model must be interpreted by providing a set of correspondence rules that relate formal terms of the theory to empirical concepts. For example, first derivatives are interpreted as marginal products, marginal utilities, etc., and in this way the theory attains empirical content. A theory, therefore, is merely an abstract model that has one or more interpretations. "Rules of interpretation do make a truth claim; they claim that the structure of relations in a calculus is the same structure that exists in some part or aspect of the empirical world."[3] Thus it is assumed that the structure of reality is approximated by the logical structure of the calculus, or set theory, or difference equations.

Formal methods produce models that are capable of yielding law-like statements. These formal laws are not empirical generalizations but are logical deductions that make a priori statements about necessary connections between abstract entities. For example, the beginning postulates of the standard theory of the firm define the firm as a rational decision-maker that attempts to maximize expected returns and has the information and ability to do so. Law-like statements that can be deduced from this include the proposition that firms will continue buying inputs and producing and selling outputs up to the point where expected returns are maximized—where marginal cost equals marginal revenue. This statement does not describe how actual firms behave, but how an ideally rational firm would behave, and is determined not from observation but from logical deduction, in fundamental contrast to the pattern model approach described later. Implicit in standard theory, therefore, is the position that truth about reality lies in the logic of the theory.

Beginning in the 1940s, economists such as Paul Samuelson attempted to reconstruct this formal body of economic theory in a way that would make deduced implications empirically testable. They attempted to show that empirically falsifiable propositions could be derived from formal models. Due in part to the development of the computer and statistical techniques, most economists have become positivists; that is, they see empirical verification of propositions deduced from formal theories as the key to economic science. The resulting formal model requires that explanation and prediction be symmetrical. Explanation occurs when the hypothesis is derived after the event, whereas prediction occurs when the hypothesis is derived before the event takes place. Due to the ahistorical and universal nature of general laws, there is a logical necessity that explanation and prediction be symmetrical. Moreover, it is critical to the viability of this symmetric relation that tentatively held hypotheses, in practice, be potentially falsifiable, but as yet nonfalsified. Indeed, the explanation is not considered adequate unless it would have served as the basis of prediction.

In the words of Milton Friedman, the goal of positive economics "is to provide a system of generalizations that can be used to make correct predictions about the consequences of any change in circumstances. Its performance is to be judged by the precision, scope, and conformity with experience of the predictions it yields."[4] Predictability, then, is the crucial element in positive economics, whereas, as we shall show, it plays a minor role in pattern modeling.

Since correct predictions imply correct explanations, scientific explanation in economics proceeds by tentatively accepting those theories which yield hypotheses (or predictions) that, when tested, exhibit a high degree of correspondence with the real world. Testing the models' predictions against experience serves to validate or verify the "system of generalizations" and leads to the accumulation of laws that constitute general theory. However, successful prediction of economic phenomena has been consistently lacking over past years for at least two reasons. First, the position of positive economics is that knowledge, whether in the physical or social sciences, is distinguished solely on the basis of the empirical subject matter and not by methodology. An implicit assumption is that the subject matter of economics is comparable to that of the physical sciences, where the subject matter and its response to external factors is characterized by its high degree of stability over time. Thus, the successful application of the theoretical methods used in the physical sciences to the subject matter of economics is contingent upon the stability of the data which, especially in development economics, are highly unstable. Second, the high degree of insulation afforded to standard theory arises because of the highly conditional nature of its predictions, which are dependent upon the ceteris paribus clauses holding and upon the data's being representative of economic reality. The economist is able to rationalize the failure of his predictions by blaming the ceteris paribus clauses, the data, or the specific testing procedure itself. These three mechanisms, examined below, make it easy for economists to reject a disconfirmation as invalid and, thus, insulate their theory from refutation.

First is the ceteris paribus problem. As mentioned briefly above, economists rely heavily upon ceteris paribus clauses when constructing their hypotheses in order to "control" their subject matter. Such hypotheses in economics are typically stated in the form of "if . . . then" propositions. Since the "ifs" do change, an econometric test that disconfirms the theory can always be rejected as "misspecified."

Second is the difficulty of constructing a clear-cut test of an hypothesis in economics. Most of the traditional statistical techniques, such as null hypotheses, are very weak ones which a variety of different theories are capable of passing. Thus, when empirical tests fail to discriminate adequately among competing theories, economists tend to assess theories on the basis of desirable logical qualities such as simplicity and generality, all qualities inherent in formal models.

Third, both the methods of collection and construction of economic data are unreliable. Typically, economic data are statistically constructed and are not conceptually the same as the corresponding variables in the theory. Therefore, econometricians and statisticians engage in data "massaging." If a test disconfirms an hypothesis, the investigator can always blame the data—they have been "massaged" either too much or not enough.

Positive economics thus becomes insulated from refutation. It cannot be harmed by demonstrating that the assumptions and laws of the formal model are abstract and unrealistic, and the model is not rejected when its predictions fail to fit the facts. What is left of "normal economic science"? When a theory is able to obtain such a high level of insulation that its substantive hypotheses are, in practice, nonfalsifiable, we contend that the theory collapses into an a priori formal model that compels assent by its logic, not by its conformity with empirical reality. As such, economic theory functions more as a *prescriptive* than *descriptive* device. That is, theory functions as a parable to elucidate the ideal toward which we should strive.

The final outcome of the use of formal methods in economics is that those methods fail to generate the hoped for results, and the investigators end up engaging in what Ben Ward calls "story-telling."[5] Instead of explaining something by logically deducing an hypothesis as a specific instance of a more general law and then subjecting it to empirical verification, economists tell a variety of stories—some more plausible than others. Some take their logical models and tell a story about a world of perfect competition. Institutions are characterized by smallness, everyone has the same motive, and all problems are frictions, externalities, and other "sociological penumbra." Other economists prepare econometric studies, "massage" the data on the basis of other information, vary the auxiliary hypotheses to paribus the ceteris, develop ad hoc explanations, and thus make up a story about what happened. The use of the term *storytelling* is not meant perjoratively. Rather, it is an accurate description of most work in the social sciences. To recognize that fact should be helpful to economics. Perhaps the science could be improved if we were more honest about this matter, for practitioners might then feel under less pressure to transform their studies into models of a procedure that has not worked and which really is not even believed. The result of that practice has been to sweep under the table some of the most important and profound issues that economics faces, as well as substantially to distort much potentially useful work.[6] In light of these difficulties, a recognition of the importance of "methodological pluralism" seems in order, and the method used often by Albert Hirschman, the holistic pattern model, is a major step toward such a pluralism.

Hirschman's Method—Holism and Pattern Model

Through his works, Hirschman has stimulated debate and research across a wide range of disciplines—sociology, political science

and economics. The way in which Hirschman has gone about re-
searching questions, developing ideas and extracting conclusions from
a lifetime of observation and reflection is the focus of the following
discussion. We are interested not so much in what Hirschman wrote,
although that certainly is important, but in how he constructed his
particular views on economic development. Hopefully, by shedding
light on Hirschman's methods we can come to an understanding of
the relevance, importance and truth-value of his work.

Hirschman appears to have recognized that formal economic
methods often fail to explain the nature of social reality. Thus he has
been engaged in the task of developing his own explanations of social
phenomena—particularly of economic development. The nature of
Hirschman's approach has ruled out other than incidental use of
formal methods. Instead he has engaged in a systematic form of
storytelling that Abraham Kaplan calls a "pattern model."[7]

Holism

At the most general level, Hirschman's method of inquiry can
be characterized as holistic, systemic and evolutionary. Social reality
is seen as more than a specified set of relations; it is the process of
change inherent in a set of social institutions known as a political-
economic system. The process of social change is not purely mechanical; it is the product of human action which is definitely shaped
and limited by the society in which it has its roots. When Hirschman
investigates the development of Brazil's Northeast, land reform in
Colombia and inflation in Chile,[8] he does so, not with the tools of
traditional microeconomic techniques and macro variables, but
through a considerably detailed discussion of each country's historical,
political and economic situation. Within that context, Hirschman
analyzes the particular role of public policy in order "to learn something about the problem-solving capabilities of public authorities in
Latin America."[9]

Hirschman's methodology is holistic because it focuses primarily
on the relations between the parts of a system and the whole.[10] It is
systemic because those parts make up a coherent whole and can be
understood only in terms of the whole. Hirschman's method is evolutionary because changes in the pattern of relations are seen as the
very essence of social reality. There is an interconnectedness between
the elements that make up an economic system and the political and
social context in which they function. Thus, in a review of the field
of development economics[11] Hirschman claims that the inability of

the field to take into account the "political disasters that struck a number of Third World countries . . . that were clearly somehow connected with the stresses and strains accompanying development"[12] led to the failure of development economics to adequately explain historical events. It is the ability to explain that is paramount in the holist method, as opposed to the ability to predict which logical positivists hold in high esteem. Later chapters show Hirschman's attempt to incorporate an analysis of political factors such as authoritarianism and social inequalities into an explanation of economic phenomena.[13]

For the holist, the explanation of reality cannot be achieved through the application of universal laws. Rather, an event or action is explained by identifying its place in a pattern that characterizes the ongoing processes of change in the whole system. Hirschman has criticized the application of mechanistic processes which were discovered in a developed country context to problems in the developing world. In describing the rejection of what he calls "monoeconomics" Hirschman supports:

> The view that underdeveloped countries as a group are set apart, through a number of specific economic characteristics common to them, from the advanced industrial countries and that traditional economic analysis, which has concentrated on the industrial countries, must therefore be recast in significant respects when dealing with underdeveloped countries.[14]

Traces of this rejection of universally applied laws can be found in Hirschman's earlier works as well, in which Hirschman questions the "applicability" of the then new macro-growth models of Harrod-Domar to the less developed world,

> theories which, because of their high level of abstraction, (may) look perfectly "neutral" as between one kind of economic system and another, (and) often are primarily relevant to the conditions under which they are conceived.[15]

Hirschman explores whether the use of growth theories is a help or a hindrance to economists trying to understand development processes and concludes that they may be far less useful in LDCs than in developed countries:

> Its (the growth theory's) predictive and operational value is low. It does not really tell us much about the key mechanisms through which economic progress gets underway and is carried forward in a backward environment . . .[16]

Hirschman suggests that "the economics of development dare not borrow too extensively from the economics of growth . . . it must work out its own abstractions."[17]

In the remaining chapters of *The Strategy of Economic Development* Hirschman does just that: works out his own abstractions about the development process which are based less on general laws and center more on the interrelations of various aspects of development within the whole social system. Thus, backward and forward linkages are identified as important elements of dynamic development processes that proceed in "sequences" or spurts of growth activity. The focus of his schema is not on macroeconomic variables but on imbalances that exist in the society and the way in which they operate to energize human action in a certain direction. The forces of development are not those that have been identified by the logical positivist approach in "monoeconomic theory" (i.e., savings rates, capital/output ratios and the like) but are powerful development stimuli such as mechanisms to induce investment, "pacing devices," imbalances in supply and demand, and important social side effects of "the creative role of imports in the development process."[18] The insights one discovers in this important work could only be elucidated by a method that rejects a rigid, disciplinary approach to development based on universal laws and proceeds by identifying the dynamics of development in a pattern that characterizes the ongoing processes of change in the whole society.

Hirschman's view of development is one that explains complex, interrelated processes rather than one that predicts specific results. This emphasis on the explanatory rather than predictive power implicit in Hirschman's method is typical of the holist approach. Holist theories are couched in the belief that the whole is not only greater than the sum of its parts, "but that the parts are so related that their functioning is conditioned by their interrelations."[19] As if to confirm this view, Hirschman writes on the effects of linkages,

> the joint linkage effects of two industries, say beer and cement, considered as a unit, are likely to be larger than the sum of their individual linkage effects . . . [20]

Recent attention to holism by philosophers of science has led to a coherent expression of its methodology. Most notably, the works of Abraham Kaplan and Paul Diesing each contain explicit presentations of the holist model of explanation which will be used to characterize Hirschman's work. These two authors seek to uncover the implicit structural framework which facilitates holist theorists' explanations of reality.[21] Diesing finds a commonality among such theories which includes the holists' conception of reality, the structure of their explanations, the primacy of their subject matter, and their particular form of logic. While all holist approaches may not conform completely to Diesing's ideal-type, as Hirschman does not, Hirschman's method includes elements of these four categories.

Conception of Reality

First is the holist conception of reality. Holistic social scientists argue that social reality must be studied as a whole human system in its natural setting. Obviously, human systems will tend to differ greatly with respect to size, complexity, degree of self-sufficiency, and relationships to the larger wholes that include them. However, the crucial element of this view is the concept of interrelationship or unity. That is, according to Diesing, "the holist standpoint includes the belief that human systems tend to develop a characteristic wholeness or integrity."[22] This unity may take the form of a set of values that expresses itself throughout the system, or it may be that a particular socioeconomic structure tends to condition everything else. Holists may disagree on whether this unity derives from some basic source (for example, religion, ethics, technology, personality) or from some complex interweaving of a number of factors, but they all agree that the unity is there.

The implication is that the characteristics of a part are largely determined by the whole to which it belongs and by its particular location in the whole system. Thus, if two superficially similar parts of different systems, let us say markets, are compared closely, they will be found to vary in characteristic ways.

In one provocative work,[23] Hirschman observes the neglect by the economist of the role of voice, typically associated only with politics, in response to the decline in quality of a firm's product, and he notes a similar neglect of exit (i.e., ability to leave) in the realm of politics. An analysis of the role of voice and exit together in relation to the economy as well as the body politic is undertaken, and Hirschman argues that the incorporation of both into a unified look at the political-economic system is vital to improving our understanding.

Some policy conclusions drawn from a unified analysis are quite striking, and run contrary to traditional economic prescriptions derived from general laws. Monopolies may not become more efficient if broken up or by allowing competition, because such action would tend to reduce the role of voice in improving the firm's performance.[24]

Through the use of consumer surplus analysis, Hirschman argues that the consumers who exit are likely to be the ones who would ordinarily exercise the loudest voice and prompt improvement of the firm's product. In this example, we see a result of holistic methodology that runs counter to "traditional economic wisdom."

The holist believes that it is inappropriate to take parts of an interdependent system out of context, and indeed that such an approach leads to erroneous conclusions. Hirschman argues that Milton Friedman's voucher plan for education whereby private schools compete with public education disregards the role of voice in the performance of public schools. He maintains that the first to leave the public school under such a system at the first sign of quality decline may be those who have the strongest voice in improving the school's quality. Thus, the plight of public schools and the general public may not be served by greater competition.[25] The neglect of the role of voice in this case is the culprit in such a proposal. The whole has been broken up into its parts and the policy conclusions are questionable in Hirschman's view.

Hirschman himself may deviate at times from this principle of not taking the parts out of context. In *Development Projects Observed,* Hirschman looks at eleven projects in various parts of the world and extracts policy "lessons" from them. In his analysis, he molds the successes and failures of the projects into his self-defined categories, as if the projects could be viewed in isolation from a socio-political analysis. This is a departure from the holistic approach, particularly since each project was undertaken within a unique political, economic and social system, and lessons learned in one may not be easily applied to other situations. Hirschman, however, attempts to gather from the various projects identifiable common themes and, as shall be shown, this is acceptable in forming a "pattern model" if certain procedures such as contextual validation, are followed.

Moreoever the holist conception of reality is that reality is a process of evolutionary change driven by the dynamic interaction between the parts and the whole. Hirschman's early view of inflation— "inflationary impulses are communicated to the economy by certain types of development sequences rather than indiscriminately by the general desire for development"—is one that contributes to an understanding of the dynamic process of unbalanced growth.[26] Hence, imbalances in the economy, supply shocks and bottlenecks are an essential part of the development process and motivate the expansion of human activity leading to sequential economic development. The parts of the system are at once conditioning and conditioned by the whole.

The Structure of Explanation

Holist theory is distinguished by the structure of its explanations. To use Kaplan's terminology, the structure of holistic theories is concatenated (linked together) rather than hierarchical, as in formal theories. Several relatively independent parts are linked together in composing holistic theories, rather than logically deducing an hypothesis from a formal theory. As such, a concatenated theory with its relatively independent subsections provides a many-sided, complex picture of the subject matter. Much of Hirschman's earlier work appears to be composed this way. The theory of unbalanced growth, for example, links together clearly identified themes such as the scarce resource of "genuine decision-making,"[27] imbalances on the supply side, bottlenecks, balance of payments disequilibria, and demand imbalances, and combines these themes to form a theory of development characterized by unbalanced growth.

> Development has of course proceeded in this way, with growth being communicated from the leading sectors of the economy to the followers . . . the balanced growth that is revealed by the two still photographs taken at two different points in time is the end result of a series of uneven advances of one sector followed by the catching-up of other sectors.[28]

Hirschman further steps outside the discipline of economics and links market forces to nonmarket forces in the unbalanced growth process, and contrasts his view to that of classical economics this way:

> Tradition seems to require that economists argue forever about the question whether, in any disequilibrium situation, market forces acting alone are likely to restore equilibrium . . . As social scientists we surely must address ourselves to the broader question, is the disequilibrium situation likely to be corrected at all? It is our contention that nonmarket forces are not necessarily less "automatic" than market forces.[29]

Here, Hirschman has not only linked together economic phenomena but he has also connected those economic forces to broader societal concerns and in the holistic tradition has created a coherent, multi-dimensional view of the development process.

A hierarchical theory, in contrast, is always one-sided. It takes one set of relations, one structure, or a single process and abstracts it out of the coherent whole, and then subjects it to logical study. For example, standard economists will focus on the process of exchange or resource allocation in isolation from the society in which the process is embedded.

The linked structure of holist explanations is necessitated in part by the holist's conception of reality. The holist maintains that we have an explanation for something when we understand its place in the whole, as opposed to the formalist's approach which maintains that we understand something when we can predict it. Consequently, to the holist, reality cannot be understood simply by exhibiting it as a concrete reflection of some universal principle; instead, the best one can do is to identify it as part of an organized whole by constructing a model which links its particular function to the whole network of themes and connections.

Primacy of Subject Matter

The primacy of the subject matter is a crucial element of holist methodology. Their concepts are relatively concrete, particularized and close to the real system being described. Throughout Hirschman's work the analysis is close to a particular situation, although in his later more theoretical work he becomes further removed from specific observations. Although the ostensible purpose of *Development Projects Observed* was "to learn something about project behavior in general,"[30] Hirschman conducts his study through specific, detailed analysis of concrete project experiences. In the introduction, Hirschman writes:

> It will, I hope, be apparent that almost all of these observations owe their very existence to a year of looking at projects and talking about them with their originators, builders, administrators, financiers, and customers.[31]

Hirschman appears to depart from the primacy of subject matter in his later works, however. In *Exit, Voice, and Loyalty,* the first significant departure from development analysis for Hirschman, he becomes more abstract in his analysis, and further removed from his subject matter—the firm, the state and organizations. Nevertheless, throughout the discussion the reader is constantly brought closer to the subject matter through frequent references to specific examples of the functioning of voice and exit.

Formalist economists assert that whatever else method is, it should first and foremost be "scientific." For them, if the canons of the scientific method are violated, or worse, if the method is radically altered or a new one adopted to fulfill the specific requirements of the subject matter, then the result cannot be science. Holists, on the other hand, do not predetermine the appropriate framework in which to explain their subject matter. In fact, holists would not object to those who would attempt to recast holistic theories into a more traditionally "acceptable" form, but they would insist that the end product not distort the uniqueness and individuality of the system. Hirschman affirms this view:

> I am very conscious that many of my statements must be considered hypotheses which remain to be tested ... I certainly hope that some of my propositions—on efficient sequences, on linkage effects, on productivity differentials, etc.—will lend themselves and be subjected to critical empirical research.[32]

In fact, many others have responded to that challenge and recast Hirschman's hypotheses into testable form.[33]

A final point with respect to the primacy of subject matter is that external formulas such as general laws or other universal categorizations are never imposed on the subject matter a priori. No statement within the pattern explanation need be generalized beyond the particular system. In this sense, holists allow the nature of the subject matter to dictate the specific method most appropriate to the task of interpreting, understanding and explaining it. Kaplan makes the point with his usual clarity and preciseness.

> The point is that the attainment of acceptable explanations is not the accumulation of eternal and absolute truths; we have not, in attaining them, laid another brick on the edifice, not fitted another piece into the mosaic. What has happened is that we have found something which serves the ends of inquiry at a particular time and place, we have gotten hold of an idea which we can do something with—not to set our minds at rest but to turn their restlessness into productive channels. Explanations do not provide us with something over and above what we can put to some use, and this statement is as true of understanding as it is of prediction.[34]

Hirschman's use of "possibilism" and his insistence upon the element of surprise in the development process is not contradicted by his use of holistic methods. On the contrary, the holist resists the temptation to construct a mosaic of truth, to use Kaplan's term, and uses ideas to constantly startle the mind rather than "to set our minds at rest." Hirschman's penchant for the surprise element at work in development processes certainly corresponds to this characteristic of holistic thought.

Form of Logic

The fourth and final characteristic of holist concepts is that they are frequently, though not always, related dialectically. The use of the dialectic is the particular form of logic of the holist approach. Diesing describes the use of the dialectics by the holist:

> Two concepts are dialectically related when the elaboration of one draws attention to the other as an opposed concept that has been implicitly denied or excluded by the first; when one discovers that the opposite concept is required (presupposed) for the validity of the first; and when one finds that the real theoretical problem is that of the inter-relation between the two concepts, and the real descriptive problem that of determining their inter-relations in a particular case.[35]

The use of the dialectic in this manner is found throughout Hirschman's work but is particularly apparent in the contrasting nature of exit and voice. Voice has been implicitly denied by the economist's focus on exit (i.e., competition) yet when the two are considered together equally, which is precisely the focus of Hirschman's book, they shed light on the responses to decline in firms and organizations with a quite different result than if only one had been employed. A quote by Hirschman illuminates the importance he attributes to both exit and voice in observing particular situations.

> Exit and voice . . . have been introduced as two principle actors of strictly equal rank and importance. I hope to demonstrate to political scientists the usefulness of economic concepts and to economists the usefulness of political concepts.[36]

To use Diesing's terms, the "real descriptive" problem later in the book becomes one of showing the interrelationships between exit and voice in specific cases. The contrasting nature of exit and voice is used to illuminate ideas concerning monopolies, public education and urban-suburban movements. In another application[37] it is the tensions and conflicts inherent in the development process that contain the incentives to further development growth. In this view, "development also draws new strength from the tensions it creates,"[38] and, quite remarkably, bottlenecks become signals for action, linkage effects stimulate investment activity, obstacles to development become incentives, and unbalanced growth creates its own forces to further the development of society. In this book and subsequent articles, Hirschman criticizes the approach of balanced growth paths and concentrates instead on seemingly paradoxical situations where disequilibria call forth the actions necessary for true development to occur.

What explains the frequent occurrence of dialectical concepts in holist theories? One reason is that they serve to counterbalance the human tendency to be biased, one-sided, abstract. They make thought and theories more concrete. "One begins with some historically or empirically suggested viewpoint and develops it until its shortcomings are clear enough to suggest the outlines of an opposing, formerly excluded viewpoint; then the latter is developed and related back to the first."[39] In effect, dialectic is the logic of the concrete.

The Participant/Observer Method

The particular exploratory method by which Hirschman constructs a holistic model, better known as a pattern model which will be explained later, is through analysis as a participant observer. In Diesing's view, the participant-observer method has achieved the greatest success in constructing holistic explanation in which the primary subject matter is a single, self-maintaining system. As an advisor to the Colombian government in the 1950s Hirschman describes his role as a participant-observer,

> I was engaged primarily in an attempt to elucidate my own immediate experience in one of the so-called underdeveloped countries. In the course of this attempt, the various observations and reflections I gathered began to look more and more like a common theme. So I undertook to discover this theme and then used it in reinterpreting a variety of development problems.[40]

The book is the result of a distillation of observations Hirschman obtained while working as a consultant to the Colombian government from 1952 to 1956. He went to Colombia as a relative newcomer to the field of economic development, as he says in an upcoming World Bank publication,

> When I returned to the U.S. after four years' intensive experience as an official advisor and private consultant, I began to read up on the literature and discovered I had acquired a point of view of my own that was considerably at odds with current doctrine.[41]

His book, *The Strategy of Economic Development,* is the fruit of years of observation as well as a generalization of the themes Hirschman encountered observing Colombian experience.

The first step of the participant-observer method is the "socialization" of the theorist. As participants, investigators allow the subject matter to impress its norms and lessons upon them. Unlike positivists, who impose external formulas upon the subject matter, the participant-observer attempts to remain close to the concrete form of the system. In describing his approach to observing Colombian development patterns Hirschman relates that "my instinct was to try to understand better their patterns of action, rather than assume from the outset that they could only be "developed" by importing a set of techniques that they knew nothing about."[42] In addition to Hirschman's obvious reluctance to impose ideas and norms from outside Colombian development experience, he views his initial role as an observer, to "look for elements and processes of the Colombian reality that did work, perhaps in a roundabout and unappreciated fashion."[43] And Hirschman finds "hidden rationalities" for development practices which the logical positivist would have overlooked.

In research for *Development Projects Observed* Hirschman steeped himself in the experiences of eleven projects in Asia, Africa, and Latin America, and first allowed the projects to impress upon him the lessons of each particular success and failure. In later works, however, it appears that Hirschman backed away from the participant-observer approach, particularly in his theoretical books. In *Exit, Voice, and Loyalty* Hirschman takes a more distant analytical tack and in *Essays in Trespassing* he picks up on themes in previous works which are based on concrete observation, albeit once-removed. In Hirschman's latest book, *Shifting Involvements,* he becomes the most distant observer of all his works, analyzing the shifts in society from public to private involvement. This attempt to engage in more general theorizing will be discussed later in the section on typologies and universal laws.

In remaining close to the concrete reality of the system under study, the theorist is in a unique position to perceive a wide variety of recurrent themes that appear in a variety of contexts. In one essay[44] Hirschman tries to form a "body of principles and meaningful generalizations which would permit the economist to be concretely helpful in the location and elaboration of promising, specific investment projects."[45] In this example, Hirschman draws upon his experience in Colombia in order to identify themes relevant to investment planning and to organize them in a unified, more general context (i.e., general guides such as the capital extensiveness of the process, the penalty of failure to maintain equipment, etc.) which help "elaborate criteria which may enable him [the economist] to make a highly useful contribution to the process of detailed investment planning."[46]

The use of abstract, general laws and universal categories is especially unsuited to the task of unifying themes. Hirschman has on more than one occasion expressed his dislike for universally applied laws and approaches which do not take into account the particular traits of the society being observed.[47]

To the participant-observer, a theme is more important the more connection it has with other themes, because the ultimate end is the construction of a model which emphasizes the interconnectedness or unity of the system. Thus, loyalty becomes an important theme because the "presence of loyalty makes exit less likely" and gives scope to voice.[48] It is the connection between loyalty, voice and exit that makes the theme more important and relevant to the observer's analysis. The next step after initial observation is to make explicit the information which, as a participant, the researcher is not able to perceive. Initially, this process is rather haphazard. The researcher constructs tentative hypotheses about parts of the system out of the recurrent themes that become obvious to him or her in the course of the "socialization" process. The themes are then woven into a complex, multi-dimensional story which includes some generalizations from observed experience. In *Development Projects Observed,* Hirschman constructs hypotheses about the importance of latitudes or "the characteristic that permits project planners and operators to mold a project."[49]

> Instead of looking at these decisions from the point of view of the "objective" analyst and his optimizing techniques, our inquiry shall deal with the propensities and pressures to which decision-makers themselves are subject.[50]

As a result, in a detailed look at why Nigerian railroads failed to respond to competition from highways, Hirschman attributes the problem, at least partially, to the latitude for poor performance permitted by the existence of an alternative method of transport. Incidentally, this theme is picked up later in another book[51] to elucidate an explanation for the special difficulties in combining exit and voice.

The hypotheses or themes are tested by consulting a wide variety of data which is different in form and substance from the data of the logical positivists (previous case studies, survey data and personal observations, rather than strictly "hard facts" and quantitative material). Evidence in support of an hypothesis or interpretation is evaluated by means of contextual validation—a process of cross-checking different kinds and sources of evidence to validate the themes. In Hirschman's work, examples of contextual validation can be seen when his earlier themes are elaborated on and expanded in later works. In fact, *Essays in Trespassing* is organized in thematic categories based on Hirschman's previous work, and as one reads his work chronologically a remarkable thread of consistency runs throughout. Exit and voice are applied in different contexts,[52] the elements of unbalanced growth are extended,[53] and backward and forward linkages are expanded to include consumption and fiscal linkages.[54] Hirschman goes one step further in his contextual validation with an extension of the linkage concept to a generalized linkage approach to development.[55] As a specific example of contextual validation, Hirschman describes a revision of his original formulation of linkage effects,

> In my original treatment of the subject, the relation between market size and the economic size of the plant was singled out as the key variable that would trigger the private or public entrepreneurship needed ... Further reflection and observation have made it clear, however, that other variables are also at work and help explain the differential speed with which these investments come into being.[56]

Hirschman goes on to identify "technological alienness" and other compelling technical characteristics as additional key variables in the linkage "hypothesis." The importance of this example is the way in which Hirschman has altered his original linkage idea and, upon further reflection and observation, expanded it to a more generalized approach. Contextual validation serves as a means of crosschecking different kinds and sources of evidence, and it serves as an indirect means of evaluating the plausibility of one's initial interpretaions. If the researcher is unable to secure evidence in support of earlier hypotheses, or if the validity of the evidence or its source appears questionable, the interpretations and/or hypotheses are revised or discarded. The technique can never produce the rigorous "certainty" espoused by logical positivists; it can only indicate varying degrees of plausibility. However, a test of a particular theme at the initial stages of development need never be conclusive to have importance for the holist, since later tests are likely to catch errors that were missed by earlier ones. Consequently, Hirschman's later reflections on exit and voice reminded him that the costs of voice (i.e., in time and effort) can quickly turn into a benefit and become a "sought-after, fulfilling activity."[57] There are numerous other examples of "contextual revisions" in Hirschman's work but, curiously, precious few examples where an earlier theme is completely discarded.

Certainly a weakness in Hirschman's work is the failure to specify in detail the process of contextual validation followed. Too often one is left with the feeling that his "themes and patterns" were not subjected to extensive cross-checking of different types and sources of evidence.

The Pattern Model and Generalization

We now turn our attention to the way in which Hirschman builds a more general thematic model from particular observations and hypotheses which have been tested contextually. This type of model, with its emphasis on recurrent themes, is known to philosophers of science as the pattern model of explanation. It is constructed by linking validated themes into a network or pattern. In the pattern model, the theorist's account of a particular part should refer to the multiplicity of connections between that part and the whole system. In this way the holist attempts to capture the interactive relationship between the part and the whole system. In his essay on the political economy of import-substitution,[58] Hirschman weaves together various themes concerning the evolution of the principal difficulties encountered by import-substitution. The importance of interrelations between economics, politics, and social factors is stressed:

> Some purely economic aspects of the problem will be discussed, but particular attention has been directed to interrelations with social and political life. The ease with which such interrelations could be suggested—mostly in the form of tentative and untested hypotheses—indicates serious neglect by social scientists of a fertile terrain.[59]

From this passage, Hirschman's concern for the interrelationship of themes is evident, and his subsequent analysis shows the pattern modeller at work. Hirschman goes on to describe the "typical" process of import-substituting industrialization and its development, incorporating his previous themes of backward linkages and their role in furthering industrialization beyond the initial import-substitution strategies in a generalized pattern of explanation. He examines the economic, political and technological factors related to backward linkages and connects them to import-substitution strategies in a generalized pattern of explanation. Though he admits the hypotheses are untested, the model has developed an internal consistency because it is linked to his previous works, including the recurring themes of linkages and sequential development, as well as being linked to the socio-political situation in a "type" of developing country.

As the holist constructs the system model, his earlier descriptions of the parts are continually tested by how well they fit together in a pattern, and to what extent new evidence can be explained with the pattern. As an example, the pattern developed by Hirschman in *Strategy of Economic Development* is brought into play in an analysis of import-substitution over ten years after initial publication. The holist is seeking to obtain a finer and finer degree of coherence between his account of the system as a pattern of interconnected parts and the real system. However, since new data and observations are constantly evolving, the model is continually being revised and can neither be completed nor rigorously confirmed.

Verification of the pattern model as a whole consists of expanding it further and filling in more details. Indeed, looking at the historical evolution of Hirschman's writing one can see this process at work. The themes elaborated in *Strategy of Economic Development* show up continually in later works, sometimes in slightly revised form; the notion of unbalanced growth, importance of "pacing devices" and, of course, linkage effects appear in nearly all of his later works. An observation and its accompanying theme in early works can be the takeoff point for an entire book, as the Nigerian railway experience was the basis of *Exit, Voice and Loyalty.*

Holists argue that their explanation is a correct one if, as the pattern becomes more and more complex and detailed, a greater variety of evidence easily falls into place. At this point, it is more difficult to imagine an alternative pattern or explanation which manages to include the same themes. As a consequence, the explanation of the whole system is tentatively held as "true," until an alternative or revised pattern is able to supersede the old model by incorporating an even greater variety of data or observation. And finally, the pattern model may be used to enable understanding of a theme in a different context, clearly Hirschman's approach in the following passage,

> I was eager to explore whether concepts such as linkage effects and exit-voice I had developed in quite different contexts could shed light on old problems.[60]

Furthermore, the accuracy of predictions, central to formalist methods, cannot be the main form of verification in the pattern model. Hirschman's themes are meant to explain, not to predict specific quantitative results, although as mentioned previously he may have no objection to someone attempting such a feat as long as the unity is not disturbed. His models can be used to recommend policy alternatives and to construct hypotheses which can be tested empirically; by itself, the pattern model cannot be used to predict because knowledge of the whole pattern and of some of the parts does not necessarily enable the holist to predict any or all unknown parts. The explanation still explains even though it leaves open a range of possible outcomes. The primary function of laws and theories within the pattern model is to provide understanding; whereas from the viewpoint of the logical positivist it is to allow accurate predictions. Hirschman's "principle of the hiding hand" explains the tendency to underestimate the problems encountered in a development project but it can't be used to predict or estimate which problems may arise.[61] Since the ultimate goals of the holist and the logical positivist are not identical, it is difficult to fault one method for failing to live up to the ends of the other. If pattern models are not very good at predicting, it is quite understandable since their purpose is to explain and create validated understanding through the use of themes drawn from concrete experience.

Few holistic social scientists have attempted to construct more general theory from the pattern model approach. Throughout the process of building a pattern model the holist is continually comparing his case with others known to him, thereby using one case to suggest areas to explore in another. One potential result of such a process of comparison is the development of a typology: "exit, voice and loyalty" in Hirschman, for example. The use of typologies can guide the researcher in asking relevant questions of a new case. However, there is always the risk of converting the type into a stereotype, which usually results from inadequate empiricism.

The apparent tendency of Hirschman to become more speculative in his later works, and more distant from specific observation, represents in our view an attempt of the pattern modeler to generate general themes or typologies that can be applied to a variety of contextual situations. In this attempt to construct general theories in a way significantly different from formalism, the pattern modeler risks being accused of uncontrolled speculation. Hirschman has not escaped entirely this accusation; however, since the pattern is always open to revision, he will no doubt continually recast his speculations should new evidence deem it necessary. Comparison of widely varying types enables one to identify still more general characteristics of many human systems—universal or nearly universal values, institutions, system problems, mechanisms and the like. Needless to say, few have been found. General theorizing of this kind attempts to transcend the relativity inherent in the pattern model approach by seeking general characteristics of human systems.

Problems with Hirschman's Holistic Methodology

Hirschman has found holist concepts more useful than formal models for dealing with considerations of power, conflict, distribution, social relations, nonmarket institutions and processes, and the like. However, there are severe limitations to holism. First, because of their lack of precision, the use of holist concepts must be continuously monitored by reference to observation, cases, and examples. Holism separated from its empirical base easily becomes loose, uncontrolled speculation. Hirschman's use of the themes of unbalanced growth, linkage effects, pacing devices, and the principle of the hiding hand were empirically derived from extensive observation. His later writings exhibit themes more distant from observation, and thus, he has not entirely escaped this fate.

A second problem is that the imprecision and generality of holist concepts make any definitive verification of hypotheses impossible. Warren Samuels points out that "it is uncertain as to the degree to which the holistic conception of the economy can be (1) specified, (2) separated from the rest of society, and (3) made manageable for analytical purposes, quite aside from its being made operational for testing purposes."[62] As a consequence the social scientist using holist theories should remember that these theories are always tentative and subject to change.

The precision and rigor that characterize formal theories are not unqualified virtues. If a school of thought, for example certain traditions within standard economics, begins to overemphasize precision and rigor it will tend to fall into theoretical stagnation and preoccupation with logical and empirical detail. Diesing points out that "every scientific tradition I have examined contains a balance of precision and vagueness, rigor and suggestiveness, but . . . different traditions apportion the two elements in different fashions."[63] Balance serves the conflicting scientific needs of creativity and control. Precision and rigor provide empirical or logical control. Vagueness and suggestiveness facilitate creativity. If a school of thought begins to overemphasize vagueness and suggestiveness it will tend to fall into diffuse and uncontrolled speculation. A central problem of any methodology is how to strike a balance between precision and rigor, on the one hand,

and vagueness and suggestiveness, on the other, and how to relate the two so that they synergize rather than cancel each other.

Conclusion

In conclusion, Hirschman's methodology can be characterized as holistic in approach, proceeding by the linking of themes together into a pattern model based upon observations obtained in the field close to the subject matter at hand. His continual reference to the political and social realm as important and vital factors influencing economic development, despite the narrowing world-view of the field of economics, is testimony to the resilience of the holistic method and pattern modeling as an alternative method. The method is distinctly different from the approach of the logical positivist in several ways. In general, the emphasis in formal models is on general laws and universal principles, while in pattern models it is on facts or on low-level empirical generalizations. Empirical facts are included as part of a formal model, but only as circumstances that condition the applicability of general laws. Deductive laws and abstract empirical generalizations are sometimes used in a pattern model but only as suggestive guides in the search for observable concrete connections or patterns; and these laws and empirical generalizations are open to modification in the process.

Use of the pattern model appears appropriate when an explanation involves many diverse factors, each of which is important; when the patterns or connections among these factors are important; and when these patterns can be observed in the particular case under study. Use of the formalist model appears more appropriate when one or two factors of laws are better known and understood than the specific instance.

Hirschman attempts to generalize from the facts of experience about the working of the development process as a whole. Traditional development economists do not generalize from the facts of experience; rather, they attempt to construct models based on assumptions about how economic agents would behave if they acted rationally in their self-interest and this rationality is bounded by the competitive equilibrium model of economic theory. If one is interested primarily in how the real world with all of its imperfections does in fact behave, the Hirschman approach may prove to be more fruitful.

The intent of this exploration into Hirschman's methodology and the "truth-value" of his work was not meant to force his writing into an inappropriate ideal form, but to explain how Hirschman often explores the world around him and how his method presents lessons to us all, in a way that is strikingly different from traditional economics but nonetheless just as valid. His explanations have "truth-value" much as some of those "truths" obtained through the formalist approach, and hopefully we have shed some light on his process of explanation.

Hirschman has been, and no doubt will continue to be, the eternal heretic, casting doubt upon our discovered "truths" and presenting his unique interpretation of society; exciting some, inciting others, but always "trespassing" on other disciplines and in the process stimulating many of us to carry on with what he calls the "passion for the possible."

NOTES

1. Albert O. Hirschman, *The Strategy of Economic Development* (New Haven and London: Yale University Press, 1958), 98–120.

2. Albert O. Hirschman, *Exit, Voice, and Loyalty* (Cambridge: Harvard University Press, 1970).

3. Paul Diesing, *Patterns of Discovery in the Social Sciences* (Aldine-Atherton, Inc., 1971), 36.

4. Milton Friedman, "The Methodology of Positive Economics: in *Essays in Positive Economics* (Chicago: University of Chicago Press, 1953), 4.

5. Ben Ward, *What's Wrong with Economics?* (New York: Basic Books, 1972), 188–90.

6. Ibid.

7. Abraham Kaplan, *The Conduct of Inquiry: Methodology for Behavorial Science* (San Francisco: Chandler Publishing Co., 1964).

8. Albert O. Hirschman, *Journeys Toward Progress* (New York: Twentieth Century Fund, 1963).

9. Ibid., 1.

10. It must be emphasized at this point that Hirschman is not a conscious holist in that he recognizes the characteristics of holist methodology and sets out to practice holistic inquiry. Noting that Hirschman's method often differs from that of mainstream economics, this article attempts to explain Hirschman's method as reflecting many of the characteristics of holistic pattern modeling, and does not suggest that Hirschman always follows these characteristics. Indeed, Hirschman himself has resisted attempts to place his thought in one category or another. His method is more varied and escapes complete categorization, but reflects much of what is described below as holistic pattern modeling.

11. Albert O. Hirschman, *Essays in Trespassing: Economics to Politics and Beyond* (Cambridge University Press, 1981), Chap. 1.

12. Ibid., 20.

13. Ibid., Chaps. 3 and 4.

14. Ibid., 3.

15. Hirschman, *Strategy,* 29.

16. Ibid., 32–33.

17. Ibid., 33.

18. Ibid., 129.

19. Allan Gruchy, *Modern Economic Thought* (New York: Prentice-Hall, 1947), 4.

20. Hirschman, *Strategy,* 103.

21. Diesing, *Patterns of Discovery,* Chap. 7.

22. Ibid., 137.

23. Hirschman, *Exit, Voice, and Loyalty.*

24. Ibid., Chap. 5.

25. Ibid.

26. Hirschman, *Strategy,* 156–66.

27. Ibid., 63.

28. Ibid.

29. Ibid.

30. Albert O. Hirschman, *Development Projects Observed* (Washington, D.C.: Brookings Institution, 1967), 1.

31. Ibid., 3.

32. Hirschman, *Strategy,* v–vi.

33. For a recent example see K. Shahid Alam, "Hirschman's Taxonomy of Industries: Some Hypotheses and Evidence for a Tested Model of Hirschman's Product-Oriented Industry," in *Economic Development and Cultural Change* (Jan. 1984).

34. Kaplan, *Conduct of Inquiry,* 355.

35. Diesing, *Patterns of Discovery,* 212.

36. Hirschman, *Exit, Voice, and Loyalty,* 19.

37. Hirschman, *Strategy,* 62–72.

38. Ibid., 209.

39. Diesing, *Patterns of Discovery,* 278.

40. Hirschman, *Strategy,* v.

41. Hirschman, "Pioneers in Development" (World Bank, forthcoming).

42. Ibid., 10.

43. Ibid.

44. Albert O. Hirschman, *Bias for Hope* (New Haven and London: Yale University Press, 1958), 41–63.

45. Ibid., 44.

46. Ibid., 61.

47. See *Bias for Hope,* 342–60, for a view of two different research approaches. Hirschman criticizes one of these approaches for precisely these reasons.

48. Hirschman, *Exit, Voice and Loyalty,* 77.

49. Hirschman, *Development Projects Observed,* 86.

50. Ibid., 87.

51. Hirschman, *Exit, Voice and Loyalty,* Chap. 4.

52. See Hirschman, "Further Reflections on Exit, Voice and Loyalty" in *Essays in Trespassing.*

53. See Hirschman, *Bias For Hope,* 64–66.

54. See Hirschman, "A Generalized Linkage Approach to Development, with Special Reference to Staples" in *Essays in Trespassing.*

55. Ibid.

56. Hirschman, *Essays in Trespassing,* 71.

57. Ibid., 215.

58. Hirschman, *Bias for Hope,* 85–124.

59. Ibid., 86.

60. Hirschman, *Essays in Trespassing,* 212.

61. Hirschman, *Development Projects Observed,* 9–35.

62. Warren Samuels, "Journal of Economic Issues and the Present State of Heterodox Economics," Report to 1974 and 1976 AFEE, 24.

63. Diesing, *Patterns of Discovery,* 221.

Rationality, Interest, and Identity[1]

Amartya Sen

I. Consistency and Interest

There are various concepts of rationality extant in economics, in particular those concepts which deal with choice behavior. One approach concentrates on *internal* characteristics of choice—more specifically, *consistency*. Another focuses on the *correspondence* of choice with interest. In the former approach, a person is rational if he chooses consistently.[2] The criteria of consistency can vary, but very often they boil down to the choice function being representable by a binary relation (typically called the "revealed preference").[3] In the internal *consistency approach*, the interpretation of that binary relation is a separate exercise and does not affect our view of the rationality of the person. Under the approach by correspondence, the choice function of a rational person is required to correspond to some non-choice feature of the person, and the feature that is commonly invoked in this context in economics is the interest of the person. I shall call this the *interest-correspondence approach*.

It is hard to believe that the internal consistency approach to rationality can be adequate. A person who—with remarkable internal consistency—does exactly the opposite of what he himself thinks would be the sensible thing to do may have many virtues, but rationality can scarcely be one of them. To take another case, consider a person who is judged to be impeccably rational in his choices. Now, keeping his non-choice characteristics the same (e.g., what he thinks, feels, etc.), "reverse" his choice function, in the sense that he now chooses in line with the exact "opposite" of the binary relation of the previous choice function.[4] It would be bizarre to insist that he must have remained exactly as rational as before. But of course his choices are exactly as consistent.

Consistency cannot itself be an adequate test of rationality of choice. The basic ideas associated with the notion of rationality demand more. In fact, it is plausible to argue that some feature of correspondence is necessary. However, it does not follow that the interest-correspondence approach provides the right feature. Indeed, it can be argued that the interest-correspondence approach is based on a basic confusion between rationality and egoism. There can be many good reasons for thinking that one alternative rather than another is to be chosen, and the pursuit of self-interest is at best one such reason.[5] Non-egoistic reasons for choosing an action may be based on "the possibility of altruism".[6] They can also be based on specific loyalties or perceived obligations, related to, say, family ties, class relations, caste solidarity, communal demands, religious values, or political commitment.

II. Correspondence-Rationality

To identify rationality with the consistent pursuit of self-interest in choice involves taking, inter alia, a very restricted view of the motives and passions of human beings. In his classic historical study *The Passions and the Interests,*[7] Albert Hirschman has discussed, with his usual insight and vision, the remarkable story of "the progressive impoverishment of the prevailing concept of human nature over a period of some three centuries."

> In the early modern age, man was widely viewed as the stage on which fierce and unpredictable battles were fought between reason and passion or, later, among the various passions. At mid-eighteenth century, some hope was held out that the interests, which were increasingly understood in the purely pecuniary sense of the term, would be able to tame the disastrous, if aristocratic, passions. But by the latter part of that century, the passions were collapsed into the interests by Adam Smith who pronounced "the great mob of mankind" to be safely programmed: From the cradle to the grave, its members were to be exclusively concerned with "bettering their condition.[8]

This "impoverished" concept of human nature is now common to a good deal of formulaic thinking on social matters, and specifically it is dominant in economics.[9]

In going beyond internal consistency and asking for external correspondence as a characteristic of rationality of choice, care has to be taken not to insist on a correspondence that is unreasonably tight and narrow. I propose to adopt a more permissive criterion of correspondence. On reflecting carefully on the choice over a set S of alternatives, if a person were to decide that no element from a subset R(S) be chosen, then R(S) would be called the "rejection set" of S. If the person, in fact, chooses some alternative from R(S), then that choice can be described as *correspondence-irrational*. The underlying idea is that a choice that would be rejected on reflection has some irrationality. This characterization has a "negative" ring—focusing on irrationality, which I believe is a more sensible procedure. But I shall not pursue the point further here. Choices that are *not* correspondence-irrational will be called, stretching a point,[10] *correspondence-rational*.

The nature of correspondence-rationality requires more elaboration and closer examination. First, the criterion must not be based entirely on the person's actual reflections, since a person may well have acted without careful reflection one way or the other. The criterion invokes what a person would reflect if he were to do so carefully (but with the same information, and other external constraints, as he had when he actually decided).[11] The purpose of the correspondence-rationality criterion is to bring a self-examination feature into the assessment of choice. Careful reflection is not, of course, a spectacularly precise concept. It would be a mistake to try to make it very precise by specifying some alleged feature of carefulness in spuriously exact terms, (e.g., "at least 7½ minutes of reflection"). Carefulness of reflection is a broader description and may be usable more exactingly *or* less. The same, of course, is true of the idea of rationality itself.

There is nothing very puzzling about this use of counterfactual reflection. For example, if we were to say that choices and lotteries that conform to the "Allais paradox" are irrational, one sensible way to proceed to examine that claim may take the form of asking the chooser to reflect seriously on it and *then* to decide what should have been chosen. Reflecting on the implications of the choices could alter the "first-blush" selections. But if, even after such a reflective exercise, the person were to maintain that he or she would have thoughtfully chosen in the same (apparently paradoxical) way, then despite the violation of the Bayesian and other so-called rationality axioms, it would be right to concede that in this case there is no irrationality, in the particular sense of correspondence-irrationality.

Second, correspondence-rationality is, by its very nature, a partial notion of rationality. It demands seriousness of reflection and that, of course, is an important condition, but it does not impose some particular notion of rationality of *thinking*. As far as thinking goes, the demand of correspondence-rationality takes, in a sense, a "procedural" form. This leaves open the question as to whether the serious reflection may itself be judged to be irrational in some—"deeper"— sense. If it is, then a person who is impeccably correspondence-rational might still be taken as "irrational" in that "deeper" view. In this sense, correspondence-rationality can be seen to be a partial—but possibly useful—approach to this difficult subject.

The possibility that correspondence-rational choices may be still irrational in some deeper sense (related to some "defect" of thinking, despite its "serious" character) suggests another (in fact, the "opposite") question. Can some choices be correspondence-irrational and still be rightly describable as rational? I believe the answer has to be in the negative, but let us consider a case that may give some superficial plausibility to an affirmative answer. Take a person who thinks fuzzily even when he thinks seriously and fails to see what he should do to achieve the results that he wishes to achieve (or what in some unspecified "deeper" sense he "really wants"). It is, of course, quite possible that in this case a person may end up doing better (perhaps in that unspecified "deeper" sense) by *violating* correspondence-rationality. Would it be reasonable to see him as just "rational" since he is doing so well? I think not. Rationality is not merely a matter of choices ending up being right. It is also a matter of coherence of choices and reasons. A person who cannot think straight and cannot translate the fruits of his thought into actions cannot really be a model of rationality, even if the two failings together make his actual choices fine and dandy.

It is, of course, not required that every act of choice must be reasoned through. A person may have learned to use rules of behavior dealing with classes of choices, without having to think them through in each case. He or she may even be able to "intuit" in line with what he would think. Nor is it required that there must not be "contrary rules" (e.g., "my impulse is always wrong, and I must try to do the opposite of what I am tempted to do"). A contrary rule ·may well be supported by serious thinking, even though in particular acts it may look *as if* an action contrary to thinking is being taken. There is room for considerable variations within the format of correspondence-rationality to admit these cases.

Third, correspondence-rationality differs from the interest-correspondence approach in not justifying the rationality of choice in terms of correspondence specifically with the interest of the chooser. Indeed, there is no prior "patterning" of rational choice related to any specific set of motives or objectives. Reflective choice is not required to correspond to the maximization of some particular thing (such as desire-fulfillment, or happiness, or interest satisfaction, or utility in some other sense).[12] To demand that choices be reflectively justifiable is not the same as to demand some particular substantive maximizing position. Passions, of which Albert Hirschman speaks, can figure just as easily as interests. The maximand explicitly or implicitly present in the chooser's thinking, can vary from person to person, and there might not even be any "everything considered" maximand.

Fourth, nor is there any presumption that the person should be able to rank, after serious reflection, every alternative against every other. There can be incompleteness of ranking, arising from, say, practical difficulties of discrimination, or from informational lacunae, or from intrinsic non-comparabilities. Correspondence-rationality does not demand that such incompleteness must be removed and a partial ranking must be completed at least to the extent of there being a best alternative to choose. Incompleteness is not only consistent with serious thinking, it can be argued (if we were to go on to discuss the question of rationality of thinking) that incompleteness need not compromise rational thinking either.[13]

It is important to emphasize that correspondence-rationality was specified in terms of the chosen alternative not being picked from the "rejection set." In the case of incompleteness, the rejection set may or may not be empty. When there are rejectable alternatives despite the incompleteness, choosing one of those elements, from R(S), would violate correspondence-rationality. Take the case of Buridan's ass, which failed to decide which of two haystacks was better, and thus died of starvation, which it clearly wanted less than having either of the two haystacks.[14] The irrationality here does not consist in the inability of the ass to decide which of the two haystacks was better, but rather in ending up "choosing" starvation which it would have least liked to happen. It is the choice from the rejection set that makes the behavior of Buridan's ass definitely irrational.

Finally, it should be noted that the purpose of using the concept of correspondence-rationality is not "operational use" only—at least not in the narrow sense in which operational use is often defined. It is easy to see that any approach that relies on comparing choices with results of reflection—possibly even counterfactual reflection—is not off to a flying start in the race of "operationalism"! Indeed, narrow operationalism has had the effect of predisposing the approach of rationality towards easily observational "tests," or at least towards tests that have the reputation of being easily observational, though that reputation may not always be altogether well-deserved. For example, judging the rationality of choice in terms of internal consistency is often favored on such operational grounds (no nonsense about what the person thought or would think). However, the simple view of "testability" of consistency of choice is severely compromised by difficulties of observation of comparable circumstances, as well as by interpretational problems. For example, on the one hand, temporal *proximity* can lead to apparent inconsistencies, when what is in fact being observed is just a taste for variety (e.g., fish at lunch and meat at dinner), while on the other hand, temporal *distance* may intensify the difficulties of changing tastes. The complexities of behavior in situations of group interdependence are also enormous.[15]

The approach of correspondence-rationality is not even aimed at getting something immediately operational. Rather it tries to provide an understanding of one aspect of rational choice. It can, of course, be used to examine particular choices, or indeed—more ambitiously— particular theories of choice (e.g., "rationality axioms" of choice under uncertainty), by subjecting those axioms to scrutiny by serious reflection on these and other possible choices. But most importantly, the approach is concerned with asserting the role of thinking in the concept of rationality and with insisting on the relevance of questions that are not even asked in some of the more standard approaches to the rationality of choice. The prime object is to move the discussion of rationality out of the narrow limits, on the one hand, of internal characteristics of choice, and on the other, of the "impoverished concept of human nature" (to use Hirschman's words) in the form of simple interest-maximization.

II. Interest and Identity

It was argued earlier that the pursuit of self-interest is not the only possible objective that serious reflection might support. It cannot, however, be denied that it is a common and important objective. Indeed, even the much-maligned hedonistic view of human choice— the maximization of happiness—has obvious relevance to human conduct. If I were to ask you whether you would like to come to dinner, and you were to say, "I would be happy to come," I am unlikely to respond, "Please answer the question: not whether this would make you happy, but whether you will come!" Happiness is not a bad reason for choice, and if nothing else is mentioned, the intended choice can be deduced from the statement about happiness. The recognition that happiness is not the *only* perspective in which even the person's own advantage may be seen, does not compromise the important role that the pursuit of happiness, and—more generally—the pursuit of individual interest, may have in the understanding, explanation and prediction of choice.

One difficulty in analyzing interest arises from an issue to which Marx made an insightful reference. He argued that while economists tend to assume that "each person has his private interests in mind, and nothing else," in fact "the point is rather that private interest is itself already a socially determined interest."[16] That point relates, of course, to Marx's well-known and important analysis of "ideology" and of "false consciousness." However, the relevance of the remark goes well beyond the particular use Marx himself made of that general diagnosis.

It is not easy to think of an individual's concept of self-interest without seeing the person in a social setting. The relationship of persons to groups can be very complex, and what a person sees as self-interest may well be closely linked with groups with which the person identifies. In fact, we all have many identities, given by our relationships with various groups to which we belong and of which we see ourselves part. As members of a family, a community, a class, an occupation group, a nation, etc., we have a complex perception of "our interests."[17] So the point, made earlier, that the pursuit of what we see to be our interest is not the only possible motive for choice, has to be supplemented by the *further* point that even what we see to be our interest may have various "social" components.

In some cases the extent of indentification may be such that the very idea of a perceived individual interest may be hard to use. For example, in the context of the strong links between individuals and the family in South Asia (including India), it has been claimed by some sociologists that the use of the notion of individual interest would be quite illegitimate.[18] The point might be a disputable one if it is meant, which it need not be, to imply that there is no sensible way of discussing the relative advantages of different individuals within such a family.[19] But certainly, as far as the notion of *perceived* interest goes, there may indeed not be—often enough—any sense of a distinct personal interest, or even of relative advantage, within the family.

These issues raise important political and moral dilemmas regarding policy and social action. But, happily, I am not concerned with them in this paper.[20] In the context of rationality of choice, and specifically of correspondence-rationality, it is important to recognize that the exact characteristics of perception of interest will play an important part in the person's own assessment of choice and, thus, in the identification of the rejection set.

The point may be of fairly general relevance to the analysis of choice and its rationality. For example, in understanding behavior patterns in situations of the type of the "Prisoner's Dilemma,"[21] the issue of identity may be quite central.[22] In explaining the observed propensity of the players to depart from the pursuit of strictly individual goals in the direction of "other-oriented" behavior, various different types of causations have been considered. While there is considerable scope for getting such explanations in terms of moral reasoning involving metarankings and "as if" preferences,[23] or in terms of strategy with repeated games,[24] they are not quite adequate explanations of actual behavior. Explanations have also included the possibility of stupidity on the part of the players, e.g., "Evidently the run-of-the-mill players are not strategically sophisticated enough to have figured out that strategy DD is the only rationally defensible strategy, and this intellectual shortcoming saves them from losing."[25] A different line of explanation may look instead at the issue of identity and what the person sees his interest to be and what the effects of that might be on his choices (despite admonitions by the organizers of the experiment to maximize this or maximize that). The sense of identity of interest among people placed in a similar situation (and subjected, in this case, to the same experiment) may offer an alternative line of explanation.

In real-life Prisoners' Dillemmas, the sense of identity may be, in some cases, more explicit and quite possibly stronger among the different individuals involved. I am not concerned here with exactly how often the behavior featured in these situations may or may not be affected by such a sense of identity. But I would argue against describing such behavior, when it occurs, as necessarily irrational, or even seeing it as really puzzling. Acting implicitly as a member of a "team" may indeed have profound effects on the nature of these games, but they may nevertheless be explicable even without departing from the interest-pursuit framework, since the perception of self-interest itself may include the team connection. The issue of identity can go well beyond that of "externalities" in the way that concept is typically seen in economics, e.g., "sympathy" in the sense of suffering in the others' suffering and enjoying the others' joys (or "antipathy" with opposite reactions). The concept of "personal interest" may include a good deal of identity, even before the question of sympathy arises.

A team member who pursues the interests of the team even when it is not best for him (given the actions of others), is not necessarily acting against "self-interest," in a suitably broader sense. This is not just because a person may be sympathetic to others in the group, but also because the choice of actions may be seen as a group choice and "self-interest" in that context may involve a correspondingly wider sense of identity. "We" may be the natural unit of first-person decision.[25]

In explaining the behavior of voters in a large election, or of workers in team-work without supervision, or of soldiers in a battlefield, the question of identity is of obvious interest, as it also is in the context of the family. Indeed, the issue of identity is a very general one and requires much more extensive investigation than it has tended to receive.

IV. Concluding Remarks

In this paper, I have argued against two of the standard views of rationality, viz., *the internal consistency approach* and the *interest-correspondence approach*. I have also outlined a different—and fundamentally partial—approach to rationality in terms of *correspondence-rationality*. Among the advantages of this approach is the broadening that it allows in the characterization of objectives, motives and identities. The opportunity to resist what Hirschman has called "the progressive impoverishment of the prevailing concept of human nature" is itself a reward. Rationality has to make more room for a wider concept of human nature.

NOTES

1. For helpful comments I am grateful to John Bennett, Max Black, Terrence Fine, Michael McPherson, and Henry Wan, Jr.

2. See Paul Samuelson, *Foundations of Economic Analysis* (Cambridge: Harvard University Press, 1947); M. K. Richter, "Rational Choice," in J. S. Chipman, L. Hurwicz, M. K. Richter, and H. F. Sonnenschein, eds., *Preference, Utility and Demand* (New York: Harcourt, 1971).

3. On the interrelations between (and, frequently, equivalence of) various proposed criteria of consistency, see my "Choice Functions and Revealed Preference," *Review of Economic Studies* 38 (1971), reprinted in *Choice, Welfare and Measurement* (Oxford: Blackwell, and Cambridge, Mass.: MIT Press, 1982); H. G. Herzberger, "Ordinal Preference and Rational Choice," *Econometrica* 41 (1973); K. Suzumura, "Rational Choice and Revealed Preference," *Review of Economic Studies* 43 (1976).

4. The "opposite" of a binary relation admits of some ambiguity, but one simple case consists in just reversing the strict rankings (e.g., x being above y to be converted to y being above x).

5. See my "Behaviour and the Concept of Preference," *Economica* 40 (1973), and "Rational Fools: A Critique of the Behavioural Foundations of Economic Theory," *Philosophy and Public Affairs*, 6 (1977); both reprinted in *Choice, Welfare and Measurement*.

6. See T. Nagel, *The Possibility of Altruism* (Oxford: Clarendon Press, 1970); H. Margolis, *Selfishness, Altruism and Rationality* (Cambridge University Press, 1982). See also E. S. Phelps, ed., *Altruism, Morality and Economic Theory* (New York: Russell Sage, 1975).

7. A. O. Hirschman, *The Passions and the Interests* (Princeton: Princeton University Press, 1977).

8. A. O. Hirschman, *Essays in Trespassing: Economics to Politics and Beyond* (Cambridge: Cambridge University Press, 1981), 288.

9. Some of these issues are discussed in my *Choice, Welfare and Measurement*, "Introduction" and essays 2–4.

10. The ambiguity arises from the fact that an alternative that is not rejected (i.e., does not belong to the rejection set) need not necessarily be thought to be sensibly choosable. So a point *is* stretched when the choice of a non-rejected alternative is seen as positively correspondence-rational, as opposed to just *not* correspondence-irrational.

11. The case for keeping the information and the external constraints as *given* is easy to understand (see H. A. Smith, *Models of Man* (New York: Wiley, 1957)). To make a mistake because one did not know enough, when deciding, is unfortunate but not obviously irrational. However, the decisions regarding *information gathering,* while different from choice *given* the information, are themselves assessable in terms of rationality. But there is a question as to how far back we may sensibly go. On this see Dieter Helm, *Enforced Maximisation: Competition, Evolution and Selection* (Oxford, 1984).

12. See my "Plural Utility," *Proceedings of the Aristotelian Society* 80 (1980–81).

13. See my "Interpersonal Aggregation and Partial Comparability," *Econometrica* 38 (1970), reprinted in *Choice, Welfare and Measurement,* in which see also "Introduction." Also see Simon, *Models of Man* (1957).

14. See my "Behaviour and the Concept of Preference," *Economica* 43 (1973), reprinted in *Choice, Welfare and Measurement,* 61–2.

15. See *Choice, Welfare and Measurement,* "Introduction" and essays 2–4

16. K. Marx, *Grundrisse.*

17. Hirschman discusses some of the complexities in *The Passions and the Interests* (1977), and in *Shifting Involvements* (Princeton: Princeton University Press, 1982). See also G. Akerlof, "Loyalty Filters," *American Economic Review* 73 (1983).

18. See, for example, Veena Das and Ralph Nicholas, "'Welfare' and 'Well-being' in South Asian Societies," ACLS-SSRC Joint Committee on South Asia, SSRC, New York.

19. For reasons for disputing that view, see my "Family and Food: Sex-Bias in Poverty" to be published in P. Bardhan and T. N. Srinivasan, eds., *Rural Poverty in South Asia,* and also in my *Resources, Values and Development* (Oxford: Blackwell, and Cambridge, Mass.: Harvard University Press), and "Carrots, Sticks and Economics: Perception Problems in Incentives," *Indian Economic Review* 18 (1983). Relative disadvantage may have objective interpretations that are eminently discussable, e.g., the lower longevity of the female compared with the male, or the higher mortality rate of girls vis-à-vis boys, in South Asia.

20. See, however, my "Rights and Capabilities," in T. Honderich, ed., *Morality and Objectivity* (London: Routledge, 1984), reprinted in my *Resources, Values and Development;* and also, with (J. Kynch), "Indian Women: Well-being and Survival," *Cambridge Journal of Economics* 7 (1983).

21. See Luce and Raiffa, *Games and Decisions* (1957); and A. Rapoport and A. M. Chammah, *Prisoner's Dilemma: A Study in Conflict and Cooperation* (Ann Arbor: University of Michigan Press, 1965). See also the analyses of rationality problems in this context; particularly, J. W. N. Watkins, "Imperfect Rationality," in R. Borger and F. Cioffi, eds., *Explanation in the Behavioural Sciences* (Cambridge: Cambridge University Press, 1970), and M. Black, "The 'Prisoners' Dilemma' and Limits of Rationality," *International Studies in Philosophy,* 10 (1978).

22. Neglect of this issue of idenity plays an important part in Mancur Olson's justly famous, pessimistic analysis of individual actions in situations of the type of the Prisoners' Dilemma. "Indeed, unless the number of individuals in a group is small, or unless there is coercion or some other special device to make individuals act in their common interest, *rational, self-interested individuals will not act to achieve their common or group interests" (The Logic of Collective Action,* Cambridge,: Harvard University Press, 1965, 2). Often such pessimism would be exactly justified, but not invariably so (e.g., people learning not to litter the streets, or not to give total priority to saving their own lives in wars, or to vote even in large elections). The question of identity is particularly important in cases of these other types.

23. See my "Choice, Ordering and Morality," in S. Körner, ed., *Practical Reason* (Oxford: Blackwell, 1974), reprinted in *Choice, Welfare and Measurement.* See also John Watkins' rejoinder and my reply in *Practical Reason.*

24. See S. Smale, "The Prisoners' Dilemma and Dynamic Systems Associated to Non-Cooperative Games," *Econometrica,* 48 (1980). See also R. Radner, "Collusive Behaviour in Non-cooperative Epsilon-Equilibria of Oligopolies with Long but Finite Lives," *Journal of Economic Theory,* 1980.

25. Rapoport and Chammah, *Prisoner's Dilemma,* 29.

26. This issue is discussed in my "Goals, Commitment and Identity," forthcoming in the *Journal of Law, Economics and Organisation.*

Some Other Kinds of Otherness: A Critique of "Rational Choice" Theories

Alessandro Pizzorno

I. Why Loyalty Has a Value

The following episodes are puzzling. A theory is required to explain the facts they describe.

FIRST EPISODE: *Defense expenditures.* A certain country was at war (no nuclear blast was envisaged). Without a very heavy increase in defense spending chances were high that the country would lose the war. For reasons of morale, maybe for fear of revolt, the government agreed upon a referendum that would decide the new tax burden. Were the country to lose the war, she would almost certainly lose independence and her existence as a separate cultural entity. But this was not the first time in history that that country had faced a similar fate, and it was confidently predicted that no more substantial private loss would be suffered by any single citizen in the case of defeat than in the case of victory. Further, the private loss due to the proposed tax burden would be heavier than that expected from the damages of the war. The final figures of the referendum are not known but, as anticipated, some voted in favor of the proposed tax, others voted against. This behavior is complex. We need a theory to explain its occurrence.

Some would suggest that those who voted in favor preferred paying more taxes to having their country lose the war, and that the others preferred the opposite option—and that this, or what can be drawn from this, is theory enough. Revealed preferences are all that there is to argue about social action. This view must be rejected. We need a real theory.

SECOND EPISODE: *A mere name in common.* A political party is very close to coming to power. To form a coalition with other parties, or to enlarge its electoral appeal, important planks of its program

355

must be changed. It is not the first time that this has happened and, added to the previous ones, the new alterations will not leave much intact of what were the original program and image of the party. If the party upsets the government, its followers will receive many advantages. Social prestige will accrue to the members of the party and economic and administrative spoils will be distributed among the party officers and militants. However, some militants (perhaps some of the founders or very first members of the party) quit, feeling that the party, by so radically changing its program, is now only nominally the party they originally founded, or adhered to. Others remain loyal. This fact again requires explanation.

THIRD EPISODE: *A mere signature.* In the years after Mussolini came to power in Italy, many persons were arrested. One of these was the leader of the Catholic party, De Gasperi; another was the leader of the Communist party, Gramsci. Freedom was offered to both if they petitioned Mussolini for release. De Gasperi signed and went free; Gramsci did not and remained in prison for almost ten years, became ill and died a few months after being released. Some would say that Gramsci was more courageous and strong-willed than De Gasperi. Whether or not this is so is beside the point. I will claim that what is significant is the difference between what signing that petition meant to De Gasperi and what it meant to Gramsci. But this statement advances us only a little. We still need categories of thought that allow us to differentiate the meanings of an act for a person. We also need a theory to explain why certain acts, or the refusal of certain acts, may be of more value to a person than freedom.

FOURTH EPISODE: *Badges of honor.* A country is at war and many of its citizens take part in the battle. Some fight bravely, are wounded and receive medals or other badges of honor. These badges have high value for them and for the persons around them who recognize the importance of the acts for which they were conferred. After the war, the mood of the population changes, the dominant opinion turns against everything linked to the war, and acts of valiancy performed during the war are vilified or belittled rather than held in esteem. So are medals and persons decorated with them. Some of these persons are themselves persuaded of the reasons that lie behind the new public opinion, and their own view of their past actions conforms to the new mood. Others are not and together with like-minded persons form associations and movements. Within these new circles medals and the acts that they symbolize have value, and the persons who have performed those acts derive prestige from them and are gratified by the recognition of which they are the object. Now there are two groups of persons: they have all performed the same type of acts and won the same type of rewards for those acts, but the persons in one group value those rewards in a way different from the persons in the other group. It may well be not unusual that somebody sells certain goods and receives an amount of money in a certain currency, while somebody else receives the equivalent amount in a different currency; then the first currency is devalued, while the second is not and the two sellers find themselves at the end with different amounts of rewards. But for the case of the badges of honor, the currency was the same for all. These facts need explaining.

These facts are about countries at war, political parties, ideologies, badges of honor: it seems that in each case a theory of loyalty is needed and one such theory is Albert Hirschman's (1970, 77 ff.). In it, loyalty is a special attachment to an organization which makes exit from that organization less likely. Hirschman argues further that loyalty gives more scope to voice, which is the activity aimed at influencing the decisions of the organization. These two circumstances have important consequences. Since it is likely that the most active and influential members of an organization have more attachment and are more loyal to it, and hence will incur a higher personal cost for leaving it, the presence of loyalty will prevent the exit of the members that the organization needs most. Loyalty is specially needed, that is, "its role as a barrier to exit can be constructive . . . when organizations are close substitutes, so that a small deterioration of one of them will send customers-members scurrying to the other." (Hirschman 1970, 81).

So far, the theory assumes that an organization includes two classes of members:

a) the *"low-loyalty" members,* for whom exit is practically costless;

b) the *"high-loyalty" members,* for whom exit is *subjectively* difficult, hence costly; these are likely to be "locked" in their organization a little longer.

But the theory also states that the barrier to exit constituted by loyalty is of finite height. When the *"Bauchschmerzen"* of the loyal member become too acute, he will exit. On the other hand, he will also be the first to reenter when the organization improves according to his wishes. This to-and-fro implies that the organization goes on working even when its most loyal members have abandoned it and, therefore, that a third layer of members exists, who are assumed never to leave either because for them exit is inconceivable, or because if they leave, the organization ceases to exist. These are:

c) the *"identifiers,"* for whom exit is not conceivable and for whom the barrier to exit is, as it were, of infinite height.

This development of the theory is unexpected and paradoxical. It seems, however, irresistible. Hirschman's theory aimed originally at explaining "the decline in firms, organizations and States" and the response to it: to this end, the development I propose is redundant. But the episodes I set forth above have a wider scope. They call for an extension of this theory of loyalty.

It will help to examine why the loyal member "feels that leaving a certain group carries a high price for it" (Hirschman 1970, 98). Why has loyalty a value? It seems that an answer can be given if the nature of the "identifiers" is unriddled. If the identifiers leave, the group (the organization, etc.) ceases to exist as such. This case is not difficult to conceive: the owners of a firm may sell it or go bankrupt, the core leaders of an association may decide to dissolve it. But the existence of a group or of a relation, as such, may also represent a *subjective* end for a member. When an "identifier" leaves a group, the group ceases to exist *for him*. The identifier is clearly different from the loyal member. The *loyal* member leaves an organization when he does not receive from it what he desires. He feels that the organization still delivers the same kind of goods, only of a lesser quality. He threatens to leave and if the threat has no effect he leaves. If the services of the organization improve, he may reenter. A member is *loyal* to a certain group (and he may be loyal to many groups at once, if they do not compete) because he approves of the goals of the group. A member *identifies* himself *in* a group not for a specific end, but for its collective reality, and thus receives from it his own identity. He will leave not when the organization is inefficient, but when it has become for him a different entity. He will leave when the identity of the organization is changed. He will not care, then, whether the organization totally deteriorates; on the contrary, this will only prove his case. This is true of one who has lost his faith. Whereas the loyal member may bargain about his own leaving, the identifier cannot. The faithful cannot threaten to lose her faith, the lover to cease to be in love. These threats would not be credible. They would be threats against oneself. Once the identity, the faith, or the love are lost, then a new person is born. If some attachment returns, it will be for some new identity, some new faith, some new lover, even if these bear, for the sake of registration, the same names.

But we can fully understand the nature of identification only when we consider the other side. If the identifier leaves, he himself ceases to exist.[1] This case seems to refer to terroristic organizations of a sort which kill their members when they leave. But we do not need to go so far. A person who leaves a group can become a "different person." This seems to be said merely figuratively. But suppose that the habits, the values, the beliefs, in a word, the order of the preferences by which that person was known, and by which his actions and reactions could be, more or less accurately, anticipated by those who had to deal with him, are radically altered. Should not an observer be led to conclude that, for what concerns him, that person is another person? Of course, body and memory would continue to appear more or less the same. For some this is an important fact, but not for those who believe that people can be understood only as rational choosers. For, what is the use of having the same body and the same memories if what distinguishes a person are the criteria he uses in his choices and evaluations, and these are no longer the same?[2]

To look insightfully at this last point, we now turn to the Fifth Episode.

FIFTH EPISODE: *Proust and the lover.*

> Our dread of a future in which we must forego the sight of faces, the sound of voices, that we love, friends from whom we derive today our keenest joy, this dread, far from being dissipated, is intensified if to the grief of such a privation we reflect that there will be added what seems to us in anticipation an even more cruel grief: not to feel it as a grief at all—to remain indifferent: for if that should occur, our self would then have changed. It would be in a real sense the death of ourselves, a death followed, it is true, by a resurrection, but in a different self, the life, the love of which are beyond the reach of those elements of the existing self that are doomed to die . . . [3]

Why is it that not to feel a grief can be "an even more cruel grief" than to feel it? How can one go about one's actions if an anticipated contentment is a state to be avoided? "We are incapable, while we are in love, of acting as fit predecessors of the next persons who, when we are in love no longer, we shall presently have become . . . " Our future selves may indeed be other persons.

A person becomes a different person, a self becomes a different self, when the group, the couple, the organization or the movement which bore out the values that allowed that person to act, to choose, to judge of persons or ideas in a certain way, to feel certain emotions, does not exist any longer *for him*. This is because it seems difficult to hold values, to be gratified by rewards, to enjoy satisfactions, without referring to other individuals who are able to *recognize* those values, rewards, satisfactions, and to respond in some terms to them. Propose this pact: that an individual would receive everything he wants in money or goods, on the condition that he should not have any human contact any longer in his life. Few, probably none, would accept.

II. Identity and Free-riding

Loyalty can therefore be understood as a degree of identification. One identifies with a group to the highest degree when the cost of one's acting together with others for the same collective ends is zero. From this point the value of voice decreases. Indeed, since voice must be understood as collective action meant to produce a public good (a specific policy, a more efficient organization, etc.), participation in it has been shown to be irrational. The rational course of action, when a public good is needed, would be to ride free, stay put, and enjoy the benefits brought about by the action of others. But many do act collectively, protests are expressed, individuals spend money, time and effort, to bring about situations whose benefits they could enjoy at no costs. It is time to explain this contradiction.

Hirschman proposes that "it is in the nature of the public good, or the 'public happiness,' that striving for it cannot be neatly separated from possessing it" (Hirschman 1970, 216). There should be no cost in "voicing" therefore, but rather pleasure. Why so? Because, when a desired policy is not easy to bring about, the next best thing to having that policy is "striving for it." This "strange transformation of means into ends," Hirschman says, is due to the painful presence of uncertainty. When the outcome is uncertain, at least anticipation in the collective action aiming at bringing that outcome about does appear certain; and this certainty "negates the uncertainty about the desired outcome" (Hirschman 1970, 216). If this is a realistic description of a mental state, it is of one we generally call "self-deception." Is self-deception always needed to generate collective action? We ought to look closely at the whole question.

Discontented members of an organization can resort either to voice or to exit. Voice is more likely, says Hirschman, when things like health or safety are at stake. Deterioration in the taste of a firm's food, or an unattractive design in a car will give rise to exit, but health hazards or safety problems will bring out voice. Voice seems to be linked with concern with people's fate. This concern makes people act together with others who wholly or partially share that fate. Should they forgo that collective concern, they feel they will lose control over that fate and will become something different, maybe something less, than what they were before. This they do not want.

The following example will make my point clearer.

Suppose you are a member of a linguistic minority. There are demonstrations to obtain the status of official language for your tongue. Participation seems to you too costly and you refrain from it as from other forms of collective action aimed at that objective. Suppose also that you speak only your language and that the status of official language for it would facilitate several operations in your daily life and that this is what you were really interested in. Your not acting collectively is a rational decision since you will obtain your benefits if the rest of the community will. If you take part in the action, your personal contribution will not affect the outcome, and you will incur costs for no added benefit. But suppose instead that you speak both languages and that no personal advantage derives to you from the official status granted to the language of your minority group. This status has only a symbolic value to you: It is meant to be a protection against the extinction of a community of speakers who, by using that language, preserve an identity you cherish. Thus you will continue to sort out things and to understand persons through values you know will be recognized. These values would be lessened and your recognitions jeopardized, if you remain estranged from the collective action. Participation in it, not the outcome of it, is needed for confirmation of your collective identity and of the renewed efficacy of the circle of persons within which you can continue to act and continue to be seen as the same person. This cannot be taken to be the "next best thing to having the desired measure." It is a state of affairs altogether different from the outcome the action is intended to bring about.

There is irony here. Staying put, letting others act, is the right choice when your interests are affected: being active, participating in collective endeavors, is correct when your interests are *not* affected. But consider. When a public good is the only goal of a collective action, you can ride free because you are, without threat or need for reconfirmation, one of those who will be entitled to the consumption of the produced good: playing in the park, driving in the street, being protected from invaders by your national army or from thieves by your local police. You *already are* a member of the union which is negotiating the agreement that will bring about higher wages for you even if you do not strike, or of the group of firms which will obtain a protectionist measure and be protected from an association to which you do not pay your dues. What is at stake in these cases of collective action is whether you will or will not receive a certain benefit, and *not* whether you belong or do not belong to the right collectivity, have or have not the required identity. Were this an outcome of the action, then you would have to participate in it if you wanted that outcome. This class of outcomes we may call the forming, or confirming, or collective identities. Of these outcomes it can be said further:

a) That they may, or may not, be willed as such by the participants. An old union militant may clearly expect that a strike will not succeed in obtaining a wage increase, but that a stronger solidarity and a confirmation of collective identity will result from that action. The young union member will start by wrongly believing in the possibility of success; and will end up belonging to a more solidaristic group.

b) That they do not belong to the class of "process benefits." These are the benefits an agent receives from performing the action. It is in the nature of any benefit to be comparable, at least nominally, with other benefits. Not so with what we call an identity. I have no way of knowing whether a person is better or worse off when one or another identity can be attributed to him. Some will say that he has chosen to act together with those persons and no others and this is a proof of a revealed preference. It is not. The forming of the collective identity was not the objective he pursued.

c) That they do not belong to the class of "aggregation" or "emergent" effects, although they seem to belong to this class because they are often unintended. But aggregation effects are the property of a system. They are brought about by non-concerted, although interdependent actions. They can be measured only by an observer who possesses criteria for tracing in a certain way the boundaries of the observable system. The forming of identity instead modifies the individual agent. It is the outcome of a process that at the same time brings about the system of recognition of that identity, and hence possesses meaning for the agent as well as for the observer.

d) That they explain collective action in a way and in cases in which selective incentives (in an Olsonian sense) do not. Often collective action takes place without selective incentives being present.

A different explanation is therefore needed. Even when selective incentives are present, it is unlikely that they can explain lasting collective action. Given their individual nature, they are unequally distributed. Individual goals will therefore emerge that will conflict with each other and hamper collective action. If this lasts, it can only be because the action is becoming an end in itself for the new identities it is forming. Or, as in the case of rites and ceremonies, because collective experience shows them to be necessary for a reconfirmation of collective identity.

Still I can see some difficulty in the argument. Let me postpone it for the moment and return briefly to another theory of loyalty to which Hirschman refers.

It seems that one can make sense of loyalty by considering it a function of the investment a person makes in the group to which he becomes loyal. The higher the investment a person feels was needed for entering into the group, the stronger his loyalty to the group will be. This is the reason behind groups requiring severe initiation, clubs requiring higher fees for membership, tribes requiring painful rites of passage. In these cases, the person performs acts that do not seem to be in his own interest, rather than leaving the group, betraying it, infringing its norms. It is as if remaining loyal adds a value to actions that can be considered loyal. If this value is produced by a past action that the person does not want to disown, we conclude that in this disowning resides the negative value, in the appropriation of the past action resides that positive value. Continuity of the self, i.e., personal identity subjectively felt, is here the reason for action.

This interpretation is very close to, but not the same as, the explanation given by the theory of cognitive dissonance, which deals technically with this type of episode. It is not the same because in that theory what becomes a negative, unbearable, state of the subject is the dissonance between a belief and an action, or between two beliefs when at least one of them is expressed (which makes it an action).[4] I find the notion of a dissonance between a belief and an action rather unclear, because it is based on a comparison between objects of different nature. My interpretation points to an inconsistency between objects of the same nature. These objects are the criteria that the person applies in orienting his actions. When the criteria appear to be inconsistent (or merely "different") then the identity of the person through time seems to have broken down. Or, in other words, when the self must make a decision, an open awareness that the criteria he is using are not the same as those that some of his former selves applied in the past threatens the perception of continuity in time that seems necessary to evaluate the consequences of any decision.

The theory behind this second view of loyalty, therefore, is consistent with the one I propounded in the first view. The value of loyalty depends on the degree of identification it expresses.

III. The Boundaries of Identity

We are able to see now at least one element that the episodes described in the first part of this article have in common. They all deal with persons who seem to have the alternative of choosing either some private utility of their own, or the commitment to some collective (even if dyadic) identity (sacrifice for one's nation or one's party, fidelity to one's ideal, solidarity with one's comrades). This is, however, not the real alternative because if persons act, they always act with reference to some identity.

Consider, first, the distinction between an identity which appears exclusive and an identity which appears to leave open further choices, as in the case of the so-called "symbolic goods." Imagine, again, the members of a minority being offered the right to have an educational system teaching their language, or, as an alternative, a program of substantial investments that will make each member of their families perceptibly wealthier. Or imagine the employees of an organization being offered the abolition of badges and rituals differentiating superior from inferior functions, or, as an alternative, a raise in wages. In these two cases, the first offer may be called symbolic, the second monetary. In both cases, the symbolic offer (transmitting one's language; being free from organizational humiliation) can be received and consumed only if the collective identity in question is maintained and felt relevant. The second terms of the two alternatives refer to monetary goods. It seems that they can be enjoyed individually, and can be evaluated in terms of the maximization of utilities, without further reference to some collective identity. But can they? Suppose that a further clause is stipulated, the already mentioned clause of the suspension of all possible identification: that the persons receiving the increase in income spend the rest of their lives with no human contact (all services would be provided, sexual satisfaction would be granted at will but with no social communication, and freedom of movement, wherever no human being is to be found, would be absolute). These have been called "robinsonades." We cannot take seriously the possibility that a benefit be enjoyed "individually." This is only the impression one receives when a benefit is paid in money. Although it is a symbol, money seems to have had the effect of making compatible the most diverse identifications, that is, to make possible the transfer of individuals from one to another collectivity, and their keeping of membership in several. Being a generalized symbol, it is recognized almost everywhere, and a person with money can move from circle to circle with the assurance of being recognized. Not always, though, as can be seen in the following episode.

SIXTH EPISODE: *Reductio ad Amazoniam*. A wealthy businessman, alone in his own private plane, lands among an Amazonian tribe. He is obliged to spent the rest of his life there. So far his life had been a succession of rational choices oriented by expected utilities. The wealth he had accumulated was recognized on any market, except by savages. This person was what the succession of his rational choices had made him to be. Now nothing has changed in him, nonetheless he must become another person. From now on he will be recognized in a different way, by people who pay attention to different values, who look for different signs to construct the identity of a person. Maybe the best capital that that businessman has brought along with him is some ill-defined skill, a by-product of some unsuccessful rational calculation: the capacity of recognizing the unexpected otherness of human beings.

This case seems unrealistic, absurd. I have placed in operation a *reductio ad Amazoniam*. But it helps to show that even the most widely recognized currency, that which is valid on the economic market, might be refused recognition. In our daily life, we operate in much narrower systems of exchange, dealing with currencies which are person-specific and which only small groups of people are willing to recognize: prestige, trust, courage, capacity for affection, friendship or solidarity. We repeatedly experience small, but sorrowful *reductiones ad Amazoniam,* sudden falls from seemingly well-secured states of recognition, sudden plunges into new tribes, sudden perceptions of the absurdity of our calculations.

IV. Uncertainty and the String of Selves

In some of the cases I have so far imagined people were confronted with situations of uncertainty. People were uncertain, or became aware that they should have been uncertain, about what *their own evaluation* of the states of the world, and hence of their own interests, would become. This uncertainty, however, was not about future states of the world, but about future states of the evaluating self. This was so because the future states of the self were seen, or should have been seen, as dependent on the recognition, by some other selves, of the validity of the criteria by which the states of the world would be evaluated.

It will help now to restate the whole question. I have claimed that any theory that explains social action in terms of rational choice must be self-defeating. A person who chooses "rationally" must be able to evaluate the consequences of his choice in terms of his own interest. But, first, the interests of his own self *now* are not the same as those of his future selves. One *now* would prefer to smoke rather than to refrain from smoking, but this is probably not in the interest of some future self who, when he comes about, would prefer to be healthier. Or one would prefer to enjoy good food and good clothes now, rather than buying stocks, but this is not in the interest of some future self who probably would enjoy eating good food and wearing new clothes that he could have afforded had his predecessor saved money instead of spending it. We may imagine some umpire, some superself, allotting benefits with equal concern for the different successive selves.[5] But then we should also have to imagine this superself possessing rules of distribution that are constant in time, or which change predictably.

A similar assumption is needed to take care of change in values. The consequences of a certain choice made by me now will occur when my way of ordering preferences has changed. In the future a certain self of mine will rate the badges of honor, the fidelity to certain ideals, the solidarity of certain friends or comrades, the love of a certain lover, with weights different from the ones that have led me to sacrifice other goods. The principle of rationality requires us to anticipate the utility of the choices we make. The anticipation may take place under conditions of incomplete information about the occurrence of certain events, but of this we may take care with the weighting, objective or subjective, of the chances of the occurrence of those events. When one is anticipating consequences, however, he must also consider that these will not be consequences for the choosing self, but for a successive one. And since comparing utilities intertemporally is as arbitrary as comparing them interpersonally, normally a state of choice is a state of uncertainty about how a future self will evaluate the situation in which the choice made now is placing it.

This type of uncertainty (let us call it "value uncertainty") is different from the uncertainty considered by the theory of probability. There, is however, an analogy in the procedure to overcome both.

Uncertainty exists when situations are too unique to form in any way groups of instances of sufficient homogeneity to make possible a quantitative determination of true probability. To overcome this situation one must form groups of instances and then proceed to evaluate, subjectively, or by calculating frequencies, the probability of occurences of those instances. In "value uncertainty" one must also create a sort of regrouping. One must form "groups of selves."

Remember the fourth and fifth episodes. They dealt with persons who seemed to have lost the values which had previously helped them make important choices. Those persons had lost their values because these had ceased to be recognized as such by the group, or collective entity, to which those persons belonged. Other persons had kept those values as working values by reconstituting situations in which they continued to be recognized. If a person can be assured that he will perpetuate his belonging to the group of persons which will hold the same values with respect to a certain class of choices or, in other words, if he thinks that his future selves will all belong to that group of selves to which his own current self now belongs, there is no reason for him to suffer from uncertainty.

The argument so far follows from the above mentioned impossibility of comparing the utilities of different selves intertemporally. The special condition that allows a comparison of some sort to be drawn is the constitution of a state of identity of a person through time. This state depends on the stability of what could be called a "circle of recognition." What this "circle" is required to recognize are the values that a person is using in his choices which make him a certain recognizable, self-identical agent.

Suppose that I am anxious about a decision I have to make. I am anxious because of what may become of me if I fail. What kind of sanctions will fall upon me? How will I bear them? These and other concerns that the uncertainty about my action provokes in me amount to one essential question: Who will recognize me and how will I be valued? If some stability of the circle(s) of recognition around me is secured, possible failure does not make me anxious. If no stability is in view success will not gratify me, in fact I will not be able to gauge it. We must conclude that uncertainty about one's action amounts to uncertainty about the stability of one's circle(s) of recognition.

To negate anxiety due to value uncertainty one may resort to action directly aimed at preserving or forming a circle of recognition. This is the type of collective action that, as was demonstrated, does not allow free-riding.

It now becomes easy to understand how a certain conception

of personal identity goes together with the idea of a circle of recognition. A person is a succession of choosing selves that may have something in common only if they are located in a common circle of recognition. Personal identity consists in some intertemporal, vertical connectedness among successive selves of a human being that is made possible only by some interpersonal, horizontal, connectedness among different individual selves.

We may imagine a univocally achieved full personal identity as a limiting case, when a sort of absolute indentification of a person with a collectivity is taking place. This person's ends are the ends of the collectivity, the person itself is no more than an instrument in view of those ends. Analogously, the current self is no more than an instrument in view of the ends of future selves, those who will consume and enjoy the fulfillment of the ends pursued by the collectivity. There is here full integration, both horizontal and vertical, collective and personal. Economists speak of "time preference" when the deciding self favors its closest successors: The further ahead in time the selves of a person lie, the less their interests weigh for the deciding self. But in the case of the fully integrated self the opposite is true. The curve of the discount rate is flat or, rather, negative. Some future self dictates choices; no weakness of the will is allowed, the current self is responsible to some future self as it is to the collective will from which the secure recognition proceeds.

I have described a limiting case. Real cases are located at a certain distance from it. But this limiting case is assumed as the norm by several ideological conceptions of society. Consider revolutionary ideologies or religions of salvation. In them, the "true" interests of a person are his long-term interests—the interests of his future selves, and to them the deciding self must sacrifice immediate benefits. These long-term interests coincide with the interests of the collectivity within which the individual forms his values and acts.

But consider also the constitutional ideology of liberalism and the practice of representative government derived from it. According to this practice, a representative does not represent the interests of his constituency but the interests of the nation. His electors cannot bring him to court on the ground that he has not fulfilled his mandate. He is not an attorney on behalf of his electors, as the representatives in pre-liberal parliaments could be considered to be. His mandate is defined by the furtherance of the interest of the Nation, or of the People, in general. This principle seems to be at odds with the majority principle. If the interest of the People were the interests of its majority, the single representative should be free to represent particular interests (and not be sued if he receives payments from them). But this is not so and, contrary to appearances, there is no contradiction. The principle of representation implies a unified state. A state is like a person, it is composed of successive selves, of successive generations of selves. The currently deciding selves may be divided about what course of action to take. But if they act as members of a state, if they act through a political institution, they are supposed to be divided not about their particular immediate interest, but about opinions of what their "true" interest as members of a collectivity, which includes present and future selves, present and future generations, could be. This is why the principle of majority rule among interests cannot hold. Changing and non-represented interests of successive selves must be interpreted. The process of representation in the modern state is assumed, by the constitutional doctrine, to be about the interpretation of the collective identity of the nation.

As political institutions operate assuming and assuring the identity of persons in time, so do other institutions. Consider the notion of legal responsibility. A person—a succession of selves—will receive just deserts for the decision of some past self. This is judged right and proper. It is probably only expedient for the sake of deterrence or for the higher probability that the future selves of the person who has committed a crime have of committing some crime again. Legal systems also know statutes of limitations. For certain crimes, a distant successor cannot be held responsible for a crime committed by a past self. On the other side, legal systems impute responsibility for past selves also to selves that are not physically connected, as in cases of inheritance.

Like the law, morality holds future selves responsible for past selves. But morality also knows confession, contrition, conversion. These are cases in which existing identities are interrrupted, or new identities constituted.

In the view I have held here, social action is not the product of selves maximizing instantaneous satisfaction nor of selves devising strategies aimed at procuring benefits for future selves or future generations of selves. It is rather the product of selves aiming at securing horizontal ties with selves of other persons or vertical ties with future selves. Persons are indeterminate, as nations and parties and movements are. This means that our commitments are uncertain and have to be continuously renewed. For the group of disappointed founders in our second episode, there is no sure way of knowing whether their party is always the same party or not, and whether they have to stay or leave it. Nor is there a sure way for me to know whether the friend who asks me to lend him some money because he cannot stand one minute more without heroin is the same person who asked me a few hours ago not to lend him money whatever he would ask, and hence to know whether the commitment I took with that previous self holds for the new one.[6]

Is the view that individual action has its end in the formation of social ties more likely to clarify social facts than the view that individual action has its end in the satisfaction of utilities? To this last view it is objected that either it has to rest on the unempirical notion of happiness, or that, if it is conceived as being expressed in preferences, it becomes tautological. Not to be such, it has to assume the pre-existence of certain structures. For instance, a world of pre-labeled objects, within which preferences can be ordered in a transitive way. But of these structures no theory can be formed using the concept of utility.

When I think on the other hand of interpersonal or intertemporal connectedness among selves, I can think of ties forming structures, and these structures I can describe and classify. When I read Hirschman's propositions on exit and voice, I understand them as actions constituting or dissolving horizontal, interpersonal ties. They form examples of how to distinguish structures that can be understood through the logic of identity. Hirschman's reasoning employs the logic of utility. But I have shown above that certain of the phenomena he discovers imply that a logic of identity is at work.

As Hirschman built a typology of structures according to the effects they were likely to have on the strengthening or weakening of the *interpersonal* connectedness of selves, one may ask how the *intertemporal* connectedness of selves may be reflected in types of social structures. Consider a traditional family, a productive organization and a religious sect. These are three types of structures which can ensure to the individual some personal identity. But the relative position of the deciding self with regard to its predecessors and successors will be different in the three cases. In the traditional family the ancestors are important, inherited culture and property are important, prescriptions absorbed by the young are important: The past selves command the deciding selves; the important collectivity of selves to which to refer is located in the past. In an occupational role the deciding self is future oriented, but what he received from past selves (his education, experience, formation of skills) still counts. In a religious sect, in a "belief group," in which persons are undergoing conversion, or second birth, the past is negated, every decision is taken for the sake of the future selves that will live in eternal salvation: The future selves command the deciding self.

It can be surmised that these different ways of achieving identity are not unrelated. The command of future selves becomes probably more encompassing when the hold of the past selves grows weaker. In other words, when the personal identity anchored in the past provides the deciding self with less and less security of recognition from the people among whom he must act, new identities grounded in common future destinies are sought. When the traditional circles of recognition are stable, when identity is secure, there is no need to resort to future selves to settle our standards of action for today.

If my criteria of choice are well rooted in the patterns of recognition both of a long string of ancestral selves, having built family identity for generations, and of a contemporary family of selves sharing the same past selves, and if this vertical and horizontal stability of recognition does not seem to be touched by larger historical movements, it is unlikely that I shall vote for an increase of expenditure to defend a national identity which is not relevant for that security of recognition. Or if I am a member of several groups from which I draw recognition for the success of my choices, it is unlikely that I will be so concerned by the loss of identity of my political party or for the loss of meaning of some badge of honor I have received in the past. If a movement is young and precarious, and if all the tension of its action is toward creating ideal conditions for future selves, it is likely that I have joined it knowing that I am adopting an exclusive identity, that in it my present self counts merely as a tool for future selves, that my membership is continuously threatened by alternative possibilities, and that a mere signature can be for me a symbol of total abdication. If a movement is old, has undergone much change and many compromises, but still keeps a relevant connectedness with the past and a recognizable identity, it is likely that I feel that temporary weakness will also be absorbed in that long-lasting identity.

The previous hypotheses help explain why strong ideological commitments are in general meant to overcome a state of weakness. Ideology defines the optimal state for future selves, for the person and for the collectivity, and subjects current action to the achievement of that state. It therefore organizes action, individual and collective, tightly and instrumentally. Identity through time will be securely defined by the standards of recognition anticipated for the future selves. Ideological commitment is like intense and concentrated investment in a developing country. It operates by sacrificing a stretch of selves and concentrating on a chosen one, because identity is secured and hence the connectedness between the sacrificed and the chosen selves is not in doubt. The efficacy of action led by ideology is therefore strongly enhanced and weak persons or weak groups can thus face strong enemies or difficult passages. People cannot act without an identity. When nobody questions the one they have received, they use it; when this is threatened or worn out, without even being aware of it, they fight for one.

Romantic love is also a form of ideology which strengthens dyadic identity by letting the state of future selves and the condition of their reciprocal recognition determine the view of the current selves. This seems imperative when the deciding self becomes responsible for its decision now for future selves. It was not the case in the traditional family, where past selves set the conditions for the choice. In romantic love a new identity through time is grounded, and this helps to overcome the uncertainty surrounding a decision that was traditionally made by the family of origin, a collectivity whose identity was not, or only slightly, threatened by the decision.

Conclusions

It seems that if one holds this view, one can explain facts and relations between facts that were explained only ad hoc, or left unexplained. But I am also interested in widening or clarifying awareness of the significance of certain facts.

If I know that the meaning of my action is not the acquisition of utilities but the securing of recognition, then I will hold the use of categories like "altruism" and "egoism" as merely stereotypical and deeply undiscerning.

I will also more easily understand the reasons that lead me to perform acts that cannot be calculated—like voting or contributing to causes. These reasons are not of a different nature from those that lead me to calculate the best means for some ends. Behind both types of reasons there is always the common need of securing recognition for the identity of my successive selves.

When someone speaks of self-interest, I will be aware of how muddled this notion is. Of whose interests is he thinking? Of the self he is now? Of some future selves of his? Of the bundle of selves with whom his current self is tightly connected? I will also know that the "selves" of that "interest" are so dispersed that no one of them, nor of those of some other string, can ever assume to be the "best judge."

This is a refreshing thought. A too fierce self-reliance can be scary or pretentious. The principle of autonomy of self, if it is not meant to operate temporarily, cannot stand alone and not be a sham. Behind "autonomy" some other self recognizing me is necessary. I now know that beyond every decision of my current self, "some other kind of otherness" must be sought.[7]

NOTES

1. This makes the reasons for identification of two kinds. For the one, the organization cannot exist without the identifier; for the other, the identifier cannot exist without the organization. It is an important distinction, but not relevant for the arguments I am developing here.

2. In other words, the question here is about the social identity of the person, not the identity of the mind. Elster's objection (unpublished, p. 9) confuses the two questions.

3. I owe the rereading of these passages of Proust to their quotation in Parfit, 1984, pp. 305.

4. Many well known experiments illustrate this theory (cf. Abelson 1968. Also Pears 1982).

5. See Schelling 1984; Elster 1979.

6. For similar arguments see Parfit 1984.

7. Whatever view we hold, it must be shown
Why every lover has a wish to make
Some other kind of otherness his own
Perhaps, in fact, we never are alone.
W. H. Auden

REFERENCES

Abelson, R., ed. 1968. *Theories of Cognitive Dissonance: A Sourcebook*. Chicago.

Elster, Jon. 1979. *Ulysses and the Sirens*. Cambridge University Press.

————. No date. "Weakness of will and the Free-Rider problem." Unpublished manuscript.

Hirschman, Albert O. 1970. *Exit, Voice, and Loyalty: Responses to Decline in Firms, Organizations, and States*. Cambridge: Harvard University Press.

Parfit, Derek. 1984. *Reasons and Persons*. Oxford.

Pears, David. 1982. "Motivated Irrationality, Freudian Theory and Cognitive Dissonance." in R. Wollheim and J. Hopkins, eds., *Philosophical Essays on Freud*. Cambridge: Cambridge University Press.

Schelling, Thomas C. 1984. "The Intimate Contest for Self-Command." In his *Choice and Consequence*, 57–82. Cambridge: Harvard University Press.

Albert O. Hirschman Bibliography

Books

National Power and the Structure of Foreign Trade. University of California Press, 1945 (reprinted 1969; paperback edition with new introduction, 1980); translated into Spanish.

The Strategy of Economic Development. Yale University Press, 1958 (reprinted 1978 by The Norton Library); translated into French, German, Italian, Spanish, Portuguese, Swedish, Japanese, Indonesian, Bengali, Korean.

Journeys Toward Progress: Studies of Economic Policy-Making in Latin America. Twentieth Century Fund, 1963 (reprinted 1973 by The Norton Library); translated into Spanish and Portuguese.

Development Projects Observed. Brookings Institution, 1967; translated into Spanish, Portuguese, Italian, Japanese.

Exit, Voice, and Loyalty: Responses to Decline in Firms, Organizations, and States. Harvard University Press, 1970; translated into Spanish, Portuguese, French, German, Italian, Swedish, Japanese.

A Bias for Hope: Essays on Development and Latin America. Yale University Press, 1975 (reprinted 1985 by Westview Press); translated into Spanish.

The Passions and the Interests: Political Arguments for Capitalism Before Its Triumph. Princeton University Press, 1977; translated into Spanish, Portuguese, French, German, Italian; being translated into Japanese.

Essays in Trespassing: Economics to Politics and Beyond. Cambridge University Press, 1981; translated into Spanish.

Shifting Involvements: Private Interest and Public Action. Princeton University Press, 1982; translated or being translated into French, Italian, German, Spanish, Portuguese, and Japanese.

Getting Ahead Collectively: Grassroots Experience in Latin America. Pergamon Press, 1984; being translated into Spanish.

Rival Views of Market Society and Other Recent Essays, Viking/Penguin, 1986.

Editor and coauthor, *Latin American Issues.* Twentieth Century Fund, 1961; translated into Spanish, Portuguese, Italian.

Ascesa e declino dell'economia dello sviluppo e altri saggi, a collection of essays, with an introduction by Andrea Ginzburg. Torino: Rosenberg & Sellier, 1983.

L'économie comme science sociale et politique, a collection of essays, with an introduction by François Furet. Paris: Gallimard/Le Seuil, 1984.

Articles and Other Papers

"Nota su due recenti tavole di nuzialità della popolazione italiana." *Giornale degli Economisti,* January 1938.

"The Commodity Structure of World Trade." *Quarterly Journal of Economics,* August 1943.

"On Measures of Dispersion for a Finite Distribution." *Journal of the American Statistical Association,* September 1943.

"Inflation and Deflation in Italy." *American Economic Review* 38, no. 4 (September 1948).

"Disinflation, Discrimination, and the Dollar Shortage." *American Economic Review,* December 1948.

"Devaluation and the Trade Balance: A Note." *Review of Economics and Statistics* 31, no. 1 (February 1949).

"Postwar Credit Controls in France" (with Robert V. Roosa). *Federal Reserve Bulletin,* April 1949.

"Movement Toward Balance in International Transactions of the United States" (with Lewis N. Dembitz). *Federal Reserve Bulletin,* April 1949.

"International Aspects of a Recession." *American Economic Review,* December 1949.

"The European Payments Union—Negotiations and Issues." *Review of Economics and Statistics* 33, no. 1 (February 1951).

"Types of Convertability." *Review of Economics and Statistics,* February 1951.

"Industrial Nations and Industrialization of Under-Developed Countries." *Economia Internazionale,* August 1951.

"Effects of Industrialization on the Market of Industrial Countries." In *The Progress of Underdeveloped Areas,* ed., Bert F. Hoselitz, University of Chicago Press, 1952.

"Guía para el análisis y la confección de recomendaciones sobre la situación monetaria." *Economia Colombiana,* October 1954.

*"Economics and Investment Planning: Reflections Based on Experience in Colombia." In *Investment Criteria and Economic Growth.* Center for International Studies, M.I.T., mimeo. 1954; published by Asia Publishing House, New York, 1961.

"Colombia: Highlights of a Developing Economy" (with George Kalmanoff). Booklet, Banco de la Republica Press, Bogotá, 1955.

"Demanda de energia eléctrica para la C.V.C." (with George Kalmanoff). *Economia Colombiana,* June 1956.

*"Economic Policy in Underdeveloped Countries." *Economic Development and Cultural Change,* July 1947.

"Investment Policies and 'Dualism' in Underdeveloped Countries." *American Economic Review,* September 1957.

Note: Items with asterick (*) are included in A. O. Hirschman, *A Bias for Hope: Essays on Development and Latin America,* Yale University Press, 1971.

"Investment Criteria and Capital Intensity Once Again" (with Gerald Sirkin). *Quarterly Journal of Economics,* August 1958.

*"Primary Products and Substitutes: Should Technological Progress be Policed? *Kyklos* (Vol. 12, fasc. 3), 1959.

"The Strategy of Economic Development." *Farm Policy Forum* 12, 1959–60.

"Invitation to Theorizing About the Dollar Glut." *Review of Economics and Statistics,* February 1960.

"Exchange Controls and Economic Development: Comments." In *Economic Development for Latin America,* ed. H.S. Ellis, 457–65. New York, St. Martin's Press, 1961.

*"Second Thoughts on the 'Alliance for Progress.' " *The Reporter,* May 25, 1961

*"Ideologies of Economic Development in Latin America." In *Latin American Issues—Essays and Comments,* ed. A.O. Hirschman. New York: Twentieth Century Fund, 1961.

*"Abrazo vs. Co-existence: Comments on Ypsilon's Paper." In *Latin American Issues—Essays and Comments,* ed. A. O. Hirschman. New York: Twentieth Century Fund, 1961.

*"Analyzing Economic Growth: A Comment." In Robert E. Asher et al., *Development of the Emerging Countries. Washington D.C.:* The Brookings Institution, 1982.

*"Economic Development, Research and Development, Policy-Making: Some Converging Views" (with Charles E. Lindblom). *Behavioral Science,* April 1962.

"Models of Reformmongering." *Quarterly Journal of Economics,* May 1963.

*"The Stability of Neutralism: A Geometrical Note." *American Economic Review,* March 1964.

*"Obstacles to Development: A Classification and a Quasi-Vanishing Act." *Economic Development and Cultural Change,* July 1965.

"Out of Phase." *Encounter,* September 1965 (special issue on Latin America).

"The Principle of the Hiding Hand." *The Public Interest,* no. 6 (Winter 1967).

*"The Political Economy of Import-Substituting Industrialization in Latin America." *Quarterly Journal of Economics,* February 1968.

*"Foreign Aid: A Critique and Proposal" (with Richard M. Bird). *Princeton Essays in International Finance,* July 1968.

*"Underdevelopment, Obstacles to the Perception of Change, and Leadership." *Daedalus,* Summer 1968.

*"Industrial Development in the Brazilian Northeast and the Tax Credit Scheme of Article 34/18." *The Journal of Development Studies,* October 1968.

*"How to Divest in Latin America, and Why." *Princeton Essays in International Finance,* November 1969.

*"The Search for Paradigms as a Hindrance to Understanding." *World Politics,* March, 1970. Also in P. Rabinow and W.M. Sullivan, eds., *Interpretive Social Science: A Reader.* Berkeley: University of California Press, 1979.

*"Ideology: Mask or Nessus Shirt?" In Alexander Eckstein, ed., *Comparison

of Economic Systems, Theoretical and Methodological Approaches. University of California Press, 1971.

†"The Changing Tolerance for Income Inequality in the Course of Economic Development" (with a mathematical appendix by Michael Rothschild). *Quarterly Journal of Economics,* November 1973.

†"An Alternative Explanation of Comtemporary Harriedness" (contribution to a symposium on time in economics). *Quarterly Journal of Economics,* November 1973.

†"Exit, Voice and Loyalty: Further Reflections and a Survey of Recent Contributions." *Social Science Information,* February 1974.

†"Policy Making and Policy Analysis in Latin America—A Return Journey." *Policy Sciences,* December 1975.

†"On Hegel, Imperialism, and Structural Stagnation." *Journal of Development Economics,* March 1976.

†"Exit, Voice and Loyalty—Comments." *American Economic Review, Papers and Proceedings,* May 1976.

†"A Generalized Linkage Approach to Development, with Special Reference to Staples." *Economic Development and Cultural Change,* Vol. 25, Supplement 1977 (Essays in Honor of Bert F. Hoselitz).

†"Beyond Asymmetry: Critical Notes on Myself as a Young Man and on Some Other Old Friends." *International Organization* 32, no. 7 (Winter 1978).

†"Exit, Voice and the State." *World Politics,* October 1978.

†"The Turn to Authoritarianism in Latin America and the Search for Its Economic Determinants." in David Collier, ed., *The New Authoritarianism in Latin America.* Princeton Universtiy Press, 1979.

**"Welfare State in Trouble: Systemic Crisis or Growing Pains?" *American Economic Review,* Papers and Proceedings, May 1980. Reprinted with slight changes in *Dissent,* Winter 1981.

†"The Rise and Decline of Development Economics." In Mark Gersovitz et al., eds., *The Theory and Experience of Economic Development,* Essays in Honor of Sir W. Arthur Lewis. London: Allen & Unwin, 1982.

†"Morality and the Social Sciences: A Durable Tension." Acceptance Paper, The Frank E. Seidman Distinguished Award in Political Economy, P.K. Seidman Foundation, Memphis, October 1980. Also in Norma Haan et al., eds., *Social Science as Moral Inquiry.* New York: Columbia University Press, 1983.

Note: Items with a dagger (†) are included in A.O. Hirschman, *Essays in Trespassing: Economics to Politics and Beyond,* Cambridge University Press, 1981.
Note: Items with double asterisks (**) are to be included in Albert O. Hirschman, *Rival Views of Market Society and Other Recent Essays,* Viking/Penguin, 1986.

**"Rival Interpretations of Market Society: Civilizing, Destructive, or Feeble?" *Journal of Economic Literature* 20, no. 4 (December 1982).

"The Principle of Conservation and Mutation of Social Energy." *Grassroots Development* (Journal of the Inter-American Foundation) 7, no. 2 (1983).

"University Activities Abroad and Human Rights Violations: Exit, Voice or Business as Usual?" *Human Rights Quarterly* 6, no. 1 (February 1984).

"Grassroots Change in Latin America." *Challenge* 27, no. 4 (September/October 1984).

†"Inflation: Reflections on the Latin American Experience." In L.N. Lindberg and C.S. Maier, eds., *The Politics of Inflation and Economic Stagnation.* Washington D.C.: Brookings Institution, 1985.

**"Against Parsimony: Three Easy Ways of Complicating Some Categories of Economic Discourse." In *American Economic Review* 74, no. 2 (May 1984). Expanded versions in the *Bulletin of the American Academy of Arts and Sciences,* 1984, and in *Economics and Philosophy* 1 (1985).

**"A Dissenter's Confession: Revisiting *The Strategy of Economic Development.*" In Gerald M. Meier and Dudley Seers, eds., *Pioneers in Development.* Oxford University Press, 1984.

**"In Difesa del possibilismo" (In Defense of Possibilism). In R. Scartezzini et al., eds., *I limiti della democrazia.* Naples: Liguori, 1985.